JAPAN REBORN

Japan Reborn

RACE AND EUGENICS FROM EMPIRE TO COLD WAR

Kristin Roebuck

Columbia University Press
New York

Columbia University Press wishes to express its appreciation for assistance given by the Hull Memorial Publication Fund of Cornell University in the publication of this book.

Columbia University Press
Publishers Since 1893
New York   Chichester, West Sussex
cup.columbia.edu

Copyright © 2025 Kristin Roebuck
All rights reserved

Library of Congress Cataloging-in-Publication Data
Names: Roebuck, Kristin author
Title: Japan reborn : race and eugenics from empire to cold war / Kristin Roebuck.
Description: New York : Columbia University Press, [2025] | Includes bibliographical references and index.
Identifiers: LCCN 2025023787 | ISBN 9780231204385 hardback | ISBN 9780231204392 trade paperback | ISBN 9780231555517 ebook
Subjects: LCSH: Eugenics—Japan | Multiracial children—Japan—Social conditions | Multiracial children—Government policy—Japan | Nationalism—Japan | Japan—Race relations | Japan—Population policy | Japan—History—1945-
Classification: LCC HQ755.5.J3 R64 2025 | DDC 363.9/20952—dc23/eng/20250820
LC record available at https://lccn.loc.gov/2025023787

Cover design: Anson Wigner
Cover photo: *China Incident at One Year* (Shina jihen isshūnen), 1938. Photographer unknown. Nihon shashin hozon sentā (Center for the preservation of Japanese photographs).

GPSR Authorized Representative: Easy Access System Europe, Mustamäe tee 50, 10621 Tallinn, Estonia, gpsr.requests@easproject.com

CONTENTS

LIST OF FIGURES   VII

ACKNOWLEDGMENTS   IX

NOTE ON LANGUAGE   XIII

Introduction
Sex, Race, and Rebirth   1

Chapter One
In Praise of "Mixed Blood":
Imperial and Racial Expansion in Asia and the Pacific, 1895–1944   18

Chapter Two
Biologizing Defeat:
Racial and Sexual Anxiety Amid Imperial Crisis, 1937–1945   61

Chapter Three
From No Abortion to Proabortion:
Rape, Race, and the Eugenic Protection Law of 1948   92

CONTENTS

Chapter Four
Sex, Censorship, and SCAP:
Debating "Blood Mixing" Under Occupation, 1945–1952   123

Chapter Five
Cold War *Konketsuji*:
Partisan Politics, Hot Presses, and US Alliance, 1950–1955   151

Chapter Six
Orphans by Design:
Ethnic Cleansing and International Adoption in the 1950s   187

Afterword
Race and the Myth of "Absent Nationalism" in Postwar Japan   217

NOTES   229

BIBLIOGRAPHY   265

INDEX   287

FIGURES

FIGURE I.1 "Japan's Lines of Overseas Expansion." Ministry of Welfare, 1943. 10

FIGURE 1.1 *Lt. (?) Higuchi Saving a Child in the Midst of Battle at Backaigai*, ca. 1895. 45

FIGURE 1.2 "Captain Higuchi, in the Midst of the Attack, Personally Holds a Lost Chinese Child." Ogata Gekkō, 1895. 46

FIGURE 1.3 Japanese soldiers rush to save a Chinese baby "abandoned" in a field near Wuhan. Cabinet Information Bureau, 1938. 48

FIGURE 1.4 Japanese soldiers fondle the Chinese baby they have "rescued." Cabinet Information Bureau, 1938. 50

FIGURE 1.5 Illustration of a mother holding a helmeted baby holding a rising-sun flag. Ministry of Welfare, 1942. 51

FIGURE 1.6 Illustration of women filing into a maternity center as a mother holds aloft her beaming baby. Ministry of Welfare, 1942. 52

FIGURE 1.7 A kneeling Japanese soldier teaches Chinese children to salute. Cabinet Information Bureau, 1938. 55

FIGURE 3.1 A blindfolded woman endures gynecological care at Futukaichi Sanatorium. Iiyama Tatsuo, ca. 1946. 105

FIGURE 3.2 An emaciated Japanese man crouches in the ruins of his house in Yokohama, 1945. 109

FIGURES

FIGURE 3.3 A proud mother shows off her baby to a US Army photographer, 1945. 110

FIGURE 4.1 The "wedding portrait" of emperor Hirohito and US general Douglas MacArthur, 1945. 124

FIGURE 4.2 The number of articles with "blood mixing" (*konketsu*) in the title published per year in Japanese periodicals, 1931–1963. 130

FIGURE 5.1 Young protestors march in Tokyo holding a "Go Home Yankee" sign. Michael Rougier, 1952. 154

FIGURE 5.2 Japanese women on holiday with British Commonwealth soldiers in Miyajima, 1952. 169

FIGURE 5.3 Fumika Clifford and her "mixed blood" daughter Mary smile as they sit for an Australian passport photograph, 1953. 170

FIGURE 5.4 A Japanese woman walks hand-in-hand with an American soldier near a bilingual hotel. Kageyama Kōyō, 1951. 171

FIGURE 5.5 A Japanese bride marries a US serviceman at Heian Shrine in Kyoto, 1952. 174

FIGURE 6.1 US troops holding "mixed blood" children marry Japanese brides at the US consulate in Tokyo. Max Desfor, 1952. 190

FIGURE 6.2 Sawada Miki and "mixed blood" social orphans at the Elizabeth Saunders Home. Margaret Bourke-White, 1952. 207

FIGURE 6.3 "Detailed Print of Yokohama Honchō and the Miyozaki District." Utagawa (Gountei) Sadahide, 1860. 215

ACKNOWLEDGMENTS

Writing this book would not have been possible without the support of many fine people and institutions. First, I am deeply indebted to Gregory Pflugfelder, who took a chance on me as a doctoral applicant with more ambition than sense. And to Carol Gluck, Christopher Leslie Brown, and Naoyuki Umemori, who supported me as a graduate student and in subsequent years. I owe these mentors deep debts of gratitude and remain in awe of them as scholars and humans.

I could not have wished for a more warm and inspiring community of colleagues than I have found at Cornell University. I am grateful to everyone in the Department of History, as well as my colleagues in Asian Studies and the East Asia Program, for making this a workplace worthy of our labor. To Sandra Greene and Tamara Loos: special thanks for your leadership and mentorship from day one. To Edward von Aderkas, Andrew Campana, Mara Yue Du, Oren Falk, Cristina Florea, Durba Ghosh, TJ Hinrichs, Mayer Juni, Ruth Lawlor, Mostafa Minawi, and Casey Schmitt: Your material support, sage advice, good humor, and occasional dog-sitting have been precious to me. May I find ways to repay you in years to come.

Special thanks to my Cornell University undergraduate research assistants: Elijah Emery, Shawn Hikosaka, Hal Reed, David Sheng, and Jordine Williams. Their proofreading and source-hunting labor was funded in part by the Laidlaw Undergraduate Leadership and Research Program of the

ACKNOWLEDGMENTS

Einaudi Center for International Studies, the Office of the Vice Provost for International Affairs, and the Society for the Humanities.

For image permissions, I must thank the Australian War Memorial; Museum of Fine Arts, Boston; Metropolitan Museum of Art; National Archives at College Park; Trout Gallery of Dickinson College; and Mead Art Museum of Amherst College. Thanks also to *Japanese Studies* for allowing me to republish parts of my 2016 article in this book.

Over the years, I have benefited from sharing my work at various workshops and conferences. I am deeply grateful to those who have organized such opportunities: Shinju Fujihira, Kathryn Goldfarb, Aya Homei, David Howell, Colin Jones, Yumi Kim, Jennifer Miller, Young Sun Park, Ken Ruoff, Jennifer Tappan, and Benjamin Uchiyama. Thanks also to the questions, corrections, and insight offered by fellow scholars at these events: Fabian Drixler, Sabine Frühstück, Laura Hein, Nathan Hopson, Hwansoo Kim, Sarah Kovner, Wendy Matsumura, Marlene Mayo, Ian Miller, Hiromu Nagahara, Joshua Schlachet, and Igarashi Yoshikuni, among others. I cannot name you all, but I have learned so much from each of you.

I also want to thank Ben for organizing what I call the Uchiyama Book Club. At the start of COVID-19 lockdown, Ben convened a group of scholars over Zoom to meet monthly and keep scholarly exchange alive. The group outlasted the pandemic and became one of the highlights of my early career. Thanks to those who joined in and added so much to my intellectual life over the past few years: Paul Barclay, Nick Kapur, Kyu Hyun Kim, John Leisure, Hiromi Mizuno, John Person, Seiji Shirane, Tsuguta Yamashita, and Kirsten Ziomek, among others. What an intimidating and inspiring bunch of scholars. I hope to live up to the high bar set by each of you.

I would be remiss if I did not also thank the incredible faculty and staff of the Inter-University Center in Yokohama and the once-thriving Full-Year Asian Language Concentration (FALCON) program at Cornell University. Without programs like these, early-life monolinguals such as myself would never be able to acquire Japanese language competency sufficient for international research and communication. Special thanks to Robert Sukle, Naomi Nakada Larson, Sahoko Ichikawa, and Akizawa Tomotaro. You are role models in pedagogical excellence and human generosity.

In addition to innumerable personal debts, I am indebted to several organizations for funds that made writing this book possible. A Fulbright

ACKNOWLEDGMENTS

US Scholar Grant for research in Japan enabled me to transform my work on the postwar era into a book manuscript on transwar transformations. Grants from the Society for the Humanities at Cornell University and the Northeast Asia Council of the Association for Asian Studies offered further research support. A two-year postdoctoral fellowship was generously funded by the Mellon Foundation. As a graduate student, I received vital support from Shinchō Foundation and Foreign Language and Area Studies (FLAS) fellowships. In addition, the History of Science Society, the Southern Association for the History of Medicine and Science, and the Japan Studies Association awarded me funds to travel, present my research, and learn from colleagues at academic conferences. In a time of declining funding for scholarly research, I am more grateful than ever for the financial support that makes intellectual inquiry, community, and communication possible.

Finally, I wish to thank my family. No page can hold all my debts to you. To Greg and Kennie: Thank you for being there over the long haul. You're always in my thoughts.

To Anson: Thank you for your work on designing this book cover, crafting my head shot, and enduring—even enjoying?—countless conversations about Japanese grammar, racism, war, and history. Thank you for playing the trailing spouse in Tokyo, Yokohama, and Ithaca, and for countless other acts of labor and love. We married twenty-five years ago, when no one thought it would last. Thank you for our life together.

To my mother: Thank you for keeping us alive and afloat as a single mother with a high school education. Thank you for modeling what a career woman looks like, and how she gets ahead and brings her family with her. Thank you for going back to school, for shouldering that double or triple burden, and for sometimes letting me sneak into a university lecture or study with you during evenings and weekends. Perhaps you thought it was a second-class upbringing, but I know I was a fortunate kid. Thanks also for teaching me how to write. You've been reading my shoddy drafts since I was seven years old. I hope what's published here is some recompense for your efforts. If there is a heaven for mothers and proofreaders, you will be their queen.

To my father: I wish you had survived. Thank you for teaching me at an early age to love history, used bookstores, free inquiry, and intellectual dialogue. Thank you for modeling curiosity and labor, ethics without close-mindedness, rigor without competitiveness, strength without dominance, and protection without control. I wish I could live up to your pedagogical model. Although you never had the chance to earn a doctorate, in some ways, you might have been better at this job. Of course, I always saw the best in you. This book is a love letter to you.

NOTE ON LANGUAGE

The names of Japanese people are given in Japanese order, with family name first. However, for people with Japanese names who live in Western countries or publish in English, names are given in Western order (family name last).

This book is an analysis of racial ideology centered on the idea of "mixed blood" (konketsu) and "pure blood" (junketsu), categories of great importance in Japan. I place quotation marks around these terms each time I use them to emphasize that they are not mine. They are translations from primary sources. Moreover, they are fictive, normative, racial categories used to dominate and discriminate. "Race" is also a fictive, normative category used to dominate and discriminate. So too is the category "Japanese."

Authors often forego quotation marks around such terms after the first instance, expecting that readers will remember not to reify them. I fear that places an undue burden on the reader. Given the extent to which racial ideology and biases about "race mixing" are already naturalized, using such language without setting it off in scare quotes runs the risk of reinforcing the system of thought I seek to challenge.

I use quotation marks to signal the artificiality of "mixed blood" as a category throughout this book. In this regard, I follow the practice established by scholars such as Shimoji Rōrensu Yoshitaka. Many other scholars who study nationalism and identity formation insist on placing "Japanese" in quotation marks in every instance. They do not want to slip up even once and reify the category "Japanese." My own experience reading such scholarship has been that, at first, all those quotation marks look like needless clutter. But the longer this pattern repeats, the more seriously one has to think about why authors and editors are going to such trouble to do something so apparently strange. On pages 1–10, all those scare quotes may look silly, but by page 100–200 they look serious indeed.

Refusal to accept discriminatory language achieves a powerful effect when it is *relentless*.

JAPAN REBORN

Introduction

SEX, RACE, AND REBIRTH

Race and nation are made by sex. People have sex. Babies are born. In the modern world, those babies are immediately racialized, rendered national citizens and imperial subjects, gendered as future fighting men or mothers-to-be: defenders and progenitors of the nation, the race, the contested future. Seeking to control the future, humans engage in the politics of sex. Through the politics of sex, we aim to control many things—above all women, their reproductive labor, and the fruits of that labor: the children they bear. A fertile woman's body is occupied territory of urgent biopolitical concern. As for the next generation, they too are occupied even before birth. The moment a birth-to-be is known, imagined, projected, or suspected, the fetus or zygote, oocyte or seminal fluid is racialized, nationalized, and claimed by rival states and powers eager to reproduce themselves, to be reborn.

We may prefer that sex were a private matter, that family were apolitical. Regardless, acts of sex and procreation are irreducibly racial and political, national and imperial. Without sex, and specifically *certain kinds of sex*, neither races nor states can sustain themselves. Most sex does not lead to childbirth. But the biological possibility and political necessity of childbirth persistently structures sexual ideology and governance. The international order, global economy (whether capitalist, socialist, or other), and assorted militaries and their states would all perish without certain kinds of sex and reproductive labor to sustain them.

INTRODUCTION

Border politics start in the womb. By defining some children as *ours* and other children as *Others*, political actors and ideologues reproduce into the future imagined communities of race, nation, and empire. Disputes over sexual sovereignty and the possession of women and children are as crucial to racial, national, and global politics as conventional contests over territory and other natural resources. Human bodies and fertility, too, are natural resources subject to state sovereignty. Sexual sovereignty is a form of border politics meant to decide who may (or must) engage in sex, and with whom; who may (or must) reproduce, and with whom; with whom sex is forbidden, and to whom reproduction is forbidden; which mothers and babies to nurture, and whose birth and nurturance will be denied. As fundamental as the imperative to "make live" is the complementary urge to impede reproduction and forestall biopolitical rebirth among one's rivals.[1] Who "we the people" are depends critically on who we are not, and such national and racial boundaries are often drawn through the bodies of women and the disposition of children. Nowhere is this dynamic more apparent than in cases of border-crossing sex and family formation.

Between 1868 and 1945, Japan emerged on the world stage as both a nation and empire. As "the Japanese" were nationalized into an imagined community, they built an empire hungrily expanding and incorporating fresh lands and peoples into their polity. From the Ainu in the north to Ryūkyūans in the south, from Indigenous peoples and Han Chinese settlers in Taiwan after 1895 to Koreans after 1910, onward into the South Seas, northeast Asia, and southeast Asia in the 1910s to 1940s, the borders of "Japan" and of "the Japanese" were relentlessly unstable and strategically destabilized. In using these quotation marks, I follow the conventions of scholars who highlight the artificiality and historical changes in definitions of "the Japanese" as well as the severe consequences of naturalizing particular boundaries drawn around that community.[2] I deliberately retain quotation marks around key phrases, such as "mixed blood," in order to highlight their artificiality and centrality in Japanese discourse. In this book, by attending to the boundary-drawing politics of sex and reproduction, I unravel how "the Japanese" constructed themselves as a multiracial and "mixed blood" people in a time of imperial expansion, then reconstructed themselves as a putatively "pure race" after defeat and loss of empire in World War II. Key to understanding the birth and rebirth of transwar Japan and its Others is the eulogized and demonized figure of the *konketsuji* (mixed-blood child).

INTRODUCTION

If borders on a map never moved, if armies never marched, and if navies never set sail, boundaries would still be unstable. Sex guarantees it; sex is a primal act of boundary-crossing and body-blending. We were born to cross borders. Migration too is a fact of human life: we move. When we move, we meet. When we meet, we have sex. Sometimes, children are born. Sometimes, families are formed: a bride brought in, a concubine bought in, a child adopted. Lovers meet; men swear oaths of brotherhood. To fashion kin in any of these ways is to redraw boundaries. Kinship formation need not proceed through heterosexual sex and childbirth, as homosocial communities (the fathers and brothers in monasteries, fraternities, and barracks) are also crucial to sociopolitical reproduction. Yet all human institutions presume prior acts of sex and giving birth. No polity perdures without reproduction, and human reproduction requires two genetic partners and the recombination of genealogical differences between them. In this sense, every child is born of mixture. With every birth, boundaries shake.

A neo-Mendelian thinks in terms of the recombination of genes. In a child are preserved but a slim selection of any parent's genes; the other genes come from somewhere else, someone else's "line." That other line is not straight and narrow, but rather a record of constant encounter, interruption, and recombination. As we will see, many researchers, policymakers, and pundits in twentieth-century Japan (as in Europe and North America) looked to the "mixed blood" child for evidence of how neo-Mendelian genetics worked. With such knowledge, they aimed not only to explain but also to control the reproduction of races, nations, and empires. Far from neutral, neo-Mendelian analyses of "blood mixing" often functioned as prescriptions for how to facilitate the eugenic reproduction of "the Japanese." Every child is in fact born of genetic mixture. Biopolitics, however, marks only some children as "mixed."

A racialist thinks of the mixture of races. As Barbara K. Fields and Karen E. Fields explain, it is crucial, however, not to make the errant move "from the concept 'mixture' to the false inference that unmixed components exist."[3] A religious community may similarly prize endogamy and cast a suspicious eye on intermarriage or reproduction with nonbelievers. A jurist may think of international children whose parents hail from separate sovereign territories. The jurist may wonder where that child belongs: a citizen of either *here* or *there*, or else a dual citizen, or perhaps a stateless being entitled to exist nowhere. Adoption raises similar juridical concerns and identarian confusions, most acutely when adoption crosses national or racial borders. Children marked as "mixed" in any of these ways have to negotiate membership in the parent communities or have membership negotiated for them. They may have some say in the matter, but much will be beyond their power to decide as the collective embraces or repudiates children of this kind.

When a "Japanese" person has sex with a person of a different "race" or nation, is the child born "Japanese"? Is Japan reproduced through such acts of "mixture"? Or does Japan diminish or even perish when nationals "mix blood" (*konketsu*) with outsiders? No idle questions, these are life-and-death matters for people having sex and being born on the shifting horizons of "Japan." Japan's borderlines do not preexist so much as they are adjudicated through these questions—and the enforcement of contrived answers. The answers enforced may shift rapidly as the political winds turn. Whichever way the wind blows, the status of the border-crossing and "mixing" minority holds urgent interest for the majority that constitutes itself as unmixed by contrast. The majority construct themselves as sovereign and "Japanese" in claiming the right to decide what mixture means and on what terms such biopolitical border-crossing shall be licensed, encouraged, or prohibited.

In a "mixed" family, does it matter whether the Japanese parent is the father or the mother? Does a "half" (*hāfu*) Japanese child with a Japanese mother count as "less Japanese" than one with a Japanese father? In a society that prizes patrilineal kinship, the answer is yes. Sociologist Shimoji Rōrensu Yoshitaka describes the "gendered racial project" that obscures the reality of "mixture" in Japan by naturalizing the Japaneseness of "mixed" children of Japanese fathers while rejecting as foreign the children of Japanese mothers.[4] Shimoji focuses on contemporary Japan, but as we will see, the borderlines of race and nation have been gendered—with children of Japanese fathers being privileged in ways children of Japanese mothers have not been—since the imperial era. Many other factors have historically come into play in adjudicating the Japaneseness or Otherness of the "mixed blood" child. From the 1930s through the 1950s, key factors were the doctrines and findings of eugenics, neo-Mendelian genetics, and race science; imperial assimilation policies, stiff Chinese resistance to conquest and assimilation, and imperial collapse in World War II; occupation by foreign armies thereafter; the outbreak of the Cold War, in which domestic and international debates over "blood mixing" played a powerful yet underrecognized role; and the commercial and persuasive reach of mass media operating in conflict or cooperation with government censors during the imperial era and the Allied occupation (1945–1952) that followed.

"Blood mixing" is a mode of seeing, interpreting, and governing the world. Rather than a natural fact, "blood mixing" is a man-made lens that brings biopolitics into focus, surveilling and subordinating sex and reproduction to political interests. Those who invent and deploy the lens and language of "blood mixing," as do the Japanese actors in this study, hail *races* and *nations* into being, reifying their biopolitical boundaries while also admitting they are open to tidal shifts. As a way of seeing and constructing kinship, "blood mixing" renders race and nation liquid and mobile, open to the construction of fresh channels or fresh dams, depending on resource demands and political plans. The complex possibilities of blood mixing made it a mode of governance of urgent importance to transwar Japanese striving to build a multiracial empire, then to rebuild a pure nation in the wake of imperial collapse. Centered at the heart of these conflicting political projects was the "mixed blood" child.

When Japan's wartime leaders surrendered to the Allies in August 1945, they agreed to occupation by the multinational forces of the Supreme Commander for the Allied Powers (SCAP), US Army general Douglas MacArthur.[5] All at once, Japan lost its overseas empire, enjoyed liberation from domestic military dictatorship, and endured subordination to a foreign military and racial power. The fact that most *konketsuji* born after 1945 were sired by foreign soldiers from enemy armies forever changed the meaning of "blood mixing" in Japan. As democracy and partisan politics were resurrected, both the left and right in Japan exploited controversy over "blood mixing" for political gain. They did so in the context of emerging Cold War rivalries and the inauguration of a fraught security alliance between Japan and the United States in 1951, which guaranteed that foreign soldiers would remain in Japan in perpetuity. Reaction against the treaty in Japan often fixated on the fact that foreign soldiers were debauching Japanese women and siring "mixed blood" children. Kanō Mikiyo identifies the 1950s uproar over *konketsuji* as an origin point for the "myth of the monoracial nation" in Japan—the same "myth" that Oguma Eiji, in his classic work, argued emerged only after and through the loss of colonial empire.[6] Defeat, occupation, and postwar alliance with the erstwhile enemy, the United States, sparked a broad, negative reaction against "blood mixing" in Japan and a profound devolution in the social status of the "mixed blood" child and his

Japanese mother. The meaning of being Japanese was transformed in the postwar process of rejecting "blood mixing."

I came to the study of interracial sex and "mixed blood" children in Japan from an unexpected angle. I initially sought to understand why, in 1956, scarcely a decade after losing World War II, Japan banned prostitution nationwide for the first time in its history. The ban came after centuries of regulating and taxing—and in the case of wartime comfort stations, organizing outright—the trade in women and girls, commercial sex and patriotic sex.[7] My hunt for answers led me to the scholarship of Sarah Kovner and Lori Watt, who repeatedly reference a postwar uproar over "mixed blood" children.[8] These *konketsuji* were children born to Japanese mothers and sired by foreign soldiers in the context of Japan's defeat and occupation after World War II. Japanese women who had sexual contact with foreign soldiers were often despised by other Japanese, as were the "mixed blood" children they conceived. So intense was the acrimony that illegal abortion, often deliberately targeting *konketsuji*, was widely practiced even by government agents. The will to abort "mixed blood" fetuses contributed to the selective decriminalization of abortion in the Eugenic Protection Law (*Yūsei hogohō*, EPL) of 1948, enacted halfway through Japan's experience of Allied occupation.[9]

Peace was secured and occupation ended in 1952. To the dismay of many Japanese nationalists, US troops stayed on as Japan's new allies in the Cold War—or as colonizers, in the view of left-wing and right-wing critics. The formal transition of US soldiers from enemies to allies did little to assuage Japanese outrage over interracial sex and *konketsuji*, which peaked in the 1950s. A few years after inauguration of the US-Japan alliance, prostitution abolitionists secured a criminal ban on sex work. The reform was fueled in part by outrage against countrywomen who indulged in interracial sex and reproduction with US soldiers.[10]

Why all the acrimony? Why pass new laws to suppress interracial sex and reproduction in Japan after World War II? From a certain point of view, nothing could be more natural. Similar cases are not hard to find in world history. For instance, after World War I, defeated German nationalists stirred up outrage over interracial sex and childbirth between German women and French-African occupation soldiers, the better to chasten those women, alienate their children, and delegitimize the postwar international status quo in which Germans had lost pride and standing.[11] The pattern repeats during World War II and its aftermath, when throughout Europe,

INTRODUCTION

partisans on all sides decried and punished countrywomen who engaged in "horizontal collaboration" with foreign soldiers. Patriots denounced children born of international liaisons not only as illegitimate offspring foreign to the fatherland but also as eugenically inferior to children fathered by conationals. Wartime and postwar nationalists thereby enforced, writes Nicholas Stargardt, the "common conviction that women's bodies belonged first to the nation and only then to themselves."[12] Japanese too participated in this global movement to reify and defend a gender-hierarchized, racialized, and eugenic nation against sexually insurgent countrywomen, foreign aggressors, and their unwanted offspring. That Japanese reacted much like Europeans to the sexual facts of occupation should not surprise us.

Japan's postwar reaction against "blood mixing" appears less natural, however, if we look not outward toward European experience but inward toward Japan's history. As Oguma Eiji has shown, after the annexation of Korea in 1910, the weight of scholarly and journalistic opinion in Japan swung decisively toward the notion that the Japanese were a constitutionally "mixed blood" people with a world-historical gift for assimilating diverse "races" into a harmonious imperial whole. Imperial policy supported intermarriage, adoption, and "blood mixing" to fuse new populations and old-stock Japanese, sometimes called Yamato, into one happy family-state.[13] This is not to say that the Japanese empire was a paradise of equality and inclusion: assimilation was coerced, and inclusion did not negate hierarchy.[14] Historian Takashi Fujitani describes a late-imperial transition from "vulgar" to "polite" racism, the latter a system that "respected" colonized and conquered peoples enough to demand that they fight as conationals, as "Japanese."[15] As nationalized Japanese, all subjects of the empire, whether they were Korean, Ainu, Okinawan, Indigenous Taiwanese, or people of "mixed blood," were expected to breed, fight, and die for their country in World War II.

In Benedict Anderson's classic formulation, a nation boasts two key features: It is an *imagined* community; and it is a *bounded* community "beyond which lie other nations. No nation imagines itself coterminous with mankind." Exactly how any group of nationalists imagine and police their territorial, cultural, or reproductive boundaries varies, but the impetus of boundary-drawing is essential. Anderson asserts that "The most messianic nationalists do not dream of a day when all the members of the human race will join their nation in the way that it was possible, in certain epochs, for, say, Christians to dream of a wholly Christian planet."[16]

Yet as historian Naoki Sakai notes, many wartime Japanese "harbored a messianic mission to end all imperialist violence by violent means and to unify all nations under one roof."[17] Ishiwara Kanji, the Kwantung Army leader and pan-Asian ideologue who helped engineer Japan's takeover of Manchuria in 1931, prophesized and planned for a near future in which all races and nations would become one under Japanese leadership.[18] Accordingly, whereas Anderson suggested that imperialism and universalism are anathema to nationalism, Sakai insists that "universalism and nationalism can easily be synthesized."[19] After Japanese imperial forces erupted from Manchuria in an attempt to conquer all of China in 1937, the universality of Japanese culture was touted by a broad range of officials and intellectuals.[20] Japanese who celebrated "blood mixing" fleshed out the biopolitical and eugenic meanings of universal assimilation. The universalist dream of multiethnic, multiracial, globe-spanning Japan was shattered by defeat in the Asia-Pacific War, but we should not take imperial Japanese universalism any less seriously for its short life and brutal end.

As I demonstrate in this book, discourse on "blood mixing" as a mode of racecraft and empire-building boomed as Japan's occupation of Manchuria in 1931 metastasized into full-scale war in China in 1937, and then expanded further in invasions of southeast Asia and the Pacific in 1941–1942. During the war, millions of Japanese moved overseas to fight, farm, fornicate, and fashion lives and kinship among a kaleidoscopic variety of foreign "races." Meanwhile, millions of newcomers migrated into Japan's labor-hungry home islands. As global war mixed previously far-flung populations together, "blood mixing" loomed larger in the imaginary of "Japan" than ever before.

According to Sakai, "a nation is a particular form of modern community whose imaginary constitution is closely tied with a geographic enclosure," that is, a sacred soil or fatherland with clearly drawn and sharply defended borders.[21] But what happens when geography is not enclosed, borders are not settled, and the nation is moving hungrily into new realms? If imperial Japanese migrants and invaders could no longer be known by the territory they inhabited, they would have to define themselves in some other way: by their "blood." Blood was a medium capable of elevating some people over others in the nominally universal imperial hierarchy, preserving a privileged place for old-stock Japanese over conquered and colonized newcomers. Yet "blood talk" was not designed only to foment division.[22] On the contrary, as Japan cultivated the allegiance of many peoples who did not appear to be Yamato—the subgroup often conceived as the original Japanese—talk of "blood mixing" provided a way to imagine a pan-Asian or even global community with Japan at the center of humanity. Citing deep evolutionary histories of racial blood ties between Japanese, Asians, and the wider world allowed wartime Japanese to transcend the narrow and artificial borders erected by nations and states and naturalize Japanese expansion. Far from alien invaders, Japanese in this blood-based imaginary were "coming home" to reunite with diverse kin in countless lands. Better even than relying on ancient blood bonds, Japanese could forge stronger blood ties in the present through intermarriage and "blood mixing." In the minds of proponents, breeding *konketsuji* enabled Japanese to reproduce their "mixed blood" selves overseas while building kinship and community with diverse people in conquered lands.

In 1943, mapmakers at Japan's Ministry of Welfare (MOW) helped to visualize the imperial geographic imaginary in which all of Asia and the Pacific might soon be converted into Japanese satellites and settlements. The MOW map in figure I.1 depicts "Japan's Lines of Overseas Expansion" throughout northeast Asia, southeast Asia, and the Pacific, including New Guinea and Australia.[23] Around the world, mapmakers routinely inscribe borders demarcating sovereign territories. This map, however, visualized Asia and the Pacific as terra nullis, denuded of prior claimants and political boundaries. The Asia-Pacific region is defined instead by the unifying force of Japanese expansion, dramatized by a borderless map dominated by arrows emanating outward from Japan's home islands. With this minimalist map, in which the only boundaries visualized are those between land and sea, MOW technocrats presented a potent visual argument that there were no prior limits to Japanese expansion. Bloodshed and battle lines are not visualized. Those who would die to fertilize Japan's advance are not denoted; nor are those born amid that advance. But both populations, the dying and the newborn, are implied in this cartographic exercise, as is the fact that "mixed" children multiply as Japanese invade foreign lands.

Imperial expansion meant expanded sexual contact between Japanese and other "races" and peoples of the world. More sex meant more babies: a simple natural law. Or was it? Man-made laws had much to do with the cultural conviction that sex begat babies. Modern methods of fertility control such as intrauterine devices and surgical abortion were known

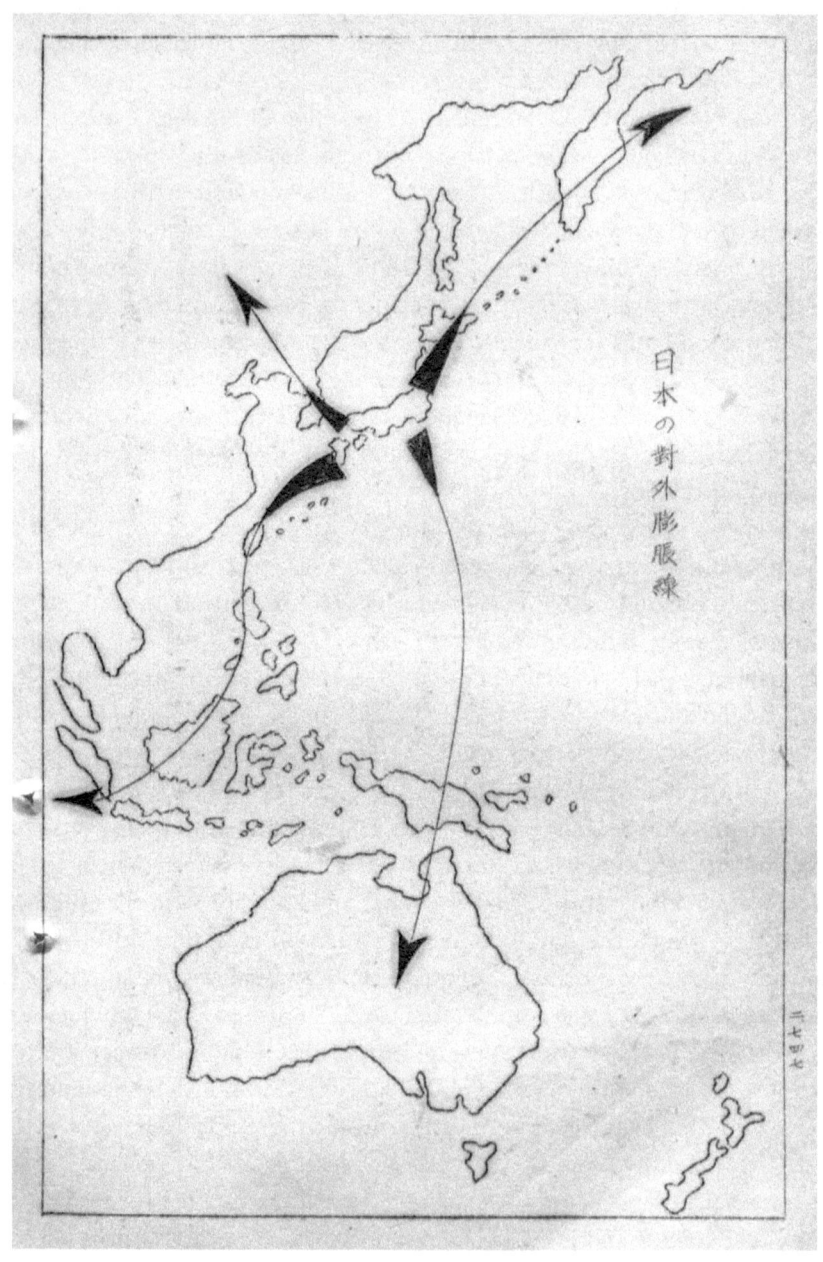

FIGURE I.1. "Japan's Lines of Overseas Expansion" (Nihon no taigai bōchō sen). Ministry of Welfare, 1943.

INTRODUCTION

but criminalized in imperial Japan. Indeed, as it rolled troops across foreign borders, Japan's government also rolled out a campaign to increase the imperial birth rate and speed population growth, thus proactively replenishing the human resources expended in violent expansion.[24] In an empire where abortion and contraception were illegal, population growth was meticulously plotted, and rapid reproduction was earnestly enjoined, policymakers and scholars vividly understood that expanded sexual contact with foreign peoples meant the proliferation of "mixed blood" children. The question was not whether such children would be born but how to evaluate and ensure their eugenic fitness, political utility, and loyalty to Japan.

To fully explain the Japanese belief that military expansion foretold a "mixed blood" baby boom, one must consider another factor: the cult of masculinity. The cultural conviction that Japanese men would have sex wherever they went with whichever women or girls were at hand fueled the imperial expectation of a "mixed blood" baby boom. Chastity or sexual continence were not expected of Japanese men-at-arms or other imperial men. Thus, rapid military expansion portended an equally rapid expansion in the variety and quantity of "mixed blood" children. What would such children look like? How would they think and feel? Where would their political loyalties lie? Few scholars, policymakers, or publishers were willing to condemn or constrain Japanese soldiers and other imperial pioneers pursuing international sex. Yet their approach was far from laissez-faire. They took a keen interest in the reproductive consequences of sexual expansion overseas: "mixed blood" children. How should they be bred and raised to ensure that they grew up eugenically fit and politically loyal allies and assets, not enemies or detriments, to Japan? Eugenicists, medical experts, population policymakers, journalists, and other Japanese mobilized to surveil and guide the "mixed blood" offspring of empire and to construct through their "mixed" bodies a medically and politically sound future.

From strangers to lovers, or from strangers to rapists—either way, war stimulates sex. Japan's global war, and the Allied occupation and Cold War that followed, moved tens of millions of bodies, male and female, combatant and civilian, across tens of thousands of kilometers of earth and ocean. Men, women, and children of nearly every imaginable race met in unexpected places, often knowing little about one another except that they were foreigners meeting in a foreign land. It was a time to learn quickly, roughly perhaps, as war forced people on all sides into sudden and sustained intimacy.

INTRODUCTION

The work of rebirth is both bodily and conceptual, for from war and occupation are born new ideas of family, race, and what it means to be related. Thus, the demographic and symbolic meaning of warfare cannot be reduced to death. War breeds life amid the ruins—the offspring of imperial friction at its most heated. The offspring of war and empire had many identities. Bastards, love children, orphans, and pampered heirs, they belonged to and were rejected from many families, races, and nations. Although their fates and reputations varied, they had one thing in common: "Mixed blood" children were born of boundary-crossing, border-demolishing sex. How should such children be integrated into a world organized in categories of race and nation that are violent and exclusive by nature? How these bouncing bundles of contradictions should be welcomed—or expelled—was a political problem that preoccupied many adults around the world throughout World War II, the Cold War, and the occupations they spawned.

Before 1945, "blood mixing" was a bridge for Japanese imperialists—principally men—to march across and implant Japanese flags and seeds in fertile soil overseas. That bridge remained dangerously intact upon defeat. Now, however, foreign armies and races of men were marching across that biopolitical bridge into the heartland of Japan—and into the beds of Japanese women. Symbolically, the "mixed" child and "blood mixing" mother were polluted by the trauma of defeat. Despite the stark reversal from imperial acclaim to postimperial repudiation, postwar obsession with *konketsuji* was redolent with imperial memory. "Blood mixing" was conflated with conquest, but from 1945 onward, Japanese men were no longer the conquerors but the conquered. Gender inversion was key to the widespread repudiation of "blood mixing" in this postwar milieu. As Japanese women became principal agents "mixing blood" with foreigners, Japanese men were deprived of that biopolitical initiative. Instead, postimperial men took on the role of spectator and often ferocious critic of mixed sexual liaisons. Many postimperial women joined in condemning the sexual and reproductive treachery of their countrywomen. In the context of defeat, Japanese eugenicists, policymakers, presses, and protestors inveighed against "blood mixing" women and redefined *konketsuji* as dysgenic and dangerous to the Japanese *minzoku*.

Minzoku is often translated as "ethnic nation," and that translation is sometimes appropriate. In this book, however, I offer an extended argument for taking the specifically racial content of *minzoku* ideology more

INTRODUCTION

seriously.²⁵ Historian Noriaki Hoshino explains that in the imperial era, Japanese scholars defined *minzoku* as self-conscious collectives linked to but not reducible to race. On the one hand, *minzoku* were related to evolutionary time with biological race as a "substratum" or "medium" for group cohesion. On the other hand, *minzoku* were subject to (re)formation on immediate human timescales through political will and deliberate action. According to Hoshino, the project of empire was precisely to formulate new and cohesive *minzoku* loyalties out of otherwise fractious Asian and global realities.²⁶ Imperial Japanese who promoted "blood mixing" aimed to overcome such divisions and breed a eugenically fit and superordinate biopolitical community in which diverse peoples could vest their loyalties. *Minzoku* consciousness had to be taught, as did the supposedly shared interests in service of which racial brethren and sisters were urged to unite and sacrifice other resources, including life itself. Japanese scholars, policymakers, presses, and propagandists dedicated tremendous resources to building and guiding *minzoku* consciousness along racial lines. Those racial borderlines were redrawn as the empire collapsed and Japan abandoned pan-Asian and universalist pretensions in favor of the politics of purity; yet efforts to foster *minzoku* consciousness on explicitly racial grounds continued. Transwar Japanese who debated, encouraged, or sought to forestall blood mixing did so with one eye on the biological consequences and one eye on *minzoku* consciousness.

As in the imperial era, so too in the early Cold War, Japanese envisioned their *minzoku* and threats to it in biological and hereditary terms. Japan's left, right, and center reconstituted themselves after World War II in the shadows of US and Soviet superpowers and on the rim of hot conflicts between communist and anticommunist forces in Asia. In an era marked by Japan's geopolitical weakness and nuclear-powered antagonisms and paranoia, many Japanese reimagined blood mixing—that age-old biopolitical bridge between Japanese and others—in a dark and deeply hostile light. Even as Japanese partisans on the left and right deepened their antipathies on other points, they converged on an increasingly narrow sense of blood-based belonging to a *minzoku* suffering sexual occupation and in need of defending. This emerging postwar consensus on being "Japanese" was rooted in a romance of "pure blood" (*junketsu*), exclusive of *konketsuji* and hostile toward women who indulged in interracial sex with the wartime enemy, now postwar ally, the United States.

The problems of sexual coercion and mass rape in Japanese-occupied lands had been suppressed and censored in discussions of "blood mixing" during the war. Upon defeat, however, rape and sexual exploitation came to the forefront of Japanese consciousness, moral outrage, and political and medical activism. Only the suffering of Japanese women and the Japanese *minzoku*, however, was seriously contemplated. The sexual violence that Japanese forces had inflicted on women during the war remained occluded, a matter of common knowledge, perhaps, but public indifference. Japanese women who had sex with foreign soldiers in the wake of defeat were forced into a false dichotomy: either pitiable victims of violence and unwilling degradation or sexual collaborators with no shame, no loyalty, and no claim on the sympathies of other Japanese. Either helpless victims of foreign rape or opportunistic race-traitors—in early postwar public opinion regarding the mothers of *konketsuji*, there was often no in-between and no alternative. Ironically, although the Japanese empire (like others) was openly hierarchical and infamously violent, its doctrine of assimilation and mixing left more space for hybridizing bodies and "mixed" families than did the nominally egalitarian and democratic nation-state of postwar Japan.

ARGUMENT AND STRUCTURE OF THE BOOK

In the chapters that follow, I trace the evolution of Japanese identity from "mixed blood" to "pure" from the imperial to postwar era. In chapters 1 and 2, I focus on the imperial era and World War II; in chapters 3 and 4, I examine imperial collapse and Allied occupation; and in chapters 5 and 6, I discuss the end of the occupation, early Cold War, and inauguration of the US-Japan alliance. In all of these chapters, I probe a paradox: that Japan embraced "mixed blood" as an authoritarian wartime empire, only to repudiate "blood mixing" in favor of xenophobic racial nationalism as a postwar democracy.

In chapter 1, I argue that ideologies and policies celebrating "mixed blood" Japanese identity and "mixed" family formation structured and sustained Japanese imperialism. Pan-Asian ideologues, scholars, mass media, and policymakers naturalized conquest as kinship when they endorsed adoption, intermarriage, and "blood mixing" with peoples classified as foreign races on the expanding imperial frontier. The extraordinary pace and scope of Japanese expansion from 1931 to 1945 sparked an unprecedented

INTRODUCTION

boom in attention to "blood mixing," widely touted as a eugenic and political tool for assimilating diverse peoples into a stronger imperial whole while breeding a larger and more powerful "race" of Japanese.

In chapter 2, I probe how even as the empire's "mixed blood" origins and future were glorified during the Asia-Pacific War, some Japanese began selectively repudiating "blood mixing" with the Han Chinese enemy in particular. Violence breeds racism, and the Japanese invasion of China in 1937–1945, in which some ten million Chinese and nearly a half-million Japanese perished, is no exception.[27] I focus on the years from 1938 onward, when expectations of a swift Japanese victory were dashed and mounting violence bred virulent racism. The war that Japan subsequently launched against the United States and British Commonwealth in 1941–1945 has long been characterized as a race war.[28] I argue that the Sino-Japanese War also took on the character of a race war, with Japanese proponents of pan-Asianism carving out a racialized exception for excluding Chinese from intermarriage and confraternity. Disavowing Chinese as kin helped Japanese metabolize mass violence, while novel neo-Mendelian arguments that Japanese genes were recessive to dominant Han genes provided a biological explanation for the empire's failure to absorb China. As the war situation worsened, this new eugenic rationale for refusing to "mix blood" won an increasing number of converts among scholars and policymakers, including a significant cohort concentrated in and around the newly formed Ministry of Welfare. Anti-mixing ideologues were unable immediately to abrogate the pro-mixing policies and practices of the empire. They found, however, new opportunities to translate racial theory into practice when the empire collapsed.

In key battles in 1944–1945 and the occupation of Japan that followed, Japanese enforced racial chastity among their countrywomen with violent conviction: first in group suicides promoted as a defense against rape by foreign soldiers, then in widespread abortions and infanticide of *konketsuji*. Race war continued under occupation, but the target of systematic violence shifted from enemy soldiers to Japanese women who had actual or imagined sexual contact with the enemy and the children conceived of such relations. Although abortion and infanticide were both illegal, "mixed blood" offspring sired by foreign soldiers were targeted for elimination by civic groups in the former colonies and the Ministry of Welfare in a nationwide eugenic campaign. In chapter 3, I detail the MOW's increasing power in the early postwar era, efforts by MOW officials and their allies to purge the body politic of *konketsuji*, and the ways in which anti-mixing activists in and outside the MOW cooperated to achieve the partial decriminalization of abortion in the Eugenic Protection Law of 1948.

Japanese diaries from the occupation era reveal venomous attitudes toward border-crossing relationships between Japanese women and Allied soldiers. Yet such sentiments could not be published when SCAP censored any media that "might invite mistrust or resentment" of Allied troops.[29] In chapter 4, I explore how discourse on race and "blood mixing" evolved under Allied surveillance and censorship. Overt commentary on the sexual conduct of Allied forces was not permitted, but debate over the history, present, and future of "blood mixing" in Japan proceeded apace. Early in the occupation, some prominent Japanese scholars and bureaucrats continued publishing celebrations of Japan's "mixed blood" identity. However, such publications came under attack from other Japanese promoting racial chastity and "pure blood" as eugenic and political imperatives. An anti-mixing ethos coalesced over the course of the occupation, setting the stage for an explosion of public grievance against foreign soldiers and their Japanese lovers once Allied occupation and press controls came to an end.

In 1951, Japan signed a peace treaty ending the state of war with the Allies and a security treaty authorizing US troops to remain in Japan past the occupation's end. In chapter 5, I examine the protests against that security treaty from a fresh angle, focusing less on the supposedly asexual terrain of Cold War geopolitics than on the intimate yet international terrain of sex and reproduction. Members of the Japan Communist Party and other left-wing groups took the lead in the early 1950s in protesting against that security treaty as abetting the sexual colonization of Japan by the United States. Right-wing politicians and mainstream presses soon joined in spreading virulent misinformation about *konketsuji* sired by US soldiers in Japan and in endorsing the end of the security treaty and removal of all *konketsuji* from the country.

At the time, US states barred many forms of interracial sex and marriage as criminal acts; the US federal government also prohibited the immigration and naturalization of members of the Japanese race, including *konketsuji*. In chapter 6, I explore the emergence of an activist movement spanning the Pacific to lower racial bars to the migration of *konketsuji* to the United States. In a movement soon joined by South Korea, the United States and Japan cooperated to facilitate adoption by Americans of "unwanted" children from East Asia. The wholesale removal of *konketsuji*, widely endorsed in 1950s Japan, was never effected, but the emerging infrastructure of international adoption provided a smaller-scale venue for excising "mixed" children from kinship and country. Interracial family formation, long illegal or taboo in the United States, was emerging as an early Cold War cause célèbre—a means to promote American universalism, shore up American moral authority and international reputation, and ameliorate the sexual and racial tensions plaguing early Cold War alliances. Ironically, as postwar Japanese became increasingly intolerant of "mixing" with Americans and other foreigners, the United States reversed course toward an increased tolerance and even enthusiasm for "mixture." For both Japanese and Americans throughout the transwar era, interracial sex and "mixed blood" children marked the biopolitical and affective frontiers of nation and empire.

Reckoning with the fallout of world war and Cold War meant, for survivors, reimagining oneself and one's country in relation to newborn children who symbolize the death of an old order and the incubation of a new world. Adults could see in the newborn dark and haunting reflections of deeds that could never be undone, bodies ravaged, cities burned, empires fallen, and futures spun out of control. What was newly born might be hopeful, adored, or inspiring; but might also be unsettling, shameful, enraging, even terrifying. Let us turn now to the politics of sex and childbirth in a time when cities burned and borders crumbled—a time of sex and world war.

Chapter One

IN PRAISE OF "MIXED BLOOD"

Imperial and Racial Expansion in Asia and the Pacific, 1895–1944

Sex and family formation between "Japanese" and conquered and colonized others started long before imperial expansion peaked in World War II. Already in the 1880s, debates were underway in Japan over "blood mixing." The key question was whether intermarriage would redound to Japan's national benefit or detriment, and the answer people gave depended on whether intermarriage would conform to gendered hierarchies, eugenic dreams, and national loyalties. Then, as later, Japanese advocates for intermarriage as a means to improve the "race" or empire preferred to imagine Japanese men bedding foreign women rather than other racial-conjugal possibilities. Anthropologist Jennifer Robertson contends that "the pureblood position emerged fairly quickly as the dominant one" in the 1880s and remained dominant through the end of empire.[1] The pro-mixing stance was more popular than such studies assume and gained increasing sway as the empire expanded in wars and decades to come.

Historian Paul Barclay traces the empire's promotion of intermarriage to Taiwan, which Japan seized as a colony upon winning the First Sino-Japanese War in 1895. For decades thereafter, Japan struggled to subjugate Indigenous groups in the island's rugged highlands. According to Barclay, the Japanese "government-general embraced interethnic marriage as a solution," urging Japanese men in government employ to take Indigenous wives for use as translators, cultural brokers, negotiators, and colonial

IN PRAISE OF "MIXED BLOOD"

officials.[2] After Japan defeated tzarist Russia in 1905 and annexed Korea in 1910, the weight of scholarly and journalistic opinion in Japan swung decisively toward the notion that the Japanese were a constitutionally "mixed blood" people with a world-historical gift for assimilating diverse "races" into a harmonious family-state. Intermarriage and adoption would accelerate this happy imperial outcome and was promoted by a wide range of Japanese scholars, pundits, and politicians.[3]

As a member of the victorious Allied powers in World War I, Japan expanded into the *Nan'yō* (South Seas), seizing the Pacific colonies of the German Empire. By the early 1940s, more than one hundred thousand settlers had crowded into these South Seas islands. Japanese settlers lived in varying degrees of intimacy with multiracial Chamorros, Carolinians, and other local peoples born of prior generations of "mixture" between Pacific islanders and colonizing Europeans. In the early days of Japanese administration, imbalanced sexual demographics encouraged Japanese men, who accounted for the vast majority of early settlers, toward sexual relations with local women. In later years, when Japanese women arrived in greater numbers, Japanese men continued taking local mistresses; others married island women and abandoned Japanese wives. In addition, roughly eighty brothels serviced men throughout Micronesia. Japanese prostitutes were reserved for Japanese men, but Japanese men could make use of prostitutes of any "race" they liked.[4] Untold numbers of *konketsuji* (mixed-blood children) were born of such relations. Such was the colonial climate that, in the late 1930s, Gondō Seikyo "cherished the notion that Micronesian women yearned to marry Japanese" men. Similarly, international correspondent Andō Sakan (1893–1938) bragged that island women "gave themselves eagerly" to Japanese men.[5] The charisma of empire and virility of Japanese men made them virtually irresistible to women of the South Seas—or so Japanese men and the mass media they created and consumed often claimed.

Japanese women also "mixed blood" with native men. But Japanese women were less prone to publicize such affairs, just as Japanese men who wrote about the *Nan'yō* seemed less eager to lionize this sexual possibility. Historian Kirsten Ziomek argues that "marriages between Japanese women and Micronesian men were rare and seen as completely taboo," a striking example of the gendered double standard of the empire.[6] We cannot say, however, that children were never born of such relations. Anthropologist

Eguchi Tamezō studied *konketsuji* born of a Japanese mother and Chamorro father alongside other South Seas *konketsuji* during World War II.[7]

In 1931, Japan's Kwantung Army seized Manchuria in northern China, establishing a puppet state dubbed "Manchukuo." In 1937, Japan launched a full-scale invasion of China, striking out into even more diverse and distant lands with invasions of southeast Asia and the Pacific in 1941–1942. Before 1937, interracial marriage and *konketsuji* were not common topics of debate in Japan, even among eugenicists.[8] Discourse on "blood mixing" with diverse peoples in far-flung lands boomed during this time of voracious imperial expansion.

Interracial filiation was strongly associated with wartime masculinity. At posh Ginza eateries in the imperial capital, waitresses donned costumes of Chinese and Manchurian women to give patrons a taste of exotic, erotic, and consumable-for-cash colonial and conquered women, conveniently served up in safe metropolitan spaces.[9] Wartime mass media routinely portrayed men in Japanese uniform in "loving" relations with beautiful women and boys in occupied lands. Key to the logic and appeal of such tales was the devotion that foreign adoptees and lovers expressed for the Japanese men who took them in and took control of their homelands.[10]

Erudite debates and high ideals regarding the role "mixed marriage" (*zakkon*) and "mixed blood" children should play in Japan's expanding empire were elaborated in eugenic, scientific, and policymaking circles. In popular culture, too, wartime Japanese consumed a steady stream of artful and erudite expressions of the allure of diverse races, interracial filiation, and multiple modes of "blood mixing." Informed by the latest scientific trends at home and abroad, guided by the latest military and geopolitical events, and inspired by their hopes for a radically new world order, wartime Japanese sought to pioneer a new "mixed blood" order and reshape the global construct of race to their advantage.

"RACIAL BLOOD TRANSFUSION" ON THE CONTINENT

At the height of Japan's imperial expansion from the late 1930s to early 1940s, researchers, policymakers, and mass media all shone an intense spotlight on *konketsuji*, a population deemed both biologically and politically significant. Most Japanese wartime commentators discovered in "hybrid" children evidence that "race mixing" was good for the body of the child and good for the body politic, too.

In the influential high-brow magazine *Kaizō*, multiple Naoki Prize-winning author and graduate of the elite Imperial Army Academy, Ijichi Susumu (1904–1966), urged that Japan pursue a deliberate program of "blood mixing" overseas. Ijichi reminded readers that the blood of several races (*jinshu*) mingled in Japanese veins, including white and yellow races from climatic zones ranging from frigid to tropical. Presuming that his audience was familiar with such commonplace anthropological theories of Japan's "mixed blood" origins, he did not pause to offer proof or persuasion. Rather, Ijichi appealed to Japanese pride. "We have been taught since elementary school about Japanese superiority." This claim to racial superiority was not premised on racial purity. On the contrary, Ijichi insisted, "for the rapid development of the Japanese *minzoku*, we need fresh blood mixing."[11] *Minzoku* is notoriously difficult to translate, for it embraces meanings ranging from nation and people to *Volk* and race, with varying inflections depending on the era and ideology of the speaker.[12] For Ijichi, like many of his contemporaries, a *minzoku* was a distinct biological subunit of humanity—a race.

Ijichi described the Japanese *minzoku* as a singular organism that must replicate and divide to survive. "The island nation known as Japan is one limited vessel. This land and the resources it contains are our culturing fluid. Over two thousand several hundred years, the cells of our *minzoku* have already divided to the outer limit" of the home islands' capacity to sustain them. Implicit in Ijichi's description of Japan's cellular need to expand was a decades-old Malthusian discourse of overpopulation, which justified as an imperative for national survival transplanting Japanese bodies to fresh territories overseas.[13]

In describing this imperative, Ijichi gendered the Japanese *minzoku* as a dynamic, penetrating, masculine organism. "Just as humans live through emission of sperm outside the body into the culturing fluid that is woman's body," he wrote, so too must the organism known as *minzoku* emit itself and divide outside its original body. Ijichi's seminal language objectified Asian women as vessels of male sexual initiative and reproductive activity at levels of both individual and race. "What can give immortal life to these dying cells?" Ijichi inquired rhetorically of his proud, but imperiled, masculine *minzoku*. "It is the vessel known as the continent, the culturing fluid known as East Asia. With Manchuria as our first undertaking, we must transplant ourselves to the fertile soil of the continent."[14]

Ijichi's vision for opening Japanese *lebensraum* (living space) like a womb in the puppet-state of Manchukuo was hardly unique in its time. Many imperial Japanese supported and participated in such schemes for overseas expansion and settlement.[15] Yet Ijichi's vision of territorial and sexual expansion differed in key respects from Nazi Germany's more infamous program for opening *lebensraum* by cleansing Eastern Europe of inhabitants, such as Jews and Slavs, deemed members of separate and inferior races. Like Nazi ideologues, Ijichi envisioned his country as surrounded by inferior races; unlike Adolf Hitler, however, he envisioned his own and neighboring races as productively intertwined. Far from promoting bans on interracial sex and marriage, like those imposed in the Third Reich or most of the United States at the time, Ijichi promoted race-mixing as the path toward a brighter, shared future. Far from xenophobic, Ijichi's program for transplanting the Japanese *minzoku* to distant soil was distinctly pan-Asianist in ethos.[16]

Like other pan-Asianist patriots, Ijichi believed the nominally independent, nascent state of Manchukuo should be governed by Japanese; the chief qualifications of such officials were to be manhood and mixed marriage. Ijichi urged that such officials should be "young, single men. It should be a prerequisite that unless they marry Manchurian maidens, they cannot be appointed as officials." Seeing parallel gendered power dynamics in marriage and military occupation, Ijichi explained that if "they can somehow bring their wives under control, we can say these young officials are able to grasp the principle of leading Manchukuo. [For] how could a man who cannot thoroughly manage a single woman, a single Manchurian woman, according to his own ideals and design, lead a great land like Manchuria?" Given the vast gap in civilizational and racial attainment he perceived between their countries, Ijichi expected disciplining Manchuria and its brides to Japanese standards would be a long and arduous task. To ease the way, he recommended establishing brides' schools (*hanayome gakkō*) to train Manchurian maidens as fit and worthy collaborators in international marriage and occupation.[17]

Tellingly, however, Ijichi did not recommend marriages between Japanese women and Manchurian men. Japanese women, he cautioned, were adaptable and conforming. For such women to marry men outside the *minzoku* entailed subjecting them to foreign domination. As historian Osa Shizue argues, intermarriage in the Japanese Empire was widely imagined—at least by policymakers and men with the power of the pen—as an exchange of women within a patriarchal system operating both domestically and transnationally.[18] But as Ijichi's gender-dichotomous proscriptions and endorsements of "mixed marriage" make clear, not all women were positioned equally as objects of exchange. To Ijichi and men like him, it was imperative that Japanese men maintain a monopoly on Japanese women—even as they denied colonized and conquered men the same monopoly over colonized and conquered women. Hence, endorsement of "mixed marriage" also entailed endorsement of sexual regulations designed to channel sperm, power, and loyalty in the proper direction. In short, Ijichi emphasized that Japan must not deviate from a position of leadership in Asia—the role of husband and father, not that of bride. Ijichi's program for patriarchal exchange of women generated multiple hierarchies—between *minzoku*, between men and women, and among the multiracial community of men—by granting Japanese men authority over all women and men of subordinated "races" alike.

If hierarchies of marriage and *minzoku* were the bedrock on which to build a pan-Asian empire, what roles would Ijichi assign to "mixed blood" children born of such unions? Ijichi held that Japanese-Manchurian *konketsuji* should enjoy all the privileges of the official class to which their Japanese fathers belonged. Treasures of the state, they should receive its protection along with special economic and spiritual support. As they matured into young men, "mixed blood" boys, like their fathers, would distinguish themselves as wise and stern officials, servants of the state, and leaders of multiracial Manchukuo.[19] What role "mixed blood" girls would play Ijichi did not specify.

Ijichi published his article less than two years after Japan launched a full-scale invasion of China. Unsurprisingly, given this timing, his plan for opening *lebensraum* extended beyond Manchukuo and deeper into "the continent," a vast territory rendered feminine by his vision of geopolitical penetration, marriage, and impregnation. Ijichi encouraged his readers to project themselves into China, Mongolia, inner Asia, India, Central Asia, and the Balkans, too. These were underpopulated, undercivilized lands, he alleged, inhabited by "extremely unintelligent" peoples who would prosper under Japanese biopolitical rule. Ijichi proposed to develop Mongolia, for example, according to a twofold program of organic improvement: on the one hand, applying Japanese scientific minds to boosting agricultural fertility; and on the other, improving Mongolian human stock with transfusions of Japanese "blood." Ijichi explained that "Reconstruction [*fukkō*] of Mongolia is reconstruction of the Mongolians. . . . We should transfuse our blood into this *minzoku*."[20]

Ijichi's slogan of "racial blood transfusion" (*minzoku yuketsu*) celebrated interracial sex as a eugenic donation from a conquering *minzoku* to "lesser races" subject to foreign military penetration. In this spirit, Ijichi offered a passing critique of Japanese policies in China, which so far had been "policies for developing Japan" rather than "policies for developing Asia." Although there was some room for policy debate in wartime media, the Criminal Affairs Bureau of the Home Ministry explicitly forbid "indications that we have territorial ambitions in China," suggestions that "new states" such as Manchukuo "are Japanese puppets," and even more capaciously, "differences of opinions with the government or military" on Japanese policy in China.[21] These prohibitions help explain why Ijichi did not elaborate on the distinction he raised between Japanese and Asian interests, much less offer any specific criticism of Japan's invasion and exploitation of China and the Chinese. Instead, Ijichi focused on the benevolent and progressive promise of "blood mixing for the development of Asia." While some wartime Japanese might doubt the wisdom of donating Japanese blood and seed for Chinese benefit, Ijichi insisted that Japan must not be stingy. To uplift all Asians and speed them along the "Japanese way," Japan must wholeheartedly implement "scientific blood mixing and racial blood transfusion."[22]

Ijichi's proposal to require Japanese officials in Manchukuo to marry local women was somewhat idiosyncratic, but his endorsement of "blood mixing" as a mode of imperial expansion was commonplace. One year before Ijichi's article, a complementary vision was promoted in the pages of *Diplomatic Revue*, a venerable journal published monthly since 1898 and twice a month from 1912 until 1943. As *Diplomatic Revue* expanded its readership and reach, the length of each edition blossomed from dozens to hundreds of pages.[23] A frequent contributor in the 1930s and 1940s was sociologist Nanba Monkichi, a prolific author and translator fashioning himself as a public intellectual qualified to interpret foreign societies and international relations for Japanese readers. Nanba held forth in *Diplomatic Revue* on topics such as Chinese nationalism, population policy,

IN PRAISE OF "MIXED BLOOD"

and "Racial Battle Lines and the Greater East Asia War."[24] In 1938, he chose *Diplomatic Revue* as a platform from which to promote "fusing" the Japanese, Manchurian, and Chinese *minzoku* into one. To achieve this ideal, no method was more apt than intermarriage and "blood mixing."[25]

Nanba condemned as misguided the French theorist of Aryan supremacy, Arthur de Gobineau (1816–1882), and Gobineau's present followers in Nazi Germany.[26] To rebut such enthusiasts of racial purity, Nanba cited evidence generated by Jewish émigré Franz Boas (1858–1942) and like-minded US anthropologists that there were no valid biological grounds to oppose "blood mixing." For Japanese to claim otherwise, enforcing the malign fantasy of separate and unequal races, would be no different from the practice of "racial imperialism" that Nanba condemned in white, Western empires.

A strong proponent of Japanese expansion, Nanba preached empire of a different kind. Instead of racial segregation and the eugenic pursuit of purity, he heralded the eugenic pursuit of blood mixing. "If humanity hopes for the emergence of a supremely wise and prudent, moreover supremely vigorous and sound, superior race [*jinshu*] . . . then blood mixing of all races [*jinshu*] must occur." Strongholds of "racial imperialism," such as the United States and Germany, were obviously ill-prepared to take the lead in breeding the magnificent, "mixed blood" master race that Nanba had in mind. It was up to Japan to pursue this enlightened end.

And there was no time to waste. For as Nanba warned, Euro-American countries and their decadent, materialistic cultures were rapidly advancing on Asia. Framing Japan's war on China as a defensive war against Western empires, as was conventional in his time, Nanba argued that the best way to guard against the "fearful, evil designs of the white race" was to promote "racial [*minzoku-teki*] union."[27] Blood mixing, he contended, was the most powerful engine available for fusing diverse and warring Asians into a united super-race under the command of his government in Tokyo.

Like Ijichi, Nanba asserted that the Japanese were, by nature and custom, a "mixed-blood" people who should take pride in that tradition. "Since the country's founding, our country's culture has spread along with blood mixing."[28] As evidence, Nanba recounted the well-known tale of the mythical founder of the Japanese dynasty, the first emperor Jinmu. For Nanba and many other Japanese, Jinmu's prehistoric conquest of foreign lands and intermarriage with a series of foreign women represented the first and noble instance of imperial expansion and integration of diverse peoples through promiscuous "blood mixing." (Ijichi made the same case in his article about "racial blood transfusion.")²⁹ Some 2,600 years had passed between the time Jinmu purportedly established a dynasty through "blood mixing" and the present war for Asia. Throughout this long course of Japan's history, recurring migration and expansion sparked further "mixing." From this racial "mixture" since antiquity emerged the united *minzoku* of which Nanba was a proud member. He boasted that "this intense assimilative power" (*dōkaryōku*) to fuse many into one was a special trait of the Japanese *minzoku*.

Nanba knew that fusing diverse and often warring peoples into one was a Herculean task. For this "world-historical mission of the Japanese *minzoku*," no effort could be spared, no hardship shirked. Distinctions in climate, custom, and lifestyle would make Japanese migration to China and the formation of shared culture there difficult. Fortunately, Japan had much to gain from the effort. "Each year, our country sees a population increase of one million people, more or less. And that excess troubles us. But if it were possible to establish a policy sending the vast majority of that population, or even more, to migrate to China's vast lands each year, it would not only be useful in solving the domestic population problem," Nanba prophesied, but would also help resolve Japan's international crises. Mass migration to China of a million or more Japanese per year would spark mixed marriage on an unprecedented scale. In Nanba's diplomatic vision, it was not military strength, but rather such "blood mixing" and transborder family formation that would "furnish the most reliable material basis and condition for the eternal fusion of the Japanese and Chinese *minzoku*."³⁰ This racial diffusion and familial fusion would dissolve pernicious borders and pockets of anti-imperial resistance, clearing the way for lasting peace under Japanese hegemony.

Watsuji Tetsurō (1889–1960), one of Japan's most prominent philosophers, had long emphasized that Japan was born of "blood mixing" centered on the imperial family. Watsuji established his academic and public reputation as a spokesman for nationalism and pan-Asianism in the 1910s–1920s, when he insisted that "all would agree" that Japanese were a "mixed" people.³¹ According to Watsuji, both the first emperor Jinmu and his forefather Ninigi, as they explored and conquered foreign lands, took women from other *minzoku* as their "prize." The highest dynastic ranks were not distinct in indulging in sexual conquest. Watsuji argued that the "Japanese *minzoku*" was forged through such "liberal miscegenation" among conquering men and conquered women. Downplaying the violence inherent to this narrative of Japanese origins (and present expansion), Watsuji insisted that the engine of "assimilation" and source of *konketsuji* was "love of a woman" by a "strong man."[32]

Pioneering feminist historian Takamure Itsue (1894–1964) made a similar argument. She traced the seminal "blood mixing" that bound many "races" into one "Japan" back to the god-king Ōkuninushi, sometimes identified as nephew to the sun goddess Amaterasu, ancestress of the first emperor Jinmu. Takamure argued that Ōkuninushi's ability to forge an expanding polity hinged not on force of arms but on force of love: He fathered "mixed blood" children with women in 181 different matriarchal clans. Because *konketsuji* were accepted on both sides, Ōkuninushi successfully fused 181 foreign peoples into one "mixed" family-state. Takamure argued that matriarchal clans were thereby gradually sublated into the patriarchal state, which she glossed as a form of progress ongoing in the present. "We find boundless joy in the progressive nature of the great Japanese patriarchy," Takamure wrote in 1938, "a patriarchy that is positive toward marrying into all alien nations and barbarian peoples and uniting them totally under its own lineage." In 1943, Takamure again celebrated Jinmu for launching Japan down its current biopolitical path of conquest, "blood mixing," and "conversion of the whole world into one family."[33]

No mere daydreams, the model of race-mixing as empire-building propounded by Takamure, Watsuji, Ijichi, and Nanba had clear correlates in Japanese colonial policy. In the wake of the March 1, 1919 independence movement in Korea, the Japanese Government-General began promoting a policy of intermarriage under the slogan *naisen ittai*, or "the interior [Japan] and Korea as one body." A royal marriage was celebrated in 1920 between the crown prince of Korea, Yi Un, and princess Nashimoto Masako, who had been in the running to wed crown prince Hirohito. Passed over as bride to Hirohito and future empress of Japan, Nashimoto was instead transformed into Korean crown princess Yi Bangja. She soon gave birth to the first modern "mixed blood" child of Korean-Japanese royalty in a biopolitical propaganda coup. Yi née Nashimoto and her royal *konketsuji* were but the most celebrated faces of a broader imperial campaign to pair elite Korean men with Japanese brides as models of assimilation. In these cases, elite Japanese women were entrusted with the mission of transborder family formation. As governor-general Saitō Makoto explained in *Diplomatic Revue* in 1923, in an empire that valued family above all, only "mixed blood" family ties would overcome the friction between *minzoku* and stabilize the expanding empire.³⁴

In addition to such propaganda efforts, the governments-general in Korea and Taiwan pushed to ease legal and bureaucratic barriers to intermarriage between residents of the *naichi* (interior) and the *gaichi* (exterior)—in other words, between the heartland of Japan and its overseas colonies. Under Japanese law, marriage meant one newlywed (usually the bride) renouncing membership in his or her prior legal family to join the legal household of the spouse (usually the groom). Less often, men entered their wives' household registries as adopted sons of the wife's parents. The juridical and political dilemma with intermarriage was that it entailed switching the residency of one spouse from *gaichi* to *naichi* or vice versa. Japanese laws and policies regarding family and military were predicated on gender inequality, so men and women faced different barriers and opportunities when it came to contracting a "mixed marriage" and changing their residency. Unburdened by military duties and voting rights, women had scarcely any juridical standing to gain or lose in contracting a "mixed marriage." As such, the Japanese state permitted women to intermarry and switch residency between *gaichi* and *naichi* relatively freely.

The borderline was far more substantive for men, however. Men in the *gaichi* (e.g. Korea and Taiwan) were not initially entrusted with the vote or military service, whereas manhood in the *naichi* was defined precisely by such rights and duties. One might expect the Japanese state to police "racial" hierarchies by sharply regulating or barring colonial men from marrying or being adopted into a Japanese family and switching his residency to the *naichi*. After all, once they were *naichi* residents, adopted sons, in-marrying men, and their male children could claim rights and duties equal to native-born Japanese men. The boundary, however, was actually policed in the opposite way. As a legal matter, it was far easier for Korean or Taiwanese men to join *naichi* families and thereby become *Naichijin*—literally "people of the *naichi*," often translated as "Japanese"—than it was for men from the *naichi* to marry or be adopted into Korean or Taiwanese families. The latter was almost always forbidden because it would exempt a *naichi*-born man from military service. Officials were far less concerned about the acquisition of voting rights and military duties by outsider men folded into *naichi* families than they were about the prospect of *naichi* men abandoning those same duties. Regardless, men in general were less likely to leave their families and enter into someone else's household registry; it was women and girls who generally married out and acquired the legal residence of her husband's family.³⁵

After 1937, when Japan launched a war on China that proved unexpectedly difficult (indeed impossible) to win, imperial officials redoubled their efforts to assimilate and win the loyalties of Koreans, whose wartime labor was desperately needed. Part and parcel of this wartime effort was the redoubled commitment to "intermarriage" for empire. From his post as governor-general of Korea, Minami Jirō (1874–1955), the former army minister, Kwantung Army leader, and onetime ambassador to Manchukuo, sermonized that Korea and Japan's home islands (*naichi*) "should become as one in shape, mind, blood and flesh." In March 1941, Minami gave highly publicized awards to "blood mixing" families exemplifying this ideal. Minami also endorsed the "mixed blood" theory of Japanese origins, declaring that "looking back over 3,000 years of Japanese history, it is clear that our ancestors . . . were not limited only to the homogenous Yamato nation, but also included countless peoples who had migrated from various regions."³⁶ Such ideas were not novel, having circulated in anthropological and pan-Asianist thought for decades and having been marshaled to rationalize Japan's annexation of Korea in 1910 as the reunion of blood kin. The Government-General and its allies seized on the extant idea that migration and "blood mixing" were central to the formation of Japan in antiquity and updated that narrative for the wartime era.³⁷

So prevalent was this discourse that it necessarily provoked a reaction. Some Korean nationalists avowed a counternarrative according to which Korean blood was "pure" and distinct from Japanese. Certain veterans of the March First independence movement, such as Han Yong'un (1879–1944), urged his countrymen and women to avoid intermarriage with Japanese and protect the "purity of the Korean *minzoku*."³⁸ As intermarriage increased with government approval and the assistance of pro-Japanese Korean intellectuals, so too did opposition and ostracism of those who dared to "mix" with members of a foreign, colonizing "race."³⁹

But as war fever broke out amid stunning Japanese victories in China in 1937, even leading Korean nationalists such as Yun Ch'i-ho (1865–1945) and Yi Kwang-su (1892–1950) converted to Japanism, abandoning visions of a

Korean *minzoku* (K. *minjok*), bloodline, history, and polity distinct from Japan. With the Government-General's support, Yi, now an enthusiast for imperial expansion, published accounts of Japanese and Koreans as racially intermixed from antiquity and of Japan's imperial family, too, as bearers of "mixed blood." Yi's zeal for muscular Japanese expansion coincided with the Japanese army's decision to open its ranks to Korean men. Masculine, militarist, and imperial pride proved an intoxicating combination. To be a Korean man was no longer to be one of the conquered, Yi proclaimed proudly; now Korean men, too, would rank among the conquering *minzoku* of imperial Japan. "The Chosŏn [Korean] people are no longer by any means a colonized people. They are not a small and weak nation. They are not a people defeated in war. They are proud, upstanding subjects of the Great Empire of Japan."[40] As Takashi Fujitani argues, Yi and other prominent Korean artists, ideologues, and activists who promoted the twin causes of military service and Japanization during the war were not "passive receptors of an already-completed Japanese discourse. . . . Instead, they participated in its production, pushing the universalist or at least inclusionary dimension of Japanese nationalism as far as they could in order to locate themselves solidly within it."[41] Yi soon transitioned to a Japanese name, Kayama Mitsurō—a conversion many Koreans made, some only under duress—and worked to dissolve other distinctions between colonizer and colonized.

Kurashima Itaru, director of the Government-General's Information Section, contributed to this effort in his book, *Korea on the March*. In an opening section on "Blood Mixing," Kurashima emphasized that Koreans and Japanese had never been pure and separate races. He summarized the findings of "physical anthropological research in our country" that millennia of geographic and sexual intimacy between inhabitants of southwestern Japan and the adjacent regions of the Korean peninsula engendered biometric similarities spanning the Sea of Japan. In the present day, natives of southwestern Japan had more in common racially with natives of southern Korea than with inhabitants of northeastern Japan.[42] In short, race and genetic identity did not conform to putative national binaries or the illogic of racial "purity."

Kurashima described the higher unity of Koreans and Japanese as "our ancestors united in one blood." Whatever their origins or identity, Kurashima encouraged readers to think of themselves as born of a long and unifying history of "blood mixing." He preached the need to bring that history to fruition and "truly melt the twenty-four million people of the peninsula into the hundred million of Japan." Such fusion of blood and spirit was an urgent "prerequisite" for imperial expansion. For if Japan failed to realize its promise as a melting pot for the people of Korea, how could it unite the even more diverse populations of Asia and the Pacific? Even if a superficial pan-Asian fusion were achieved through military might, Kurashima doubted that a Japanese-led bloc riven by interracial rivalries would prove capable of winning the war and establishing peace on Japanese terms.

It was clear to Kurashima that "in this situation, there must be abundant mixture of blood." The need was both material and psychosocial. As the strategic bridge between Japan and Manchuria and a site of human and material resource extraction for the initial war in China and additional fronts in the Pacific, Korea was "not merely a forward base for military supply and resource mobilization. Even more, it is a spiritual forward base for promoting the Imperial Way in the continent and Greater East Asia." As an information officer charged with such tasks as education, propaganda, and spiritual mobilization, Kurashima imagined Korea as ground zero in the struggle for the soul of Asia. Hence he warned against expressions of bigotry and fantasies of racial purity, which he condemned as both scientifically unsound and grievously poor strategy at a time when the empire desperately needed the allegiance of those whose "blood" was not "pure" Japanese. If "purity" was a geopolitical dead end, better then to imagine oneself, one's allies, and even one's Asian enemies as members of a common community of blood with "ancestors united." Kurashima therefore uncompromisingly declared that "to oppose inter-racial marriage as a corruption of the pure blood of the Japanese nation or degradation of the Japanese spirit is a reflection of a narrow-minded, intolerant and insular spirit" unbefitting the modern empire of Japan.[43] It was a point on which an increasing number of Japanese and Koreans could agree.

Author and activist Ueda Tatsuo made a similar argument in *The Emperor's Korea*. Mirroring dominant scholarly theories about the Japanese, he insisted that Koreans, too, were a "mixed blood" people. Just as the Japanese imperial family bore Korean blood in their veins, he stressed, Japanese blood flowed in the veins of the former Silla monarchs of Korea. Such were the fruits of a long history of migration and intermarriage. From monarchs to masses, from antiquity to the present, the peoples of East Asia were bound by blood. In a section of his book entitled "The Absoluteness of Japan and Korea as One," Ueda asked rhetorically "how much of the blood of Koreans has entered into those called people of the *naichi* today, and how much of the blood and spirit of Japanese has entered into Koreans?" His answer was clear and compelling: "Physically and metaphysically, both *minzoku* are one; they are not two."[44] Like other wartime ideologues, Ueda interpreted biological and genetic flows as geopolitical and vice versa. Shared blood meant shared identity and justified, even mandated, unification under a single sovereign.

This mandate for unity extended beyond Korea's northern border into Manchukuo and beyond. Residents of northern Korea, Ueda argued, were clearly *konketsuji* with Chinese ancestry. Korea as a whole was born of such interregional and interracial fusion, and Korea's culture was a hybrid culture, "not the culture of Korea itself."[45] The fact that some misguided Koreans, like warring Chinese, continued to resist Japanese rule signified, in Ueda's mind, that those Koreans shared more Chinese blood and spirit than Japanese. Explaining anti-Japanese resistance as a manifestation of Chinese blood flowing in Korean veins ran the risk of destabilizing Ueda's argument that "mixed blood" was a genetic asset and instrument of imperial expansion. Although Ueda acknowledged that "blood mixing" might occasionally work against empire, he overwhelmingly framed the breadth and depth of Korea's "mixed blood" ties as a positive thing—an engine of power and progress. For him, Koreans' hybrid heritage was a point of pride. In their diversity, Koreans formed a genetic and cultural bridge spanning from the Japanese home islands into the depths of mainland Asia. As sentient planks of that organic bridge across Asia, Koreans could play a leading role in imperial expansion and the harmonization of diverse races.

Ueda published these arguments as the Japanese army, now including Korean volunteer soldiers, cut a bloody swath through China.[46] Keenly attuned to the symbolic stakes, he dated his book's foreword to August 1, 1943, "the inspirational day that military conscription is applied in Korea." While praising their growing military contributions, Ueda also emphasized that Koreans could take the lead in pacifying anti-Japanese resistance nonviolently. By deploying the assimilative power of their "mixed blood" on the frontiers of Japanese Empire, Koreans could "absorb those with Chinese blood connections" as proud children of the empire. In Ueda's analysis, it was not only Japanese who boasted the world-shaping capacity to fuse diverse *minzoku* into one. As the vanguard of imperial "blood mixing,"

Koreans could help secure peace in Asia and guarantee Japan's global preeminence for generations to come.[47]

Ueda's ideological efforts to theorize race-mixing for empire hold particular interest because he was born in Asan, Korea, as Yi Yŏng-gŭn. Not until he grew up did he, like other Korean-born men of his day, transition to a Japanese name and identity. A highly educated and cosmopolitan thinker, Ueda née Yi studied first at the prestigious Keijō Imperial (now Seoul) University in his homeland before moving abroad to study in the United States. During the war, he relocated to Tokyo to master what he termed the "Japanese spirit," a calling he pursued at the National Spiritual Culture Research Center of the Greater Japan Youth Club. By the time he published *The Emperor's Korea*, Ueda was serving in the Korean Labor Association and promoting the Japanism Youth Movement in cooperation with the governor-general in Korea.[48] As Ueda collaborated with Japanese authorities to mobilize Koreans for the war effort, he also exploited the war effort for his own advancement and that of his fellow Koreans. Many other colonial subjects in Korea, Taiwan, Okinawa, Manchuria, Hokkaido, and beyond participated in such efforts, striving to turn wartime calls for unity to their own advantage.[49]

As suggested by his insistence that Korea and Japan "are one; they are not two," Ueda was a relentless critic of "dualistic" thought. He condemned liberalism (*jiyūshugi*) on the grounds that it denied commonalities and unities between *minzoku*, recognizing instead only atomized "units of mutual national [*minzokuteki*] independence." But the *minzoku* of Korea, in Ueda's view, did not need independence, because "Korea is not a colony." He decried as "intellectual poison" the view that "Japan annexed Korea using military might and made it a colony." Ueda explained that "in this view, there is only the problem of dominion and submission, power and power. All that is contemplated is the oppositional relationship between the strong and the weak. Particularly in arguments for the pure blood of the *minzoku*," Ueda warned, proponents of Korean independence sank to a loathsome low. He decried "pure blood" as another outgrowth of dualistic and liberal thinking that pitted people against one another. "Assimilation in one body" must not be "made impossible," Ueda insisted, by such binary thinking. What Koreans needed was not the (allegedly) false anticolonial promise of a pure and independent *minzoku* but rather organic thinking and imperial holism.

"Who in the world have we received this colonization argument from?" Ueda demanded. "Who in the world's second-hand good is the argument for a pure-blood *minzoku*?" His answer was the British and American enemy. As Ueda explained it, it was Anglo-Saxon empires that governed through racial segregation, domination, and the politics of "purity." The Japanese Empire was different, and Korean separatists' arguments for "pure blood" amounted to a form of transimperial false consciousness. Ueda therefore condemned those who opposed "assimilation in one body" as victims of misbegotten "British-American colonial consciousness." He then turned the logic of racial nationalism against anyone who on the basis of "blood" sought to exclude him or others like him from Japanese community: "Japanese who are truly Japanese [*Nihon rashiki Nihonjin*] are those who deeply believe that Koreans and Japanese are one. People opposed to this truth we clearly must call un-Japanese."[50]

No tepid plea for mutual respect and reconciliation, Ueda's claims were fighting words. He depicted opponents of "blood mixing" not merely as philosophically misguided or scientifically misinformed but as threats to the Japanese Empire. He denounced "conduct of the sort that concocts divisions of Koreans from Japanese and applies Western theories of colonization and pure-blood *minzoku* to Korea" as "a great retrogression that plots upheaval in the *kokutai* [body politic]."[51] There was no charge more serious, in imperial Japan, than plotting against the *kokutai*.

Kokutai was an amorphous concept, but at base, the term indicated a polity centered on loyalty to the emperor. *Kokutai* ideology was therefore hostile to "foreign" revolutionary movements ranging from communism to independence for a "nation" or *minzoku* such as Korea. Beyond these fundaments, however, what entailed service or disservice to the *kokutai* was subject to vociferous debate. From the late 1920s through the 1940s, people ranging from communists to plutocrats, professors to retired admirals were purged, persecuted, imprisoned, and attacked by assassins for offending against someone's particular vision of *kokutai*.[52] So when Ueda accused proponents of "pure blood" of "plotting upheaval in the *kokutai*," he was using potentially deadly language. He thereby denounced and menaced both metropolitan bigots from the *naichi* and nationalist proponents of the purity and independence of Korean *minzoku*. Ueda knew that *kokutai* meant different things to different people; it could be weaponized against many enemies. At the peak of the Asia-Pacific War, with the backing of the governor-general in Korea, Ueda née Yi boldly arrayed himself as a defender of the *kokutai* while celebrating "mixed blood."

IN PRAISE OF "MIXED BLOOD"

Ueda published *The Emperor's Korea* in Tokyo, in Japanese, in 1943. At the time, authorities deemed scarcely one in five Koreans to be competent in the Japanese language. Literacy rates overall were far higher among Japanese than Koreans.[53] For whom then was Ueda writing? An elite stratum of highly educated and politically active men of Korean extraction, like himself, were surely among his intended audience. So too were younger generations of Okinawans and Ainu, educated in Japanese-language schools, who were still, like Koreans, in the process of proving their Japanese credentials.[54] But the vast majority of those who could read Ueda's argument for a mixed-blood *kokutai* were natives of the *naichi*, men and women who had grown up speaking and "being" Japanese. The primary audience largely included people who took their "Japaneseness" for granted. The assumption that such people had a monopoly on Japanese identity or a special relationship to Japaneseness was intolerable to a man like Ueda. Ueda insisted that if claims to "pure" Korean blood and biopolitical being, which doubled as anti-imperial claims for political independence, were illegal and treasonous, then claims to "pure" Japanese identity should be judged and condemned by the same standard. Such invidious distinctions of blood and birth should be condemned to the dustbin of empire.

We are all "mixed blood"; we are all Japanese. Such were the claims made by Ueda and his allies in the Government-General of Korea. Such were the battle cries of prominent Japanese and Korean men cheering imperial expansion into Manchukuo, China, and the erotically imagined depths of Asia. Like the legendary emperor Jinmu of old, Japanese men with ambitions for empire must strike out into foreign lands, tame and marry foreign women, and beget new "mixed blood" generations. In the imagined "mixed blood" community of Japan, righteous rule expanded along with Japanese bloodlines, eugenically and promiscuously organizing Asia into a vascular network with Tokyo as its beating heart.

RACE SCIENCE, *KONKETSUJI*, AND THE CO-PROSPERITY SPHERE

Despite all the fanfare about intermarriage and "blood mixing" in imperial Japan, there was little evidence as to whether *konketsuji* were healthy and thriving. Before the war, such studies had not been a priority. Mizushima Haruo (1896–1975), professor of medicine at Kyushu Imperial University, complained in 1942 that there existed few detailed, empirical studies of *konketsuji*. [55] But Mizushima knew ambitious young scientists were stepping in to fill the empirical void. He also knew that their findings might shape the future of policy and social practice. Mizushima's remark about the dearth of studies amplified the significance of their work while inspiring more researchers to join the fast-growing, interdisciplinary field of *konketsuji* studies.

At the forefront of such research was Miyake Katsuo, a medical researcher writing his dissertation at Mizushima's own university. Alert to the professional opportunity afforded by the wartime boom in popular and political attention to "blood mixing," Miyake focused his research on 428 "mixed blood" children, each born to a reproductive pairing of one Korean and one Japanese parent. In June 1941, Miyake presented his research to the Union of Hygienic Societies (*Rengō eisei gakkai*), a major scientific organization founded in 1929 to gather researchers, practitioners, and policymakers in fields ranging from bacteriology and epidemiology to public health and hygiene.[56] In hosting Miyake's talk, the Union testified to how relevant *konketsuji* now were to diverse medical and policy communities in Japan.

Miyake probed the bodies, health, and school records of his "mixed blood" subjects and then compared them to children with parentage exclusively either Japanese or Korean. Miyake judged the *konketsuji* generally superior in height, weight, and overall physique, and also in terms of being superlative students. Despite his junior status and the still in-progress nature of his work, Miyake's findings were immediately picked up and amplified by more senior scholars and practitioners hungry for data on *konketsuji*. Among these were physician-bureaucrats Ishiwara Fusao and Satō Hifumi at the Tokyo Municipal Hygiene Examination Office, who cited Miyake's research when publishing their study on *konketsuji*. Their methodology was similar to Miyake's, but rather than examining Korean-Japanese "mixed blood" children, they studied Sino-Japanese *konketsuji* growing up in metropolitan Tokyo. Ishiwara and Satō announced that Miyake's "findings resemble our own," for the physical stature and academic performance of *konketsuji* in both studies were "superior."

Like Miyake, Ishiwara and Satō attributed these positive outcomes to both biological and environmental factors, including the salutary influence of foreign cooking styles on otherwise undernourished and underdeveloped Japanese bodies. Unlike Miyake and Mizushima, however, Ishiwara and Satō raised serious doubts about the social milieu of "blood mixing."

As we will see in chapter 2, anxieties over women's chastity, gender norms, and the potentially dire influence of Chinese fathers on Japanese children's political loyalties led Ishiwara and Satō to warn against Sino-Japanese "intermarriage" at the height of Sino-Japanese war. Yet despite these concerns, these medical researchers raised no eugenic doubts about the inborn, genetic excellence of *konketsuji*.[57]

In 1942, Miyake Katsuo and Mizushima Haruo contributed a coauthored paper on "blood mixing" to *Population Policy and Territorial Planning*, a compilation of research findings and policy recommendations by the empire's leading scholars and technocrats. To win the war and build the autarkic bloc dubbed the Greater East Asian Co-Prosperity Sphere, Miyake and Mizushima wrote that "it is desirable that roughly 20,000,000 of the Yamato race advance energetically into the continent of Asia and the Pacific." As a result of this "large-scale overseas advance, blood mixing will inevitably occur." Indeed, "blood mixing" was already underway, and not just in frontiers and war zones.

The heart of the empire, too, was a contact zone, with a rising tide of migrants from Korea taking up residence in the *naichi* to perform wartime labor.[58] Mizushima and Miyake's research on Japanese-Korean *konketsuji* was thus of clear and urgent relevance. Yet for all that seems political and predetermined about their analysis, Miyake and Mizushima were serious researchers with a deep commitment to generating precise, detailed, and to their minds, geopolitically relevant medical and racial data on *konketsuji*. As a result, there was considerable complexity and variation in their findings about the comparative quality of "mixed" and "pure" children. They found *konketsuji* were often physically larger and more robust than "pure" children, a result possibly attributable to "hybrid vigor."[59] Not all *konketsuji*, however, were physically imposing specimens. The broad range of traits discovered in the children under study led Mizushima and Miyake to conclude that "whether they're pure-blood or mixed-blood is all the same."

This is not to say that Miyake and Mizushima were egalitarian in their outlook. On the contrary, they were deeply concerned with eugenic reproduction. They simply considered eugenic quality to be more a question of class than of race or racial purity. They therefore recommended that Japan adopt a policy for selecting high-quality Koreans for permanent residence in Japan to avoid dysgenic outcomes as "blood mixing" accelerated.[60]

Several months after issuing this recommendation, Miyake published an extended report on an expanded total of "449 mixed-blood students" from 326 families formed through "marriage between the interior and Korea [*naisen kekkon*]." Miyake's fifty pages of detailed data and argumentation about "blood mixing" ranged from neo-Mendelian genetics or "hard" heredity to "soft" inheritances like customs, lifestyle, and diet.[61] Despite the complex and sometimes contradictory nature of his findings, Miyake concluded that race mixing "certainly is not something to view pessimistically." After weighing all the scientific evidence available in several languages, Miyake found no grounds to support the notion that adverse consequences of "blood mixing" were accruing in the Japanese Empire. On the contrary, the *konketsuji* he studied were "in fact superior to both races, Japanese and Korean [*nai, sen ryō jinshu*]."[62]

Starting in December 1941, Japan launched offensives on several new fronts, with attacks on Pearl Harbor, Alaska, the Philippines, Singapore, Hong Kong, the Dutch East Indies, New Guinea, and beyond. The Greater East Asian Co-Prosperity Sphere now took on a vastly expanded geopolitical scope.[63] As Japan broadened its war on China into a world war, research and debate regarding race and "blood mixing" not only with Koreans and Chinese, but with far-flung and diverse populations throughout Asia and the Pacific only increased in relevance and complexity.[64]

Miyake Katsuo's mentor, Mizushima Haruo, continued in this era of global war to lend his weight to rebutting claims that "blood mixing" was dysgenic. Mizushima cited Norwegian eugenicist and politician Jon Alfred Mjöen as a leading proponent of the dysgenic point of view. Mjöen's studies on "race-crossings" between "Mongoloid Lapps and the Nordics" diagnosed in hybrids higher rates of disease, criminality, alcoholism, and "low mental ability" compared with their "parent races."[65] Yet Mizushima was far from convinced. Against Mjöen's findings, Mizushima cited the good results of his own and Miyake's research on eugenically fit *konketsuji*. Mizushima and Miyake also cited Jewish-American anthropologist Franz Boas and his recent *Race, Language, and Culture* (1940) as evidence that nothing was biologically amiss in "blood mixing." Boas was highly favored by pro-mixing advocates in Japan as an international authority whose superlative scholarship could be construed to support their racial-imperial claims. Despite his fondness for the German-American Boas, however, Mizushima chalked up the whole global scientific debate over "mixing" to white bias and white scientists like Mjöen who labored—and failed—to prove that "mixing" with colored races was deleterious. Of people "who, binding together biological ways of thinking and racial prejudice, emphasize the doctrine that blood mixing is harmful," Mizushima noted, "those are mainly white people."[66] Needless to say, this was neither a flattering estimation of white scientists nor of any Japanese who might be taken in by their bigotry and error.

To Mizushima, it was clear that there were no pure races in humankind. Casting his gaze around the Pacific, Mizushima found varieties such as Malay-Chinese and Malay-Dutch *konketsuji* to be not only numerous—evidence of strong fecundity and eugenic fitness—but also superior in both mental and physical traits. These were encouraging findings, given that Japan had recently occupied Malaysia and the formerly Dutch territory of Java. "Blood mixing" between Japanese and residents of these new territories was underway.

Mizushima argued that in a world of rampant mixture, the Japanese *minzoku* had perhaps "the greatest measure of mixed blood." Citing numerous eminent Japanese scholars—Torii Ryuzō, Kiyono Kenji, Tsuboi Shogorō, and others—Mizushima detailed Japan's blood ties to Eskimos, Indonesians, Indochinese, and Tungus peoples; to Caucasians, Koreans, Chinese, and Mongolians; and to Negritos from Bengal, Java, New Guinea, and the Philippines too. He emphasized that such genetic connections were more than a matter of ancient history or antiquarian interest. "From today forward, our *minzoku* is poised to enter into an era of even greater blood mixing."[67] It was a confident statement on imperial expansion.

Despite his optimistic outlook, Mizushima acknowledged that "blood mixing" involved risk. For instance, Mizushima wondered whether "*konketsuji* will have the same Japanese spirit as pure Japanese." The cause of his concern was not any inborn difference in *konketsuji*, but rather the threat that other Japanese would discriminate against them. Such discrimination would give rise to social and spiritual divisions between old-stock Japanese and newborn *konketsuji*. Mizushima cautioned his fellow Japanese that in mismanaged European empires, *konketsuji* were socially excluded by white people who prided themselves on "purity." The result was that *konketsuji* developed weak "*minzoku* spirit." Mizushima did not define "*minzoku* spirit," but the term appears to denote collective identity, political cohesion, and loyalty. He urged that Japan must not follow the self-defeating model of discrimination against "mixed blood" people common to European empires.

Mizushima's concern reflected his awareness, which he did not squarely confront, that it was not whites alone who discriminated on the basis of "blood." Many Japanese looked down on newly incorporated members of the empire and inhabitants of conquered lands—people deemed darker of skin, weaker of body and mind, or less "civilized," and those whose cultural and blood ties to Japan were deemed to be too remote or too recent. Such supremacist and insular attitudes among "Japanese" posed, in Mizushima's analysis, an imminent threat to imperial power and cohesion. He warned that if Japanese subjected *konketsuji* to segregation and discrimination, the "mixed" offspring of empire might internalize the prejudiced notion that they were not Japanese. This in turn would disrupt the development of *minzoku* spirit and alienate *konketsuji* from the empire. Improperly managed, Mizushima warned, such prejudice-born racial disunities could become a "great political cancer" in the heart of Japan.[68] In Mizushima's analysis, the notion of "pure blood" was potentially factionalizing, and it must not be allowed to disrupt the process of Japanese identity formation and the unification of diverse populations and co-prosperity countries under Japan's imperial banner. Mizushima was not alone in his premonition that racial chauvinists might destabilize the empire by pitting old-stock Japanese against intermixed newcomers. Historian Yi Jonson treats Mizushima's warning as prophetic, as rapidly proliferating "mixed" marriages and informal liaisons met with prejudice in the 1940s, turning "mixed blood" children into a socially recognized "problem."[69]

Despite such backlash, the spirit of high-imperial acclaim for amalgamating foreign lands and peoples into Japan's bloodlines and *kokutai* continued to flourish as the war wore on. One of the more prominent proponents of the pro-amalgamation line was professor Taniguchi Konen (1902–1963), an internationally renowned anatomist at Keio University. During the war, Taniguchi led a team of researchers to study "blood mixing" of virtually every imaginable variety throughout the co-prosperity countries in Japan's imperial orbit. As a scientist, Taniguchi dutifully emphasized that further research on all varieties of *konketsuji* was necessary before reaching a "firm determination" on their quality. His mind in fact seemed largely made up, as he consistently cast doubt on claims that "blood mixing" was harmful.

Like Mizushima, Taniguchi pointedly discredited the findings of white European scientists who mistook the temporary material advantages of their civilization for innate racial superiority, a rank to be preserved by upholding their faux "purity." At the peak of Japan's imperial expansion in the early 1940s, amid shattering victories against the United States, British, and Dutch forces in the Pacific, Taniguchi ceded no ground to such tendentious theories of white supremacy. Japanese race-scientific research had made "clear that there is no observable difference in superiority and inferiority between whites and we Japanese. Not only that, we have also even proven that on some points, whites likely possess traits closer to animals than do people of the yellow race." Like many other race scientists in Japan during the Pacific War, Taniguchi enjoyed turning the tables of racial stereotyping on "animalistic" white people. And like Mizushima, he confidently denounced white scholars for studding the potentially enlightening sciences of heredity, genetics, anthropology, and eugenics with bias and error. Taniguchi foresaw years of work ahead for Eastern researchers, whom he seemed to assume were less prone to bias, to develop a more accurate map of the races and genetic factors of the world. There was every reason to hasten fresh raciological research, but given the state of the field at present, Taniguchi concluded that it was impossible to assert qualitative differences between races. As such, there were scant grounds for opposing "blood mixing."[70]

Taniguchi sharply criticized whites for regarding any "blood mixing" as a loss of their supposedly pure traits—as "blackening" or "Judaization"— and suggested that Japanese need not harbor similar fears. His 1942 tome, *The Constitution of Eastern Races*, detailed racial mixture not only among the diverse *minzoku* of Japan, Korea, and China but also among Kanaka, Chamorro, Papua, Negrito, Spanish, and other populations in the South Seas. Occasionally, Taniguchi noted, crinkled hair appeared on Japanese heads—clear phenotypical evidence of Negrito admixture. But "among *konketsuji*, the characteristics of Japanese hair are genetically dominant, and Japanization materializes to a high degree."[71] Here Taniguchi deployed the logic of neo-Mendelian genetics to argue that because of the dominance of the stereotypically Japanese trait of straight hair over "foreign" textures of hair that he termed recessive, imperial expansion and "blood mixing" multiplied Japanese traits; it did not dilute them. Notwithstanding his sharp critique of white supremacy and the white politics of purity,

Taniguchi appealed to similar racial bias in emphasizing the appeal of reproducing stereotypically Japanese traits, such as straight hair, in *konketsuji*. Even as he legitimized "blood mixing," Taniguchi celebrated the genetic and phenotypical "Japanization" of populations subject to Japanese rule. In the process, he yoked neo-Mendelian conceptions of dominant traits to Japanese geopolitical dominance.

Taniguchi, however, did not promote "blood mixing" exclusively as a way to eliminate foreign traits through the exercise of neo-Mendelian dominance. He also emphasized the utility of "letting in the blood of *minzoku* with strong constitutions" to give birth to better Japanese. Taniguchi was as convinced as any contemporary white scientist of genetic hierarchies and the propriety of eugenic engineering. "That superior children are born of superior parents is the law of genetics." Taniguchi tended to insist that the eugenic or dysgenic quality of *konketsuji* depended on their parents, not on their parents' races.[72] Within each race, some were held more fit to breed than others and more fit to interbreed with Japanese.

Taniguchi praised the "mixed blood" children of Chinese and Cambodians as healthier than "pure" children of either parental race, exhibiting improved resistance to smallpox and cholera, in particular. On the basis of this data and far more, Taniguchi suggested that "by borrowing the power of the blood of the native *minzoku* who are amply adapted to the territory where Japanese are advancing," Japan could "rapidly secure a large number of Japanese people (mixed-blood Japanese) biologically suited to those lands." In other words, the empire should deliberately breed diverse *konketsuji* so that future generations of Japanese could master new frontiers. "Blood mixing" was an evolutionary shortcut and eugenic opportunity with geopolitical ramifications. Properly bred and managed *konketsuji* were a strategic asset. They would empower the Japanese to dominate almost limitlessly diverse foreign lands by increasing the biological diversity and inborn capacity of the Japanese.

In this spirit of evolutionarily informed geostrategic planning, Taniguchi recommended subdividing the Japanese by their adaptive traits. For as Taniguchi argued, "one can probably find more variation within a single *minzoku* than between completely different *jinshu*" or meta-races, such as white, black, and yellow. Fortuitously, the Japanese *minzoku* was a particularly "mixed blood" population with abundant internal genetic diversity. The empire should therefore dispatch those with "southerly constitutions" (*nanpōteki taishitsu*) to develop territory seized in the south Pacific and those with "northerly constitutions" (*hokuhōteki taishitsu*) to develop northern reaches such as Sakhalin and Manchukuo.[73]

By 1942, Japan's Co-Prosperity Sphere had expanded to include the Philippines, and Taniguchi and his team of researchers eagerly directed their scientific attention toward this new frontier. Taniguchi declared that a "mixed blood" population one million strong inhabited the Philippine islands and tended to outperform and outrank "pure" locals, regardless of the type of mixture. "Mixed blood children of the Filipinos and Chinese, Japanese, white Americans, and Spaniards are highly superior," he assured readers of the influential journal *Eugenics*. Taniguchi highlighted as examples of such "mixed blood" excellence Filipino presidents Emilio Aguinaldo and Manuel Quezon, among others.[74]

Marxist theorist Hirano Yoshitarō and leading anthropologist Kiyono Kenji joined the wartime chorus heralding these Filipino leaders as living proof of the biopolitical payoff of "blood mixing." They made of the exceptional *konketsuji* Quezon a general rule that "blood mixing" was a salutary practice. "Every race [*jinshu*] under heaven has each its own strengths," opined Hirano and Kiyono. "We should perfect the flourishing of the Greater East Asia Co-Prosperity Sphere by helping one another and binding ourselves together." The key to success in this project of racial "binding," they explained, was to cultivate and educate *konketsuji* properly. Care must be taken to prevent *konketsuji* from indigenizing, as "mixed blood" descendants of Japanese who had settled in New Caledonia in the southwest Pacific in the late-nineteenth century had done. Kiyono and Hirano presented these "mixed" offspring of Japan in New Caledonia as a lost opportunity to uplift Japanese and natives alike. They identified a better model in Java, where *konketsuji* born of unions between the colonizing Dutch and colonized natives worked as junior officials in the Dutch colonial government, serving the Dutch Empire and facilitating understanding with the natives.[75] In the Japanese Empire, Kiyono and Hirano urged, properly trained *konketsuji* should play comparable political roles.

Wartime scholars' emphasis on the natural and desirable reality of genetic diversity within *minzoku* and of "mixture" between *minzoku* did not proceed in ignorance of Nazi theories of the desirability of racial homogeneity. Taniguchi referenced doctrines of Nordic purity and supremacy precisely to distance Japan from such talk: "There is no scholar who doubts that we, the Yamato *minzoku*, are a mixed-blood *minzoku*. So if we take the Japanese *minzoku* to be a superior *minzoku*, then not only can a mixed-blood *minzoku* also become a superior *minzoku*, it is also conceivable that by mixing the blood of *minzoku*, a superior *minzoku* is born."[76] Confident that "blood mixing" could function as an engine of imperial growth and eugenic advancement, Taniguchi continued to emphasize Japan's advantages as a mixed and mixing *minzoku* long after the tides of war began to turn.[77]

BATTLEFIELD ADOPTION AND "MIXED" LOYALTIES

While imperial scholars and officials promoted "mixed marriage" and the eugenic reproduction of "mixed blood" children, popular media made clear that bonds of blood were not exclusively to be forged through heterosexual sex and genetic reproduction. The trope of Japanese soldiers symbolically adopting needy and adoring youths in conquered lands was already popular in the arts and mass media during the First Sino-Japanese War (1894–1895). Such tropes reappeared in the second Japanese war on China some forty years later. In the 1890s, commercial artists took the lead in propagating this popular narrative. Later, in the mid-twentieth-century era of "total war," the Japanese government produced propaganda trumpeting Japanese soldiers as adoptive fathers for the needy children and subordinate "blood lines" of Asia. Whether through "intermarriage" or the adoption of colonized peoples as kin, justifying imperial expansion and Japanese hegemony hinged on forging patriarchal family ties with diverse peoples in new lands.

One oft-repeated tale of adoptive heroism in the First Sino-Japanese War featured captain Higuchi Seizaburō. Journalists and artists feted him to transnational fame in 1895 for having allegedly rescued an abandoned Chinese child while leading an attack on Qing imperial forces near the city of Weihai. A lithograph by an unknown Japanese artist (figure 1.1) colorfully depicts the dashing captain brandishing a Japanese saber in one hand and a Chinese foundling in the other. The foreign foundling clings to Higuchi with desperate affection.

Many well-known artists recreated the tale of Higuchi's heroism, with each variation and embellishment affirming rather than undermining the manufactured sense that Higuchi and the unnamed infant embodied fundamental truths about their respective peoples or "races" and empires. As historian John Dower explains, wartime images of violence and salvage

IN PRAISE OF "MIXED BLOOD"

FIGURE 1.1. *Lt. (?) Higuchi Saving a Child in the Midst of Battle at Backaigai.* Artist unknown, n.d., ca. 1895. Colored lithograph on paper. The Trout Gallery, Dickinson College, Carlisle, PA.

fuse "denigration of the 'old' China with chivalrously rescuing 'young' (or future) China." As self-represented in popular arts and media, Japan was an adoptive father who was "actually saving China's future by forcing it into the 'modern' age."[78] Japan, the masculine invader, was redeemed from its violence through the noble work of male-male pan-Asian filiation, which tended to justify the disciplinary violence required to achieve imperial rule.

Some contemporaneous representations omitted violence from the scene altogether. An 1895 triptych by woodblock artist Ogata Gekkō (figure 1.2) beautifies Japan's invasion of Korea and northeastern China as a loving, domestic affair. Violence is not visible; instead, the artist shows captain Higuchi and other Japanese soldiers fawning over a Chinese infant "rescued" from the battlefield. The Chinese infant gazes up, reaching for Higuchi's idealized figure, heedless of the presence of a countryman to the left. A defeated Qing soldier kneels there, unable to defend his country or

FIGURE 1.2. "Captain Higuchi, in the Midst of the Attack, Personally Holds a Lost Chinese Child" (Higuchi taii shingeki no toji mizukara seishi no ishi o hoji suru no zu). Ogata Gekkō, 1895. Woodblock print triptych. Photograph © Museum of Fine Arts, Boston.

IN PRAISE OF "MIXED BLOOD"

its children. A failed patriarch, he too appears in need of Japanese leadership and succor. He raises his hands in silent supplication as the transfer of Chinese futurity to Japanese hands unfolds. That Japanese troops were the very forces shattering families and producing orphans in need of battlefield rescue is not clarified in Ogata's triptych; instead, the infant's need for kinship with powerful men appears to justify Japanese invasion as a form of benevolent, borderless filiation.[79]

A nascent narrative of "mixed blood" filiation is on display. This transracial, Japanese-initiated family formation bypassed the womb to occur spontaneously among men and boys on the battlefield. Women were not needed for this sort of reproduction of paternal lineages and imperial loyalties among conquered "races" in occupied lands. Left to themselves on distant battlefields, deprived or relieved of the company and fertility of Japanese women, Japanese men and boys forged "mixed" families on their own (figure 1.3). In the era of total war in the 1930s and 1940s, blood brotherhood and battlefield adoption loomed large in the cultural imagination. Bypassing "mixed marriage" and Mendelian gene flows, male-male lineages of "mixture" and "fusion" reproduced the Japanese Empire overseas with great symbolic efficiency. They did so far more quickly than eugenic advocates of "blood mixing" could imagine, bound as the latter were by the delays inherent in heterosexual reproduction.

Japan's first months of all-out war on China in 1937 fueled expectations of imminent and total victory. So celebratory was the home-front mood by December 1937 that even Japanese leaders complained that the Japanese public had lost sight of the sobriety suited to a time of sacrifice and slaughter.[80] The mood began to shift in 1938, when Chinese resisters sacrificed roughly a million casualties to defend the great city of Wuhan and slow Japan's advance into central China. Japanese casualties were astronomically higher than anticipated.[81] Suddenly confronted with a long-term war of attrition rather than a short war of decisive superiority, Japan's leaders rushed to mobilize more human, material, and spiritual resources. It was in this context that the cabinet propaganda project "Wuhan Lullaby" transfigured the reality of near-genocidal violence into a tender narrative of pan-Asian adoption and asexual "blood mixing" among fighting men and foundlings in China. In "Wuhan Lullaby," government agents and mass media replicated on a much larger scale 1890s-era tropes of Japanese men as adored, adoptive fathers and elder brothers to needy children on the continent.

IN PRAISE OF "MIXED BLOOD"

FIGURE 1.3. Japanese soldiers rush to save a Chinese baby "abandoned" in a field near Wuhan. Cabinet Information Bureau (CIB), photographer unknown. "Wuhan Lullaby" (Wuhan komori-uta), 1938. 35 mm nitrate.

In figure 1.3, Japanese soldiers posing before a camera pretend to have found a lone infant in the vast, empty plains of central China.[82] They lovingly set down their Japanese flag on contested Chinese soil to uplift the Chinese babe. Whose child they requisitioned for the photo shoot is not clear. The photograph dramatizes the need for Japanese men-at-arms to establish a surrogate pan-Asian patriarchy on the continent to care for future generations of Chinese.

This and similar photographs were produced in 1938 as part of the propaganda series "Wuhan Lullaby" for the Cabinet Information Bureau (CIB) in Tokyo. The series features shots of hale and handsome Japanese soldiers holding, teaching, and playing with local children in the meticulously curated warzone of Wuhan. Hunger, filth, and wounds of war are visible on neither side. The Japanese soldiers wear smiling faces and pristine uniforms; the Chinese children likewise look clean and healthy. Anthropologist Sabine Frühstück observes that such images and narratives "transmute war into a naive, emotionalized aesthetic not of battle, killing, death, and chaos but of rescue, peace, and comforting order.... Every new, gratefully smiling child gazing up at a soldier essentially mocked any critical analysis of their encounter."[83] The "Wuhan Lullaby" series was part of an ecosphere of knowledge and denial that presented Japan's war as peace, violence as kinship, and empire as in the best interests of conquered children.

This reticence to visualize violence marks a stark contrast to mass mediation of Japan's invasion of China forty years prior, when propaganda policy was more diffuse and Japanese censors had a looser grip. In the 1890s, commercial artists often reveled in visualizing the brutality of war and detailing Japanese soldiers' contemptuous treatment of racialized Chinese prisoners, even as those same artists romanticized transracial battlefield adoption.[84] By the late 1930s, by contrast, as Japanese authorities mobilized photographers, poets, visual artists, and journalists to whip up support for the war, they suppressed imagery of human bodies broken and brutalized, much less of Japanese soldiers inflicting such harm. As historian Julia Adeney Thomas observes: "The results were war images of astonishing quietude." Japanese photographs from the front "rarely depicted or even referenced actual fighting; the enemy was usually completely out of sight; and the photographer himself almost always remained at a distance from his subjects."[85] The "Wuhan Lullaby" series exemplifies the quietude of war imagery that Adeney describes, but it does so with a twist. For the anonymous photographer in this CIB propaganda series, rather than keeping his distance, gets up close to his Japanese and Chinese subjects and attempts to humanize and idealize them as a battle-born, "mixed blood" family.

In figure 1.4, two beaming soldiers embrace and play with the Chinese "orphan" they allegedly rescued from an empty field. It almost looks as if photographer, soldiers, and unknowing child cooperated to restage the famous scene from 1895 woodblock prints in which captain Higuchi "rescued" a Chinese babe while routing and killing that boy's countrymen. The Japanese photographer innovates by zooming in more closely on the battle-born "mixed blood" family than did woodblock print artists in the 1890s. He (for the anonymous photographer was almost certainly a man,

50
IN PRAISE OF "MIXED BLOOD"

FIGURE 1.4. Smiling Japanese soldiers dandle and play with the Chinese baby they have "rescued." CIB, "Wuhan Lullaby," 1938.

like his primary photographic subjects) shot his subjects in medium framing, close enough to individualize persons and personalities and register the affective subtleties of gesture and facial expression. In effect, he shot his Japanese and Chinese subjects in the intimate terms of family portraiture. In the iconography of "Wuhan Lullaby," the two soldiers dandling their "rescued" Chinese baby could be a happy heterosexual couple, married and fondling their "natural" child. What is naturalized, however, is not heterosexual reproduction within chaste marriage, but rather asexual reproduction of "mixed blood" bonds among men and boys in foreign battlefields.

In nineteenth-century Japan, male kin, such as fathers, grandfathers, and elder brothers, along with nonkin, such as hired apprentices and neighbors, played a prominent role in childrearing. But Japanese men and boys retreated from childrearing in the late-nineteenth to twentieth century amid the rise of sex-segregated "separate spheres" typified by the masculinized university, government, military, and other mass institutions, contrasted against the increasingly femininized household.[86] In time, Japanese men were ritually evicted even from paintings and other visual iconography

IN PRAISE OF "MIXED BLOOD"

FIGURE 1.5. A mother holds aloft her baby boy, who salutes while smiling down at her. The patriotic baby wears a helmet and holds aloft a rising-sun flag. This image of the reproduction of empire graces the cover of the Ministry of Welfare, Mother-and-Child Section's tract, *Kenmin daiippo* (First step toward a healthy people), 1942.

of the normative family. Historian of art Wakakuwa Midori argues that World War II–era Japanese paintings and popular magazines represented "family" as a sacred unit of mother and child, likened in some respects to the holy mother and child depicted in European paintings. This iconic mother and child (see figure 1.5) were visually and symbolically separated from the father, whose very invisibility likened him to a god. The implied but invisible and "godlike" Japanese patriarch was relocated outside the frame of family to international sites for waging war and shrines for the war dead.[87] The patriarch reappeared, however, in CIB photographs that conjured a world in which Japanese soldiers adopted Chinese children as surrogate kin in all-male "mixed blood" families.

One finds the same visual pattern that Wakakuwa identified in paintings and popular magazines in pronatal educational materials produced directly by Japanese government agencies. For instance, the Ministry of Welfare's 1942 illustrated pamphlet, *First Step Toward a Healthy People,* brandished

52

IN PRAISE OF "MIXED BLOOD"

FIGURE 1.6. Ranks of women file into a maternity center in the midground as a proud mother in the foreground holds aloft her beaming baby. The repeating line of rising-sun flags on the horizon mirrors the repeating line of fertile women in the midground, as if flags and fertile women are surrogates for each other. This image of the reproduction of Japan graces the interior of the Ministry of Welfare, Mother-and-Child Section's tract, *Kenmin daiippo* (First step toward a healthy people), 1942.

the Japanese mother-and-child unit in both cover art (figure 1.5) and internal illustrations (figure 1.6). These deployments of the mother-and-child icon exemplify how the Ministry of Welfare identified babies with flags and military service with sexual reproduction. Childcare and sexual reproduction were rendered women's work as able-bodied Japanese men left the family to devote themselves to the work of war.

It is in relation to this pervasive wartime iconography of mother and child that "Wuhan Lullaby" takes on its full meaning. In this alternative official vision of reproduction under total war, CIB propagandists centered men in occupied China and pushed wives and mothers outside the visual frame. In place of mother and child, they figured a frontline family composed of father and child. The visual tropes are familiar: babies and flags; military hardware and soft, round cheeks; and Japanese adults beaming as they uplift adoring children. Evacuating women from the frame, "Wuhan

Lullaby" illustrated a means for Japanese men to reproduce the empire asexually, forging surrogate kinship ties with children of foreign "bloodlines." Photographically excluding women also helped to bypass (or suppress) the question of sex and rape on the frontlines between Japanese men and women in war-torn China.

The adoptive model of imperial expansion visualized by the CIB had been explicated by scholars years prior. For instance, in lectures organized by the Ministry of Education in the late 1920s, Watari Shōzaburo argued that Japanese need not share literal "blood" with foreign peoples to integrate them into the family-state. He argued that in distinction to European empires, "our country is a blood-family body rich in the ability to embrace others" without discriminating against these foreign relations. "Even if the ancestors of these alien nations [*minzoku*] are different from us in terms of blood," they should "regard the ancestor of their foster family [i.e., Japan] as their real family ancestor."

Fictive blood ties and adoptive bonds, if sincerely honored, were just as important as "blood" kin in forging the family-state. Feminist historian Takamure Itsue agreed, insisting that "genealogical assimilation" would incorporate as Japanese kin outsiders who did not personally bear "mixed" blood.[88] If scholars and officials had long approved adoption and assimilation of those who were not "blood" kin as "Japanese," the propaganda project "Wuhan Lullaby" transformed such potentially abstruse academic theory into easily grasped visual images for consumption by everyday Japanese. The CIB photographer collaborated with Japanese soldier-actors and Chinese children to conjure just such an adoptive narrative. In these photographs, Japanese men performed the bulk of the affective and bodily labor involved in pan-Asian adoption, reproduction, and childcare, bringing into focus a male-centered "mixed blood" family as it is born on a foreign battlefield.

The CIB launched the photo magazine *Photographic Weekly* in early 1938 amid efforts to mobilize the Japanese population for war. Sold at the low price of ten *sen* (cents), *Photographic Weekly* aimed for and achieved a broad audience of two to three million per edition, as print runs in the hundreds of thousands were passed from hand to hand. The magazine's abundant photographs and straightforward human-interest stories reached beyond the limited age-groups and educated strata who might plow through a wordier propaganda tract of the kind the CIB and other government agencies had published before.[89] *Photographic Weekly* consistently showed a beatific and bucolic vision of occupied China, denuded of violence and resistance. Attractive young Chinese women often graced the magazine's cover, smiling into the camera as if welcoming Japanese soldiers, spectators, kinship, and empire.[90] As media historian Kanō Mikiyo notes, for the magazine "to express the 'equality' and 'amity' of the Greater East Asian Co-Prosperity Sphere's . . . gender politics were indispensable."[91] Asia, its women, and its children had to be constructed as needing Japan, particularly Japanese men, to act as hero and savior. Hence Japanese soldiers rescuing and nurturing Chinese children was a recurring theme.

The "Wuhan Lullaby" portraits were commissioned a few months after the magazine's launch. Throughout the "Wuhan Lullaby" series, the photographer generally kept adult Chinese outside his frame. The visual insinuation is that Chinese children were found by imperial soldiers orphaned, abandoned, or otherwise in urgent need of Japanese kinship and care. This insinuation becomes overt slander in the article, "Wuhan Lullaby," published in January 1939. The text printed alongside the photographs claimed that imperial soldiers did indeed happen upon an "abandoned child" in the empty fields of occupied China. The anonymous CIB writer(s) led the audience to believe that these paternalistic soldiers just happened to have both cameraman and toys on hand when they found an abandoned child and captured a priceless moment of tender, transracial care. In short, the CIB insisted that the "Wuhan Lullaby" photos were not staged. *Photographic Weekly* contrasted the tenderness and deep regard for life of Japanese soldiers with the callousness and carelessness of Chinese adults: "What heartless parents! We can't understand their feelings at all."[92]

Japanese who professed ignorance of how exactly children were orphaned and otherwise made to bear the brunt of war would not remain blissfully ignorant for long. When Japanese homes became ground zero in a losing war against US forces from summer 1944 to 1945, Japanese would learn how easily children were orphaned and otherwise separated from kin in the midst of catastrophe.[93] As curated for home-front readers in 1938 and 1939, the war in Wuhan was so painstakingly cleansed of conflict and carnage as to render orphaned children inexplicable, except as products of willful neglect or malice on the part of Chinese parents. The propaganda effect was to prompt moral outrage at the wickedness of such Chinese and concomitant moral confidence in Japan's masculine and militaristic mission of claiming foreign children and forging "mixed" kinship overseas.

IN PRAISE OF "MIXED BLOOD"

FIGURE 1.7. A Japanese soldier teaches Chinese children to salute. White arrows mark where the image was cropped to exclude Chinese adults from the published photograph. CIB, "Wuhan Lullaby," 1938.

One would not know it from the published article, but Chinese adults were indeed present for the "Wuhan Lullaby" photoshoot. In one such shot, a local man edged into the background. This photograph, shown in figure 1.7, disrupts the otherwise neat CIB narrative of absentee Chinese adults and needy Chinese children eager for kinship with Japanese soldiers. Tellingly, the photograph as printed in *Photographic Weekly* was cropped along the right side, erasing the Chinese adult who had intruded into the frame.[94]

In the original, uncropped photograph, a Chinese man watches stone-faced, hands clasped behind his back, as the CIB photographer stages his shot. Perhaps he was a father or kinsman to these requisitioned children.

Or perhaps he was no "blood" relation, but rather a bystander taking an adoptive interest—as the Japanese men in uniform also claimed to do. Equally plausible is that this Chinese man was working for the Japanese, helping them organize local children and other requirements for the photoshoot. Whatever the case, the Chinese man kept his distance during the shoot. He watches as a performatively friendly Japanese soldier crouches to the Chinese children's level. Smiling, the soldier entices the children with a toy balloon while teaching them to salute him. The moment is affective, pedagogical, and disciplinary, like empire itself. Some of the older children smile back, looking eager to engage in this transnational play.

The downturned, dubious face of the young child in the center, rendering a reluctant and ill-formed salute, suggests a story at odds with the CIB narrative of zealous pan-Asian filiation. The uneasiness exuded by this child and the unplayful posture of the Chinese man pushed to the cropped edge of the frame evokes the atmosphere of coerced kinship that Japanese propagandists were laboring to obscure as they visualized a borderless, male-centered, "mixed blood" empire.

The following year, *Asahi* newspaper profiled a "mixed blood" soldier captured in enemy uniform in China. This young captive no longer remembered his Japanese mother's personal name, but he believed her family name was Takahashi. Although he had forgotten much, he remembered Japanese well enough to surrender in that language, recount his blood ties, and befriend the Japanese soldiers who took him captive. *Asahi* reported that the Japanese soldiers grew fond of their "mixed blood" prisoner, expunged his Chinese patronym, and bestowed on him the name Takahashi Kitarō, restoring the "mixed blood" enemy soldier to Japanese kinship.[95] Frühstück finds wartime children's literature replete with such tales of Japanese soldiers informally adopting Chinese boys on the battlefield.[96] In adult-oriented media, too, such narratives were popular fare.

Throughout the war, Japanese news reports emphasized the heartfelt loyalty of diverse "mixed blood" peoples of Asia to Japan. Press reports made clear that "mixed-blood children" need not boast Japanese ancestry to heed Japan's call to arms; adoptive and affective bonds of voluntary filiation could be equally potent. For instance, in 1932, *Asahi* publicized the case of a *konketsuji* of US and German parentage who approached the Japanese consulate in Honolulu, hoping to join the Japanese army and from there, the fight in China. (As a non-citizen, he was refused.)[97] In 1939, under the headline

IN PRAISE OF "MIXED BLOOD"

"Mixed-Blood War-Wounded Soldier," *Asahi* profiled Higuchi Kaneo, a veteran of the China war currently recuperating in an imperial army hospital. Higuchi's grandfather, the paper reported, was renowned British engineer Henry Spencer Palmer (1838–1893), himself a child of imperialism born in Bangalore. After a long and peripatetic career in the British Empire, Palmer settled in Yokohama in 1885, married a Japanese woman, fathered Japanese children, and designed for his adopted homeland cutting-edge municipal waterworks and sewage systems.[98] Many people of European heritage were living in Japan during World War II, negotiating prejudice and persecution as well as continued warmth and welcome as "Japanese."[99] It is possible that Higuchi's loyalty, as a "mixed blood" soldier, to Japan would have been even more celebrated had he found himself in the news three years later, amid imperial war on the British homeland of his grandfather, than he was while nursing war wounds sustained in China in 1939.

Japanese news outlets also celebrated "mixed blood" people of enemy ancestry, provided they proved friendly to Japan. In this spirit in 1942, *Asahi* extolled forty-year-old "mixed-blood child" Dorothy Siddens, born in Singapore to an English father and local mother. Although she had no Japanese "blood," Japan's noble cause apparently inspired her to join the pan-Asian struggle against her father's countrymen. Although she never joined a Japanese family, she was affectively adopted by the empire. In 1942, Siddens received a highly publicized commendation from Japan for her contributions, as a spy, toward Japan's pacification of Singapore and ouster of British forces.[100] Japanese reports on such cases were enthusiastic, the perceived propaganda value of such stories on the home front considerable. They evidenced the justice of Japan's war effort as people of all "races" and "mixes" rushed to serve the empire and its "new order" in Asia. If even foreign women with no Japanese "blood" were giving their all for Japan's victory, how could *naichi*-born Japanese balk at any sacrifice?

Not all wartime news reports on *konketsuji* were flattering, however. As liminal beings, "mixed-blood children" were capable of many things, including deception and double-dealing. News reports on *konketsuji* criminals and con artists were not uncommon, and newspapers often featured the accused person's "mixed blood" identity in the headlines as a crucial element in the story and the crime.[101] The dark side of liminality was especially salient in reportage on "mixed" children born of enemy European bloodlines. For instance, after Japan's conquest of Java, *Asahi* reported that gaudily dressed blondes were flocking to government archives in Jakarta. These *konketsuji* had lorded their Dutch ancestry over indigenous people during Dutch rule, the paper sneered. Now under Japanese rule, these same *konketsuji* abruptly reidentified as Indonesian and frantically dug for archival evidence to prove their Asian ancestry.[102]

Despite the newspaper's haughty tone, one might read against the grain to sympathize with "mixed blood" Eurasians who were rocketed into identity crises by Japanese invasion. Headlines such as "Warning to Mixed-Blood People in Java" made clear that people of Indonesian-Dutch ancestry were under strict military surveillance and suspicion.[103] The sudden craze among Dutch-Indonesian *konketsuji* to seize an Asian identity was therefore no idle faddishness or slick opportunism. It was a deadly serious effort to evade detainment by Japanese authorities as enemy nationals.

"Mixed blood" families and communities were no rarity in wartime Asia and the Pacific. As a result, similar scenes played out wherever Japanese troops took control of formerly European colonies and treaty ports. In a front-page op-ed in 1942, Murata Takaharu claimed that Japan had liberated "mixed blood" people in the Philippines from racial discrimination and that the latter now enjoyed high status as members of government and leaders in the reconstruction of Asia.[104] But for preexisting "mixed" communities, Japan's arrival often spelled disaster.

In the British colonies of Shanghai and Hong Kong, stable "mixed blood" communities that once proudly identified as Eurasian scattered in the face of Japan's invasion. Eurasians who might pass as Chinese often decided to do so. Like *konketsuji* in the "liberated" Dutch Indies who sought to secure Asian status, these Eurasians sought Chinese status less out of cynical opportunism than in an effort to survive in a bewildering, volatile, and potentially deadly racial climate. Eurasians who could pass as Chinese and bury their British heritage might stay put in their hometowns and adapt to Japanese rule, whereas Eurasians more stereotypically "white" in appearance or publicly marked with British identity were more likely to flee into the depths of China. There they might try to blend in, avoid internment in Japanese camps, and keep their "mixed" families and selves alive and intact.[105] Despite imperial Japan's professed tolerance for "blood mixing" and its highly choreographed performance of affection for the world's diverse *konketsuji*, Japan's arrival as the "liberator" of multiracial Asia was far from an unmitigated blessing.

IN PRAISE OF "MIXED BLOOD"

Japan's new "mixed blood" order in Asia shattered long-held identities and hard-won social bonds, delegitimizing and endangering some of the liminal identities and hybrid peoples it claimed to champion. One tragic result was to shatter "mixed" families and communities along the lines of racialized phenotypes and binary political identities. It was left to each "mixed" person, family, and community to decide how to (mis)represent themselves, hide, and survive in these perilous and polarizing times. These agonizing calculations and forced identity switches were not distinct to "mixed blood" people. Other liminal populations, such as colonized Koreans, also had to prove their worth, loyalty, and belonging in a highly racialized wartime order. As historian A. Carly Buxton argues, Japanese-American *Nisei* who happened to be in Japan at the time of the attack on Pearl Harbor were stuck in a similar limbo. Unable to go "home," they had no choice but to survive by proving themselves loyal subjects of Japan, true to their "blood" rather than to the enemy land of their birth.[106] Taiwanese, too, were liminal subjects who had to negotiate overlapping and competing identities as "Japanese" and "Chinese" during this era of imperial expansion and racial rebirth.[107]

Yet despite premonitions of mixed-up loyalties among the liminal peoples of Asia and the Pacific, Japanese press reports generally evoked more optimism than paranoia about their utility and loyalty to the empire. Japanese readers were repeatedly assured that *Nisei*, Koreans, Taiwanese, *konketsuji*, and other such borderline beings were much better off under Japanese rule than under the boots of Chinese, British, Dutch, or US governments. Japanese audiences were further assured that most *konketsuji* instinctively knew that Japanese rule was ideal and euphorically embraced Japanese soldiers as they arrived in land after war-torn land. This wartime orthodoxy of optimism, indeed overconfidence, regarding the universal appeal of Japan's imperial and racial project left little publishable room for doubt that the diverse peoples of Asia and the Pacific were clamoring to collaborate with empire. That "mixed blood" populations naturally favored, and followed, Japan was a piece of imperial orthodoxy not lightly to be challenged.

As historian Emma Teng argues, "the fetishization of 'blood' as a criterion for group membership does not necessarily entail a concomitant fetishization of 'purity.' In other words, 'mixedness' can coexist with models of identity founded on race as biology or lineage."[108] Indeed, hybridity can do much more than coexist with biological essentialism—"mixedness" can muscularly bolster identities rooted in the idioms and ideologies of "race" and "blood." According to wartime Japan's pro-mixing racialists, it was precisely because Japanese were a "mixed blood" people that they enjoyed a special destiny and mandate to rule over limitless territories and peoples throughout Asia and the Pacific. These eugenic imperialists argued that new breeds of *konketsuji* could and should be bred and reared to serve Japan's expanding interests. It was not despite, but because of, their diverse and divergent "blood" ties that *konketsuji* would serve the empire better in key roles and regions than would Japanese with weaker and fewer "blood" ties outside the *naichi*. To harness the power of hybrid blood and foster "mixed blood" identities was a long-term strategy of integration, stabilization, and governance across Japan's vast internal territories and imperial frontiers. Explicit in such recommendations was the notion that "mixed blood" and "Japanese" were overlapping and mutually productive rather than exclusive categories.

Nevertheless, Japanese had to confront the reality that not all Asian or Pacific people were eager, or even remotely willing, to filiate with Japanese in a Japanese-dominated pan-Asian empire. The dogged resistance of Chinese in particular prompted an anxious reconsideration of "blood mixing" in the final years of the empire. In the face of militant rejection of Japanese overtures for racial and political "fusion" in China, some Japanese began singling out Han Chinese as a "race" uniquely unsuitable for intermarriage, "blood mixing," and pan-Asian fusion. The worse went Japan's war, the more opponents of Sino-Japanese "mixture" elaborated a new vision of the Japanese as a race imperiled rather than empowered by "blood mixing."

Chapter Two

BIOLOGIZING DEFEAT

Racial and Sexual Anxiety Amid
Imperial Crisis, 1937–1945

Japan expected to win its war on China in a matter of weeks after large-scale fighting commenced in July 1937.¹ The surrender of Chinese Nationalist forces would prove once and for all that Japan was Asia's future, resistance futile, assimilation imminent. 1938 was to be the year of Japanese triumph. But the new year dashed imperial expectations as Chinese soldiers and civilians rallied in a mass movement to defend their homeland. In defense of the single city of Wuhan in 1938, Chinese forces suffered up to one million casualties. Military historian Stephen Mackinnon identifies this as "a key turning point in the course of the war." Japanese too suffered more casualties than in any subsequent battle.² By the time Chinese defenders retreated from Wuhan, they had inflicted such carnage on their assailants that the battered Japanese Army declined to pursue them. The Nationalist regime retreated into its new stronghold of Sichuan, carrying the hope of ultimate victory with them, out of Japanese reach.

China had delivered an unmistakable rebuttal to the conceit that Japan would enjoy an easy victory over inferior Chinese forces and a Chinese people with no will to resist. Japan's leaders and public declined to come to terms with this reality. Refusing to negotiate terms with Chinese Nationalist leader Chiang Kai-shek, prime minister Konoe Fumimaro (1891–1945) instead promulgated a "Greater East Asian New Order." It was an order he was in no position to enforce. Thereafter, Japan continued to escalate the war in China with no path to victory in sight.[3]

Conscription, casualty lists, and material costs of invasion continued spiraling upward. From 1939 to 1940, Japan invested more than ten billion yen in the attempt to vanquish Chinese resistance; imperial soldiers and sailors suffered more than one hundred thousand deaths. Hundreds of thousands more were left disabled, disfigured, widowed, orphaned, and grieving. Soldiers who suffered and inflicted mass trauma on Chinese battlefields spread their fear and animus toward the Chinese people among their kin and countrymen on the homefront.[4] Even as Japan declared it was constructing an idyllic Greater East Asian Co-Prosperity Sphere, an intra-Asian enmity was metastasizing.[5] Historians Yoshimi Yoshiaki and Louise Young argue that the shared experience of inflicting and suffering violence in China brutalized moral sensibilities among the Japanese and turned attitudes toward Chinese virulently racist.[6] The dominant model of imperial expansion as benevolent incorporation of diverse others into the Japanese family-state did not survive intact the brutal racialization of war on China.

By October 1941, Japanese casualties in China exceeded one half million. It was a scale of devastation unknown to Japan in prior wars. Washington was ratcheting up economic pressure on Tokyo to force a withdrawal from China, as well as southern Indochina, which Tokyo had seized for raw materials that summer. Beleaguered Konoe was considering it. In defiance of the belligerent, hypermasculine, antidefeatist posture of the Imperial Army, general Hata Shunroku, commander-in-chief of Japan's forces in China, was pleading for prompt withdrawal from a war his country had no capacity to win. Arrayed against such calls for reason and peace were Japanese leaders and members of the public who demanded victory, vengeance, and even extirpation of the Chinese enemy. If Konoe could not deliver, perhaps war minister and army leader Tōjō Hideki (1884–1948) could. When Tōjō denounced the politics of "surrender" in China, he helped to push Konoe from power and secured his own promotion to prime minister.

Tōjō's regime then embarked on a quixotic quest to wrest victory from China by expanding the war to targets that Konoe had prudently avoided: the British and Dutch colonial regimes in Southeast Asia and the Pacific, the sovereign states of Australia and New Zealand, and the United States with its pro-Chinese sentiments and Pacific bases in the Philippines and

BIOLOGIZING DEFEAT

Hawaii. Initially, Tōjō's regime achieved a series of grand successes over unprepared British, American, Dutch, and Filipino forces in 1941–1942, much like Konoe's regime had achieved over unprepared Chinese forces in 1937–38. But early victories once again proved impossible to replicate, and the war turned ever more decisively against Japan.[7]

At the wartime peak of imperial expansion, as we have seen, many Japanese celebrated "blood mixing" and interracial kinship as modes of pan-Asian unification and eugenic futurity. Yet even as this triumphalist narrative of "blood mixing" flourished, doubts began to fester. Takashi Fujitani argues that the war's pan-Asian patina and pragmatic imperatives to embrace all possible allies helped shift Japanese attitudes toward colonized Koreans from segregationist and supremacist "vulgar racism" toward a more inclusionary "polite racism."[8] Yet the war also fostered bloody new dividing lines in pan-Asian rhetoric and practice as Japanese reimagined their Chinese adversaries as beyond the pale of confraternity and racial solidarity. When it came to the Chinese enemy, "vulgar" and exclusionary racism intensified over the course of the war. A growing number of Japanese repudiated Sino-Japanese intermarriage and *konketsuji*, while some propagated novel neo-Mendelian arguments that "blood mixing" with Chinese was tantamount to race suicide.

HEREDITY AND CHINESE RESISTANCE

From 1938 onward, politicians, scholars, pundits, and Japanese on the ground in China began to realize that many, if not most, Chinese violently rejected the ideal of "fusion" with Japan. Some Japanese began circulating narrowly tailored arguments for excluding Chinese from intermarriage, kinship, and "blood" ties with Japan. Once imagined as disunited, heterogeneous, and pliable Asian brethren, Han Chinese in particular were reimagined during the war as a singular organism uniquely hostile to Japanese blood and empire.

In the spring of 1940, Sakurai Hyōgorō (1880–1951), the leader of the Minseitō Party, which held, by a narrow margin, more seats in Japan's House of Commons than any of its rivals at the time, took a stand in the ongoing debate over "blood mixing." He began by citing what he framed as popular opinion: "They say that 'for the construction of New East Asia . . . the Japanese *minzoku*, Chinese *minzoku*, and so on must mix together blood with blood. That the union of Japan and China will be perfected by Japanese youths taking Chinese girls as brides, and Yamato girls becoming brides of Chinese youths." Despite Sakurai's claim, enthusiasts of "blood mixing" who addressed the gendered division of labor inherent in sexual reproduction generally endorsed Japanese men spreading seeds in foreign wombs—not the reverse (chapter 1). It is telling that Sakurai named no one in particular who endorsed "Yamato girls" taking Chinese lovers. If he could have, he likely would have, given that he proceeded to discuss in detail the opinions of several authorities on race and intermarriage whose names he cited as a matter of course.[9]

Far from endorsing, Sakurai's intent was to discredit Sino-Japanese "blood mixing." Sakurai conjured the image of "Yamato maidens" bedding down with "Chinese youths" precisely because he expected this conceptual fare to turn Japanese stomachs. Sakurai's rhetoric exposes the gender strictures fundamental to politics, warfare, and race formation, in his day and ours. The racial line in the sand is often drawn through the bodies of women. Historian Kirsten Ziomek has shown that, even in the imperial heyday of pro-mixing ideology, Japanese women who considered intermarriage with racially foreign men could face a backlash sufficient to dissuade and discipline them in "the limits of colonial desire."[10] The ethos of interracial sexual license for Japanese men coexisted with a disciplinary regime of racialized chastity for Japanese women.

Sakurai, the Minseitō leader, was well aware of the sexual double standard of the empire and played deftly on it. He toyed with images of lost chastity among "Yamato maidens" to stoke imperial and masculine anxieties about inverted power hierarchies in which young Chinese men might exercise power over Japan through its women, and Japanese women might slip the leash of imperial patriarchy and offer their bodies, loyalties, and reproductive labor to hostile foreign powers. Yet despite the incendiary power of the dystopian image of cross-marrying women that Sakurai conjured, he otherwise said little about women or gender roles. Sakurai used racialized chastity as a launching pad for an argument that proceeded swiftly toward another target—namely, preserving Japanese supremacy on the world stage by preserving the "pure blood of the Yamato *minzoku*."[11]

Since the late 1920s, Sakurai had been promoting Japanese expansion and emigration to virtually every corner of the world, from Manchuria and Mongolia in the north to the South Seas, India, Africa, and the Middle East.

BIOLOGIZING DEFEAT

He was not an isolationist or a segregationist. Over these years, he traveled widely, laboring to build transnational capital and transracial bonds between Japanese and other pan-Asian peoples. Sakurai served as parliamentary undersecretary of the Ministry of Commerce and Industry under prime minister Wakatsuki Reijirō, then leader of the Minseitō, when the Kwantung Army staged a takeover of Manchuria in 1931. When Wakatsuki proved powerless to prevent the takeover, his cabinet fell; the principle of government responsible to elected representatives, rather than to military officers, was crumbling.[12] In these years of democratic collapse and mounting Japanese violence in China, Sakurai earned a reputation far from that of a China-basher. As late as February 1937, US ambassador Joseph C. Grew cited Sakurai as a voice of reason in the Diet promoting "Sino-Japanese friendship" and economic cooperation over the "chauvinistic" and "pugnacious" military domination championed by some other Japanese.[13]

A few months after Grew issued this assessment, the Imperial Japanese Army launched an all-out war on China. As leader of the Minseitō, Sakurai did not long delay his conversion to support Japanese expansion. He published his repudiation of Sino-Japanese "blood mixing" in 1940, shortly before the Minseitō and other political parties were dissolved by prime minister Konoe, who deemed factionalism anathema to the unity required for victory in the war.[14] Far from abandoning the halls of power, Sakurai found new ways to support the empire as director of the Imperial Rule Assistance Association (*Taisei yokusankai*) and in other elite posts in Japan and occupied Burma. Sakurai's wartime leadership led to his arrest by the Allies as a class-A war criminal after the cabinet of Suzuki Kantarō—on which Sakurai served—surrendered in 1945.[15]

Although Sakurai spoke from within government circles in 1940 when he endorsed protecting the "pure blood" of the Yamato from intermarriage, he did not speak *for* Japan's government, which was deliberately promoting intermarriage and "blood mixing" with colonial subjects.[16] In fact, Sakurai did not criticize those policies. Nor did he define the limits of the nebulous "Yamato *minzoku*," except to emphasize difference and distance from China. Sakurai readily admitted that the Japanese were already a "mixed blood" people. He emphasized, however, that further "blood mixing" of the wrong kind—specifically with Chinese—would dilute the superiority of Japanese blood and derail Japan from global leadership. Sakurai insisted that race-scientific research had proved that "Japanese people are decisively superior" in terms of both intelligence and key bodily metrics. On the basis of these scientific findings, he assured his Japanese audience that "[we] are not only the leader of the East; in fact, we are the leading *minzoku* of the world."[17]

Perhaps his long-standing rhetorical and financial investment in fostering pan-Asian bonds explains why Sakurai tailored his call to curtail "mixed" marriage in early 1940 narrowly against the Chinese enemy. As Japan struggled to secure a Co-Prosperity Sphere and win its war on China, Sakurai continued to address people in the South Seas and Southeast Asia as siblings—as *kyōdai* and *dōhō*—the latter meaning literally people of the "same placenta."[18] Even his calls to biologically dissociate from China were tempered with pan-Asian pleasantries, for Sakurai rejected intermarriage only to propose that "we should firmly bind Japan and China in union only in the spiritual dimension." He admitted Chinese to "spiritual" brotherhood and singled out no other people—whether Koreans, Africans, Jews, or Javanese—for exclusion from the bonds of Japanese matrimony.

As inspiration for his selective stance on transracial unification, Sakurai cited professor Takagi Tomosaburō (1887–1974), who suggested that "we should reject marriage between Japan and China."[19] Takagi was chair of economics at Hōsei University and a frequent commentor on the increasingly dismal war in China. However, Takagi was not a rabid opponent of "blood mixing" in general or a proponent of racial purity as a prime value. Like politician Sakurai, economist Takagi had come to oppose intermarriage with the Chinese *minzoku* in particular.

Takagi imagined *minzoku* as units formed through both political and evolutionary history. In some cases, he used *minzoku* to translate "nation" from European languages, meditating on questions of national self-determination (*minzoku dokuritsu*) and liberation from empire. After World War I, Takagi noted, Czechoslovakia became independent of the defeated Austro-Hungarian Empire under the name of Wilsonian national (*minzoku*) self-determination. But Czechoslovakia had since deteriorated into a situation in which Germany seized part of its territory under the same name of *minzoku* liberation, on the grounds that members of the German *minzoku* lived there. Clearly, *minzoku* were not natural or self-evident units; they were tools and products of political, affective, and military struggle. Looking back over the past twenty years from World War I to the present, Takagi seemed to conclude that notions and practices of *minzoku* were both inescapable and incoherent, incapable of resolving problems that boiled down to ideology and military power.[20]

Takagi was one of many late-imperial Japanese who regarded *minzoku* as dynamic and alterable groups. Historian Noriaki Hoshino explains that these scholars viewed *minzoku* as linked to but not reducible to race, because "race" might be precognitive or inborn, but *minzoku* were self-conscious groups acting on their perceived political interests. On the one hand, *minzoku* were related to evolutionary time with biological race as a "substratum" or "medium" for group cohesion; on the other hand, *minzoku* were subject to (re)formation on immediate human timescales through political will and self-determination. According to Hoshino, the project of empire was precisely to formulate new and cohesive *minzoku* loyalties out of otherwise fractious Asian and global realities.[21]

Takagi's take on *minzoku* aligns with Hoshino's analysis, with the caveat that war began to transform and harden imagined boundaries of the *minzoku*. Takagi and others explicitly racialized those rigidifying boundaries. Takagi defined *minzoku* as a people that differed from others not only in customs, language, and thought but also in anatomical and bodily characteristics. Even so, he warned against a tendency to treat *minzoku* as pure lines or branches of a larger race, because "*minzoku* form from a degree of mixture between every race [*jinshu*]."[22] Every *minzoku* was a mixed-race community. Yet Takagi's embrace of multiracial realities and awareness of the contested boundaries and membership of *minzoku* did not undermine his commitment to racial hierarchies and distinctions—both between Asians and worldwide.

The degree and type of "blood mixture" in each *minzoku* was, in Takagi's view, profoundly consequential. Like many Japanese observers of German and European politics, Takagi was a sharp critic of theories of Aryan racial supremacy and purity. Takagi contended that countries where Aryan traits such as blue eyes and blonde hair were most common, such as Norway, were not generators of world culture. He described England, Germany, and France as Europe's powerhouses of cultural creation and as sites of abundant "blood mixture" between Aryan, Alpine, Oriental, and Semitic "races."[23] Japan, too, was a "mixed blood" polity since antiquity. Takagi asserted that "blood mixing" in Japan had slowed from the medieval to the early modern era, but that Japan's cosmopolitan modern history continued to prove "the assimilative power of the Japanese *minzoku*."[24] Yet in China, he drew strict limits on Japan's assimilative mission.

Like other Japanese in his day, Takagi recognized continental China as a vast, disunited land inhabited by many peoples. Among these, Takagi singled out the Han *minzoku* as the enemy most responsible for impeding Japan's "advance" on the continent.[25] One effect of singling out the Han *minzoku* was to rationalize Japan's invasion, for other *minzoku* on the continent might welcome Japanese rule as preferable to Han hegemony.

Extant studies of the contested and shifting meaning of Han *minzoku* [Ch. *minzu*] detail the construction of a Han majoritarian identity within China, its borderlands, and frontiers across a long period of late imperial, then nationalist, then communist rule.[26] "Han" was first promoted as a mass racial-national identity in the late nineteenth and early twentieth century by revolutionaries against the Qing dynasty (1644–1911). Ideologues such as Zhang Binglin and Zou Rong rallied Chinese against the Qing by defining the ruling class of Manchus as a foreign "race." They defined themselves by contrast as members of a proud "Han race" (*Han minzu*) that must no longer submit to subjugation: "I had rather see the Han race extinct, killed to a man, dead to a man, rather than that they should live and prosper . . . under the heel of the Manchus," declared Zou in 1903.[27] Initially decocted and imbibed by a narrow circle of revolutionaries as an antidote to Qing subjecthood, Han subjectivity was popularized by Chinese Nationalist (*Kuomintang*, KMT) leaders who built the Republic of China (1912–1949) out of the ashes of the fallen Qing. By the 1930s, Han nationalism, originally premised on repelling a "race" of Manchu invaders, was reoriented toward repelling a "race" of Japanese invaders.[28] Given these developments in Chinese racial consciousness, it is not surprising that wartime Japanese also zeroed in on the "Han" as their most fearsome biopolitical rival.

Japanese researchers and government agents rushed to document non-Han "races" in territory seized from China. For example, Kutsuna Shōa, an anatomist from Taipei Imperial University, researched the "racial nature [*jinshusei*]" of the Tanka people living in Pearl River region of southern China, now under Japanese occupation. He declared the Tanka to be "extremely different" in biological metrics from northern and southern Chinese, yet "scarcely different from Koreans"—a population already well integrated into the empire.[29] The implication seemed to be that the Tanka were a natural candidate for dissimilation from China and assimilation into Japan. In a parallel ideological effort, Ide Kawata, a career bureaucrat in the Taiwanese Government-General, described southern China as a hodgepodge of many intermarrying *minzoku*, among whom the Han accounted for a minority. Ide and like-minded imperialists envisioned Japanese expansion as the liberation of various oppressed *minzoku* in China from Han hegemony. To bolster this self-aggrandizing point, Ide cited Hakka anthropologist Xu Songshi, whose family had helped finance the revolution against the Qing, but who did not subscribe to the Han identity or Han supremacy of many northern Chinese revolutionaries. On the contrary, Xu decried that Han racism was the bitter fruit of "four thousand years of northern hegemony." Although it is unlikely that most southern Chinese decrying Han hegemony hoped to trade in for Japanese hegemony, complaints like Xu's were music to Japanese imperial ears. As sociologist Huei-Ying Kuo argues, for Japanese imperialists, there were "obvious political implications" of Japanese researchers' discoveries of multiple *minzoku* in China. Namely, that "since a singular Han Chinese race did not really exist, the Chinese nationalist demand for building a Chinese nation-state was rendered invalid."[30]

Beyond rationalizing imperial aggression, the second effect for Japanese of singling out the Han *minzoku* as the enemy was to lay the groundwork for promulgating racial limits to pan-Asian assimilation, brotherhood, and intermarriage. Even as economist Takagi Tomosaburō dismissed the idea of the superiority of pure races and called for further research on the many "mixed blood" *minzoku* of Asia, he advanced a strong argument against "blood mixing" with the Han.

Takagi framed the problem this way. The great common trait between Japanese and Han was their strong assimilative power, which correlates to the vast expanse of territory under their control. Yet their methods of assimilation were not the same. According to Takagi, that foreign ideas and practices were continually reborn as Japanese showed the strength of the Japanese in sublating foreign materials into a superior whole. By contrast, "the Han *minzoku* . . . is absolutely diametrically opposed to Japanese people, and is not remotely interested in foreign culture, foreign ways of life, or absolutely anything else from a foreign country." These solipsistic Han were clearly poor candidates for assimilation as Japanese. The evidence Takagi offered for his sweeping claim was thin, but if one accepted the premise, it raised an interesting problem. If the Han *minzoku* was so insular, how could the Han emerge as one of history's great assimilators and civilization builders, comparable to or even outperforming the Japanese?

Takagi explained the paradox of Han insularity yet assimilative power in terms of military and evolutionary history. For four thousand years, the Han suffered wave after wave of invasion and incursion. Unable to keep foreigners out, the Han adapted by relentlessly absorbing foreign people—not their ideas, but their bodies—through intermarriage. Generation after generation of "blood mixture" strengthened the Han racial ability to absorb other *minzoku* biologically. The economist was hazy on the details, but he seemed convinced that a superior capacity to digest and diminish intermixing peoples was a hereditary trait of the Han *minzoku*. This evolutionary accomplishment, the ability to extirpate invaders through apparent submission and sexual out-reproduction, made the Han a formidable race indeed. They could weather nearly any invasion by any foreign "race" only to emerge more numerous and reproductively potent.

In describing Han evolution into a people who could not be assimilated, Takagi adduced high eugenic costs. For even as the Han gained reproductive potency, they lost their original genius and degraded, Takagi alleged, into the mentally inferior *minzoku* found in China today. Promiscuous mixture with invading barbarians and other inferiors launched the once-illustrious Han *minzoku* down a path of racial degeneration. Only among the upper classes, where elite Han men were able to concentrate and preserve their hereditary genius through polygamous use of multiple wives and concubines, was the original eugenic excellence of the Han *minzoku* still to be found. Or so Takagi alleged, recasting Japan's war on China as a war between two unequal *minzoku* engaged in mixture and assimilation in diametrically opposed modes.

Although Takagi was an economist, he framed Japan's incapacity to conquer China not in terms of deficits of labor pools, natural resources, food supplies, or industrial capacity, but rather as a deficit of another material substrate: the reproductive capacity of the "race." Takagi dared not suggest that Japan was facing military defeat in China. But he did suggest that biological defeat at the hands (or rather, the genitals) of the Han might befall Japanese even as they pursued military victory. Takagi asked: "Will the physiological power to assimilate of the Chinese masses grind us up with numbers and triumph? Or will the Japanese *minzoku*, strong in its cultural capacity to assimilate, triumph?"[31] By biologizing the possibility of defeat, Takagi ushered his pessimistic argument past censors into print while minimizing potential backlash.

Biologizing defeat made defeat both thinkable and utterable in a wartime empire where people continued to speak of certain victory (*hisshō*) even to the brink of surrender in 1945.[32] In fact, long after the war, many Japanese continued to resist the idea that Chinese people had defeated them militarily. Postwar denial preserved a widespread, racialized contempt for Chinese while reserving credit for imperial defeat to a late-coming enemy, the United States.[33] Given this long arc of postwar denial, Takagi was prescient in suggesting Chinese capacity to defeat Japan as early as 1938. He explained the military disaster as it unfolded by racializing a Han *minzoku* as monstrous in its ability to resist the supposedly superior genes, culture, and military of Japan. Biologizing defeat also sidestepped the reality that Japanese were responsible for waging a war of invasion that was both unwinnable and a humanitarian disaster. Racialized rhetoric helped exculpate ill-advised and mass-murderous Japanese conduct and strategy while redefining the war as a disaster caused by the Han *minzoku*—by a people racialized as insular, backward, and pitiless aggressors, rather than as people defending themselves against pitiless invasion. Such racialization of the Chinese enemy proliferated in wartime Japan amid warnings that even if Chinese land were conquered, Chinese people could not be trusted or treated as kin. They must not be conjoined to the Japanese *minzoku* through intermarriage and "blood mixing."

Hence in 1940, politician Sakurai Hyōgorō cited both economist Takagi and German leader Adolf Hitler as authorities worth heeding in the backlash against Sino-Japanese "blood mixing." Although Takagi had carefully rebutted Nazi arguments for the superiority of "pure blood," Sakurai presented Hitler and Takagi as if they were all on the same page. Despite this significant and perhaps deliberate oversight, Sakurai did accurately reproduce professor Takagi's position on two points. First, that intermarriage was inadvisable because "if Chinese people's hereditary power is stronger, the Japanese *minzoku* will end up fully Sinicized." In other words, Chinese could conquer and absorb Japanese at the level of genes. Second, that generations of "blood mixing" with barbarians and invaders had degraded the once-resplendent Chinese race. Sakurai warned that "if the highly evolved Japanese *minzoku* intermarries with the Chinese *minzoku*, with its inferior character, ultimately both *minzoku* will end up with inferior characters.

This clearly resembles the lesson to be learned from Hitler intently appealing to 'pure blood.'" Sakurai presented Hitler's position as reasonable because, when light-haired Aryans intermarry with dark-haired Jews, the former "are assimilated, and end up with black hair and brown eyes." Best to trust the Nazis on this point and protect Japanese from a similar peril.[34]

Even sociologist Nanba Monkichi, who had prophesized the imminent "fusion of the Japanese and Chinese *minzoku*" into one eugenic "mixed blood" family early in 1938 (chapter 1), saw his confidence deteriorate into a sense of crisis within a few years. Such was the impact of Chinese military resistance on Japanese racial thought. In late 1940, Nanba warned repeatedly that "Chinese *minzoku* consciousness has been transformed into anti-Japanese consciousness." With the ill temper of an imperialist suitor spurned, Nanba decried the "stupidity and disutility of directing Chinese *minzoku* consciousness solely against Japan" when, he insisted, Asians must instead unite to defeat "Anglo-American imperialism."[35] Years of bloody warfare had made him painfully aware that most Chinese did not agree with this imperative.

Nanba did not explicitly renounce his earlier endorsement of eugenic intermarriage to unify Japan and China. Yet by 1940, he did discontinue making such proposals to refocus on why Chinese people refused them. Nanba held that *minzoku ishiki* (racial or national consciousness) used to be the "monopoly of a minority of the governing class, intellectual class, and students." But the revolution and Chiang Kai-shek's subsequent efforts to unify China spread *minzoku* consciousness to a broad base. Far from checking this trend, Nanba observed with dawning horror, Japan's current "war and its effects disseminate and strengthen Chinese *minzoku* consciousness among the masses." Nanba, once ready with bold "blood mixing" policy proposals to unify East Asia genetically and politically, now seemed helpless to generate concrete suggestions for how Japan could salvage its situation in China. The dream of *minzoku* fusion had turned into a nightmare with no end in sight.[36]

The same month Nanba published his pessimistic new take on the dim prospects for fusing China with Japan, and several months after Sakurai published his screed against Sino-Japanese "blood mixing," the fourth annual All-Country Conference on Population Problems convened in Tokyo. The conference was organized by the Foundation-Institute for Research on Population Problems (*Zaidan hōjin jinkō mondai kenkyūkai*), a semigovernmental think tank established in 1933 by technical bureaucrats (*gikan*), cabinet leaders, diet members, and donors representing Japan's wealthiest corporate conglomerates, the *zaibatsu*.[37] By 1940, the All-Country Conference was dedicated to surveilling and governing populations not only within Japan but throughout the Co-Prosperity Sphere.

In his opening conference remarks, welfare minister Kanemitsu Tsuneo informed his learned audience that "population growth and improvement" were the "fundamental long-term policy for a century for our state." The term "population growth" reflected the regime's commitment to pronatalism and antipathy toward voluntary birth control and abortion. The language of population "improvement" was the language of eugenics, of technocratic reproduction and coerced limits on who could breed and who could be born. After endorsing these twin pillars of population policy, Kanemitsu surrendered the podium to prime minister Konoe. Konoe rallied his learned audience to turn their scientific minds to constructing a fecund and eugenic "new order of co-prosperity in the heaven and earth of East Asia." The prime minister did not clarify what role "blood mixing" should play as he championed "population growth and improvement" as the twin engines of empire and pan-Asian futurity.[38]

In his conference talk, physician-bureaucrat Ishiwara Fusao of the Tokyo Municipal Hygiene Examination Office tackled the delicate question of Sino-Japanese "blood mixing" head on. Ishiwara presented the results of "medical research" conducted with fellow physician-bureaucrat Satō Hifumi on *konketsuji*, specifically 204 children born to "mixed-blood families" composed of a Japanese mother and Chinese father. Most of the fathers hailed from occupied Shanghai and its environs. Ishiwara foregrounded the lower-class backgrounds of both parents, noting that the fathers generally worked in barber shops and Chinese restaurants and that Japanese women who consorted with Chinese men generally had low educational attainment. In light of this educational disadvantage, he judged the *konketsuji* under study to be particularly praiseworthy. He noted the children's "grades are extremely good" with especially strong showings in mathematics. In addition, these *konketsuji* boasted agreeable personalities and robust, healthy bodies. Like other doctors researching "mixed" children in Japan at the time, such as Miyake Katsuo and Mizushima Haruo (chapter 1), Ishiwara and Satō judged the *konketsuji* they studied to be physically and mentally "superior" specimens. They voiced no doubts about the inborn, genetic fitness of *konketsuji*.

In line with dominant arguments that Japanese were a "mixed blood" people, Ishiwara and Satō framed "blood mixing" with China as a recurrent trend rather than recent rupture in Japan's long history. They reminded their audience that the second shogun in Japanese history, Sakanoue no Tamuramaro (758–811), was a "Sino-Japanese mixed-blood child." A great general who served his emperor and led Japan to conquest in antiquity, Sakanoue seemed a promising symbol of contemporary "mixed blood" geopolitics. Conceivably, equally loyal and useful—even world-historically significant—subjects and soldiers might be expected to emerge from the ranks of *konketsuji* born during Japan's present era of expansion. Ishiwara and Satō's findings of positive eugenic and military outcomes of Sino-Japanese "blood mixing" in the past and present might give their audience grounds to hope that Japan's grinding struggle with China would end in victory. Better even than military victory over a decimated Chinese foe, eugenically fit and loyal "mixed blood" children signified that the war might end in moral and medical victory, too.

Despite all these positive points, Ishiwara ended his conference talk on a sour and defensive note. "Intellectually and physically, *konketsuji* are not bad. We aren't saying they're good, but we're saying they're not bad." Perhaps the duo felt constrained by rising public skepticism and hostility toward the very Sino-Japanese families they studied. Ishiwara demurred that he did not intend "to stimulate blood mixing or say it's alright."[39] How could he square such reluctance with his team's positive empirical findings? Having found no fault in the bodies or minds of *konketsuji*, Ishiwara redirected attention from genes to the social milieu. Anxiety over gender inversion and political power, rather than eugenics or genetics, fueled Ishiwara's expressed disquiet over "mixed blood" families.

Many of the Sino-Japanese *konketsuji* whom Ishiwara and Satō studied were born "illegitimate" to unwed Japanese mothers. Ishiwara termed this family situation "tragic." *Konketsuji* raised in such families would be legal members of their mothers' households, bearing their mothers' Japanese family names and acquiring Japanese nationality through their matrilines. They might be indistinguishable from any other Japanese child. When they came of age, the boys would have the same voting rights and military obligations as any other Japanese man. Under the law, then, these *konketsuji* were fully Japanese, and under eugenic scrutiny, too, they proved to be fully fit and worthy members of Japanese society. But these researchers seemed

BIOLOGIZING DEFEAT

to believe that the sins of the mother outweighed the merits of the child. Even in an era prizing rapid population growth and enjoining women to "give birth and multiply" (*umeyo fuyaseyo*), bearing eugenically fit children outside arranged marriage was strictly taboo.

Feminist scholar Ueno Chizuko identifies in wartime Japan's population policy "a blind spot . . . euphemistically referred to as 'the family system.'" For all the emphasis on driving up birth rates and promoting eugenics, the empire selectively celebrated the births of healthy children, embracing only those born to a chaste wife and husband. When the goal of population growth conflicted with the goal of stabilizing the "family system," Japan's government and like-minded scholars and eugenicists opted to sacrifice growth and preserve the family system. Unlike in Nazi Germany, where Aryan women were encouraged to reproduce even outside marriage, in Japan, containing women's sexuality within the family and strictures of chastity was prioritized over rapid reproduction. According to Ueno, the grounds for this privileging of "family" over "fertility" was the priority assigned to cultivating masculinity, for "family itself was the stronghold where the masculinity of the soldiers of the Imperial Army" was defined and daily sustained.[40] Unmarried mothers might breed healthy children quickly—but they also violated norms of chastity, ruptured patrilines, and disrupted patriarchy. It was in defense of this male-dominated "family system" that Ishiwara and Satō found grounds to condemn Sino-Japanese "intermarriage"—which in practice, they warned, was not proper marriage at all.

Needless to say, not all Sino-Japanese *konketsuji* were born to unwed Japanese mothers. Some were born of Japanese fathers and Chinese mothers. Tellingly, however, Ishiwara and Satō never discussed or critiqued such unions. They did not acknowledge the countless children sired by Japanese men overseas—children born sometimes of marriage, but more often of extramarital relations, brothels, comfort stations, and mass rape in wartorn China. Keeping their blinders carefully in place, they addressed Sino-Japanese "mixture" only within Japan, characterizing it as a type of moral error committed by lower-class Japanese women.

Within Japan, Ishiwara noted, some "mixed blood" Japanese boys took Chinese names in honor of their fathers. Ishiwara approved of this patrilineal practice. Yet he proved no more comfortable with "mixed" families centered on Chinese patriarchs than "mixed" families centered on unwed Japanese mothers. He fretted that calling *konketsuji* by Chinese names impeded the formation of Japanese identity and loyalty. "If war occurs," as Ishiwara euphemistically put it, pointing to a future war perhaps ten years out when these "mixed" boys would come of age to fight, the adverse consequences of such spiritual malformation would manifest to Japan's disadvantage. Such *konketsuji* might even "return" to China to fight for their father's country. It appeared that only families led by Japanese fathers would meet with these researchers' approval—but no such families appeared in their study.

Ishiwara's fear that sons of Chinese fathers might someday join China's fight against their motherland, Japan, was one logical reason not to endorse "blood mixing." But his political pessimism was capacious. He judged *konketsuji* under the influence of Chinese fathers of dubious loyalty, but did so on unspecified grounds and dubbed the households of *konketsuji* under maternal leadership "extremely doubtful" in their patriotic credentials, as well. It was a lose-lose situation for these "mixed" families. Whether *konketsuji* raised in Japan by Japanese mothers received the proper patriotic upbringing might seem to be a peculiar concern, given that their family life, names, and schooling were thoroughly Japanese. But the combination of malign influences on such children—low class, gender deviance, foreign paternity, illegitimacy, and intermarriage—unsettled Ishiwara to a high degree.

Was it possible to save such *konketsuji* from their families? Although short on details, Ishiwara suggested that political intervention might salvage the endangered Sino-Japanese "mixed blood" child. To this end, he noted that in the United States, "one born in that country enjoys all the rights of citizenship." The US model for inculcating a unifying identity and loyalty irrespective of race or paternal origin was relevant to imperial *konketsuji*. As Ishiwara observed, "If we don't treat them as Japanese people born in Japan, love of country toward Japan will not emerge."[41] What use were *konketsuji*, even of the highest eugenic quality, if they did not love Japan?

Ishiwara and Satō's analysis of Sino-Japanese "mixture" combined biological optimism with political pessimism. The crisis of blood mixing, as Ishiwara and Satō framed it, lay not in the genes but in the social milieu—in threats to patriarchy, patriliny, and patriotism. Political countermeasures were therefore necessary, though not necessarily adequate to the challenge. Despite finding Sino-Japanese *konketsuji* eugenically fit, and finding political hope in US models of race-blind jus solis citizenship, they also found gendered grounds to accommodate the anti-mixing furor gaining steam amid the war on China. Absent dramatic improvement in family formation and patriotic subject formation, they suggested Sino-Japanese "blood mixing" was best avoided.[42]

In 1941, *Japan Medical News* staged a debate on "blood mixing" among four experts: Ministry of Welfare (MOW) bureaucrat Koya Yoshio (1890–1974), anatomist Taniguchi Konen, geneticist Komai Taku (1886–1972), and medical doctor Ōyuki Yoshio. Koya had graduated from Japan's top medical program at Tokyo Imperial University, completed advanced training in Berlin in the late 1920s, then returned to Japan to serve as professor at Kanazawa Medical University. There he taught and published prolifically on race and reproduction, heredity and eugenics. In 1930, he collaborated with eugenic-minded bureaucrats and scholars to found what soon became Japan's premier scientific institute for eugenic research, popularization, and lobbying, the Japan Race Hygiene Association (*Nihon minzoku eisei gakkai*, RHA).[43]

Then Japan seized Manchuria, established Manchukuo, and several years later, embarked on all-out war. The Ministry of Welfare was founded in January 1938 as the empire plunged deeper into war on China. To the MOW was designated the task of achieving "population growth and improvement," or eugenic and pronatal policies in service to the war effort and "family system."[44] Among the men who arrived to staff and shape the wartime MOW were medical elites such as Koya Yoshio, whose training and worldview included eugenics. Like technocrats in other ministries examined by historian of science Hiromi Mizuno, Koya and other medical elites in the MOW embraced the opportunity to build their careers and advance their ideological visions while serving their country under the banner of "scientific patriotism."[45]

In 1939, Koya Yoshio moved from academia to government with a post as a technical bureaucrat at the new ministry. By December 1940, he was director of a department, and his rise through the ranks had only begun.[46] That year, Japan's national broadcaster, *Nihon hōsō kyōkai* (NHK), invited Koya to speak on a radio show where he took the opportunity to warn about the dangers of "blood mixing." Minseitō party leader Sakurai Hyōgorō cited Koya's radio address in his article decrying Sino-Japanese "mixture" (quoted earlier in this chapter).[47] Koya was well on his way to becoming one of Japan's most influential opponents of "blood mixing."

Koya's complaints about intermarriage predate the war. In 1935, Koya had groused that "blood mixing" had recently been normalized to the point that some Japanese women "take pride" in their Western husbands.[48] Koya seemed put off that women in Japan might prefer a foreign to a native lover or husband, and he was not the only Japanese man complaining along these lines.[49] In this heyday of pan-Asianist intermarriage, however, Koya did not condemn Japanese women who formed unions with Korean or Taiwanese men, and he had even less to say about "mixed blood" children born to such unions. Koya's early complaints about intermarriage expressed less eugenic dread than gendered grievance and wounded masculine pride. It was Japanese women's ethics that needed improving, their pride that needed humbling. At the time, Koya proposed no countermeasures, such as segregation, penalties for interracial sex or marriage, or abortions for women who crossed the race line. Despite his broadside against race-crossing women, Koya's objections to intermarriage in 1935 were relatively moderate and decoupled from policy proposals.

Total war was a turning point for Koya, as it was for many men and women of his time. The war on China turbocharged Koya's sense of racial grievance and redirected it toward Asian others while expanding the audience for his ideas. By 1941, the "mixing" with Westerners he had warned against in 1935 was no longer what concerned him. For as Koya announced in *Territory, Population, Blood*, "Today our country is bestowed the destiny of advancing upon the continent."[50] That continent was Asia, a vast and biologically diverse landmass with no recognized limits in terms of extant political boundaries to Japanese military expansion.

Koya pitched *Territory, Population, Blood* to a broad lay audience. In a section devoted to race-mixing, he opened by observing that "there are all kinds of conjectures flying about confusing ordinary people." Koya treated public opinion toward "blood mixing" in Japan as confused and in a state of flux, and consciousness of a distinctly Japanese "blood" identity as anemic and even on the wane. Under these (to his mind) troubling conditions, Koya acted on a sense of urgent scientific and patriotic duty to redirect racial thought and praxis in Japan. "Naturally with regard to blood mixing there arise strange phenomena that are hard for amateurs to understand," he wrote, at once sympathizing with the presumed perplexity of his audience and positioning himself as a reliable guide. "There are even people who say things like we should welcome blood mixing because a mixed-blood *minzoku* is of higher quality than either mother *minzoku*." In order that readers would "not be confused by such amateurish points of view and conjecture," Koya opined, "it is necessary to examine the phenomenon of blood mixing from a proper scientific angle."

While maintaining a pretense of scientific and political neutrality, Koya proceeded in 1941 to regale his audience with supposedly ironclad evidence that *konketsuji* were dysgenic types, prone to bodily ailments, low intelligence, and other mental and social disorders. Many of these he described as a consequence of neo-Mendelian "disharmony" between the allegedly incompatible genes of separate races. Furthermore, because "blood mixing" violated the "intimate relation" between a "*minzoku*'s nature and its culture," Koya warned, social maladaptation among *konketsuji* was inevitable. As Koya framed it, "mixed blood" was a biologically dangerous and sociologically miserable condition that no humane or sensible scientist or layperson would sanction.[51]

Koya also warned of a biopolitical risk he dubbed "racial 'back-stabbing'" (*minzoku no "uragiri"*). This was a phenomenon he had mentioned in earlier work in 1935, but dwelled on with dark urgency in *Territory, Population, Blood*. Originally, Koya had argued that when one race "enters" the territory of another race and lives side by side, "blood mixing" was inevitable. Over time, through neo-Mendelian assortment of genetic traits, new and varied combinations of genes would appear in *konketsuji*, who would be quite diverse as a result. Among these diverse *konketsuji*, Koya held that those more closely resembling the native race would be better adapted to the territory in which the natives had evolved. By contrast, *konketsuji* resembling the newcomer race would remain adapted to a foreign land and climate. So over time, natural selection would cause the newcomer race and its genes to vanish, leaving only the native race behind.

In *Territory, Population, Blood*, Koya spun out this argument at greater length while editing a few key phrases. Instead of writing about "entry" of a foreign race, he now wrote about the "conquest" of foreign lands. And instead of describing newcomers and *konketsuji* who resembled them naturally vanishing, he wrote that the "conquered *minzoku* take their revenge biologically," ascribing agency and ill intent to foreign *minzoku* framed as to-the-death adversaries. The result of such "intermarriage," Koya warned apocalyptically, was not to achieve harmony and union but rather to empower a militarily impotent race to "drive the conquerors to extinction." He adduced evidence from European history, but the conquerors he worried for in the present were the Japanese in China.[52]

It is testament to Koya's political and medical stature at the forefront of debate that he was not only cited by Minseitō Party leader Sakurai in 1940, but that in the debate over "blood mixing" staged among experts in 1941, *Japan Medical News* printed Koya's argument first. Koya opened by railing against "blood mixing" in Manchuria and China. "Isn't it too pitiful and too precious to cast away the Japanese spirit into Chinese blood, which is like the waters of the Yangtze River?" Leaving no room for doubt, Koya insisted that if Japanese pursued "blood mixing" in China, the *konketsuji* born in that land would end up entirely Chinese.[53] Justifying his stance with references to neo-Mendelian genetics, disharmony, and racial backstabbing, Koya expressed much the same biological defeatism as economist Takagi, politician Sakurai, and other war-worried Japanese.

Like his contemporaries, Koya complained far more often about race-crossing Japanese women than men in publications spanning the 1930s to the 1950s.[54] In *Japan Medical News*, he groused that "having a father from a different *minzoku* is a totally different situation than having a mother from a different *minzoku*."[55] Koya did not bother to explicate the difference, but he seemed convinced that even those with a benign view of "blood mixing" by Japanese fathers must disapprove of Japanese mothers making babies with foreign men.

Yet it is crucial to note that the neo-Mendelian arguments against "mixture" elaborated by Koya and some of his contemporaries strongly resisted a gender-specific regulation of interracial sex. The more seriously one took the possibility that "Japanese" traits were either recessive or too fragile to survive evolutionary competition on the continent, the more dangerous any form of mixture might appear. This neo-Mendelian logic cut against a gendered logic that licensed Japanese men to "mix blood" freely while imposing racial chastity on Japanese women. A Chinese mother was equally capable as any Chinese man of passing on dominant genes that would eliminate Japanese traits in *konketsuji*. Koya's warning that "racial backstabbing" would allow Chinese to "drive the conquerors to extinction" over generations of mixing admitted no exception for Japanese men bedding Chinese women. Anyone who took neo-Mendelian genetics or evolutionary science seriously—as many contemporary Japanese scholars, policymakers, and scientifically informed laypersons did—knew that these arguments against "blood mixing" held true regardless of whether the Japanese partner in a "mixed" relationship were male or female. Koya Yoshio was advancing a far more radical, total repudiation of "blood mixing" than gendered objections to Japanese women crossing the race line had ever entailed.

A competition was afoot over the methodology for evaluating "mixture." Should the patriarchal and patrilineal "family system" and attendant gender norms license Japanese men's sexual activity outside the "race" (and marriage) while constraining Japanese women from pursuing similar relations? Such was the implication of Ishiwara and Sato's study of Sino-Japanese *konketsuji* born to unmarried Japanese mothers, which found the children to be eugenically fit but their families politically undesirable. Or should novel takes on evolutionary theory and neo-Mendelian genetics restrict even Japanese men's sexual conduct? The latter argument was gaining ground precisely because, unlike the "family system," neo-Mendelian logic could mark the Chinese as utterly alien, deporting them beyond the borderlines of kinship.

Such was the new eugenic line advanced by Koya Yoshio and other wartime opponents of miscegenation. From the perspective of Japanese women, the distinction might be moot, as both gendered and neo-Mendelian arguments against "mixture" overlapped and reinforced the norm of racial chastity. The thrust of Koya's neo-Mendelian argument against "mixture" was definitely not liberatory for Japanese women. From the point of view of Japanese men, however, the two arguments had different implications, as the neo-Mendelian argument introduced constraints on men's reproductive prospects.

Koya made this point explicit when he bluntly decried "discarding Japanese *sperm* into the blood of Chinese people."[56] With this guttural expression, Koya exposed the real bodily fluids and male sexual initiative driving "intermarriage" in China. It was a rare case in which a critic of "blood mixing" acknowledged that Japanese men were the overwhelming military and sexual vanguard advancing onto the continent. Japanese women who "mixed" with foreign men came in for the first and most abuse, while race-crossing Japanese men often went unchallenged or celebrated. In this exceptional instance, Koya appeared almost evenhanded, criticizing his countrymen for "discarding sperm" into Chinese bodies. Koya was coming close to criticizing the empire's soldiers for sexual incontinence. The subtext of Koya's critique was that the empire should not be responsible for the offspring discarded by its soldiers. Such *konketsuji* should not be esteemed as Japanese, their Chinese mothers not honored as mothers to Japanese sons.

Yet despite his disavowal of imperial soldiers' overseas bloodlines and disdain of their sexual conduct and dysgenic offspring in China, Koya conformed to the imperial ethos of sexual double standard and self-censorship in other regards. To wit, Koya steered clear of acknowledging the violence undergirding Japanese men's seminal conduct on the continent, where coercion, trafficking, mass rape, and sexual enslavement of women had become standard military practice.[57] In the heated wartime debate over "blood mixing," rape and coercion of women subject to Japanese rule were not acknowledged as even passing concerns. The concern was rather to deny kinship to the Chinese victims of violence and to the *konketsuji* born of such relations.

Koya's evolving argument against "blood mixing" in China incorporated an eclectic range of rationales ranging from gender and neo-Mendelian genetics to anti-communism and anti-Semitism. Anti-Semitism was an old thread in Koya's race science.[58] As with Chinese, so too with Jews, the war seemed to exacerbate his racial animus and paranoia. Drawing a dark parallel between the supposed Jewish enemies of Germany and Chinese enemies of Japan, Koya insisted that failure to implement a proper policy against "blood mixing" would force Japan into a racial and cultural crisis like the one Germany supposedly confronted with Jews. "That individualistic and liberal essence of the Jews is an extremely dreadful thing," Koya warned. Linking Jews to Marxism and to a racial "essence" he deemed spiritually corrosive, Koya justified Nazi policies of ethnic cleansing. "Both Marx and Trotsky are of the bloodline of this *minzoku*. Expelling such a race [*jinshu*] may be unavoidable. So it will be terrible if in Japan, too, we carelessly bring about blood mixing with other *minzoku* without either sufficient scientific research or proper political research."[59] Koya's blitz-speed transition from justifying ethnic cleansing of Jews in Nazi Germany to denouncing "blood mixing" in his own empire evinced his interest in European politics and peoples primarily as an allegory for imperial Japan. Koya regarded German policy as a useful model for an expanding power to refuse cohabitation and intermarriage with foreign *minzoku* in favor of segregation, domination, and, if necessary, ethnic cleansing.

The next three experts published in *Japan Medical News* were not in agreement. None replicated Koya's anti-Semitic tropes or revulsion against "blood mixture." Geneticist Komai Taku was an old colleague of Koya, as both men were founding members of the RHA and frequent contributors to its eponymous journal, *Race Hygiene* [Minzoku eisei]. But unlike his fellow-traveler in race hygiene, Komai expressed no paranoia about "blood mixing" or defensiveness about the future of the Japanese "race." Instead, Komai dwelled on the imprecision of racial categories, the weakness of evidence for adverse genetic outcomes from intermarriage, and the possibility that racial hybridization was a force for breeding genius, achieving historical progress, and fostering a flourishing civilization. Ironically, in a separate wartime publication, Komai propounded an "urgent duty" to investigate the results of "mixed marriage" between Japanese and many others, including Koreans, Chinese, Filipinos, Malaysians, and Westerners. Like other imperial Japanese, he sensed that the scale and stakes of "mixture" were high and believed that salient biological and sociopolitical data about *konketsuji* remained to be discovered and applied.[60] Yet in his debate with Koya in *Japan Medical News*, Komai downplayed any unresolved issues, insisting that "blood mixing" was not an urgent problem and that no new policies were needed. There was certainly no reason to bar "blood mixing" with Chinese. The wartime empire had more pressing concerns—and so should, he implied, MOW technocrats such as Koya Yoshio.[61]

The next expert to weigh in was Taniguchi Konen, whose enthusiasm for "blood mixing" (explored in chapter 1) we need not rehash. But one aspect of his remarks in *Japan Medical News* is notable. Taniguchi did not engage in ad hominem refutation, but he did pointedly challenge the scientific basis of Koya's racist logic. Koya claimed that the Japanese *minzoku* was narrowly evolutionarily adapted to the islands of Japan and would be bred out by natives, such as Chinese, if they dared "mix blood" in foreign lands. Taniguchi questioned the evidentiary basis of that claim. Even if Koya's point were conceded, purely as a thought experiment, Taniguchi insisted that the opposite normative and policy conclusions would result. A *minzoku* so severely handicapped that it could scarcely survive and reproduce outside a few Japanese islands had all the more need to pursue eugenic "blood mixing" in newly occupied territories. Taniguchi rhetorically asked, "Without borrowing the strength of the blood of *minzoku* adapted to those lands, biologically, wouldn't the Japanese be unable to expand?"[62] With scientific confidence and a deft rhetorical touch, he turned Koya's racist logic on its head to favor "blood mixing" for empire once again.

The final word went to physician Ōyuki Yoshio, who joined his more famous colleagues in rejecting racial segregation. Like Taniguchi, Ōyuki argued that *konketsuji* could prove to be assets to the empire as they proliferated with new adaptive strengths in new environments. He added that it would be wise to reduce prejudice and socioeconomic barriers confronting *konketsuji* before discarding them as unfit or justifying such prejudice with specious biological arguments. Overall, he voiced skepticism at the certitudes that some educated men were propounding in the guise of science. "On the topic of blood mixing, the opinions of biologists and eugenicists are at best no more than food for thought. What is of the utmost necessity is rather to Japanize customs, manners, language, and economy. We must surely advance toward shared thoughts, shared mentalities, and shared ideals. With narrow hearts despising blood mixing, we will be utterly unable to achieve the expansion of the Yamato *minzoku*." Ōyuki challenged the reduction of "blood mixing" to biology and rejected biological defeatism. A humanitarian and an imperialist, Ōyuki defended *konketsuji* from scientific racism in the name of shared human values and Japanese expansion.[63]

The results were in. If *Japan Medical News* were holding a vote, it would be three to one in favor of "blood mixing." The rising wartime chorus of antagonism toward "blood mixing" clearly had not convinced all parties, not even on the narrow and incendiary topic of intermarriage with Chinese.

As the war dragged on and war dead increased, arguments against Sino-Japanese "mixture" found new converts. Moriyoshi Yoshiaki, leader of the Imperialization Alliance (*Kōka renmei*), adduced such an argument in 1942 even as he fervently condemned racial inequality in Nazi Germany and other Western states. Moriyoshi cited Adolf Hitler and like-minded European theorists solely to rebut their doctrines of racial purity and racial superiority. He asserted that "blood mixing produces a superior race, produces a superior culture." He insisted that no government should be in the stranglehold of a single race and no country should elevate race as its supreme value. In Japan, the supreme value was loyalty to the imperial court. Compared with such transcendent loyalty, racist pride was a paltry, pathetic thing.

Yet Moriyoshi paused in his defense of "blood mixing" to note that Chinese were a special case. Moriyoshi was convinced that the narrow-minded racism and exclusionary ethos of Germany and other white powers illuminated what was incomparable and superior about the Japanese empire—a model of benevolence, harmony, and inclusion for which there was no Western model. Now, however, he excluded Chinese from that model. "Scientists say that the blood of Chinese people is dominant over our blood," Moriyoshi noted, boiling down a neo-Mendelian argument over Chinese heredity to its invidious essence. To interbreed with Chinese was to eliminate Japanese traits. There was no reproductive future in such "unions," only death for Japan. Moriyoshi remained open to "blood mixing" with other people, provided they "adopt the *minzoku* spirit" of Japan and affirm their fealty to the emperor. With Chinese, however, there could be no compromise and no kinship.[64]

In 1943, Nagai Hisomu (1876–1957), a leading medical professor and popularizer of eugenics, waded into the debate. Nagai had secured his stature at the forefront of Japan's eugenics movement by publishing prolifically from the 1910s to 1950s, training innumerable medical doctors at top universities, serving as government adviser and lobbyist, and cofounding and leading the RHA with Koya Yoshio.[65] Yet for all his effusion about race hygiene (*minzoku eisei*), starting in the prewar era, Nagai initially made little initial effort to draw geographic and genetic borders around the *minzoku*.

In 1933, he issued one relevant statement, "On Blood Mixing Between *Minzoku*," a paper not even two pages long. Even when Nagai bothered to address "blood mixing" in this midpoint in his career, he did not evince much passion or go into much detail. In this paper, Nagai asserted that "our superior ancestors emerged from intermarriage with other *minzoku*." Nagai added that successive generations, by intermarrying among themselves, had distilled and passed down a concentrated line of "pure blood" from their "mixed blood" ancestors. The reproductive consequence of first "mixing," then "purifying" their blood was that Japanese now enjoyed a "position preeminent over all countries." As a "superior *minzoku*," Nagai suggested that Japanese should avoid "mixed marriage with inferior *minzoku*."[66]

Historian Sakano Tōru interprets this paper as definitive evidence that Nagai Hisomu opposed "blood mixing."[67] True, Nagai's hereditarian and hierarchical logic were unambiguous. But the implications of this short paper for "mixture" in the heartland, colonies, newborn Manchukuo, and the expanding imperial frontier were not immediately clear. As anthropologist Eika Tai notes, Nagai did not designate any group in Asia as inferior, "leaving unclear his position on intermarriage" in the colonies and borderlands of Japan.[68] In fact, Nagai was known to count among the Japanese *minzoku* the entire population of the empire—including Korea, Taiwan, northern China, and Sakhalin.[69] Given this capacious imperial vision of reproductive community, it is not surprising that Nagai singled out no *minzoku* in particular as unfit for intermarriage with Japanese.

Instead, Nagai focused his 1933 discussion of "blood mixing" on the West. Nagai depicted "black-white *konketsuji*" as inferior to white people but as "far superior compared to black people." Though suffused with racism toward Black people, the point Nagai was trying to make was that *konketsuji* were genetic averages of two racial types – neither inherently superior nor inferior. Nagai asserted that "from the perspective of genetics, the consequences of blood mixing" depend on the "good or ill of the genes of individuals." Not all members of the same "race" were of the same quality—one point on which every eugenicist, with their classist obsessions and paranoia of hereditary disease, could agree. Hereditary elites from divergent *minzoku* might breed better offspring through intermarriage than by marrying "lesser" members of the same "race." This was precisely the argument made by many proponents of intermarriage in Japan, who insisted that selection of eugenically fit partners in "mixed" marriages would guarantee eugenically fit *konketsuji* (chapter 1). Nothing in Nagai's short statement on "mixing" refuted that conclusion, although he did not endorse it, either. Far from a policy statement, Nagai's paper was designed simply to explain the heredity of "blood mixing." At this stage, Nagai's notion of avoiding "mixed marriage" with "inferior *minzoku*" remained a hazy and generic principle rather than a clear-cut policy position with immediate relevance for the empire.[70]

By 1936, Nagai had risen to the post of dean of the faculty of medicine at Tokyo Imperial University, Japan's most prestigious institute of higher education. From that eminent position, he published an *Introduction to Eugenics* designed to inform broad audiences about the cutting-edge applied science of human genetics and the ethical and political imperatives of eugenics. In this nearly three-hundred-page tome, Nagai relentlessly called on his fellow Japanese to decrease the empire's "bad elements" (*soshitsu*) and increase good elements through practice of race hygiene. It is telling that he barely mentioned "blood mixing." Once again, Nagai centered a brief discussion on the genetics of interracial unions in the United States. Nagai observed that "the intelligence of black *konketsuji* is on the whole superior to pure black people and inferior to pure white people." Two points are worthy of note. First, Nagai was one of many learned men replicating and transmitting to Japanese audiences the anti-Black bias of white race scientists. Second, and despite this fact, Nagai did not transmit to his Japanese audience

BIOLOGIZING DEFEAT

a white-supremacist tenor of alarm over miscegenation. In a book replete with normative directives, Nagai offered none on the topic of "blood mixture." He simply observed that from a genetic standpoint, "blood mixing" tends to produce intermediate types, and moved on.[71]

At the age of fifty, in 1937, Nagai retired from Tokyo Imperial. Past the age of mandatory retirement yet still energetically building his career, Nagai moved overseas to take charge of medical education at Taipei Imperial University in Taiwan. Given that Japan had colonized Taiwan in 1895, intermarriage with Chinese was an old topic of debate by the time Nagai arrived. Despite early opposition, the governor-general in Taiwan was now promoting intermarriage as a mode of imperial union and assimilation. Of course, not all Japanese or Taiwanese supported such unions. As had been true of his career in the *naichi*, Nagai remained relatively aloof and did not declare himself for any side of that debate during his time in Taiwan. That time was soon cut short by war.[72]

Shortly after his arrival in Taipei, the Japanese army seized the old capital city of Peking (Beijing) in northeastern China. So Nagai embraced a new challenge for a new era and moved overseas once more, determined to help build the New Order in Asia. Thus Nagai took over as dean of the medical school at Peking University as Japan strove to imperialize thought in occupied China. From that time until the end of the war, when he evacuated to Japan, Nagai preached the gospel of eugenics, pan-Asianism, and pro-Japanese ideology to medical students and other captive audiences in occupied China.[73] He also dispatched, from time to time, his evolving thoughts on race and "mixture" to the metropole to be published and discussed among his fellow Japanese. Whatever his initial optimism, after a few years in occupied China, Nagai joined the chorus of pessimism about Japanese prospects there.

Deep in an unwinnable war in the early 1940s, Nagai began brooding over the perils of "blood mixture" with Han Chinese. The military and reproductive history of China, a matter of little interest to Nagai in earlier decades, was now a topic of urgent interest, and Nagai began reinventing himself as an expert on that problem. Like other Japanese in his day, Nagai identified recurrent waves of incursions and "blood mixing" as Chinese dynasties rose and fell, centuries came and went, and—through it all—the Han *minzoku* perdured. Clues to Japan's inability to wrest victory from chaos on the continent must, Nagai believed, be sought in the evolutionary history of that *minzoku*.

The year was 1943, and Japan was desperately promoting a pan-Asian united front against Anglo-American enemies. Sensitive to that imperative, Nagai, unlike some of his countrymen, did not publicly deride all other *minzoku* or continental Asians as innately inferior to Japanese. On the contrary, he praised the powerful role of the Mughal Empire (1526–1857) on the world stage, when Mongols had scattered their blood across Eurasia. Possibly Nagai saw in the former Mongolian Empire a model for multi-*minzoku* unification under one imperial banner and an inspiring precursor to present-day Japanese expansion. Ever the hereditarian thinker, Nagai was certain that heroic genetic elements lingered in present-day Mongolian blood. Mongolians might be a *minzoku* worthy of intermarriage. Yet late-war pessimism darkened his outlook. "One gets the feeling that even the iron sinews of the Mongols have completely softened in the curious melting pot known as the Han *minzoku*." If the Han had so thoroughly "softened" and digested the conquering Mongols in their reproductive cooking pots, Nagai feared, they might also digest, like racial cannibals, the conquering Japanese.

Like several prominent compatriots before him, Nagai had become convinced that the Han *minzoku* boasted a special racial trait, an assimilative power that marked them as distinct and dangerous on the world stage. The Han seemed always to digest and outlast their invaders, be they premodern barbarians or "advanced" *minzoku* such as the Japanese. To illuminate this point, Nagai reviewed the history of the Qing dynasty, in which Manchurian conquerors united and ruled the "varied *minzoku*" of a rapidly expanding continental empire for more than three hundred years. The conquering Manchurians were finally overthrown, and in their place rose the Chinese Republic with which Japan was now locked in an unwinnable war. Nagai read all this history as racial and as testimony to the uncanny assimilative power of the Han. "History repeats itself, and those Manchurian tribes, too, are completely Hanified [*hanka*]. Nowadays the blood of the Manchurians can no longer be seen except in extremely remote, undeveloped lands." According to Nagai, the Manchurians, like the Mongolians, had been cooked up and digested by the Han. The cost to conquerors of imperial expansion on a continent inhabited by the Han verged on racial extinction.

BIOLOGIZING DEFEAT

The implication for Japan was dire. From his post in occupied Peking, Nagai urged further research to determine "how much the mental and bodily tenacity and vigorous assimilative power of the Han *minzoku* are to be feared." The overall picture was already clear: "We Japanese, as appointed leaders of the Greater East-Asia Co-Prosperity Sphere, must realize that this [fearful assimilative power of the Han *minzoku*] has exceedingly grave meaning."[74] The purported history of the Han as an omnivorous "race" consuming even the strongest invaders foretold Japan's military defeat in biological terms.

Thus, Nagai Hisomu belatedly joined his colleague in the metropolitan MOW, Koya Yoshio, in denouncing Sino-Japanese "blood mixture." Some scholars have depicted Nagai as a relentless proponent of anti-mixing ideology in Japan, where it is often claimed that dogmas of "pure blood" and "pure race" were the mainstream if not the only sentiment.[75] In reality, Nagai was a latecomer to anti-mixing activism, converted to a more pessimistic eugenic outlook and xenophobic racism by the horrors of a failing war effort. Even in 1943, Nagai tailored his repudiation of "blood mixing" narrowly against the Han Chinese enemy. Like an increasing number of Japanese over the prior five years, Nagai now claimed that the Han were, by some dire quirk of nature, inherently more virile and prolific than the Japanese—destined to neo-Mendelian dominance at the level of genes.

Nagai's conversion from unconcern to selective horror at "blood mixing" encapsulates a broader shift in Japanese culture. Foreboding over the unconquerable Han eroded pan-Asian optimism and eugenic worldviews that had once celebrated or at least tolerated "blood mixing" as a mode of imperial expansion. Thus began the redefinition of "blood mixing" as the very opposite of racial expansion. To an increasing number of Japanese, "blood mixing" now meant race suicide.

GENERALIZING RACIAL PERIL

Oguma Eiji argues that, in 1944, "when the tide of war had obviously turned against Japan, the mixed nation theory almost completely disappeared from the pages of major magazines." The propaganda value of pan-Asianism declined as the borders of the Co-Prosperity Sphere collapsed under Allied assault. Prominent pan-Asian nationalists such as journalist Tokutomi Sohō, who had "used the mixed nation theory to argue for overseas expansion and assimilation at a time when the areas under Japanese occupation were expanding," now reversed course and "emphasized homogeneity... once Japan was driven on to the defensive." Leading philosopher Watsuji Tetsurō, famed for promoting "liberal miscegenation" as the font of Japanese "race" and empire, likewise reversed his stance to declare that no country that "permitted intermarriage has ever been successful."

Perhaps it was psychologically necessary to reframe disunion as the will of a proud, independent, "pure" Japan rather than the will of hostile foreign "races." Certainly there was late-war propaganda value in emphasizing that Japanese required no outside help and had never required such help to sustain and defend their country—for no outside help was coming. As US bombers darkened the skies and Japan braced for invasion, appeals for unification in "one body" with other *minzoku* ceased to have much meaning. By 1944, some government textbooks omitted references to the once-celebrated variety of *minzoku* cohabiting in the empire. In this sense, Oguma writes, "the Great Japanese empire had already collapsed internally before its military defeat."[76]

This ideological collapse began years prior in the unwinnable war on China. Eventually, escalation of Japan's war on China into a war throughout Southeast Asia and the Pacific brought about the collapse of Japanese Empire. Long before collapse was realized, premonitions of defeat darkened the horizon. Economist Takagi Tomosaburō, eugenicist Nagai Hisomu, politician Sakurai Hyōgorō, and like-minded Japanese, however, were afflicted by an inability to confront the real reasons for sustained and successful Chinese resistance and for the spectacular failure of Japan's Co-Prosperity Sphere. Hence the ideological and emotional recourse to biologizing defeat. Racialization of the Han was one means to metabolize enmity with Asian "brethren" and the long, slow, agonizing process of defeat while purifying the Japanese self of strategic and moral accountability for invasion, atrocity, and the self-inflicted implosion of empire.

Imperial rhetoric justifying the war as a means of liberating and unifying pan-Asian brethren in one utopian family did not entirely cease. Imperial policies supporting intermarriage were not reversed, despite mounting critique. Proponents of "blood mixing" as a form of transracial empire-building did not go silent all at once. Yet such talk did come under challenge under the increasingly bleak circumstances of a misbegotten war. As imperial confidence decayed amid mass violence, grief and privation, and serial strategic disasters, many Japanese lost trust in their capacity to assimilate and in other peoples' willingness to be assimilated. The climate of wartime opinion shifted from extroverted optimism to paranoid pessimism, from confidence that the Japanese Empire had broad appeal to conviction that Japanese were alone in their fight, surrounded by enemies and irreconcilably foreign "races." All the while, the continued assertion that "blood" mattered to one's identity, role in world history, and place on the geopolitical map set the stage for a radical reappraisal of "blood ties" as the empire collapsed. When foreign armies invaded Japanese territories at the war's end, paranoia and enmity toward other "races" metastasized into denunciations of mixing with any *minzoku* whatsoever.

Chapter Three

FROM NO ABORTION TO PROABORTION
Rape, Race, and the Eugenic Protection Law of 1948

It has often been said, with wonder and retrospective relief, that the Allies met no military resistance in occupying Japan upon the latter's surrender in August 1945. Writes historian John Dower, "it is impossible not to be impressed by the speed with which a war of seemingly irreconcilable hatred gave way to cordial relations." However, there is a subtle distinction between accepting defeat and accepting foreign rule. Japanese who felt constrained to be cordial to Allied soldiers did not feel equally constrained to be cordial to Japanese women who flirted or fornicated with the former enemy. Dower argues persuasively that well beyond tactical necessity, "race hates" motivated much of the reciprocal brutality inflicted by Japanese and Allied forces throughout World War II. At war's end, "the war hates and race hates did not go away; rather they went elsewhere."[1] Dower traces "race hates" between Americans and Asians forward in time to the Korean War, Vietnam War, and late-century economic rivalry between Japan and the United States. One need not skip past the occupation or move outside Japan's borders, however, to find race hates alive and well. When racialized power over and animus toward conquered and resistant foreigners could no longer be expressed in imperial domination and military violence, racism in Japan was redirected toward softer domestic targets. Japanese women who cozied up to Allied soldiers would prove irresistible targets for many resentful Japanese, as would the "mixed blood" children born of such relations.

Such sexual and reproductive tensions were common around the globe during wartime and postwar occupations. In Europe, partisans on all sides decried and punished women who engaged in "horizontal collaboration" with foreign soldiers. Children born of such liaisons were despised not only as illegitimate offspring "foreign" to the fatherland but also as eugenically inferior to children fathered by conationals. By targeting women and children for ostracism, abortion, and social death, wartime and postwar nationalists enforced the "common conviction that women's bodies belonged first to the nation and only then to themselves."[2] Japanese were no laggards in this regard. As we have seen, Japanese condemned "mixing" with Han Chinese with increasing furor during the war when the latter refused to surrender to Japan. Although Japanese men were the agents of most border-crossing sex during the war, race-crossing Japanese women, rather than men, were the targets of most recrimination.

In the final year of the war, which overlapped with the start of Allied occupation, US and then Soviet troops first set boots on soil inhabited by Japanese civilians in Saipan, Okinawa, Manchukuo, and Korea, before finally landing in the home islands. Japanese animus against "mixing" quickly refocused toward those oncoming enemies. Even more ferociously than during the war on China, Japanese hostility also turned against countrywomen who got too close to the enemy and the "mixed blood" children conceived of such relations. In key battles in 1944–1945 and the occupations that followed, Japanese soldiers and civilians enforced patriotic chastity with violent conviction, first in group suicides promoted as a defense against rape by foreign soldiers, then in widespread abortions and infanticide of *konketsuji*. Although abortion and infanticide were illegal in Japan, "mixed blood" fetuses were targeted for both procedures from 1945 onward in a campaign coordinated by the Ministry of Welfare (MOW). In 1948, the selective elimination of "undesirable" children won legal sanction with the partial decriminalization of abortion in the Eugenic Protection Law (*Yūsei hogohō*, EPL).

SEX, SHAME, SUICIDE... AND ABORTION

For two and a half years starting in December 1941, overwhelmingly male US forces fought the exclusively male members of the Imperial Japanese Army and Navy for control of the Pacific. This gendered dynamic in the Pacific War, in which women participated principally as supporters on the home front (*jūgo*, literally "behind the guns"), was obliterated from the battle of Saipan onward. From summer 1944 until the end of the war in summer 1945, battles for Saipan and neighboring South Seas islands and the subsequent US and Soviet invasions of Okinawa, Manchukuo, and Korea put enemy soldiers in close contact with Japanese women and girls for the first time. The orgy of violence, terror, and racialized animus that marked the final year of the war sharpened norms of racialized chastity and drove up the death rate among female Japanese.

Paranoia over Japanese women's sexual contact with foreign soldiers fueled Japanese-on-Japanese violence on Saipan and adjacent islands when US forces landed in 1944. As invading Americans tried to coax civilians to surrender, numerous Japanese women and girls instead killed one another, their children, and themselves. According to historian Shimojima Tetsurō, their "country ordered them to die before their bodies were soiled, and they had internalized that order." Fathers killed their daughters, sons their mothers. Others were murdered by Japanese soldiers. In Tinian, an island adjacent to Saipan, an estimated 20 percent of civilians in one community perished by suicide, with single men the least likely to die.[3] The line between "good girls" and "bad girls" was drawn in blood on battlefields and inked in government statements and press coverage that put female subjects of the empire on high alert as to what was expected of them when they encountered foreign soldiers: death before sexual dishonor. In the home islands, Japanese newspapers printed hagiographic descriptions of these chastity martyrs as "the pride of Japanese women!" performing the "finest act" of the war. In *Asahi shinbun*, esteemed professor of imperial history Hiraizumi Kiyoshi extolled the auto-eradication of civilians on Saipan as "a hundred or thousand instants of bravery emit[ting] brilliant flashes of light." As the light of so many lives faded from Saipan, he romanticized the distant dying as "an act without equal in all of history." In truth, more women on Saipan chose to live than to die, but that is not how Japan's wartime government or presses told the story.[4]

Such propaganda had a powerful effect in subsequent battles. Japan's military insisted that all civilians in the *Nan'yō* had died honorably rather than surrender to US forces, and many throughout the empire believed this misinformation. Shortly after US troops landed in Okinawa in April 1945, in one small community on the front lines in Chibichirigama, eighty-two people killed themselves, their kin, and their neighbors in conscious imitation of the autogenocide they had been told occurred in the South Seas. The victims were overwhelmingly women and children.[5]

Another powerful motivator for mass suicide was late-war propaganda that vividly portrayed US men as sex-crazed beasts and rapists.[6] Government-sponsored bashing of the enemy's sexual reputation had a terrorizing effect on Japanese women and girls who confronted foreign troops in Saipan and elsewhere in the final stages of war, and teenagers at the battle of Okinawa sincerely believed that US troops offering food and soliciting surrender were "demons" determined to rape, torture, and massacre them. One such eighteen-year-old at Chibichirigama begged her mother to kill her while she was "pure." Her mother complied. Elsewhere, groups of Okinawan schoolgirls opted for death by hand grenade rather than submit to sexual contact with foreign soldiers.[7] All this, writes Shimojima, was not madness, but rather the logical result of government propaganda that demonized the enemy, an educational system that indoctrinated girls in twin duties of patriotism and chastity, and widespread cultural contempt for women. Women and girls "were *made to choose* group suicide to escape the shame of rape" by foreign soldiers.[8] As Japan grudgingly metabolized defeat in 1944–1945, war hates and race hates directed toward enemy soldiers were sublated into gendered violence within the nation and within Japanese families.

On August 8, 1945, Josef Stalin declared war and Soviet troops descended over the northern rim of the Japanese empire. Swiftly they swept south, driving Japanese soldiers and settlers out of Manchuria and down the Korean peninsula. Of the 1.3 million Japanese who did not quickly escape, some three hundred thousand would perish.[9] Hunger, disease, exposure, and overwork in Soviet camps for prisoners of war (POWs) took many additional lives.[10] Among civilians, a significant portion of the high death rate was due to kin-killings and mass suicides among women and children.[11]

Rape was already normalized as a weapon of war among Soviet forces who had been fighting equally rapacious German troops for the past four years.[12] Transferred eastward to fight Japan after Germany's defeat, men in Soviet uniform brought Europe's militarized rape culture with them. Rape culture was nothing new to the region, as Japanese troops had inflicted mass rape on conquered women and "comfort women" throughout the war. Japanese men expected no better from enemy soldiers than they had behaved. One survivor of Japanese exodus from Manchukuo, Fukushima Yoshie, testified that "Japanese soldiers gave us women hand grenades and told us to die . . . They also gave us cyanide. There probably wasn't a single Japanese woman who didn't receive a little packet from military men with the admonition, 'It would not be good for a Japanese woman to be raped.' "[13]

Those who refused inducements to die and instead surrendered or fled for their lives had to navigate, on top of the terrors of the male refugee (hunger, homelessness, and violence), the added hazards of rape, unwanted pregnancy, and attendant social stigma. Yet such women were not entirely abandoned to their fates. In Dalian, word spread that abortions were available to victims of foreign violence at the local Japanese-run hospital. Doctors from Manchuria Medical University (*Manshū ika daigaku*) began performing abortions with little delay. In Pyongyang too, hundreds of Japanese women were said to be requesting relief from "Russki [*Rosuke*]" babies. Farther south, the Seoul Japanese Assistance Association (*Keijō Nihonjin sewakai*) sprang to life and established an internal medical division, the Mobile Relief Union (*Idō iryōkyoku*), in early September 1945. To provide or obtain an abortion in any condition other a medical emergency was a crime under Articles 212–216 of Japan's penal code and article 16 of the 1940 National Eugenics Law.[14] Yet doctors and nurses on the front lines of a failed empire were improvising exceptions to statutory law and providing illegal abortions on the grounds of rape, race, and national emergency.

Across the straits in Japan, accounts of rape were soon so widespread that it became common, if spurious, knowledge that if a woman had returned from Manchuria, she had been raped by a foreign man. In reality, the rape repatriates suffered was not always inflicted by foreigners. Refugee women and girls who made it out of enemy territory to a repatriation ship bound for the home islands were sometimes accosted by their countrymen at sea.[15] Assaults by Japanese men on repatriate women, however, were underreported and rarely sensationalized. It was assaults by foreign men that preoccupied postwar presses, politics, and medical authorities. Omura Takehisa, who became section chief of Japan's National Hospitals after the war, boldly asserted that "250,000 Japanese women are coming home after being raped by bandits and such on the ground in Manchuria."[16] "Bandits" was how Japanese described Chinese and others who dared resist the empire while it expanded, and the usage did not cease upon defeat.[17] On the contrary, the content and wording of this official's claim highlights the wounded imperial sense that it was not only uniformed Soviet troops but also vengeful Chinese and Korean insurgents who were raping and impregnating Japanese women amid the ruins of empire.[18] The outcome of this sexual "banditry," according to *Asahi shinbun* in April 1946, was that 40 percent of female repatriates "had been given the burden of bearing a mixed-race child."[19]

As rape and pregnancy born of rape were linked to foreign invaders, so too was venereal disease (VD). One repatriate aid worker who specialized in advising women and girls arriving in the port of Sasebo bluntly asserted that VD caught from "someone of a different race" (*jinshu no chigau mono*) was more malignant. Such racially foreign VD threatened not only to harm the patient but also to "ruin the country." If "40 percent" of repatriate women were assumed pregnant with *konketsuji*, it was also said that 40 percent of repatriate women were infected with VD. Later data suggested that only 2 percent of repatriates were in fact infected with VD, with pregnancy rates even lower.[20] However low the actual numbers, the symbolic filth attached to repatriate women through their assumed experience of sexual violation by foreign men was not easily expunged. Although not numerically accurate, the pattern of statistical inflation regarding VD and *konketsuji* bespeaks the moral panic over the violation of national chastity and racial patrilines in defeated Japan.

Prewar suffragette Kubushiro Ochimi (1882–1972) echoed the same sensational claims of mass VD and impregnation with *konketsuji* as she reemerged as a political activist after the war. Kubushiro urged the MOW to solve this eugenic crisis "for the future of the Japanese *minzoku*."[21] Because it was difficult for the government which surrendered in 1945 to control foreign men, the political and medical target was Japanese women. The war had been lost, but the battle to save the Japanese *minzoku* from enemy "races" was on. The anticipated threat and defensive tactics thus shifted from military to medical and hereditary. As historian Robert Kramm argues, many Japanese "imagined the arrival of occupation forces in sexual terms and as a sexual 'invasion.'"[22] With the Japanese army and navy no longer resisting that invasion, it was up to women and girls to stage the resistance. When they could not or would not, eugenic intervention was justified, even in defiance of the law. The situation in Japan was similar in many respects to occupied Germany, where medical activists and bureaucrats "driven by a complicated set of health, eugenic, racist, and humanitarian motives" collaborated to provide German women impregnated by foreign "races" of soldiers with "mass abortions."[23] When sovereignty over Japanese borders was lost, attempts to reassert sovereignty over Japanese women and wombs redoubled.

Initially, local medical agents, rather than the central government, took the initiative in reasserting such sexual and racial sovereignty. To meet local needs in southern Korea, professor of anthropology Izumi Seiichi (1915–1970) and colleagues from the medical faculty of Keijō Imperial University established the Mobile Relief Union. They were pioneers in what became a widespread campaign to abort and cleanse the body politic of "mixed blood" fetuses and children. Later, when Izumi and his colleagues repatriated to Hakata, they played a key role in systematizing VD checks and abortions for female repatriates returning through the same port. The Izumi group's efforts are especially significant because more repatriates flowed through Hakata than any other Japanese port: 1,392,429 people by late 1948.

Early on, Izumi petitioned Tokyo for a special law to authorize abortions among repatriates. In the absence of a law, they provided abortions anyway. After repatriation to Hakata, the Izumi group initially operated out of Shōfukuji, a Buddhist temple minutes from the shoreline, facing the liberated Korean peninsula. By February 2, 1946, they reorganized as the Medical Care Unit (*Kuryōbu*, MCU) under the Overseas Compatriots Support Foundation (*Zaidan-hōjin zaigai dōhō engokai*) affiliated with the Foreign Ministry. Although they failed in securing prompt legislative sanction for their work, these elite repatriates succeeded in making inroads among bureaucrats supportive of their mission. In late March, with support from the MOW and Foreign Ministry, the MCU took control of a better provisioned and more secluded site some forty minutes removed from Hakata's harbor: Futsukaichi Sanatorium. With a deficit of medically trained government personnel in the right places, the MOW relied on such medically trained volunteers and civic groups to implement its vision of race hygiene among repatriate women.[24]

The history of Futsukaichi Sanatorium reveals in microcosm how the MOW achieved unprecedented biopolitical control over Japan's population and reproductive-age women and girls, in particular, after the war. Futsukaichi was a hot-spring town renowned for its healing waters. During the war, servicemen wounded in China were brought to the sanatorium to recuperate under the care of the Patriotic Women's Association (*Aikoku fujinkai*). After defeat, such nationalistic organizations disbanded; furthermore, by October 16, the Supreme Commander for the Allied Powers (SCAP) had dissolved the Imperial Army and Navy in their entirety.

In November, SCAP opened such former military medical facilities to civilian use. In the coming weeks, these facilities were reorganized as a network of National Hospitals and Sanitoria under the jurisdiction of the new national Medical Bureau (*Iryōkyoku*), affiliated with the MOW.

As SCAP handed over former military medical facilities to the MOW, it simultaneously directed the MOW to manage the influx of often malnourished, diseased, and destitute repatriates arriving on Japanese shores. To that end, the MOW established a Repatriate Aid Division and Repatriate Aid Bureaus (*Hikiage engo-kyoku*) at major ports such as Hakata, Uraga, Maizuru, Kagoshima, and Sasebo. As Japanese repatriates flowed in, more than a million Koreans, Chinese, and other former subjects of the empire left through the same ports for their liberated homelands. Reshuffling of "races" was underway, a more "pure" Japan being born. The MOW did everything it could to speed the process through its governance of repatriates. The Repatriate Aid Bureau in Hakata helped Izumi's group of medical activists take over Futsukaichi Sanatorium and transform it into a site specializing in the genital rehabilitation of female repatriates.[25] From March 1946, instead of soldiers wounded on the front lines, it would be women and girls who suffered a different kind of nationalized wounds—pregnancy with *konketsuji* and VD—who received government-supported medical care at Futsukaichi.

The MOW was staffed and led by medical officials with a eugenic worldview and by population policymakers who likewise harbored instrumental attitudes toward sex and reproduction. They did not hesitate to use the power of the state over the bodies of women and girls to achieve political and racial ends. Fortunately for the eugenicists concentrated in and around the MOW, SCAP was staring down the barrel of countless public health crises in Japan. For one thing, SCAP was keenly concerned that Asian plagues ranging from VD to cholera would overspill the native population and infect Allied personnel. In addition, the defeated Japanese appeared to SCAP to be so malnourished, diseased, densely crowded, and perversely fecund as to be potentially ungovernable. Sickly, teeming masses were vulnerable to riots and, one might infer, to Communist contagion.[26] To counter this array of bodily and political threats, SCAP needed the help of local medical authorities. Who better to tap than the MOW, conveniently based in MacArthur's own Tokyo and densely networked with political and medical authorities and institutions across the country?

In the early stages of the occupation, SCAP further strengthened the MOW's hand by weakening, abolishing, and purging rival centers of power within Japan's government. SCAP obliterated older and more powerful units of government to which the MOW had been either subordinated or sidelined since its establishment less than ten years prior: the War Ministry, Army Ministry, Navy Ministry, Imperial Rule Assistance Association, colonial governments-general, Home Ministry, and so forth. SCAP also purged nearly every influential member of those organizations while charging their leadership with war crimes.[27] The imperial military had forcefully promoted assimilation as they integrated colonized men into the war machine. The colonial governments-general were leading proponents of intermarriage and "blood mixing" during the imperial era. As anti-mixing ideology metastasized during the war, the superior power of these older ministries guaranteed that racial purists such as Koya Yoshio could not use his position in the MOW to transform that ideology into policy. When SCAP abolished these institutions and purged their leadership, however, the political core of support for building a "mixed blood" Japan vanished from the halls of power.

By contrast, the MOW's relative weakness as an organ of the imperial state turned out to be a strategic advantage under foreign occupation. No one overseas or in SCAP's headquarters in Tokyo assigned much blame to the MOW for Japan's wartime aggression. The MOW was spared the weight of the purge; after a little bureaucratic shuffling, its personnel carried on into the postwar era. In fact, some of the wartime MOW's hardest-core opponents of "blood mixing," such as rising star Koya Yoshio and his colleague Koyama Eizō, were even promoted.[28] In the wake of victory in World War II, SCAP inadvertently freed the "pure blood" faction at the MOW of its domestic restraints while granting it massive new resources.

The rise of anti-mixing activists in and around the MOW, followed by the MOW's assumption of authority over repatriates, produced powerful postwar effects. So too did the fact that SCAP left population policy almost entirely under Japanese jurisdiction, especially when radical steps were to be taken. US secretary of war Robert Patterson Sr. warned president Harry Truman in March 1946 that "the most unsolvable problem in Japan at this time is its high birth rate."[29] Keenly concerned over the pressure Japan's growing population put on limited food supplies and a devastated economy, US authorities, sensitive to potential charges of genocide as well as American antipathy to contraception and abortion, proved unwilling to spearhead population control in Japan. Yet they were willing to look the other way if Japanese pursued such methods on their own.[30] Thus empowered by a combination of SCAP's active support and benign neglect, MOW agents and local medical activists were able to consolidate a postwar regime promoting abortion of *konketsuji* in defiance of statutory law.

In the first nine months of operation after March 1946, Futsukaichi Sanatorium took in more than 450 patients—a few dozen with VD, the vast majority pregnant. The latter were subdivided into "normal pregnancies" (*seijō ninshin*) and far more numerous "illegal pregnancies" (*fuhō ninshin*). Nothing in Japanese law defined a pregnancy as "illegal." But as a badly desired alternative to positive law, the term emerged as a political and medical staging ground for counter-reproductive resistance to foreign incursion. Exactly who coined the term is not clear. By late 1945, however, an MOW official was already instructing doctors at Kyushu Imperial University near Hakata to find and treat "unlawful pregnancies" among repatriates. Many of these faculty were former military doctors. (Pregnant repatriates arriving in Sasebo, too, were turned over to medical staff directed by a former military officer.) A senior colleague passed the instruction on to junior colleagues, urging one another to break the law "for the sake of the future of the Japanese race." It was imperative to find and abort *konketsuji* to stop blood mixing "at water's edge."[31]

Because abortion remained illegal, many details of the postwar campaign to abort *konketsuji* remain opaque by design. We do know that by spring 1946, activists were petitioning the Diet to authorize abortion of "illegal pregnancies" incited by foreigners. Meanwhile, the term "illegal pregnancy" proliferated in MOW records related to repatriates and national hospitals, and a novel statistical category appeared in MOW records tallying repatriates "in need of an artificial miscarriage."[32] Medical practitioners, government officials, and activists were all casting about for some way to justify abortion of *konketsuji* despite strict laws outlawing the practice. Defining the pregnancy itself as "illegal" was one such tactic.

It appears that welfare minister Ashida Hitoshi decided on a comprehensive policy of "artificial miscarriage" for pregnant repatriates by March 15, 1946.[33] It had been seven months since surrender. Women and girls who had been raped or otherwise succumbed to sex with foreigners in those early days of defeat and occupation, and who had conceived and sustained a pregnancy on the long road home, were now coming to term. Frontline medical groups had long been urging their government to authorize abortion of children conceived of such relations; news outlets and political activists were also protesting the allegedly vast numbers of women bearing such embryonic "burdens." With SCAP soldiers on Japanese soil, "blood mixing" was underway in the heartland, too. There was a clear public appetite and no more time to waste to implement reproductive control against "blood mixing."

Under Ashida's direction in March 1946, the Medical Bureau and National Hospitals and Sanitoria hurried to gather requisite materials: forceps, laparoscopes, obstetrical stethoscopes, neonatal scales, rubber bougies to induce labor, and tools for collapsing the skull of a fetus. Posters were hung, leaflets distributed, ships boarded to identify women and girls who needed such "aid." In April, Repatriate Aid Bureaus were directed to establish Women's Consultation Offices. There, medical staff and social workers would impose VD and pregnancy checks on female repatriates ages thirteen to fifty-five. Those found infected or pregnant would be transferred to National Hospitals and Sanitoria or to semiprivate organizations like the MCU at Futsukaichi Santaorium. The Medical Bureau also circulated a directive to "implement interruption of pregnancies" on repatriates when "due to given conditions, normal childbirth is inappropriate." Exactly which conditions made childbirth "inappropriate" was not specified.[34] Some discretion was in order; after all, abortion was illegal and the country was occupied by Allied forces. To specify in writing the aim of illegally aborting children sired by the Allies risked provoking an unseemly and counterproductive conversation.

As this new, nationwide system of reproductive surveillance and quarantine gained steam, tens of thousands of repatriates were treated each month, peaking at 30,406 in May 1946. Even so, government agents complained that targets were not met. They confronted a frustratingly high rate of resistance among repatriates and deliberate flight from bodily examination. In summer 1946 in Maizuru, where repatriates arrived from Huludao, medical agents were able to capture only 12 percent of women and girls for "consultation." Aid Bureau staff grieved that they were unable to achieve "great results" despite their best efforts because "it was difficult for women to present their problems."[35] If shame fostered silence, one might infer that Medical Aid Bureaus might achieve better results by creating a less judgmental environment; alternatively, they might achieve "great results" through greater coercion.

The latter approach was strongly endorsed by deputy minister of welfare Hattori Iwakichi (1885–1965). Hattori testified in the Diet in August 1946 that women and girls confronting government demands to undergo genital exams and interrogations regarding their sexual history before reentering Japan exhibited "no small tendency" to "escape." He reassured legislators that the MOW and its allies "are doing everything in our power to force medical inspection" on such unwilling patients.[36] The moral panic over VD and *konketsuji* fostered a medical-government regime of obstetric and gynecological surveillance and control that some repatriate women and girls proved determined, others powerless, to resist.

Repatriates at Maizuru who refused to cooperate were likely keenly aware that they did not need the "aid" that MOW agents sought to "force" upon them. Of 24,430 women and girls targeted for such interventions by the Maizuru Repatriate Aid Bureau in summer 1946, scarcely three thousand underwent consultation. Of these, only thirteen were pregnant and forty-one infected with VD. The moral and medical panic over interracial rape and "blood mixing" with marauding foreign soldiers far exceeded the actual incidence, as women on the front lines knew. Coerced genital examinations were the more pervasive form of sexual abuse.

Although they would never admit that forced obstetric and gynecological exams and treatments including illegal abortion were a form of sexual abuse, rather than a legitimate exercise of sexual sovereignty, MOW officials eventually came to a similar statistical conclusion. Rape and VD among repatriates had never been as prevalent as alleged. In the same House of Representatives hearing in which deputy minister Hattori attested to the MOW's use of "force" on repatriating women and girls, Abe Toshio, an MOW technical expert, testified that his Ministry was "extremely relieved" that earlier rumors of "40 percent" of repatriate women infected with VD were utterly unfounded. On some ships, rates were lower than 1 percent. But repatriate women might bear other reproductive burdens, so even as Abe declared VD a nearly vanquished enemy, the MOW pledged to intensify its coercive efforts. Accordingly, by December 1949, the MOW had dramatically improved on its early poor showing at Maizuru. Nationwide, 78 percent of women and girls of childbearing age underwent VD and pregnancy exams on repatriation. In the postwar struggle for sexual sovereignty, the MOW and its agents won considerable power.[37]

There were multiple reasons to fear that carriers of a "mixed" fetus might elude detection at the port, whether because women and girls evaded exams or dissimulated under questioning, or because their pregnancies were too early to detect. Inspired by such concerns, in summer 1946, the Hakata Repatriate Aid Bureau and medical team at Futsukaichi opted to defy the general media blackout on illegal abortions. In carefully worded article in *Nishi Nihon shinbun* (Western Japan news), they reached out to repatriate women who, "having returned to your old home haunted by the repulsive shadow of an abnormality in your body, have not let your parents or brothers know, much less your husbands." The MOW and its civic allies would neither urge such women to seek support from their families or communities nor urge families and communities to support such women. Instead, the article urged repatriates to seek a cure for their shame, stigma, and bodily stigmata at Fustukaichi Sanatorium, which "admits exclusively this sort of unhappy lady." Using MOW funds and a confidential and unspecified medical procedure, Futsukaichi promised a "new life" to these "unhappy women." The sanatorium asserted: "We have fully equipped a comfortable medical facility. We are waiting for you all."[38]

Some women and girls did arrive at Futsukaichi on their own initiative or that of their kin, thanks to this article and word-of-mouth referral. In some cases, women and girls traveled from as far as Tokyo or Kagoshima for abortions they could not secure closer to home. The proportion of patients who complained of rape declined over time, and the clinic proved to be broadly accommodating. There was a logic to the sanatorium opening its doors to such clients; after all, Tokyo and other major cities were occupied by Allied soldiers, prostitution and fraternization were booming, and "mixed blood" babies were being conceived on Japanese soil. Indeed, the published advertisement suggested that stigma and poverty were equally powerful reasons as rape to desire abortion.[39] Once again making ad hoc, extralegal decisions, clinicians at Futsukaichi gradually expanded their view of what made childbirth "inappropriate" or pregnancy "illegal" in a time of national disaster.

Despite this apparent largesse, the promise of a medically provided "new life" for pregnant women and girls could not always be kept given the conditions that reigned at Futsukaichi. Despite the published claim that Futsukaichi was "fully equipped" and "comfortable," the clinic lacked even basic medicines. Late-term abortions were largely performed without anesthesia,

FROM NO ABORTION TO PROABORTION

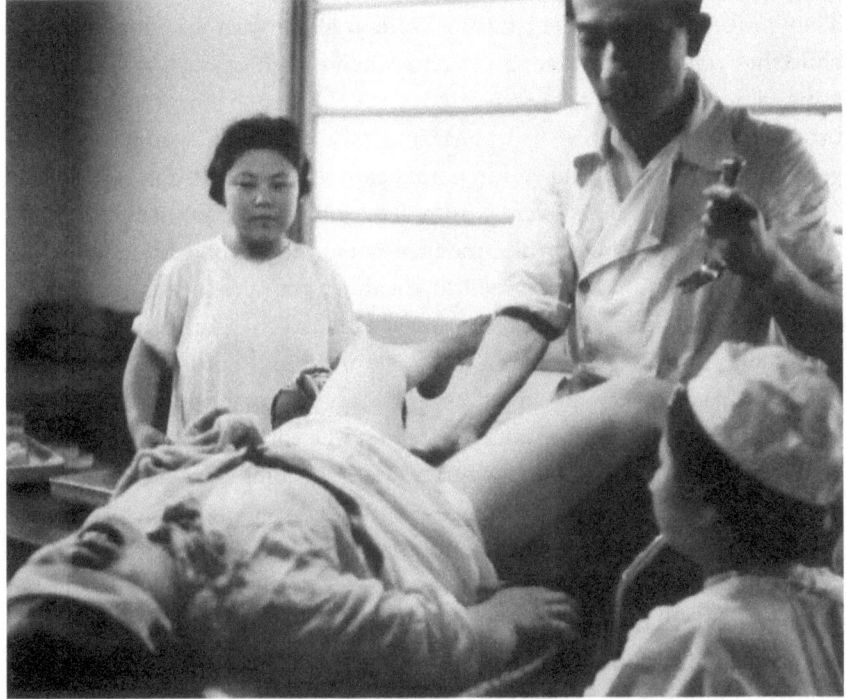

FIGURE 3.1. A woman endures obstetric care at Futukaichi Sanatorium. Photograph by Iiyama Tatsuo, ca. 1946.

and worse still, by doctors with little or no prior experience in the illegal procedure.[40] It was a lack of expertise felt keenly nationwide as abortion became the preferred solution to rape, "blood mixing," and shortages of food and housing.

One of the first young women treated by the MCU in Hakata was a former student from Korea of one of the MCU's founding professors. Her pregnancy was not detected at the port, but her parents later took the initiative to approach her former professors for help. After graduation, they explained, their daughter was dispatched to work at an elementary school in northern Korea. When Soviet soldiers occupied the region, they raped her, not once but several times over the course of weeks. At some point, she became pregnant. Her parents now asked that the family be spared the shame of bringing a "mixed blood" child of the enemy to life in Japan.

Sympathetic, her former professors agreed to terminate the pregnancy. They proceeded to kill their former student along with the "mixed blood" child they removed from her body. After their daughter's death on the operating table, her parents confessed in tears, "No matter how much shame it brought, the right thing was to bear and raise the child."[41] For these three generations of parents and children, that conviction came tragically too late.

Decades after these events unfolded, journalist Kamitsubo Takashi spent years tracking down the medical personnel involved and soliciting their testimony. One who agreed to speak on the record was Hashizume Hiroshi, who oversaw most abortions at Futsukaichi Sanatorium. He told Kamitsubo that his work there was an "unpleasant memory. I don't like to recall it." Hashizume had served as a military doctor on the front lines in the Philippines during the war. He was no novice in bloodshed and horror, but he was a rank novice in obstetrics and gynecology. In the Philippines, all his patients had been men. Once Hashizume signed on to work at Futsukaichi, he trained in obstetrics and gynecology as he practiced it.[42] The same held true in other facilities, where inexperienced personnel paged through medical textbooks as they performed abortions.[43] The results were not always salubrious.

Hashizume strove to override his concerns, and those of the nurses he directed, by reframing their task as merely managing "miscarriage." One should not underestimate the violence entailed in such procedures. In reality, many of the women treated at Futsukaichi Sanatorium and similar facilities were late term. The term "miscarriage" would not apply even if it occurred spontaneously rather than through surgical manipulation. The method that staff often used was to induce labor and then deliver "mixed blood" babies directly from the womb to the grave. At Futsukaichi and other military hospitals now affiliated with the MOW, where the use of crushing forceps, toxic injections, and fatal neglect of newborns marked as racially other became routine, the euphemism "abortion" (much less miscarriage) is best abandoned in favor of "infanticide." Nishimura Fumiko, who worked at Women's Consultation Office in Sasebo, remembered separating repatriate women in advanced pregnancy from their companions, then delivering any babies born with features such as "red hair" or "pure white bodies" to a former naval hospital to be euthanized. Like Hashizume, she carried the memories uneasily for decades, confessing them to Kamitsubo shortly before her death. "Women were the ones who suffered the worst wounds on account of defeat in the war," Nishimura reflected.[44] Perhaps—or perhaps the "mixed blood" infants systematically murdered on government orders and civic initiative suffered even more.

There is some dispute about whether the illegal abortions and infanticides performed by doctors and nurses at such facilities were entirely consensual. In response to a Japanese journalist's suggestion many years after the fact that they were not, one woman wrote an anonymous letter of protest. She and others were grateful, she insisted, to have been granted access to such services despite the criminal ban still in place.[45] No doubt this was often true for women who found themselves pregnant after rape, scavenging for food and housing, or otherwise unable or unwilling to care for a newborn at that bleak moment in their lives. Yet the high rate of refusal of medical "care" among repatriates processed at Maizuru suggests another side to the story. We cannot hope to piece together retrospectively what proportion of repatriate women and girls secretly treated at Futsukaichi Sanatorium, National Hospitals, and elsewhere after the war were grateful to medical practitioners for performing abortion and infanticide, and what proportion might have been, if ambivalent, persuaded, or in the worst cases, coerced. Coercion and consent are not so neatly subdivided.

Women and girls who risked their lives—or who were made to risk their lives—to obtain risky and illegal "miscarriages" and medically managed infanticides in the immediate aftermath of defeat were operating in a twilight zone of force and freedom. If national chastity was so highly valued by the end of the war that women and girls were expected to die rather than risk sexual contact with enemy soldiers, such norms did not simply evaporate at war's end. True, collective suicides of entire communities abated after Japan's leaders belatedly surrendered in August 1945. If surrender was good enough for the emperor, army, and navy, perhaps it was good enough for the average Japanese girl. But not if she got pregnant by a foreign man. As repatriate ships arrived in Japanese ports, chastity suicides recurred among women and girls who, as fellow repatriate and elected representative Okamoto Yoshito remarked in the Diet in 1948, "bear the kinds of pregnancies that become a crisis on return to the *naichi*." In one of the deadliest incidents in 1947, more than ten women and girls on a single ship died violently upon arrival on the shoreline of Hakata. Okamoto seemed convinced that abortion was the best way to save these women from suicide.[46] As on the front lines, so too on the repatriate ships after the war's end, chastity suicide was a collective and nationalist rather than individual enterprise. Pressured by neighbors, strangers, doctors, government, and kin, and desperate to escape stigma and bodily or social death, some women and girls "chose" abortion or infanticide to be reborn as Japanese.

In this sense, the chastity killings and kin-killings notorious from the battles for Saipan, Tinian, Guam, Okinawa, and Manchukuo in 1944–1945 cannot be said to have stopped that August. As historian Shimojima wrote of battlefield group suicides, so too of abortion and infanticide after August 1945: Women and girls "were *made to choose* . . . to escape the shame" of sex with enemy soldiers.[47] Although no longer deployed on battlefields as a weapon of mass destruction, the underlying ethos of death before sexual dishonor shambled on. Systemic military violence was replaced by a form of medically managed bloodletting unique to women and girls and the babies they conceived.

While the sense of crisis around repatriate women faded over years of successful medical management at the shoreline, the sexual threat posed by occupation soldiers stationed in the heartland of Japan remained. Extralegal abortion of *konketsuji* was normalized in the context of Japan's defeat. The time was ripe for legislation to authorize the new norms and institutions already enacting eugenic abortion.

CODIFYING EUGENIC ABORTION

Upon surrender in 1945, Japanese were expelled from every territory claimed by the empire since 1895, from Sakhalin in the north to Sumatra in the South Seas. In the months and years following surrender, nearly seven million Japanese men, women, and children who had been fighting, farming, or fashioning other kinds of lives overseas were suddenly shipped back into the shrunken heart of Japan. Foreign troops too were shipped in by the hundreds of thousands, with US troops deployed to Japan in late 1945 and tens of thousands of British Commonwealth Occupation Force members landing in early 1946.[48] Consensually and otherwise, these foreign soldiers and civilian personnel soon began cavorting and creating babies with Japanese women.

The pressure of all these bodies was enough to overwhelm Japan, with its cities and economy already leveled by war. Rations were steadily being cut, and all too often, were not distributed at all. Crops failed. Inflation

FROM NO ABORTION TO PROABORTION

FIGURE 3.2. A Japanese man crouches in the charred ruins of his house in bombed-out Yokohama. Hunger is visible in his emaciated frame, and food shortages would only worsen in the months to come. "A Elderly Japanese Ekes Out The Bare Necessities Of Life Amid The Wreckage And Rubble That Was Once His Home." Photographs of Activities, Facilities and Personnel ca. 1940 - ca. 1983; Records of US Air Force Commands, Activities, and Organizations 1900-2003, Record Group 342; National Archives at College Park, Still Pictures. September 1, 1945.

was rampant; in the first year of occupation alone, wholesale prices rose 539 percent. Pestilence was spreading—cholera, smallpox, typhus, tuberculosis—and famine was on the horizon. Even those Japanese lucky enough to escape disease and find enough to eat might not find a place to live, given a severe shortage of both housing and materials with which to rebuild. Some nine million Japanese, accounting for more than 12 percent of the postwar population, were homeless at war's end. Displaced families crowded together in any structures still standing, from salvaged buses to underpasses, train tunnels, bomb shelters, and other subterranean havens not meant for human habitation. Orphans and vagrants slept in the streets, and shantytowns sprang up in the bombed-out cities of Japan.[49]

Amidst this devastation, there were signs of renewed life. A baby boom began in Japan as couples divided by war reunited, and menstrual cycles disrupted by air raids resumed with prewar regularity.[50] Yet to many at the time, the baby boom appeared less auspicious than ominous. The dire predictions of English demographer Thomas Malthus (1766–1834) that population growth must outstrip food supply were well known in twentieth-century Japan. Neo-Malthusian theory had been propounded with vigor before the war by socialists and birth control advocates such as Katō Shizue (1897–2001). She and other Japanese concerned with economic distress, class struggle, "overpopulation," and the subjection of women had issued calls to limit family size, curb population growth, enfranchise women, promote contraception, and disseminate eugenics. Some even called to decriminalize abortion on select grounds. Yet Japan's overlapping socialist,

FIGURE 3.3. A forerunner of the postwar "baby boom." A proud mother shows off her baby to a US Army photographer outside her shack in the ruins of Ebisu, October 1945. US Army Signal Corps, RG-342-FH-287372, National Archives, College Park, Maryland.

suffragist, and birth control movements were crushed in the late 1930s, with Marxists rounded up and birth control clinics shuttered by police. As William LaFleur, a scholar of religion and medical ethics, notes of the late-imperial era, the "whole ideology of the period was bent on producing a sense of motherhood that would make women feel a kind of sacred, patriotic obligation to bear all the children they possibly could."[51] Wartime feminists joined in endorsing patriotic motherhood and "childbirth as service to the state" (*sanji hōkoku*). They were eager to raise women's status by making maternity the font of a eugenic *minzoku* and expanding empire.[52]

After August 1945, there were no more colonies to people or frontiers to conquer. Instead, an "excess" population once dispatched overseas was coming home to roost—and much of the roost had been burned to cinders. A neo-Malthusian sense of population crisis began to haunt occupied Japan with a vengeance. The warnings of Katō Shizue and other prewar proponents of birth control suddenly seemed prescient. The wartime ethos of "childbirth as service to the state" was in tatters; in its place emerged a norm of *not breeding* as service to the state. The scope of Japan's disaster was such that a consensus quickly emerged on the need for radical measures to bring down the birth rate, particularly among subpopulations deemed dysgenic or otherwise undesirable. One category widely deemed undesirable were spawn of the foreign occupiers.

Midwife Satō Ei recalled that as Japan's economic situation deteriorated during the war, fewer people wanted to have children and more wanted to abort. Heedless, the government and MOW demanded fecundity and punished abortions. Soon after the war, however, the same officials that had demanded Japanese "give birth and multiply" (*umeyo fuyaseyo*) began retraining midwives as birth control counselors. In the face of such rapid reversals, Satō felt disgusted by her government's hypocrisy, its unapologetic use of women and families to fulfill one short-term goal, then the opposite, all while claiming to be enforcing moral propriety and high ideals. She was equally dismayed by the virulent turnabout in public opinion and professional opinion among her fellow midwives. After defeat, Satō recalled, "You started hearing people say things like . . . 'women who have babies are bad,' that they were traitors—they started to use the word 'traitor.'"[53] If giving birth under postwar conditions exposed a Japanese woman to grassroots charges of treason, how much worse to give birth to a *konketsuji* sired by a foreign man, an Allied soldier, an enemy of Japan?

FROM NO ABORTION TO PROABORTION

In October 1945, MOW official Koya Yoshio, wartime Japan's most vociferous opponent of "blood mixing," was appointed head of the postwar government's New Committee for Population Countermeasures. Koya's mission, in light of the catastrophe of defeat, was to craft a radically new population policy for the early postwar government of Japan. Soon the MOW established a parallel committee, on which Koya also served. Appointees from outside the ministry included Koya's colleague Nagai Hisomu, cofounder and fellow leader of the Race Hygiene Association (RHA), who slid into biological defeatism and joined Koya in denouncing "mixing blood" in the final years of the war (see chapter 2). Additional committee members included Katō Shizue and Ichikawa Fusae (1893–1981), leaders of the prewar women's, eugenics, and birth control movements. Although New Committee members had to be circumspect in 1945, at the occupation's end in 1952, Ichikawa publicly endorsed ethnic cleansing of *konketsuji* sired by US soldiers along with their Japanese mothers. Nagai and Koya likewise leveraged their medical authority to denounce "blood mixing" (see chapters 4–5). Meanwhile, Nagai Hisomu continued, as he had before defeat, to deride voluntary birth control on the orthodox eugenic grounds that it would be overused by the upper classes, leading to "reverse selection." Among methods to suppress human fertility, only compulsory eugenic sterilization and abortion on select targets met with Nagai's approval.[54] Katō, by contrast, remained committed to liberalizing access to contraception. In another world, these two might have been bitter enemies, but they found a way to get along. After all, Nagai and Katō were old colleagues from the Japan Society for the Promotion of Eugenic Marriage (*Nihon yūsei kekkon fukyū kyōkai*).[55]

Members of the New Committee could work together despite their differences because everyone at the table spoke the common language of eugenics. Before the war, activists like Nagai, Koya, and Katō had been united by a commitment to eugenics but divided over liberalized birth control. In the wake of defeat, they set aside their differences and forged a common plan. Medically trained eugenicists such as Koya were persuaded to lend support to family planning for the first time, provided that advocates of birth control such as Katō committed to coercive eugenics. Commit she did. But despite the keenly felt urgency of the eugenic population crisis and a clear will in the MOW and coordinating sectors of government and civil society to ease the way to aborting *konketsuji*, Koya, Nagai, Ichikawa, and their colleagues on the New Committee were in no position unilaterally to decriminalize abortions of undesirable children.

The reforms they planned required buy-in from legislators, but Japan's legislature was in a state of disarray. Lawmakers in occupied Tokyo were beset by crises on all sides and negotiating an unprecedented relationship with SCAP. Cabinets were struggling to form and survive. The short-lived cabinet of prime minister Suzuki Kantarō, who oversaw surrender on August 15, 1945, resigned in ignominy two days later. The successor cabinet of prince Higashikuni Naruhiko clashed with SCAP over civil liberties and collapsed in less than eight weeks. The next cabinet, formed by diplomat Shidehara Kijūrō in October 1945, implemented SCAP's directives on civil liberties and assisted in democratization—presiding over the resurrection of political parties and the passage of a new elections law in December—only to be ousted in the first general election of April 1946.[56]

The size of the electorate more than doubled under the new election law, which enfranchised women and lowered the voting age to twenty. This law also granted women the right to hold government office. Never before had so many people in Japan been eligible to vote and run for office, and run they did. Of a record 2,782 candidates, 2,638 had no prior experience in the national legislature. Only thirty-seven incumbents retained their seats. Clearly, Japanese voters were ready for a change. But the strikingly poor showing among incumbents was also preordained by SCAP, which purged a full 82 percent of incumbents from office. Incredibly, incumbents were now outnumbered by thirty-nine women elected to the House of Representatives. Some of those women, such as Katō Shizue, would go on to play key roles in codifying eugenic abortion.

The result of all this tumult was new voices and new ideas in government—but not, perhaps, a government designed for maximal legislative efficiency. Compounding both innovation and inefficiency in the Diet was the fact that political parties, after dissolving in a self-eradicating display of wartime loyalty in 1940, had risen from their graves in what US intelligence deemed a "weak and disorganized" state. Fewer than half of candidates who ran for the Diet in 1946 were members of any of the five largest parties. To build from this confluence of national policy novices and enervated political parties a coalition of legislators to renovate population policy would take time.[57]

Appetite for such change was expressed at the outset, particularly among newly elected women. One such legislator, Tomita Fusa, submitted a petition to loosen extant law outlawing abortion in August 1946. Her reasoning was that many repatriates were pregnant, and many in the *naichi* crushed by poverty; above all, the government must act to "protect the purity of Japanese blood." Tomita had held office in the Patriotic Women's Association during the war, but that organization was now disbanded. In legislative action to protect Japan's "pure blood," she found a new mode to express her nationalism. On August 7, MOW official Satō Hisao assured Tomita in the Diet that pregnant repatriates were already treated to abortions as needed. He demurred that authorizing abortions more broadly would have an "extreme impact" on "public morals" and thus required "careful thought" and "ample research."

Another newly elected legislator, prewar suffragette Sugawara En, pushed Satō and his colleagues to take the petition more seriously. To clarify the stakes in expanding access to abortion, Sugawara focused not on impoverished mothers forced to give birth under unsustainable economic conditions, but rather on the "blood mixing" mother who would *choose* to give birth if not deterred. Sugawara warned that "a mother's heart is truly blind. . . . There is something in her love that transcends national borders, fearing neither water nor fire." Sugawara insisted that "now, in this critical time, when we must protect the purity of Japanese blood," the single-minded love of mothers even for "mixed blood" babies posed an urgent policy problem. She assured hesitant MOW officials that it was not to encourage sexual license among women, but rather to enforce stricter rules regarding proper reproduction that she, Tomita, and like-minded women supported legislation to selectively license abortion. In startlingly obsequious language, she implored MOW officials to "properly instruct . . . us women" on when and why to abort. Otherwise, uneducated women "might run wild" and "forget national borders," bearing "mixed blood" children whom only a mother could love. "Please hand down a law" that would substitute the "cold judgment of the state" for "blind" maternal love, Sugawara demanded.[58]

Satō had not been disingenuous when he said the MOW needed time to research and plan revisions to abortion law. That was exactly the mission of Koya, Katō, and other members of the New Committee for Population Countermeasures. Sugawara and Tomita lost their seats in the Diet before they saw the fruits of such planning, when the next round of elections brought Socialist prime minister Katayama Tetsu to power. Katō Shizue, who had run as a Socialist in 1946, kept her seat in spring 1947 and for almost thirty years thereafter as a wildly popular proponent of birth control and women's rights counterbalanced by patriotic and eugenic responsibility. With this election, she gained a new legislative ally in obstetrician-gynecologist and eugenicist Ōta Tenrei (1900–1985). Like Katō, Ōta was a famous prewar proponent of birth control who won a seat in the House of Representatives under the Socialist banner. That summer, Katō and Ōta took the recommendations of the New Committee to the legislature in the form of the Eugenic Protection Bill.

The alliances Ōta formed with fellow obstetrician-gynecologists, a professional group surprisingly well represented in the postwar Diet, were essential to chipping away at the criminalization of abortion.[59] One such ally was fellow ob-gyn and Socialist Fukuda Masako (1912–1975). Like Katō, Fukuda won her seat almost as soon as postwar reforms granted women the franchise and the right to run for office. This trio of Socialists cosponsored the Eugenic Protection Bill. In the House of Representatives, Katō explained that the extant National Eugenics Law of 1940 was marred by a "militaristic, give-birth-and-multiply spirit" that made it "almost impossible to achieve the objective of forestalling heredity of bad elements." Her new bill was superior: It proposed stronger measures for compulsory and consensual eugenic sterilization and abortion while also sanctioning contraception to check population growth. Katō framed the bill as both a strong eugenic intervention in the *minzoku* and a humanitarian measure offering a form of reproductive relief from nationwide shortages of food, fuel, and housing. As Katō put it, "many women are raising their voices, saying, today we don't want to bear children."[60]

Perhaps Katō oversold her point. That Japanese women might give up on childbirth was not a pleasing prospect to many members of the Diet, whose attitudes toward gender roles, family forms, population policy, and contraception had not reformed as suddenly as Katō hoped. Her rhetoric backfired, not because eugenics was controversial (it was not), but because granting women's expressed wish to not bear children was anathema. The bill was shelved and did not pass into law.[61]

Determined to try again, Ōta and Fukuda forged a cross-party alliance with another ob-gyn and eugenicist in the right-leaning Democratic Party, Taniguchi Yasaburō. This new alliance proved decisive, particularly as Socialists lost power and Katayama's cabinet crumbled in March 1948. Now came the sixth cabinet to attempt to govern Japan since surrender. The cabinet of conservative prime minister Ashida Hitoshi would endure but half a year; in that interval, prodigious legislative changes were achieved. One decisive moment came in June 1948, when the multiparty alliance of right-wing Taniguchi and left-wing Fukuda resubmitted the Eugenic Protection Bill to the Diet, shorn of Katō's provisions for voluntary contraception.[62]

In June 1948, Fukuda summarized to the Welfare Committee of the House of Representatives the dire conditions that justified the radical new population policy envisioned in her bill. "With defeat, our country lost over 40 percent of its territory, and over 80,000,000 citizens are living in this narrowed land." Gone were the overseas colonies and feted "one hundred million" multiracial members of Japan's former empire. In their place was emerging a strictly delimited "national" subject, a Japanese citizenry numerically and racially narrowed down and crowded into a few islands of defeat.

The war had been over for nearly three years, but Japan remained mired in a state of emergency. Fukuda cautioned her fellow elected representatives that Japan was facing both "inescapable food shortages" and projected population growth of two hundred thousand per year. To weather this Malthusian storm, Japan urgently needed a new population policy to replace the high-growth policy of the early 1940s. Solving the quantitative aspect of Japan's burgeoning demographic crisis would not be enough, for the country also faced an alleged decline in the eugenic quality of its population. Eugenicists had long been convinced that lower classes and inferior breeds reproduced more quickly than "superior" people endowed with the moral and sexual restraint and intellect required to engage in family planning. Dubbed "reverse selection," this biopolitical threat from within seemed only more ominous in the context of defeat, occupation, and sexual penetration from without. To address this biopolitical crisis, the Eugenic Protection Bill would "establish a system to carry out compulsory sterilization" on "hereditary inferiors" (*akushitsu idensha*). Fukuda added that the government must also redress the threat of "impregnation through violence and intimidation."[63] The subtext—which Fukuda could not specify openly, given the strictures of foreign occupation and censorship (chapter 4)—was that Allied soldiers were stationed throughout Japan, raping and otherwise impregnating Japanese women.[64]

To redress these reproductive crises, Fukuda and several cosponsors introduced a Eugenic Protection Bill. At the same time in the House of Councilors, Taniguchi Yasaburō, leader of the powerful Japan Medical Association and legislator in the Democratic Party, advanced the same bill.[65] Despite their positions on ostensibly opposite ends of the political spectrum—Fukuda a Socialist, Taniguchi a member of the right-wing Democratic Party—these legislators had a lot in common. Both entered the Diet as novices after Japan's surrender, having built prior careers in obstetrics and gynecology. Both embraced eugenics as central to their medical and political mission. And both had visited Futsukaichi Sanatorium to observe its secret, government-supported program of illegal abortions and infanticide of *konketsuji* before sponsoring the Eugenic Protection Bill.[66] This bill was designed, in part, to provide legal sanction and structure for such abortions while tackling an array of interlocking eugenic concerns.

In 1948, Fukuda and Taniguchi coauthored a book on the eugenic legislation they sponsored, repeating for a broader audience the argument they first voiced in the Diet about lost territory and a crowded country. They had little to say about *konketsuji* fathered by foreign soldiers. There was little they could say, given the strictures of SCAP censorship (detailed in chapter 4) and the threat of being purged from office should they offend the occupiers. Even as these author-legislators sidestepped the fraught reality that the MOW and its allies in clinics and hospitals across the country were carrying out systematic abortions and infanticide targeting *konketsuji*, they elaborated on the threat of dysgenic reproduction in their beleaguered land. They warned their countrymen and women that the "phenomenon of reverse selection of the *minzoku*," in which bad elements out-reproduce eugenically desirable ones, "has begun."[67]

By eliminating provisions for voluntary contraception and emphasizing coercion and state control of reproduction, these legislators ensured that the revised Eugenic Protection Bill did not rouse the same skepticism as the original, shelved in 1947. It took just three weeks after Fukuda and Taniguchi introduced their bill in 1948 for the EPL to pass both houses.[68]

Under Articles 212–216 of the Japanese Penal Code, abortion was still a crime punishable by imprisonment and hard labor. Without abolishing those provisions, the EPL carved out narrow exceptions to the definition of abortion as a crime. As specified in Article I: "In addition to preventing the birth of offspring who are inferior from the perspective of eugenics, this law takes as its purpose protecting maternal life and health." Article 13.1 authorized abortion on the grounds of a personal or family history of congenital disease such as epilepsy or "feeblemindedness." Articles 13.2 and 13.3 authorized abortion if giving birth posed a "risk of considerable injury to the health of the maternal body." However, these health-preserving provisions were exceedingly narrow, as a woman or girl was eligible only if she already had several children or had given birth within the past year. Even then, she needed her husband's or male partner's permission to abort. In all circumstances, the EPL granted women and girls the chance merely to petition for permission to abort on specified grounds. Clearly, this was not a law passed with women's rights, autonomy, reproductive freedom, or health as its central concern.

Finally, Article 13.4 authorized a woman or girl to petition for permission to terminate pregnancies induced through "violence or menace." This final provision bore little overt connection to the stated eugenic and medical purpose of the EPL. But for Japanese who had been inundated with propaganda about enemy soldiers as rapists during the war, who experienced the occupation as "sexual invasion," and who (like Taniguchi and Fukuda) were aware and approved of systematic abortions provided to female repatriates on the grounds of race and rape since defeat in 1945, the race-hygienic relevance of Article 13.4 was clear. At last, "illegal pregnancy"—a makeshift cultural category—was given permanent statutory form.

Before 1945, women in Japan had never been allowed to seek abortion on the grounds of rape. Not only was abortion treated as a crime, but the desire for abortion by a woman "crying rape" was often seen as reason to suspect she was in fact covering up yet another sin—that of having an affair. As late as 1948, Taniguchi was assuring doubters in the Diet that the Eugenic Protection Bill, if enacted, would not entitle fornicating women who "tell lies" and fake rape to access abortion on demand, as their false claims when they petitioned to abort would be judged and discredited by (predominately male) police, judges, and welfare officials. Aware that surely not every woman who complained of rape was a false accuser, the male elites who set government policy before enactment of the EPL expected that women and girls who had actually been raped should go ahead and bear the child anyway.[69] It was the idea of rape by *foreign* men that changed the calculus of merits and demerits for postrape abortion.

FROM NO ABORTION TO PROABORTION

Far from codifying new reproductive "rights" or "freedoms," the EPL and its provisions regarding rape codified strict eugenic and sexual norms and granted medical and government authorities new tools for enforcing them. Reproduction was nationalized in a new way when rape became the object of racial-nationalist attention. The terms on which abortion was selectively decriminalized reconfirmed in 1948 that women and girls were not sovereign over their bodies. Under the EPL, women and girls remained subjects and subordinates of the men they married, medical professionals, the state, and the *minzoku*.

The language of the EPL is cautiously race-neutral, and scholars have often treated it as such. However, ostensibly race-blind laws are frequently applied in racially disparate ways. Take, for example, the Law to Prevent Hereditarily Diseased Offspring (*Gesetz zur Verhütung erbkranken Nachwuchses*) passed in Nazi Germany in 1933. Early on, Nazi leaders were sensitive to international opinion and hesitated to target racialized groups or "mixes" overtly for mass sterilization. This de jure racial neutrality helps explain why Jewish and Japanese eugenicists alike endorsed the Nazi law: It was not an explicit tool of Nordic supremacy. The primary grounds for compulsory sterilization under the *Gesetz* were feeblemindedness, schizophrenia, and epilepsy, conditions despised by eugenicists around the world. In 1935, the law's provisions for compulsory eugenic sterilization were extended to encompass eugenic abortion. Nothing in the law stipulated that particular races or "mixes" be eliminated from the gene pool. However, race hygienists, geneticists, and medical practitioners colluded with the Nazi regime to bring *Mischlinge* (mixes) within the orbit of the law. Mass sterilization of "mixed race" Germans followed.[70] At the war's end, abortions of children fathered by soldiers of enemy "races" were organized swiftly and at a large scale.[71]

The "race neutral" Nazi sterilization and abortion law was the model law used by Japanese race hygienists in their efforts to pass and enforce eugenic legislation in Japan. Leading these efforts from 1933 to 1948 was Nagai Hisomu, leader of the RHA. In 1940, Nagai and his colleagues in the RHA secured passage of the National Eugenics Law, only to lament its insufficient application to forestall dysgenic births in an empire he deemed too narrowly focused on boosting the birthrate. Defeat in 1945 gave Nagai and other leading eugenicists a chance to regroup and write a stronger law modeled on Nazi precedent. As we have seen, by the end of World War II,

Nagai had joined Koya Yoshio as a determined opponent of "blood mixing." On the New Committee, they collaborated in designing the policies that became the EPL. Integrated into the EPL, which remained in force until 1996, were nominally race-blind provisions for eugenic sterilization and abortion that would reduce the overall birth rate while weeding undesirable elements out of the breeding pool. The technocratic control over human reproduction that Japan had established in the imperial era was not being loosened, but it was being repurposed for the postwar era.[72]

That the race-neutral language of the EPL was open to race-conscious enforcement was attested by EPL cosponsor Taniguchi Yasaburō. Shortly after securing passage of the law in 1948, Taniguchi urged vigorous enforcement of the EPL among "*panpan* girls." *Panpan* was a common, derogatory term for Japanese women who consorted with occupying soldiers. Although stereotyped as degenerate streetwalkers, the term *panpan* was widely applied in postwar Japan to any woman or girl who consorted with a foreign man or gave birth to a *konketsuji*. Whether she was a sex worker, casual date, monogamous partner, or mother to *konketsuji*, all women and girls deemed too intimate with Allied soldiers were derided as whores to foreign men.[73] Outrage against such women and fears of sexual contagion manifested in draconian "*panpan* hunts," in which women on urban streets and at train stations were indiscriminately rounded up and forced to undergo VD checks. It was a practice quite similar to that imposed on repatriate women, but in "*panpan* hunts," nearly any woman or girl living in regions of the *naichi* also inhabited by foreign soldiers could be captured, tested, and "cleansed." Ob-gyn and legislator Taniguchi, far from objecting to this fusion of medical and police power, advised the minister of welfare to use "*panpan* hunts" to discover pregnant women and apply the EPL: "Conduct artificial abortions and stop them from giving birth." Taniguchi further alleged that "*panpan* girls" were mostly "feebleminded," making them lawful targets for eugenic sterilization. Collaboration between police, the MOW, and medical practitioners licensed to apply the EPL to such "suitable targets" would, Taniguchi insisted, help "prevent degradation in our genius" as a *minzoku*.[74] Taniguchi's plan to target *panpan* with sterilization and abortion lays bear the racial logic undergirding the Eugenic Protection Law.

The end of the occupation—and with it, the threat of SCAP purges and censorship—in 1952 unleashed a torrent of negative press about Japanese women who had "failed" to abort *konketsuji*. Taniguchi, for one, reissued his call to sterilize *panpan* and abort *konketsuji*.⁷⁵ Taniguchi and his cosponsor of the EPL, Socialist Fukuda Masako, seized the opportunity to denounce the reigning Liberal Party for not doing more to prevent the births of *konketsuji* (chapter 5). Katō Shizue would later deny that *konketsuji* had been envisioned as a target of the EPL. But an official from the Ministry of Justice who worked on the law, Takahashi Katsuyoshi, testified that *konketsuji* were exactly among the targets lawmakers had in mind when they crafted a system of eugenic abortion.⁷⁶ In the Diet in 1959, Socialist Ukeda Shinkichi remarked sorrowfully on Japan's failure to forestall more births of *konketsuji*, whom he described as "tragic products of an inability to use birth control."⁷⁷ With this utterance, Ukeda expressed a notion so widespread that it functioned as a kind of postwar national common sense. Mothers of "mixed blood" children should have practiced racial chastity, or failing that, they should have practiced abortion. Failure to do so was simply "tragic."

Nagai Hōji, a journalist from Japan's leading newspaper, *Asahi shinbun*, asked: Of the six hundred thousand legal abortions recorded in Japan between 1949 and 1952, the year the occupation ended, how many were of *konketsuji*? He estimated that tens of thousands of "mixed blood" fetuses must have been "cleaned up" by their would-be mothers since the end of the war. Yet he struggled to understand why the number of aborted *konketsuji* was not higher. Nagai subjected to an extended and bitter critique "blood mixing" mothers who, he said, had every "reason to seek the application of the Eugenic Protection Law before birth," but failed to do so.⁷⁸ For this well-placed journalist, who veered very close to endorsing prenatal ethnic cleansing, tens of thousands of abortions were not enough.

Nagai's proabortion, antibirth sentiment was more mainstream than fringe when it came to *konketsuji*. The tones that Japanese took in rebuking their countrywomen for bearing such children ranged from pitying to scathing. Prominent literary scholar Itagaki Naoko criticized as "foolish" and weak-willed the miscegenating mothers who "lacked the decisiveness to abort the children they were pregnant with." As a result, Itagaki complained, "the country today must bear the burden of more than ten thousand mixed-blood children born of war."⁷⁹ Takagi Masataka, famed as an international mountaineer, likewise castigated "blood mixing" mothers who "give birth to children so irresponsibly."⁸⁰ The prevailing attitude seemed to be that it was nearly criminal to give birth to a "mixed" child when the country had gone to so much trouble to provide legal means to dispose of them. An article in popular magazine *Ladies Review* ratified this consensus when it declared that *konketsuji* were "unhappy children irresponsibly given birth."[81] Negligence, rashness, immaturity, and "feeblemindedness" were attributed to "blood mixing" women who dodged eugenic abortion in favor of "mixed" motherhood.

Although it was impossible to impose abortions outright on all women who might be pregnant with the children of Japan's conquerors, such women were nonetheless targeted for eugenic intervention by Japanese government, medical practitioners, and civil society. For postwar women, abortion was not a freedom newly won in a resurgent democracy concerned with women's rights. Abortion was a directive handed down by a diverse array of governmental and nongovernmental actors uniting behind an ideology of racialized chastity and "pure blood."

That nationalist backlash against "blood mixing" was never sufficient to forestall all births of "mixed" children. Tensions over national chastity and "blood mixing" persisted—a thorn in the side of nationalists and the increasingly racialized eugenics movement in postwar Japan. Tensions over "blood mixing" also proved to be a thorn in the side of the occupiers, who did their best to clamp down on any criticism of Allied soldiers over their sexual liaisons with Japanese women. But SCAP proved unable to control the narrative. Even under the aegis of SCAP's substantial censorship apparatus, hostility toward "mixing" spread through the presses of occupied Japan. The rise of "pure blood" nationalism redefined Japanese identity and fueled an anti-American backlash by the occupation's end.

Chapter Four

SEX, CENSORSHIP, AND SCAP

Debating "Blood Mixing" Under Occupation, 1945–1952

On September 29, 1945, Japan's three largest newspapers published a photograph of emperor Hirohito standing side by side with Supreme Commander for the Allied Powers (SCAP), Douglas MacArthur. Hirohito, who had been photographed at fawning, upward angles in military uniform throughout the war, was now stripped of that masculine regalia and photographed dead-on. He stood by MacArthur's side as a mere civilian—just as Japanese women had stood beside their servicemen during the war, perpetual subordinates. Negative reaction from the cabinet of prime minister Higashikuni Naruhiko (1887–1990), prince and uncle to Hirohito, was swift. Apparently, this photograph did not satisfy the *ancien régime* requirement, inscribed in the constitution of 1889, that the emperor be "sacred and inviolable."[1]

Scholars argue that defeat in World War II symbolically "emasculated" and "feminized" Japan and its men.[2] Japan is thereby construed as "masculine" during the expansive imperial era, with "feminization" an insulting devolution in national status. We need not agree with the assumption that femininity is debasing and inferior to appreciate that many Japanese, men in particular, may have felt thus degraded by the loss of imperial power. The notorious photograph that showed MacArthur's public display of courtly dominance over a diminished Hirohito is cited as a case in point, as a "wedding photo" symbolizing the unequal and "sexualized power relations" between occupier and occupied.[3] In some respects, this "wedding"

SEX, CENSORSHIP, AND SCAP

FIGURE 4.1. The "wedding portrait" of Douglas MacArthur and Hirohito, September 27, 1945. Courtesy of the National Archives at College Park, Still Pictures.

resembled the marriage arranged decades prior between Korean crown prince Yi Un and Japanese princess Nashimoto Masako to celebrate the unification of colonial Korea and imperial Japan in "one body." But this time, the marriage was between the conquering United States and conquered Japan. Japanese responses to "intermarriage" on these terms proved as harsh as Korean nationalist reactions had been against fusion with Japan years prior (chapter 1). From the symbolic union of Hirohito and MacArthur to interracial sex at lower levels of society, border-crossing relations between conquerors and conquered proved a site of constant controversy in occupied Japan.

In the September 1945 "wedding" portrait, Hirohito appeared shorter, rigidly symmetrical and altogether spiffier in his elegant suit than the tall and relaxed general at his side, standing limbs akimbo with khaki collar casually unbuttoned (figure 4.1). If this was a wedding, it was a coerced one, in which Hirohito assumed the role of diminutive Japanese bride to masculine US power. That the US general did not bother to dress to impress his new Japanese consort, as Hirohito dressed to impress him, was no doubt part of the symbolic problem, from the perspective of the Higashikuni cabinet. A human rather than sacred emperor, alive and well but docile and subordinated, was precisely what SCAP wanted the Japanese public to see. Not so the Japanese government, which suspended publication of all three papers that published the photograph for the crime of *lèse majesté*. When SCAP reversed the cabinet's order, proclaiming press freedom and contravening the legal mandate of imperial fealty, the Higashikuni cabinet resigned and a new era dawned in Japan.[4]

Poet and novelist Takami Jun (1907–1965) experienced this turn of events not as emasculation but as liberation by foreign hands. Takami had been arrested as a Marxist in the early 1930s and suffered constant police surveillance thereafter. During the war, he began to redeem himself by working for the Japanese Empire in occupied China, Burma, and Bali. Yet even as he devoted his literary skills to building the Co-Prosperity Sphere, Takami quietly nursed his dissent, not only toward the government he served, but toward the everyday imperial arrogance and racism of his fellow Japanese. In his wartime diary, he grieved that the humblest Japanese farmer or soldier was apt to treat even the best-bred "Chinese like a dog or a pig."[5] In Harbin, Takami watched Japanese soldiers treat Russians with the same violent contempt and sexual aggression. Despite wartime slogans to the contrary, throughout Japanese-occupied Asia, he observed darkly, "there was neither harmony nor co-prosperity."[6]

Under the storm clouds of state violence and wartime censorship, he dared not air such critique outside the pages of his diary. Publication of the "wedding photo" was a sign that the skies were clearing, and Takami reacted with ecstasy. "Now one can write anything at all, freely! We can publish anything at all, freely! This is the first freedom I have known since I was born."[7] The US spent the early months of the occupation issuing civil liberties directives, enfranchising women, bolstering democracy, freeing political prisoners, demolishing the empire's secret-police and thought-control apparatus, and mandating "an absolute minimum of restrictions upon freedom of speech" in Japan.[8]

Emboldened by Allied occupiers who acted as a shield between Japanese dissidents and the old regime, author Nakano Shigeharu waxed fervidly outspoken in his critique of Japan's leadership. In the pages of the influential journal *Reconstruction* in early 1946, Nakano argued that surrender had done nothing to weaken Japanese elites' ruthless grip on power. "All of the Japanese have been enslaved by these earthly gods," he fumed. He feared those self-appointed gods were now hunkered down defending their own interests rather than working to rebuild a devastated Japan. That Nakano published this protest without fear of political retribution through state-sanctioned violence was a marvel.

Yet it was not true, as Takami initially gushed in September 1945, that "now one can write anything at all, freely!" On the contrary, Nakano launched his protest against a broader target than the published version of his article admitted. Passages implying that Allied authorities, just like Japanese authorities, systematically deprived the people of Japan of freedom were deleted by censors now working, not for the Japanese government, but for SCAP.[9]

Political scientist Toshio Nishi argues that SCAP pushed for civil liberties expecting "the Japanese people to break out in iconoclastic criticism of prewar Japan." Such criticism did pour forth, but Nishi suggests that overall, SCAP "badly misjudged the target at which criticism would be directed."[10] However furious many Japanese were at their government, they had plenty of fury to direct at foreign occupiers, too.

Far from naïve, SCAP officials anticipated such blowback from the start. Although SCAP denied Japan's government the sovereign prerogatives to censor speech, control the press, and crack down on political dissidents, SCAP claimed the same sovereign powers for itself, erecting its own Civil Censorship Detachment (CCD) to control forbidden chatter. SCAP's initial civil liberties directive on September 10, 1945, in fact mandated restrictions on speech and the press, chiefly encompassing "Allied troop movements which have not been officially released" and "criticism of the Allied powers."[11] The former point would not become a bone of much contention. The latter did. On September 21, the CCD issued a more detailed press code that enunciated two overriding restraints. First, "News must strictly adhere to the truth." Second, "There shall be no destructive criticism of the Allied Occupation and nothing which might invite mistrust or resentment of those troops."[12] The US-dominated SCAP apparatus shielded even Soviet soldiers from critique under this policy.[13] Mistrust and resentment of Allied troops was rife in Japan, so a great deal of censorship ensued.

Much of that resentment and censorship focused on relations between foreign soldiers and Japanese women and the "mixed blood" offspring born of such affairs.

CENSORING SEX AND CHILDBIRTH

Initially, when occupation soldiers landed in Japan, government officials, newspapers, and rumormongers promoted gendered panic over mass rape. They urged women and girls to evacuate, to quit their jobs and stay home, or if they must go out, to wear ugly clothing, avoid exposing skin, and refrain at all costs from speaking to foreign soldiers. But Japanese bureaucrats and police soon reversed course, recognizing that mass panic was counterproductive to public order. The same authorities who had described Anglo-Americans as "demons" and "beasts" during the war now encouraged a more benign view of the occupiers as less racist and prone to rape and other atrocities than originally alleged. Historian Barak Kushner emphasizes that this discursive shift began with Japanese authorities, who did not wait for orders from SCAP to soften and redirect domestic discourse. As women and girls came into increasing contact with occupying soldiers, the initial terrors of foreign occupation began to fade in favor of a grassroots culture of fraternization.[14]

Yet consensual fraternization proved divisive and highly offensive to many Japanese. As Allied soldiers spread out through Japan, so too did the bitter sexual politics of subdividing Japanese women and girls into categories of chaste or pure, sexual patriot or race traitor.

Budding right-wing novelist Yamada Fūtarō (1922–2001) was but one of many men intensely affronted by the way occupying soldiers spoke and waved to Japanese women. The casual or convivial responses of his countrywomen appalled him. "A normal woman would turn pale and run away," Yamada groused.[15] Disturbingly, to his mind, Japanese women often failed to run. Unable to publish his complaints against the outgoing occupiers and "abnormal" Japanese women who failed to flee them, Yamada poured out his recrimination in his diary, far from the eyes of CCD censors. A great fan of suicide before surrender, perhaps Yamada felt that a "normal woman" should kill herself rather than suffer defiling contact with a foreign soldier, as many women had during the fall of Saipan, Okinawa, and Manchukuo (chapter 3).[16]

All too many women under occupation did not seem to sense their defilement. To Takami Jun's dismay, the women he saw subjected to US soldiers' attentions "looked as if being flirted with in this way was unbearably pleasurable." So much for the performance of patriotic chastity. What was emerging instead was a culture of open feminine pleasure taken in the company of foreign men. "What an indescribably shameful sight!" Takami fumed. Like fellow author Yamada, Takami recorded unpublishable outrage in his diary, just as he used to do in the imperial era. But his postimperial outrage had new targets. As to Japanese women consorting with the conquerors, "I was appalled by the thought that these disgraceful women would have the right to vote."[17]

That women would be entitled both to vote and to hold government office was one of many democratic reforms initiated at the outset of occupation.[18] Even this democratizing move, often regarded in retrospect as one of the highlights of the occupation, generated gendered and racialized resentment. Takami, for one, doubted his countrywomen deserved the right to vote when they snuggled up to the enemy rather than resisting, as chaste and patriotic women should. The sexual resentment expressed by left-wing Takami and right-wing Yamada, who might otherwise agree on little, foretold an emerging culture of suasion, shame, and grassroots policing designed to segregate Japanese women from foreign soldiers and punish them when they strayed across enemy lines. This regime of sexual segregation, however, could not work without cooperation from both SCAP and Japanese women. SCAP proved unable or unwilling to curtail servicemen's liaisons with local women.[19] And Japanese women were clearly split on how to behave.

Japanese men were more united. One year after Takami Jun fumed over unchaste women's unfitness to vote, comedian and author Furukawa Roppa expressed similar doubts about his countrywomen's sexual ethics and national allegiance. "American soldiers, Negroes, and the shameful lipsticks of the Japanese women clinging to them"—such were his impressions of defeat.[20]

Such complaints, although commonplace in the wartime diaries of prominent men, and no doubt too in daily conversations that escape the historical record, were rarely published during the occupation. Indeed, the chatter that most vexed CCD censors often revolved less around high politics than around the intimate, interracial affairs between Allied men and Japanese women. In his study of CCD censorship, literary scholar Jay Rubin explains that "by far, the single largest group of deletions . . . concerns fraternization." Resentful remarks about Japanese women holding hands with foreigners and "mixed blood" babies born of such relations were routinely deleted.[21] Sex was a sore point, and the point where sex and race intersected was almost unbearably sensitive.

SCAP censorship was narrowly designed to shield its soldiers and their nations from vituperation and was never aimed to control, much less brighten, Japanese attitudes toward interracial sex and reproduction. As a result, even as SCAP shielded its forces from critique on the grounds of "blood mixing," anti-mixing rhetoric that appeared sufficiently abstracted or depoliticized was allowed to flourish.

A prominent test case for SCAP censors came in June 1946, when Japan's national broadcaster, NHK, publicized the birth of a certain *konketsuji* as "the first gift of the occupation." Tone and intent can be difficult to judge, but SCAP interpreted the broadcast as sneering and satirical. The animosities of war and defeat remained strong, even as the initial terrors of occupation abated. It was clear, by now, that a Japanese man did not risk his life when he defied SCAP censors. As one Japanese reporter put it, the former imperial censorship apparatus had "posed an omnipresent threat to my life, but GHQ's [General Headquarters] censorship never made me feel my life was at stake."[22]

Provoked on the question of *konketsuji*, SCAP set out to prove that soft censorship still had teeth. SCAP had the radio announcer dismissed, ostensibly on the grounds that he averred that interracial sex and breeding were something of an occupation policy.[23] Such a narrative threatened the reputation of Allied soldiers and their leaders not only in Japan but also in their home countries. After all, interracial sex and marriage were widely reviled among Europeans and Australians and criminalized in much of the United States.[24]

Another test came in August 1947, when *Japan Economic News* proposed an article under the headline, "Abandoned Mixed-Blood Child." Unlike the prior radio address, this terse piece prudently eschewed editorial commentary and emotional tone. In a just-the-facts style, it stated that a "mixed blood" girl, about two weeks old, had been found abandoned in Shinjuku. The article made no reference to geopolitical context, foreign soldiers, or the infant's suspected paternity. Yet CCD censors clearly felt that Japanese audiences would read between the lines in a mood of dark misgivings about foreign occupiers.[25] Despite its overt neutrality and "strict adherence to the truth," which met the requirements of the CCD press code, this article, too, was nixed. It appears that the article ran up against the other main injunction in the press code, as it might have had the calculated or accidental effect of fostering "mistrust or resentment" of Allied troops.[26] SCAP was censoring not only what was stated but also what was implied or might be inferred—the metatextual context in which news and rumors about "mixed blood" newborns circulated.

Such cases lead media historian Kanō Mikiyo to aver that SCAP imposed a "taboo" on *konketsuji* sufficient to "socially erase" them.[27] Scholars Yukiko Koshiro and Yuko Kawai go even further, asserting that the CCD prohibited and suppressed "any mention of race, regardless of circumstances or intentions."[28] In reality, these scholars overstate both SCAP's intentions and its powers to control, much less halt, racial discourse in Japan. Kanō is correct in observing that there are far fewer publications on *konketsuji* during the occupation than after the occupation's end in April 1952. However, that metric distorts as much as it reveals. As figure 4.2 shows, the

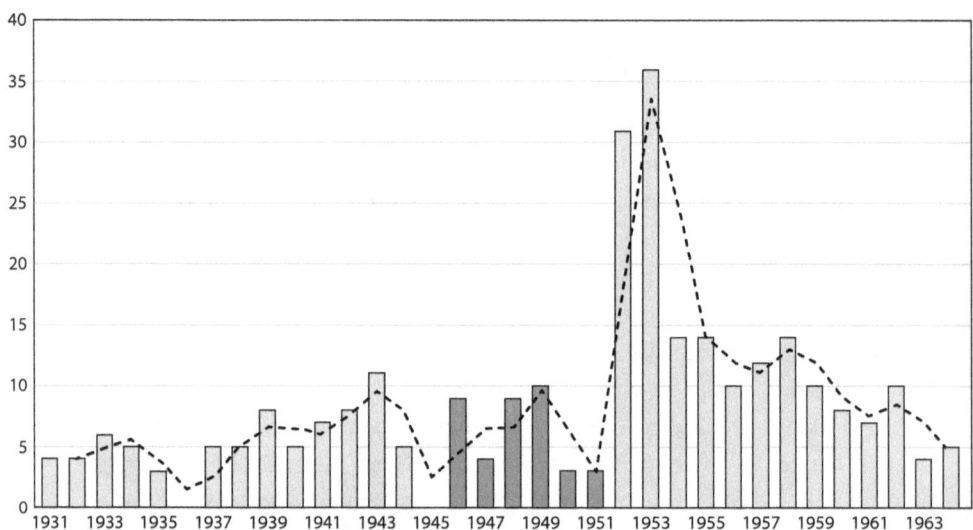

FIGURE 4.2. The number of articles with "blood mixing" (*konketsu*) in the title published per year in Japanese periodicals. "Blood mixing" featured in articles but not headlines is not captured. Other forms of media, including books, movies, and radio are not counted. As such, the data understate overall publication and must be read as suggestive rather than comprehensive. Publication in the occupation era (shown in darker gray) is not drastically reduced from that during the imperial era. Publication skyrockets at the occupation's end in 1952. Data sourced from *Zasshi kiji sakuin shūsei dētabēsu* (Complete Database for Japanese Magazine and Periodicals).

extraordinarily high frequency of publication on "blood mixing" in 1952–1953 stands out as a historical aberration compared with every prior year of Japanese history—not just those years under foreign occupation. In fact, rates of publication on "blood mixing" in 1946–1949, when SCAP censorship was in effect, exhibit considerable continuity with the late imperial era. (The absence of publications in 1945, a year split between imperial and SCAP censorship, is best explained by air raids, paper shortages, and the devastation of the Japanese publishing industry, which rebounded after the war.) Such data make clear that "race" and "blood mixing" were not topics that SCAP erased from Japanese discourse. SCAP's intervention was more partial and fine-tuned, as we will see.

To better understand postwar patterns of silence and speech regarding *konketsuji*, one must weigh more than SCAP policies—Japanese motives also matter. The flood of commentary on *konketsuji* in 1952–1953, immediately after the occupation's end, was sharply critical of foreign occupiers and their sexual and genetic imprint on Japan. As such, Japanese publishers deliberately held back much of that commentary until the occupation's end. That flood of negative commentary is analyzed in subsequent chapters. Suffice it to say that Japanese who chose to (1) lambaste "blood mixing" and the foreign soldiers deemed responsible for fomenting it, and (2) hold back that commentary until the occupation's end, produced a trough in publications in 1950–1951, then an unprecedented boom in 1952–1953. This pattern of relative quiet followed by clamor exhibits an ironic feature, in that the quiet period in 1950–1951 came after the CCD censorship apparatus was dismantled.

Media coverage of the atomic bombing offers an interesting point of comparison. Like *konketsuji*, atomic bombs were an incendiary topic that Japanese and foreign critics would levy against the US victors in World War II as evidence of their moral derangement and devastating biopolitical impact on Japan. Sensitive to this potential for bad press from the start, CCD carefully monitored media attention to both atomic bombs and interracial sex and children. Censorship of both topics followed a similar path, with coverage never fully suppressed even at the height of the CCD's power in the late 1940s, and much coverage held back by Japanese even after the CCD's dissolution in 1949, leading to a deluge of publishing on the atomic bombings and *konketsuji* in 1952.[29] As parallel biopolitical catastrophes inflicted by Americans on Japan, controversy over *konketsuji* and atomic bombs continued sotto voce until they could emerge in full force.

Even under occupation, Japanese published more on "blood mixing" than Kanō's otherwise insightful study, and those of Rubin, Koshiro, and Kawai, lead one to believe. Analyzing publications from that period exposes less consistency and rigor in SCAP quashing talk of "blood mixing" than allegations of taboo and erasure would imply. SCAP did not suppress all talk of "blood mixing"—the ban was on *negative* coverage that would "invite mistrust or resentment" of Allied forces. The relative scarcity of occupation-era publications on *konketsuji* is testimony to how little in a positive vein members of the postwar Japanese media thought to say.

In fact, the very same month (June 1946) that SCAP sacked an NHK radio announcer for his broadcast on *konketsuji* as "gifts" provided to Japan by occupation policy, SCAP permitted publication without modification of "The Pure Blood of *Minzoku* and Blood-Mixing Marriages." This article was written by demographer Okazaki Ayanori (1895–1979), director of the Institute for Research on Population Problems affiliated with the Ministry of Welfare (MOW).[30] A few months later, Okazaki discussed *konketsuji* again in his book, *Population Anguish*, in which he revealed facts about Japan's population crisis that had been classified during the war. After defeat, Okazaki was free to disclose such matters publicly. He was also free, just as he had been during the war, to apply his sociological and scientific lens both to interpreting and attempting to guide interracial sex and reproduction. With the notable exception of sharing previously guarded imperial secrets, there was much continuity on display in Okazaki's occupation-era work. He recycled for postimperial audiences the imperial common sense that of all the world's *minzoku*, none was a pure line (*junkei*). He reviewed wartime debates over "blood mixing," including research by Ishiwara Fusao and Miyake Katsuo, who documented the eugenic fitness of imperial *konketsuji* (chapter 1). Like most wartime researchers before him, Okazaki concluded that what mattered most in determining the quality of a child was not the races to which one's parents belonged, but rather the quality of the parents. Whether one's parents belonged to the same or different "races" was eugenically irrelevant.

Okazaki did harbor concerns, however, about the ramifications of "blood mixing" under present postwar conditions. He warned that Japanese must nurture the proper environment for *konketsuji* to thrive. For "racial pride and feelings of superiority exist not only among whites. In our country, too, there are likely not a few people who embrace racial prejudice [*minzokuteki henken*]." Tactfully, Okazaki condemned no one in particular, but acknowledged that even among his fellow scientists, some wished to put an end to Japan's long history of "blood mixing." Okazaki was keenly aware of the rise of biological defeatism among prominent colleagues in the MOW, such as Koya Yoshio, and the broader public sphere in the final years of the war (chapter 2). Surrender had rendered interracial sex with foreign soldiers all the more threatening and despicable in the eyes of many Japanese. Given injunctions against talk that might spark (or reflect) resentment of the occupiers, Okazaki dared not state these obvious points; but the obvious need not be stated. The palpable subtext was that wartime grudges and occupation animosities imperiled the futures of *konketsuji* being born in Japan, as well as the futures of interracial couples now forming. In the face of mounting antipathy, Okazaki took a stance on "blood mixing" that was optimistic, tolerant, and humane. Rather than take pride in "purity" and enforce segregation, Okazaki urged his fellow Japanese to support "as much as possible the partners in blood-mixing marriages."[31]

Okazaki's 1946 publications on intermarriage should not be misconstrued as evidence that SCAP, through the CCD, enforced a pro-mixing line. To take but one counterexample, in May 1947, *True Love* magazine printed a poetic paean to raven-haired Yamato maidens who "bear the pride of a many-isled country in their red blood." This sexualized and nationalistic poem, which passed through CCD censorship with no violations, closed with an injunction to "protect the eternally pure blood [*junketsu*] of our *minzoku*."[32] Clearly, CCD operatives did not treat the ideal of a "pure-blood *minzoku*" or ethos of racialized and nationalized chastity as taboo. Why should they, when paeans to "pure blood" and national chastity were hardly unknown in North America, Australia, China, the Soviet Union, or Europe? Many members of the Allied forces could sympathize with demands that countrywomen keep sex and reproduction within "racial" and patriotic bounds. White supremacy and racial segregation among the occupiers were important reasons that anti-mixing advocates in Japan might find their CCD censors permissive of strongly negative statements on "blood mixing."

It is important to recognize, however, that CCD censorship was not a purely white or Euro-American imposition. White Americans held the highest ranks in the CCD, but they could not very well censor a language they did not understand. The front line of CCD censors were more than five thousand Japanese, often men determined to enforce their values, alongside Japanese laws and policies, rather than to bolster SCAP's ideology or hegemony. These Japanese employees of the CCD often advocated stricter and more conservative censorship, especially regarding sex and "healthy" (*kenzen na*) social mores and conduct, than did their American bosses.[33] This dynamic suggests an additional reason that anti-mixing rhetoric made it into print after 1945. The SCAP ban was on negative coverage, but negativity was in the eye of the beholder. And the beholding eye was often Japanese.

As the CCD's eyes and ears, Japanese censors exercised a measure of autonomy in flagging texts and ideas as problematic. Pieces that fluent Japanese-language readers did not flag were unlikely to be noticed by higher-ranking CCD officials. Such acts of noncensorship left little paper trail, so it is impossible to reconstruct the reasoning or identities of decision-makers in most cases. In the case of the *True Love* poem "Pure Blood," we can only infer that a frontline censor, likely Japanese, identified no "destructive criticism" of the Allies in the text—or nothing overt enough that he risked his job by declining to censor it. At the height of the occupation, *konketsuji* could be repudiated in print and Japanese women urged not to bear them, to remain "pure." The taboo on criticizing Allied personnel did not shield Japanese women or their children from such rhetoric.

Like MOW demographer Okazaki Ayanori, anthropologist Kiyono Kenji, whose scholarship had favored "blood mixing" during the war (chapter 1), continued publishing on the problem under occupation. In 1946, he suffered through numerous CCD excisions of his forthcoming tome, *Theory of Japanese Race Formation*. In nearly five hundred pages of text, Kiyono presented twenty years of biological research on the Japanese in a manner he touted as accessible to the "general educated class" of readers. The stakes for propounding race science so widely were overtly political. "For the Japanese *minzoku* to possess a clear consciousness of the uniqueness of its own genus would be necessary in any kind of world, but especially today as we volunteer in the construction of Greater East Asia." Clearly, Kiyono wrote these words before the empire collapsed, not yet dreaming that foreign censors would be the ones to review them. He continued: "The people of Japan must take a scientifically grounded confidence in their own genealogy and their own development as a *minzoku/jinshu*. In short, both love of our race [*shuzoku*] and love of our homeland must thereby be deepened. It is thus that love of country is cultivated." After receiving Kiyono's manuscript,

CCD censors scrubbed the text clean of references to "Greater East Asia," the "Co-Prosperity Sphere," and "love of country." Shorn of political exposition, the race science was left substantially intact.[34]

Aside from anachronistic references to the war, SCAP censors focused on deleting passages that would "invite mistrust and resentment." Deleted were assertions that Europeans look down on Japanese as an inferior, "colored" race. Then came an extended passage, fated to provoke CCD censors, in which Kiyono attempted to turn race-scientific prejudice around on Europeans. Kiyono mimicked invidious comparisons made by white racists of other "races" to animals, but inverted such comparisons to Europeans' disadvantage. For instance, Kiyono asserted that Europeans have a stronger, more animalistic body odor than Japanese, Mongolians, or Malaysians. Europeans were hairier, thus more similar to apes, than Japanese. European toes were more similar to the toes of apes than to the more evolved toes of Japanese. As he built up a damning and laughable picture of the wartime enemy, now postwar occupier, Kiyono added that Europeans also had uncommonly long arms, like those of apes. But those sneaky Europeans, Kiyono explained, "to conceal the fact that their arms are long, say that among their own breed, torsos are short." Even the fingers of European women came in for sexist and racist critique, as Kiyono deemed them fat with bulging joints compared with the slender, sophisticated digits of Japanese. Most important, Kiyono advised readers that "with regard to brain weight, Japanese people are superior even to Europeans."[35] As Kiyono pilloried the egocentric biases in Western race science, he also reveled in redirecting race science, in all its power, to hierarchize and dehumanize the wartime Other while building cohesion and pride in his own "race." Such an ideological effort could have passed through imperial censorship, but Kiyono's attempts to build up Japanese racial pride by denigrating Europeans came a few months too late. CCD censors deleted several pages in this vein.

Despite CCD's intervention, Kiyono's race-scientific tome was printed largely as written. Changes the censors demanded were relatively few and superficial. Kiyono's promotion of racial-national pride, quixotically paired with sharp critique of racial prejudice, passed into print and the hands of Japanese readers in February 1946. These readers found Kiyono promoting Japanese pride in their "mixed blood" heritage, just as he had in the imperial era. Kiyono explained that amalgamating multiple races into one was the font of Japanese "race" formation, cultural progress, and construction of a unified country. Among Japanese since the stone age, he wrote, "blood mixing with surrounding *minzoku* has occurred without pause, both changing our physical constitution and changing and elevating us toward new culture."[36] These ideas were nothing new—but printing them in a new era attracted a new tenor of critique.

In 1949, anthropologists Ikeda Jirō and Imamura Yutaka published a paper sweeping in scope and scathing in allegations, entitled "Doubts About Dr. Kiyono's Theory of the Japanese Race." Zeroing in on alleged "contradictions" in his data and analysis, particularly regarding "blood" ties between Koreans and Japanese, these anthropologists charged that Kiyono's life's work and long-dominant "mixed-blood theory is nothing more than supposition."[37] The notion that Japanese and Koreans shared the same "blood," vigorously propounded during the imperial era, was losing purchase now that Korea had regained its political independence. Because "blood" ties between Koreans and Japanese were among the best documented and widely accepted in Japan, for prominent scholars such as Ikeda and Imamura to reject Kiyono's claims on this point opened up the possibility that Japanese had few "blood" ties to any people anywhere on earth. Perhaps, despite all that had been said during the war, the Japanese were not so much "mixed" as they were "pure."

To more swiftly overturn the old paradigm, Imamura and a team of researchers rushed to conduct new raciological studies on populations previously deemed exemplars of "mixture": inhabitants of Tsushima. From the sixteenth to nineteenth century, the rulers of Tsushima, an island located halfway between the Korean peninsula and main islands of Japan, "maintained a monopoly on Japanese-Korean intercourse and served as a diplomatic intermediary."[38] After Tsushima and Korea were incorporated into the modern Japanese Empire, Japanese scientists defined Tsushima islanders as intermediate racial types and embodied evidence of the long and productive history of "mixture" between Japanese and continental peoples. As historian Miriam Kingsberg Kadia observes, by "highlighting the continuity of the home islands and the continent, the study of Tsushima served to justify imperial ambitions in Asia."[39]

During the occupation, Imamura and other Japanese researchers descended on Tsushima determined to disprove the old intermixed paradigm and erect a biopolitical binary in its place. In the postimperial order, one could be Korean or Japanese—one could not be both. Imamura attempted to prove the point by remeasuring and reevaluating biometric factors, such as cephalic index, blood type distribution, and bodily proportions. Based on these classic racial indictors, he concluded that "from a biological standpoint, the Tsushima islanders are Japanese." Another researcher who sought to demarcate the boundaries of the Japanese on Tsushima was Izumi Seiichi, who had helped organize abortions of *konketsuji* among repatriates from Korea at the war's end (chapter 3). Far from a frontier of "mixture," Tsushima emerged in the early 1950s research of Izumi and his colleagues as "paradigmatically Japanese."[40] *Yomiuri shinbun* trumpeted such findings to readers, citing biometric and other evidence to prove: "Tsushima is Japan!" The headline announced that the findings on Tsushima proved the existence of a "pure Yamato *minzoku*."[41]

What was coming into vogue during the occupation was a more insular, even xenophobic, interpretation of the evolutionary and political history of the Japanese than had been popular in an expanding empire. "Purity" rather than "mixture" was the new foundation of racial pride and national identity.

Even more aggressive in his renunciation of any "mixed blood" origin or identity for Japanese than Ikeda and Imamura was their colleague Hasebe Kotondo, head of the anthropology program at Tokyo University. In 1948, Hasebe took his argument to *World of Science*, a youthful magazine targeting popular audiences. In an article bluntly entitled "The Japanese *Minzoku* Is Not a Mixed-Blood *Minzoku*," Hasebe denigrated the research of Kiyono and other scientists who had promoted a "mixed blood" vision of Japan. Far from scientific fact, Hasebe characterized their claims as mere "folklore," "high-handed conjecture," and "grave error."[42] Dismissing decades of scientific work by Kiyono and men like him, Hasebe contended that the Japanese had in fact evolved from a single, unadulterated line since the Paleolithic era. In all that time, they were essentially untouched by "mixing" with foreign *minzoku*. According to historian Arnaud Nanta, Hasebe had been attracted to such a vision of "pure" Japanese for many years, but had felt constrained to quiet his doubts during the imperial era. During the occupation, such constraints lifted.

In *World of Science*, Hasebe propounded a "pure," ancient, and endogamous Japanese bloodline as a matter of scientific fact. He kept perversely mum on the "mixing" that had gone on in the imperial era and that was still going on under occupation. As such, CCD censors had no reason to object to his raciological musings. To an American occupier—if any bothered to read Hasebe's article, which is doubtful—debates over Japanese evolutionary history from the Paleolithic era onward might seem merely academic. In fact, as Japanese well knew, they were profoundly political.

By 1951, Hasebe secured the presidency of the Anthropology Society of Japan, a powerful position he would hold for the next seventeen years. As he rose to dominance in the Japanese academy, he helped secure the postwar respectability and then hegemony of the once-marginal idea that the Japanese were not "mixed blood" but rather "pure."[43] In Hasebe's academic milieu, Koreans and other former imperial subjects still resident in postwar Japan, latter-day immigrants, and newborn *konketsuji* were all redefined as innately foreign, beyond the biological and therefore political boundaries of Japaneseness. Under SCAP censorship, Hasebe was able to set the stage for a thorough repudiation of "mixed blood" children as biological aliens. Such scholarship also provided support for a popular backlash against "blood mixing" adults blamed for staging an unprecedented assault on the Japanese *minzoku* and its allegedly pure "blood."

Such was the range of commentary about intermarriage, "blood," and *konketsuji* that SCAP was prepared to see published. Calls for tolerance and support for interracial families, such as those penned by demographer Okazaki Ayanori, SCAP permitted. Paeans to "pure blood" and denunciations of "blood mixing," such as those published by poets and professors, were also permitted. Kiyono's claim that the Japanese were a proud "mixed blood" people, once shorn of expansionist and Japan-supremacist rhetoric, was permitted. Challenges to that claim from Hasebe and other scholars and journalists who encouraged Japanese pride in racial endogamy and purity were also permitted. The only certain rule was that Allied soldiers be sheltered from censure—and that rule left leeway for interpretation by Japanese censors and readers alike.

As historian Kevin Doak observes, SCAP was too fixated on tackling other ideological targets in Japan, such as the military, emperor, and State Shinto, to recognize "blood" talk and *minzoku*-centered nationalism as hazards to its aims. "It was a momentous oversight, for it allowed a virulent nationalism to fester beneath the radar screen as a mere form of 'social theory.'"[44] To be clear, *minzoku* nationalism was not only a social but also a profoundly biological theory, one that deliberately rejected a race-blind constituency of Japanese citizens in favor of an endogamous, evolutionary community of "blood." Hence MOW-affiliated sociologist Koyama

SEX, CENSORSHIP, AND SCAP

Eizō's insistent declaration that a *minzoku* was a "natural community . . . a community of 'blood.' " The exclusionary and essentialist tenor of this remark did not provoke SCAP censorship. Under SCAP, the old imperial notion that anyone might become Japanese as long as they were loyal to the emperor was likely to be censored, whereas the "scientific" theory that Japanese must be defined by what Koyama termed "uniformity of blood" was perversely preferred.[45]

If medical researchers, anthropologists, and eugenicists in the imperial era often tolerated or favored "intermarriage," in the occupation era, social and medical scientists launched an about-face toward denial of "mixing" in history and repudiation of "mixing" in the present. Precisely because such commentary was nominally neutral and "scientific" rather than partisan and "political," CCD tended to give medical, anthropological, genetic, sociological, and eugenic publications wide latitude to debate and decide Japan's racial identity. Under the lax oversight of foreign occupiers, sex and reproduction with foreigners were reconfigured as racial rather than "political" threats—as an unremitting biological attack on the living organism of Japan.

RE-RACING *KONKETSUJI*

Early in the occupation, *konketsuji* sired by the occupiers became an urgent topic of biological and eugenic research and debate. One of the earliest such studies was conducted not on the living children of the occupiers, but on the dead. In 1946, a trio of Japanese anatomists began investigating the aborted bodies of six-month-old and seven-month-old *konketsuji*, each selected by the researchers because they had been conceived by Japanese women with either a "Negro" or "European" man. The anatomists' object was to determine at what gestational age there emerged measurable racial differences between the "mixed blood" and "Japanese fetus." They were disappointed to report, however, that their search for clear prenatal racial markers was a failure. "We were unable to discern racial differences," they reported, even at the third trimester. No one at the CCD objected as aborted offspring of Allied soldiers were transformed into research materials for Japanese race scientists.[46]

A few years later, obstetrician-gynecologist and director of Iwakuni Hospital, Shōji Tadashi, published two more pioneering studies on occupation-born *konketsuji*.[47] Shōji focused on those born alive, but abortion haunted his research as well. Shōji noted that one in three of the infants he studied was born after the mother "was urged to have an abortion but would not agree."[48] Shōji was far from the only scientist researching the "mixed-blood" children sired by the occupiers, but he beat most of his race-scientific competitors to publication. As a clinical practitioner, he felt no need to conduct multiyear longitudinal studies of the kind that would dominate university-based research on konketsuji published from 1952 onward. Shōji also had the advantage of being in the right place at the right time. The Japanese Imperial Navy had commissioned an air station in Iwakuni in 1940, and like other military bases, this one passed into Allied hands upon surrender. By 1948, Iwakuni was a Royal Australian Air Force base.[49] Shōji's geographic and professional position at Iwakuni Hospital, combined with his background in obstetrics and gynecology, brought him into close contact with Japanese-Allied "mixed blood" families as they began to form.

As a young doctor, Shōji had built his career far from Iwakuni, in another occupied zone where armed men clashed and mingled with native women: the Japanese colony of Taiwan. In the 1930s, Shōji had conducted research on Indigenous peoples there, evincing particular interest in "savage" menstruation and pelvic dimensions.[50] Shōji was working in the established fields of colonial medicine and comparative racial gynecology, pioneered by earlier generations of obstetrician-gynecologists in the late-Meiji era.[51] Japan's colonial sciences did not vanish with the colonies in 1945. Race-science researchers such as Shōji Tadashi neither abandoned their profession nor forgot their sense of patriotic mission and professional opportunity in linking scientific enterprise to nationalist ends.[52] As research centers in Japan's former colonies broke up and old colonial research projects plunged into obsolescence, Japanese race scientists repatriated to the newly colonized heartland of Japan.[53] Some, such as Shōji, applied the tools and techniques of their trade to a novel racial minority: Japan's foreign conquerors and their newborn, "mixed blood" children.

Just as they had in the empire of old, postwar Japanese scientists used biological data and metaphors of "blood" to trace political and patriarchal relationships between ruler and ruled, to signal where loyalty was owed, and to establish and police "natural" hierarchies. But in the wake of defeat, with important exceptions such as Okazaki, Japanese scientists became significantly less likely to celebrate konketsuji as fit and desirable members of the body politic. No longer offspring of Japanese Empire, postwar konketsuji were offspring of imperial defeat and an emasculated nation. Now more than ever, Japanese scientists elaborated on the biological defeatism pioneered during the final years of empire. But the threat of "mixing" with Han Chinese (chapter 2) was now an anachronism. The new and urgent threat was "mixture" with members of the occupation forces: Australians, Europeans, Filipinos, and especially the overabundant Americans.[54]

In the occupation era of nationalist ferment over "blood mixing," obstetrician-gynecologist Shōji Tadashi brought his practice of colonial medicine home from Taiwan to Iwakuni. His research target now was not pelvises or menstrual blood but what came out of them: "mixed blood" children. In his early 1949 publications on postwar "mixed" families, Shōji eschewed the overtly moralistic and nationalistic language that would prevail in popular and political discourse after occupation's end in April 1952. He did not describe *konketsuji* as an existential threat to Japan or denounce their fathers or mothers as scoundrels. After all, Shōji did not want to imperil his prominent position as director of Iwakuni Hospital. Whatever his private feelings, he practiced scientific circumspection in his work on *konketsuji*. Even so, he articulated clear eugenic and biopolitical grounds for opposing "blood mixing."

In May 1949, Shōji and the editors of *Heredity* cautiously ventured half a page on the potentially explosive topic of the "mixed blood" child. The child in question was Rumi, two months old, described as "cute," with fair skin and brownish-black hair. Her mother was Japanese, twenty-two years old, her father American. Shōji cataloged the anatomy of the "mixed" child Rumi and her family background without noting any malformation, ill health, or cause for medical concern. Why exactly was a report on such an unexceptional child published? Why did the Genetics Society of Japan print this slight article in its ambitious new journal, *Heredity*, as they positioned it to become one of the most prominent and long-running journals in the field?[55]

In Shōji's banal description of the healthy child Rumi, scientific interest hinged on the clinician's proclamation that her body, although healthy, was nonetheless freakish. "With her eyes closed, her appearance as she suckles a nipple is that of a baby no different from any other," Shōji opined. "But when she blinks her blue eyes, her appearance is bizarre." Nor did the freakery of the *konketsuji* end with the color of her eyes. "Her cry is not '*ogyaa ogyaa*' like a Japanese person. At first it sounded like '*aa aa*,' but lately it sounds like '*iyaa iyaa*.'"[56]

The finding that a "mixed blood" baby could not cry in the normal Japanese way received extended scientific explication in another *Heredity* article the same year. Here Shōji asserted, "What is most interesting [about *konketsuji*] is the heredity of intelligence and sound." His clinical specimens were two baby boys, one fathered by an Englishman and another by an American. "It appears that these *konketsuji* do not laugh '*ketaketa*' like Japanese children do," Shōji noted, peremptorily severing "mixed" children from the category "Japanese." Nor were cries and laughs the only spontaneous utterances that Shōji claimed distinguished "mixed" babies from "Japanese." Shōji offered an extended list of the sounds babies make in imitating the world around them, sounds that he depicted as reflexive utterances. "When you hear a car, provided you are Japanese, it is normal to answer '*buu buu*.' However, the child from the first case, although he absolutely had not been taught this, says '*bii bii*.' Similarly, on hearing a dog's call, if you are Japanese you answer '*wan wan*.' It is interesting that *konketsuji* reply with '*vaagu vaagu*.'" Shōji attributed a bizarre series of onomatopoeia to *konketsuji*, then used those attributed sounds as evidence of the "mixed blood" infant's innate and categorical distance from "Japanese." In Shōji's account, the genetics of language acquisition set *konketsuji* so far apart from the "Japanese" as to make them separate natural types, verging on mutually unintelligible.

Shōji's displacement of the ambiguity in infantile vowel sounds with clinical precision—as if infants say *buu* or *bii* but nothing in between—focused scientific inquiry on the infant's speech rather than the clinician's hearing or habits of transcription. Tightening the noose of inalterable difference, Shōji denied environmental influences on early language development. He speculated that *konketsuji* would struggle as they grew up to pronounce Japanese words, with their abundant vowels; instead, the seeds of their paternal races would predispose them to oration thick with consonants. Shōji projected future linguistic development among *konketsuji* as an inevitable deviation away from "normal" and "Japanese," speculating that "when they hear the sound of a clock, they may end up replying '*tick tock*.'" Here Shōji altered his practice of transcription, abandoning Japanese altogether to record the imagined utterance "tick tock" in English. It was as if "mixed" children would literally begin speaking in foreign tongues, acquiring vocabulary from a racial subconscious embedded in their genes.[57]

In this article, which opened with a discussion of dominant and recessive patterns of inheritance, Shōji appeared to be suggesting that languages were Mendelian units. He positioned Japanese as a recessive unit, with the implication that "mixed blood" children would struggle to acquire from their environment what was not passed down in the genes of *both* parents. Japanese mothers were not capable, on their own, of endowing the babes they bore with the gene pairs required to speak Japanese or be Japanese. Shōji was not isolated in the scientific community in proposing such genetic limitations. There was no shortage in mid-century Europe of scientists theorizing racialized disability in language learning and phonetics, as when English eugenicist C. D. Darlington insisted of European and African populations that "speech boundary . . . is a genetic boundary."[58] Shōji did not cite such foreign scholars in 1949. But he knew mid-century genetics was an international language well adapted to expressing the idea that differences in human culture, or language and pronunciation, were racially distinctive, inborn, and irremediable.

In the imperial era, when the national language (*kokugo*) of "Japanese" was consolidated in the home islands and imposed in colonies overseas, to assert that *kokugo* would be genetically impossible for newly colonized or "mixed blood" peoples to learn would have been defeatist. After 1945, the time was ripe for a former colonial scientist such as Shōji to reappraise the genetic potential for foreigners and "half breeds" to learn Japanese and be Japanese.

At the time Shōji published his neo-Mendelian argument for the recessive transmission of Japanese-language ability, Japan was already home to "mixed blood" adults with a fine grasp of their native language. "Mixed blood" celebrities Satō Yoshiko (1903–1982) and Hirano Imao (1900–1986), who had Japanese and French parents, counted themselves proud Japanese. Yet Hirano, the renowned author, grumpily reported that some of his fellow Japanese treated his ability to write haiku with a stubborn surprise. They treated him as if haiku were bound to a recessive gene distinct to "pure blood" Japanese. In a similar vein, Satō the stage star drily reminisced on being commended by her fellow Japanese on her grasp of kabuki and facility with her native tongue. These "mixed blood" celebrities spoke out after the war in the hopes of enlightening and reforming exclusionary attitudes among their fellow Japanese.[59] As their testimony made clear, the myth of the indivisibility of "blood," language, and culture predated defeat and survived it. Yet it is telling that these "mixed" adults mobilized to resist that myth *after* the war, when the imperial state that had promoted Japanese language and civilization as universal, or at least as a pan-Asian medium of communication, had collapsed.

With exclusionary nativism and anti-mixing bigotry on the rise, "mixed blood" adults stepped into the ideological breach to defend multiracial inclusion. They were bound to be outnumbered, however, and the efforts made by scientists such as Shōji Tadashi and the editors of *Heredity* to affirm and Mendelize racial prejudice undermined their efforts. "Mixed blood" Japanese have continued to attest in the twenty-first century that other Japanese alternately insult or praise their facility in their native language.[60] Such low expectations and linguistic bigotry persist, in part, because "mixed blood" adults such as Satō and Hirano, when they spoke up, were talked over and disregarded by "pure blood" scientific activists and racial nationalists in the early postwar era.

Shōji used his medical authority and neo-Mendelian expertise to promote a biolinguistic nationalism aimed at extruding Western genetic and cultural influences from Japan. To that end, instead of consulting "mixed blood" adults on their facility with Japanese, Shōji Tadashi opted to study specimens who could not speak any language at all. When "mixed" infants did try to speak, Shōji insisted that the words they uttered were gibberish. In his clinical reports on *konketsuji*, Shōji bolstered the idealized blood-language-culture nexus by adducing a causal mechanism—Mendelian recessive traits—that could explain how "mixed blood" people born and raised in Japan could wind up bereft of "Japanese" traits and abilities.

There is no community without communication, and *konketsuji*, as Shōji constructed them, were literally unintelligible. Yet the unintelligible child's meaning was clear. As Japan's constitution was redrafted, its textbooks revised—as the nation was literally rewritten by foreign occupiers—Shōji Tadashi and his colleagues in the Genetics Society of Japan inscribed a hard limit on trans-Pacific assimilation. Whether Black or white, Western men and their half-breed children could never understand Japan—they could not even learn its language. This rendered the changes the conquerors imposed both unwarranted and superficial. In this anxious era of forced assimilation and Americanization, the language of neo-Mendelian genetics offered scientific reassurance that the essentially foreign and the essentially

Japanese would remain always distinct. Even a Japanese woman could not give birth to a Japanese child if any portion of that child's genes came from a foreign father.

Shōji's specific claims about the heredity of sound did not win ultimate scientific consensus. They contributed, however, to building consensus on a more fundamental point. They helped normalize the framing of Japaneseness as a politically neutral but biologically vital essence, located in the "blood" and transmitted through Mendelian laws. Those laws made Japaneseness vulnerable to extinction upon mixing with "foreign" elements. Building on biological defeatism pioneered during the war on China (chapter 2), under Allied occupation, Japanese scientists again deployed neo-Mendelian language toward political ends of metabolizing defeat and policing the boundaries of the *minzoku*. Far from politically neutral, neo-Mendelism was rather an authoritative and safe way to comment on issues that were nationalist and geopolitical at their core: national identity, interracial sex, native women fornicating with foreign men, and the balance of power between Japanese men—who dominated hospitals, universities, and scientific presses—and foreign soldiers—who dominated the base towns and global politics of defeated Japan.

No medical authority denounced "blood mixing" more emphatically during the occupation than Nagai Hisomu, the eugenicist who helped craft the Eugenic Protection Law (chapter 3). When Nagai initially propounded "race hygiene" (*minzoku eisei*) in the era of imperial expansion, he did not define the *minzoku* as a closed unit imperiled by intermarriage or "blood mixing." But as we have seen, Nagai's benign take on "mixture" changed at the tail end of a losing war in China, when he converted to biological defeatism and fulminated against "blood mixing" with the unconquerable Han (chapter 2). Total defeat in 1945 accelerated Nagai's rejection of "blood mixing" and redirected it toward new targets.

Like Shōji Tadashi, Nagai was forced to repatriate from his elite overseas post to bombed-out Japan. In the ruins of his homeland, he repudiated his formerly tolerant stance on "blood mixing." No longer were the Han an exception to the rule that the Japanese could expand and strengthen themselves through "blood mixing"; now the rule must be overturned and the Japanese reconceptualized as a "pure" race. Hunkered down under Allied occupation, deprived of his former post as medical school dean, but still publishing prolifically, Nagai redefined the Japanese *minzoku* as a closed biological unit imperiled by outsiders. For the first time in the late 1940s, he comprehensively denounced "blood mixing" with any and all non-Japanese.

Nagai articulated this new anti-mixing doctrine in 1948, in *The Fate of the Race: I Appeal to the People of Japan*. Nagai argued that "in a country occupied by Europe and the United States," race hygiene (*minzoku eisei*) must be more rigorous than ever. Nagai explained that *minzoku* "carries a biological meaning, namely, a group of people bound by blood . . . who bear the genetic stock of the same ancestors." He contrasted this organic, eternal community of blood against the temporal community of *kokumin* or citizens, whom he defined as merely "a group of people living in the same society." Nagai had by no means abandoned his classical eugenic stance that some Japanese were superior to other Japanese by dint of class, disability, and genetic inheritance. Yet Nagai was emphasizing, as never before, a racial unity that bound all members of the *minzoku* together and separated them from everyone else—including occupation forces and *kokumin* with divergent ancestry, be they Korean, Taiwanese, or *konketsuji*. The book's cover boasted its scientific credentials, proclaiming itself "written by doctor of medicine and professor emeritus of Tokyo University, Nagai Hisomu," and "edited by the Japan Race Hygiene Association." From this position of scientific authority, Nagai endorsed the political principle, radical in its rejection of recent imperial projects, that of all possible forms of government, "the most suitable situation is one *minzoku* to one state."[61] Obviously "blood mixing" imperiled this ideal.

From start to finish, Nagai's book emphasized the threat of Japanese racial extinction and hope of racial revival. The book's second-person and first-person style of address and occasionally apocalyptic tone seemed targeted to a broad lay audience. "Beloved 70 million countrymen of Japan! Fellow countrymen who endlessly love Japan, who love the Japanese race, who wish from their hearts for the rebirth of New Japan. The poisoned cup overhangs our lips!" Such were the book's final words, driving home the urgency of Nagai's call to implement race hygiene. Only thus could the "*minzoku* gain ultimate victory" in an international battle for survival, which Nagai made clear (however severe Japan's setback in 1945) had not been lost altogether. Historian John Dower argues that racial hubris and "race hates" fueled both Japanese and Anglo-American aggression in the Pacific theater, so profoundly shaping the conflict that it amounts to a race war. However, contrary to Dower's expectation, the "race war" did not necessarily end with Japan's surrender in 1945.[62] For Nagai Hisomu, like-minded race hygienists and readers, the race war was ongoing under occupation.

In a world of finite resources and deep grudges, Nagai deemed racial conflict inevitable. In *The Fate of the Race*, Nagai piously acknowledged the value of peace—a necessity to pass through SCAP censorship—noting that "in the future, if men grow wise," they might "avoid blood-soaked competition. But competition in peace is utterly unavoidable," he added. Nagai instructed readers on how to win this postwar contest, not through military prowess, as Japan had attempted in the old days, but rather through eugenic cultivation of the race. "In order for a *minzoku* to gain ultimate victory, its members must be superior in numbers and in quality." In short, "race hygiene simply must be the foundation of long-term plans for rebuilding the nation."[63]

Nagai was a long-standing proponent of eugenic marriage.[64] His 1934 *Marriage Guidebook* was replete with medical and eugenic instruction on selecting fit mates and reproducing fit children. So popular was this handbook that it went through seven editions, the last published posthumously in 1960. Yet even amid booming public debate and promotion of "intermarriage" in the heyday of empire, Nagai's 1939 *Marriage Guidebook* skipped past the topic of "blood mixing."[65] In a strong and expanding empire, he did not deem "blood mixing" an existential threat.

Ten years and one defeat later, in 1949, Nagai published a *New Marriage Guidebook* that showed he had undergone a dramatic conversion. His indifference to "blood mixing" had not survived the onset of Allied occupation and the racial emasculation it implied. Hence he warned occupation-era audiences that "we must be aware that numerous undesirable sorts may proliferate as a result of blood mixing." To explain why, he proselytized a new vision of the *minzoku* as a closed evolutionary unit, inherently weakened by "mixing" with outsiders. "If one race has been carrying out a particular existence over the course of countless years, it will naturally have developed in such a way as to preserve the proper equilibrium of its genes and the corporeal and mental expressions thereof." He now claimed that genes had evolved in particular groups in particular environments over the course of many generations, thereby producing well-balanced genetic "races." This new genetic definition of "race" presumed a high degree of reproductive isolation over a long period. Exactly how to define or measure reproductive isolation, how long isolation must persist to create a "race," and where if anywhere such a hypothetical isolate could be found in reality, were not questions that Nagai addressed. Nor did he acknowledge that Japanese had been anything but reproductively isolated in the recent era of imperial expansion. Instead, he encouraged his postwar audience to believe a priori that the Japanese were such a reproductively isolated "race." With that assumption in play, Nagai explained that "blood mixing" threatened to undo the meticulous work of natural selection, rending the community of genes known as the *minzoku*.

Dire effects would follow. "If suddenly through blood mixing divergent genetic characters are introduced, the equilibrium maintained until then will collapse, inciting functional disharmonies of body and mind. Resistance to disease may weaken, or the efficiency of mental functions may decline, or the dyke of character may be breached." During the war, Nagai's colleague Koya Yoshio had insisted that neo-Mendelian "disharmonies" afflicted *konketsuji* (chapter 2); Nagai was now endorsing the same claim.

After listing these capacious genetic risks, Nagai acknowledged that some famous men had achieved greatness despite a "mixed" genetic heritage: Alexandre Dumas, Alexander Pushkin, Élie Metchnikoff, Booker Washington, W. E. B. DuBois, and Niels Bohr, among others. It is notable that not a single Japanese name made the list; apparently all Japan's geniuses, like Nagai himself, were "pure." Enthusiasts of "mixing" and of "hybrid vigor" had often pointed to such luminaries as evidence that intermarriage between well-chosen spouses could produce artistic and scholarly genius and cultural fluorescence. Nagai assailed as "laughable" the notion that one could justify the genetic risks of "blood mixing" by reference to these erudite "mixed blood" men, whom he dubbed "exceptions among exceptions." Having thus acknowledged and waved away the "exceptions" to the alleged genetic rule that miscegenation breeds inferiority, Nagai informed his readers that "the abilities of mixed-blood children of white and black people . . . are by and large *inferior* even to pure blacks."[66] In this, he directly contradicted his prior assertion, in 1936, that *konketsuji* were of intermediate type, generally *superior*, in his biased view, to "pure blacks."[67]

In short, Nagai asserted, contrary to the false promises of the now dismantled and discredited Japanese Empire and to his own former teachings on eugenics, that "blood mixing" was inherently dangerous. It bred shocking genetic impairment both in individual *konketsuji* and in the "race" writ large. No amount of assimilation and intermarriage could overcome inborn divisions of blood and rank between *minzoku*. On the contrary, intermarriage debased all "races" and produced offspring who were the worst of all genetic possibilities. The specter of unrestrained proliferation of genetic "undesirables" led Nagai directly to the "doctrine of avoiding blood mixing [*konketsu kihi setsu*]." Should his fellow Japanese disregard his warnings and adopt a permissive postwar attitude toward "blood mixing," Nagai warned, "there will be no alternative but for the entire *minzoku* to fall into the fate of ruin."[68] Nagai's extraordinary hostility to "blood mixing," which he alleged could destroy Japan, provoked no reaction from CCD censors, and proceeded uncensored into Japanese hands.

After the occupation's end in 1952, many Japanese researchers would explicitly link mental disabilities and genetic disharmonies to "mixed blood" children. One leading newspaper in 1952 ran the eye-catching headline, "Mixed-Blood Children Growing Up: Clearly Inferior Intelligence, Sociability." To support this claim, the paper cited race scientists Koya Yoshio and Ishiwara Fusao.[69] Ishiwara dedicated decades to studying *konketsuji* after the war, and ultimately deemed their IQs on average nearly twenty points lower than those of "pure Japanese children."[70] This pessimistic take on the innate abilities of *konketsuji* marked a stark reversal of Ishiwara's wartime stance, when he judged Sino-Japanese children eugenically fit and even superior in academic achievements compared with other Japanese children. He had, however, expressed doubts about the moral fiber of their unwed Japanese mothers (chapter 2).

Upon defeat, Ishiwara lost interest in Japanese-Chinese hybrids and began instead decades of research on white-Japanese and black-Japanese *konketsuji*, about whom he rarely found anything positive to say. Ishiwara held off on publishing his revisionist, intensely negative studies on postwar *konketsuji*, whom he defined as "an unhappy minority race, neither American nor Japanese," until the occupation ended.[71] From summer 1952 onward, in leading scientific journals and a comprehensive report published by the MOW in 1954, Ishiwara condemned those *konketsuji* as mentally and physically deficient and prone to genetic "disharmonies."[72] In his newfound insistence that "blood mixing" was dysgenic, Ishiwara found himself in good professional company. MOW official Ogawa Masahiro, too, rated a full 26 percent of the *konketsuji* he studied after the war as feebleminded (*seishin hakujaku*).[73]

Hostility and contempt toward *konketsuji* and their parents was rationalized by nominally apolitical studies repudiating "blood mixing" as biologically dangerous. Such hostility was further normalized in the 1950s as the occupation wound down and Cold War–inflected partisan politics wound up. As responsibility for determining the limits of acceptable speech and conduct passed back into Japanese hands, Japanese police, progressive intellectuals, parents' groups, and left-leaning protestors staged book burnings and other civic campaigns against a "colonial culture" in which Japanese women abandoned racial chastity and national loyalty to "mix blood" with foreign soldiers.[74] A moral panic over "mixed blood" children and their wayward Japanese mothers was underway, and partisan politicians in the 1950s were determined to make good use of it.

Chapter Five

COLD WAR *KONKETSUJI*

Partisan Politics, Hot Presses, and
US Alliance, 1950–1955

On the spring evening of April 28, 1952, the Allied occupation of Japan came to an end. The Treaty of Peace, which prime minister Yoshida Shigeru (1878–1967) had signed in San Francisco on September 8, 1951, now went into effect, finally concluding the state of war between Japan and forty-four Allied powers.[1] The Soviet Union refused to sign, but Soviet protests notwithstanding, Japan was reborn a sovereign nation. The national anthem played on the radio, temple bells rang, and raucous revelry was anticipated. Yet *Asahi* news described the atmosphere on this historic day as "quiet beyond expectation" in Japan. In no mood to celebrate, college students in the nationwide communist organization *Zengakuren* (*Zen Nihon gakusei jichikai sōrengō*) held a ritual wake for Japan's independence, mourning the flag and passing out provocative leaflets. They complained that "Japan has become a colony" of the United States and "many women that we love have fallen to become jeep girls."[2] Brandishing a sense of shared masculine grievance, these young leftists declared Japan's independence a fraud, Japanese "jeep girls" lost territory, and their country a de facto military and reproductive colony of the United States.

Such protests against Japan's "colonization" targeted the second treaty that Yoshida had signed that September day in San Francisco. The 1951 bilateral security treaty between Japan and the United States, *Anzen hoshō jōyaku* (or *Anpo* for short), declared in its preamble:

> Japan has this day signed a Treaty of Peace with the Allied Powers. On the coming into force of that Treaty, Japan will not have the effective means to exercise its inherent right of self-defense because it has been disarmed. There is danger to Japan in this situation because irresponsible militarism has not yet been driven from the world. . . . The Treaty of Peace recognizes that Japan as a sovereign nation has the right to enter into collective security arrangements, and further, the Charter of the United Nations recognizes that all nations possess an inherent right of individual and collective self-defense. In exercise of these rights, Japan desires, as a provisional arrangement for its defense, that the United States of America should maintain armed forces of its own in and about Japan so as to deter armed attack upon Japan.[3]

In short, Allied occupation pursuant to the terms of the Potsdam Declaration was ending, but under *Anpo*, US troops would stay on in Japan. They remain to this day.

In Japan, "blood mixing" and the biology of defeat had been under debate since the first setbacks of the war on China, and intolerance of "mixture" had metastasized amid defeat and occupation. As the Cold War intensified in the 1950s, fears of foreign mastery were insistently sexualized and racialized. Hence the Zengakuren college students protested that, under *Anpo*, Japanese "girls" would continue to take rides in American jeeps, go on dates with American men, and "mix blood" with US soldiers.

In this chapter, I examine the buildup of resentment toward *Anpo* in the 1950s from a fresh angle, focused less on the supposedly asexual terrain of Cold War geopolitics than on the intimate yet international terrain of sex and reproduction. Even in the late-twentieth and twenty-first centuries, Japanese resentment toward *Anpo* and US soldiers is frequently expressed in sexualized and racialized terms, with *konketsuji* marked out as a stigmatized subpopulation by association.[4] In many respects, the script for latter-day controversies over "blood mixing" and *Anpo* were set in the early 1950s, "a period when arguably the bilateral security relationship was most fraught with tensions and at its most vulnerable."[5] The 1950s was also the period when antipathy toward "blood mixing" with Americans reached its peak in Japan—not only on the left but on the right and center, too.

By signing *Anpo*, Yoshida put Japan firmly in the anticommunist camp in the Cold War. With no hint of irony regarding his regime's armed expansion into foreign lands, Soviet dictator Josef Stalin greeted this development by deploring "the horrors of foreign occupation" and wishing the Japanese people "full success in their gallant struggle for the independence of their homeland." For despite Yoshida's blandishments, Moscow warned, "the United States of America will remain the real master in Japan."[6] Moscow regularly drummed out the message that "peace" and "alliance" with Americans were but tawdry window dressing over the reality of colonization.

As *Anpo* went into effect in 1952, Japanese could be forgiven for feeling a sense of déjà vu, that Tokyo continued to answer to Washington, that April 28 was no watershed of independence. Three days later, on the international labor holiday May Day, large-scale and raucous protests against Yoshida, the United States, and *Anpo* wracked Tokyo and other major cities in Japan. College students and left-wing protestors danced and paraded through the streets, brandishing signs that demanded "Don't Forget April 28, Day of National Humiliation" and "Yankee! Go Home" (figure 5.1). By early afternoon, some six thousand demonstrators had massed in the Imperial Plaza in Tokyo. A "feeling of liberation" reportedly permeated the scene. Whatever breaks there had been during the six years of rule by the Supreme Commander for the Allied Powers (SCAP) against Japanese publicly criticizing US policies and personnel were blown out of the water at the occupation's end.

The Imperial Plaza where protestors massed was directly in front of the Daiichi Building, which served as MacArthur's General Headquarters throughout the occupation. US forces continued to work there under *Anpo*. The US flag still flew beside the flag of the United Nations on Daiichi's roof, where US and UN personnel gathered to watch the scene unfolding in the plaza below. Unbeknownst to most protestors that day, the Japan Communist Party (JCP) had deployed a paramilitary unit in the plaza "to provoke a violent clash with police" and rally potential revolutionaries to their cause. Japanese police were no pacifists, and in the ensuing melee, Japanese leftists battled Japanese police, American cars were incinerated, American servicemen attacked, a Japanese student was killed, and headlines were made around the world. Japan's press dubbed the day "Bloody May Day."[7] Leading US news magazine *Life* printed a two-page photograph of young Japanese men hurling projectiles at a US Army jeep while its

FIGURE 5.1. Young protestors in Tokyo on May 1, 1952. Michael Rougier, *Life Magazine*.

driver ducked for cover. The headline blared: "Rioting Japanese Reds Tee Off on the Yankees."[8]

The controversies over *Anpo* that broke into violent view in May 1952 have never entirely abated. The treaty established the basis of Japanese security amid slow rearmament, grounded US interests in the region, and established between Tokyo and Washington one of the most significant and abiding alliances in the contemporary world. As revised in 1960, it is still in force today.[9] Despite or indeed because of its durability, this treaty and alliance remain beset by controversy. Those controversies peaked in the massive nationwide protests of 1960, which did not prevent Japan's government from maintaining the security treaty on revised terms, but did alter the course of politics and culture in Japan along with US-Japan relations.[10]

Doubts or flat denial about whether Japan had regained its sovereignty under *Anpo* were not always expressed in sexualized or racialized terms. But very often, Japanese linked or equated sovereignty to sex, blood, and reproduction. A new nationalist script boomed forth in Japanese politics and presses: To resist "blood mixing" was to resist US imperialism. As *konketsuji* were redefined as living proof of Japan's ongoing "colonization" by the United States, they were also redefined as external to the *minzoku*. A new vision of the *minzoku* and racial-national self as homogenous and "pure" was consolidated in Cold War Japan. Historian Kanō Mikiyo identifies the 1950s furor over *konketsuji* as an origin point in the postwar "myth" of a Japanese *minzoku* composed of a single bloodline, distinct from all other peoples.[11] What has remained relatively obscure is exactly who fostered this new and narrow sense of racial-national belonging and why.

One important piece of the puzzle is to be found in electoral politics. Postwar democracy provided both motive and method to opposition politicians hoping to sensationalize sex, link "blood mixing" to *Anpo*, and improve their political prospects as they maneuvered against the governing Liberal Party. Fighting rhetorically to defend or recover the "purity" of the *minzoku* by resisting *Anpo* allowed opposition political parties to prove their nationalist bona fides, identify enemies, and rally supporters. Driven by both opportunism and conviction, Yoshida's rivals denounced the 1951 bilateral security agreement as anything but a legitimate alliance. Instead, they cast *Anpo* as Yoshida selling out the country, abetting US imperialists in the military and reproductive colonization of Japan. Controversies over *Anpo* have been well studied, albeit by scholars with little or nothing to say about the furor over *konketsuji*.[12] But these two controversies—over blood and soil, sex and sovereignty—were inextricably linked.

The 1950s furor over "blood mixing" demonstrates how inhospitable majoritarian democracy can be for unpopular minorities. In this case, the unpopular minorities who served as convenient punching bags were both sexual—"blood mixing" women—and racial—"mixed blood" children. Japanese partisans who denounced the US-Japan security treaty redefined *konketsuji* as sanguineous symbols of American Empire. They decried US imperialism and "blood mixing" as two sides of one debased national coin. Party politicians, however, did not spread this new anti-imperial racial ideology all on their own. On the contrary, they needed help from a free press, which stood to profit by selling scandal, outrage, and a new and narrow vision of a *minzoku* beset by "blood mixers," collaborators, and imperialists. Freed of SCAP press controls, mass media lost no time in marketing a "moral panic" over Americanized *konketsuji* and their Japanese mothers.[13] Never before had so many Japanese united behind ideals of national chastity and "pure blood."

COLD WAR *KONKETSUJI*

The Cold War began in Japan with an odd alliance. In late 1945, Japanese communists, who had been hounded nigh into oblivion by the old imperial regime, hailed US forces as an "army of liberation."[14] In the wake of its military victory, SCAP secured a further moral victory by freeing Japanese political prisoners, including Marxists and communists; repealing the Peace Preservation Law, under which such dissidents had long been persecuted; and promoting labor unions, redistributing land to tenants, promulgating civil liberties, and curtailing the emperor's sovereign prerogatives—all over the vociferous objections of Japanese conservatives such as Yoshida. Looking back from a later vantage, Yoshida acidly remarked that "Americans are an unsuspicious race." In the immediate aftermath of World War II, he alleged that America's global naïfs "may well have thought . . . that the Russians—and therefore Japan's Communists, who were under the aegis of the Russians—were their friends."[15]

To Yoshida's delight, however, the love affair between Japan's left and the "unsuspicious race" of Americans did not survive long. Josef Stalin and his allies were tightening their grip on occupied lands from Eastern Europe to northern Korea, with no intention of liberating subject peoples or holding free elections. Nor would the United States retreat inside its borders and idly watch the world "go Red." By 1949, the Berlin Blockade, Soviet success in nuclear testing, escalating partisan violence in Korea, and Mao Zedong's victory over US ally Chiang Kai-shek in China stoked fears of global communist ascension in Washington, London, Seoul, and SCAP's Tokyo as well as among Japanese anticommunists. Within Japan, labor unions and student radicals grew increasingly militant amid perduring economic crisis and disenchantment with foreign occupation. The outcome is often described as a "reverse course," in which SCAP and Japanese conservatives were drawn into a close embrace as they cracked down on Japan's left, while leftists rebelled against these authorities.[16] Ressentiment and resentment regarding interracial sex and "blood mixing" contributed to this friction between SCAP and Japan's leftists and to the JCP's anti-American turn in the 1950s.

Historian Kenji Hasegawa finds that JCP leaders "continued to view the American occupation as an army of liberation" until 1950.[17] Then on January 6, Moscow denounced the JCP and its leaders for cooperating with SCAP. According to the Cominform, the JCP's largely successful pursuit of labor mobilization, education, and peaceful parliamentary politics under US protection "misleads the Japanese people and helps the foreign imperialists to turn Japan into a colonial appendage." On January 17, the *People's Daily* in Mao's China issued a parallel rebuke. Only militant resistance to SCAP and the United States—now defined decisively as "foreign imperialists" rather than lawful occupiers—was countenanced in the new Moscow-Beijing consensus.[18] Ironically, international communists were coming very close to endorsing the old imperial line according to which the otherwise-peaceful Japanese must wage a defensive war to safeguard Asia from American imperialism.

In January 1950, Stalin also secretly approved the ambition of Kim Il-Sung, the former anti-Japanese freedom fighter, now communist leader in the Soviet sphere of North Korea, to invade South Korea and communize the entire peninsula by force. SCAP had occupied southern Korea to deimperialize, demilitarize, and repatriate the Japanese after World War II, so this plan risked war with the residuum of US forces still in the peninsula.[19] With preparations for a summer invasion underway, Stalin moved to demolish the amicable relationships among SCAP, the JCP, and other receptive audiences in Japan.

Within the JCP, self-criticism, purges, and factional struggle ensued. Thereafter, the JCP jettisoned both the postwar peace movement and class-based politics in favor of a revolutionary united front focused on resisting US "imperialism" in East Asia. The JCP embraced what Oguma Eiji describes as militant "racial nationalism" marked by an "extreme emphasis on the *minzoku*."[20] The principal adversary of the *minzoku* was, needless to say, the United States. Equally despised were Yoshida and any other Japanese "traitors" who collaborated with the Americans. *Panpan* and mothers of *konketsuji* would figure among the latter.

Hasegawa argues that "the standard narrative of the JCP's anti-American radicalization" circa 1950 neglects "internal factors, instead privileging the significance of the external interventions" from Moscow and Beijing. Among these internal factors was a generational schism between JCP leaders, who had defied the Japanese Empire through years of imprisonment and torture, only to be liberated by US forces in 1945, versus younger leftists with no experience of opposition to or brutalization by the old regime. These young leftists had grown up in the heady wartime atmosphere of ultranationalist and anti-American propaganda. A twenty-year-old college student in Zengakuren in 1950 would have been just eleven years old during the attack on Pearl Harbor—too young to fight for the empire, too young to resist it, but not too young to absorb its propaganda. This younger generation of radicals chafed under JCP leaders who cooperated with SCAP and they welcomed the new militant line from Moscow. They applauded the Cominform criticism for "successfully expos[ing] the American imperialists' plot to enslave the Japanese nation and transform it into a base for military adventures against the Soviet Union and China."[21] Arguably, in the minds of these young radicals, the war between the United States and Japan had not ended in 1945; it had simply entered a new phase. In the 1950s, they were finally old enough to participate, even take the lead, in the national struggle against the American enemy.

According to Hasegawa, JCP leaders embraced the Cominform criticism in 1950 largely to regain control over these young leftists who had already internalized militant anti-Americanism. Part and parcel of their anti-American nationalism was gendered ressentiment over US soldiers' sexual successes with Japanese women. "Wherever we go," student protestors grieved in 1950, "the long-legged ones walk by haughtily, holding *panpan* girls looking like monsters of white powder and red lipsticks." These young radicals decried "*panpan* politics" and offered "manly threats of political violence" to enemies of the *minzoku* whom they decried, among other things, as gender and sexual deviants.[22]

Pervasive bashing of *panpan* by postwar leftists made it seem as if unchaste, race-crossing women represented everything wrong with postwar Japan. As historian Christopher Gerteis explains, in the late 1940s, labor union posters routinely commanded left-leaning patriots to "protect *minzoku* culture" and "banish the culture of *panpan*!" Well before the Cominform criticism, union activists were denouncing Japan's government under SCAP "as a *pan-pan seifu*, or 'government of whores'"—a fine translation provided one understands that *panpan* were a special kind of whore, despised for sleeping with foreign men and bearing "mixed blood" children. Labor cartoons sometimes depicted Japan's postwar prime ministers as cross-dressed *panpan*, stripping, dancing to American tunes, and sexually servicing foreign masters.²³

From labor unions to college campuses, the postwar left was saturated with overt appeals to the racial politics of sex. If all too many young Japanese women were opting to abandon national chastity, leftist activists declaimed the need and right to reassert sexual sovereignty over them and thereby purify Japanese "blood." Radicals made clear that they aimed to rid Japan not only of metaphorical *panpan* such as Yoshida, who as head of state was "whoring out" the country to American Empire, but also of race-crossing women and girls whom they identified and shamed as *panpan*.

The JCP was not alone in the 1950s in turning from class-based identity and ideology toward a politics rooted in defending a racialized and sexualized *minzoku* from Americans. Historian Simon Avenell finds that many progressives leaned into victimhood nationalism after the war, positioning the Japanese *minzoku* as victim of US imperialism without reckoning with Japan's own recent history of imperial aggression. Likewise, historian Umemori Naoyuki details how prominent conservative Etō Jun offered a self-exculpating, anti-imperialist performance after the war, "celebrating Japan's challenge against the United States while marginalizing Japan's aggression against neighboring nations." Whether progressive or conservative, Japanese celebrating and defending the *minzoku* in the early Cold War tended to take for granted the homogeneity of that community of "blood" and its closure against foreign others. A recrudescence of pan-Asianism among postwar leftists did nothing to undermine the postimperial premise that the Japanese *minzoku* ought to be homogenous and pure. Writes Avenell, "this assumption did not lend itself to a sensitivity toward diversity within the nation."²⁴

Although spurred on to denounce the United States by leaders in Moscow, Beijing, and Pyongyang, the JCP appears to have lit on the idea of drubbing up doubts about *konketsuji* on its own. Anti-mixing animus was homegrown—not a *diktat* of international communism—a resource readily capitalized on by partisans in Japan's Cold War. Prodded by Moscow, Beijing, and younger Japanese leftists to prove their own anti-American credentials, JCP leaders in 1950 began to politicize interracial sex for their own purposes.

Hence a few weeks after the Cominform criticism, on January 29, 1950, *Red Flag*, the official organ of the JCP, issued a low-fact, high-impact exposé on *konketsuji*. Children born "mixed" in Japan's prior era of imperial expansion were nowhere to be seen in an article focused exclusively on *konketsuji* born of sex between Japanese women and occupation soldiers. Japanese mothers of such *konketsuji* were not interviewed—an elision that made it easier for the JCP to render the feminine objects of reportage exactly as desired: as skulking social outcasts, ashamed of themselves and their "mixed" children, too. In its eye-catching headline, the JCP alleged that of such *konketsuji*, "A Heartbreaking Half Are Abandoned." No evidence was offered to support this claim or most of those that followed.

With a tone of breathless anxiety, *Red Flag* warned that eighty thousand such "unhappy children" had been born in the major metropolitan centers of Osaka and Kobe, thirty thousand in the smaller military base towns of Tokorozawa and Tachikawa, and far larger numbers in the SCAP strongholds of Yokohama and Tokyo. Even these staggering figures the JCP presented as conservative underestimates, for "if we include abandoned and aborted children, it's said to be three times as many; and nationwide, it's a number of children impossible even to estimate that have likely been born during these four years." These tendentious statistics, utterly unsubstantiated, might strain credulity for some readers. But given the tenor of anti-*panpan* rhetoric already circulating, the editors of *Red Flag* could confidently bet that alarmist and outraged claims about the high fecundity and low morals of GIs and their Japanese consorts would strike a responsive chord with leftist readers.

Red Flag cast *konketsuji* as humiliation made flesh. Dubbing them "orphans born of defeat," the JCP left no room for doubt about the disgraceful geopolitical and moral framework through which Japanese should now interpret "blood mixing." With this selective characterization, the JCP edged toward endorsing racial chastity and victimhood nationalism in the vein of "pure blood."

In key respects, *Red Flag* thus converged with the anti-mixing ethos advanced by Japanese eugenicists who biologized defeat under occupation (chapter 4). It is easy to imagine cross-fertilization of anti-mixing ideas among Japanese eugenicists and communists, but *Red Flag* eschewed hereditarian debates. Soviet endorsement of Lysenkoism disinclined the JCP to endorse mainstream, neo-Mendelian eugenics.[25] As a result, any eugenic groundwater nourishing the party's newly expressed antipathy to "mixture" remained implicit rather than overtly expressed. Instead of delving into debates over biology and eugenics, *Red Flag* focused on sociopolitical problems, defining *konketsuji* as detritus of defeat and occupation, alien to the nation, and unwanted even by their mothers.[26]

The quick turnaround between the Cominform criticism on January 6 and *Red Flag*'s tendentious exposé on *konketsuji* on January 29 raises the question of whether the latter was crafted, in part, in response to the former. Was twenty-three days long enough to decide on a new policy to politicize *konketsuji* and then to research, write, and publish a partisan broadside? Perhaps not if research had been careful and serious, but the "research" in question was shallow, the statistics cited products of imagination rather than careful inquiry. In fact, the JCP's story about orphaned *konketsuji* was similar to an article by Hara Momoyo published several months prior in the nominally apolitical journal *Flag*. The JCP appears to have borrowed liberally from this postcensored exposé from 1949.

Postcensorship emerged as standard practice midway through the occupation when Japanese and Allied officials were working toward a peace treaty. In the prolonged period of multilateral negotiation before treaties were concluded, the United States aimed to minimize the "numbers of tactical, and especially non-tactical, forces" in Japan. The United States also sought "to reduce to a minimum the psychological impact of the presence of occupational forces on the Japanese population."[27] Reducing US forces and "psychological impact" in Japan meant, among other things, winding down CCD censorship. Most publications submitted to the CCD from late 1948 to 1949 were in fact never reviewed. Almost all Japanese book and magazine publishers, aside from a threatening few identified as organs of the "ultra-right" or "ultra-left," would henceforth publish on their own recognizance.[28]

One magazine in the censors' archives bearing the now-standard stamp "Processed w/o Examination" was the May 1949 edition of *Flag*. Published monthly by the Association for Japanese Literature (*Nippon bungaku kai*), the magazine was variously categorized by CCD censors as "non-political" or "center." These were exactly the categories of publication to which the CCD paid the least attention, preferring a laissez-faire model of minimal intervention in a partially free press. But editors at *Flag* gave SCAP reason to reconsider its "nonpolitical" stance—or what the "center" in Japan really stood for—when they printed an incendiary exposé entitled "Mixed Blood Orphans." Author Hara Momoyo alleged that innumerable *konketsuji* had been born unloved and unsupported by both their American fathers and Japanese mothers since the occupation began. In short, GIs were massproducing "mixed blood" orphans in Japan. Hara's denunciation of the occupiers as guilty of mass miscegenation and child abandonment foreshadowed a flood of similar commentary that would burst forth at the occupation's end, commentary replete with both racism and anti-American animus.

When *Flag* hit the newsstands, it provoked a sensation. Word of a hatchet job on the occupiers got back to CCD, which scrambled to secure a full translation of the article for higher review. Days later, CCD slapped the publisher with a violation of the now little-enforced September 1945 press code, to wit, "crit[icism] of SCAP." To what end? Hara's damning take on *konketsuji* "born unwanted between GIs and their temporary lovers," which doubled as an indictment of the occupation entire, was already in circulation.[29] The whole affair seemed designed to disprove the claim of Etō Jun, one of Japan's most prominent conservative critics of the occupation, that "Japanese newspapers and magazines were seized media. Japanese reporters could not surpass the invisible wall [of censorship], even by an inch, no matter how hard they tried."[30] In reality, the "invisible wall" was shabbily constructed and sporadically policed, and SCAP disapproval meant less with every passing day. A few months later, in October 1949, CCD ceased operations altogether.[31]

In January 1950, the JCP was looking for ways to defy SCAP and to signal that defiance to receptive audiences. Recycling Hara's allegation that "unwanted" *konketsuji* were abandoned en masse by GI fathers in Japan proved an efficient means to the end. The JCP's timing was good; by the time *Red Flag* tackled the topic, the CCD was disbanded. Thus unfettered, the JCP suggested that the occupiers had been conducting a relentless sexual assault on the Japanese *minzoku* during the last four years of occupation. "Mixed blood" children, allegedly numbering in the hundreds of thousands, were the abandoned and aborted proof.[32]

Soon after this article was published, Ezaki Kazuharu (1907–1972) submitted the first official inquiry about *konketsuji* in the Diet. Ezaki was one of thirty-five members of the JCP elected to the House of Representatives at the peak of the party's popularity in 1949, when the JCP won almost 10 percent of Japan's popular vote. From his position near the heart of government—but well outside the ruling conservative coalition—Ezaki demanded to know how many *konketsuji* had been born "of relations between Japanese and the occupying army?" Of these, "how many have been abandoned without protection?" Furthermore, what was the Japanese government, led by Liberal Party prime minister Yoshida Shigeru, going to do about it?[33] As in *Red Flag* a few weeks prior, *konketsuji* born in the imperial era were omitted from Ezaki's inquiry. It was becoming clear that *konketsuji* who lived overseas or were born in Japan up to 1945 were of no political interest to the JCP. Ezaki was advancing the allegation from *Red Flag* to a far more high-profile and multiparty venue that abandoned *konketsuji* were both innumerable and a gross abuse of Japan by rapacious foreign personnel. Implicit in his three-point query was the accusation that Yoshida's government, which was collaborating with SCAP on domestic governance, treaty negotiations, and anticommunist containment, was complicit in fomenting "blood mixing" and the mass abandonment of "mixed blood" orphans in Japan.

In 1947, SCAP's Public Health and Welfare Section (PHW) had countermanded Japanese Ministry of Welfare (MOW) plans to investigate *konketsuji* born under occupation to determine, among other things, their numbers. PHW director Crawford Sams nixed this and other projects singling out *konketsuji* on the premise that they were rooted in unconstitutional racial distinctions and would tend to exacerbate the same.[34] Sams likely sensed an unsettling current of animus in occupation-era attitudes toward *konketsuji*. In later years, certain Japanese critics asserted that Sams's true motive in nixing the MOW study was to cover up American sins—namely, the "mixed blood" children.[35] If so, Sams's intervention was ineffective. As the occupation wound down, Cold War and partisan politics wound up, and made *konketsuji* of presumed American paternity both hypervisible and exceedingly unpopular.

In response to Ezaki's inquiry, the Yoshida cabinet accurately replied that no pertinent demographic data were available. The government further clarified that its plan to care for *konketsuji* entailed treating them equally under the law, in accordance with article 14 of the postwar constitution.[36] In its brevity and constitutional clarity, this reply might have made Crawford Sams proud. If, however, one interprets Ezaki's "questions" as rhetorical—as accusations rather than inquiries—then the cabinet's terse response seems inept and out of touch. It did nothing to calm debate, allay discriminatory attitudes, or deter the politicization of *konketsuji*.

Perhaps there is nothing Yoshida's government could have done. Public opinion cannot be doused by fiat, as the long-term failure of SCAP's efforts at censoring critiques of Allied "blood mixers" amply proves. If anything, the absence of definite data about *konketsuji*, which Sams had ensured in 1947, made the wildest claims circa 1950 irrefutable, however false: hundreds of thousands of children sired by Americans and abandoned in just a few short years. Once made, the allegation would not easily be refuted, and it was often repeated in years to come.

Meanwhile, the power struggle between SCAP and the JCP deepened. In summer 1950, shortly after North Korean forces invaded the South, MacArthur—now once more a wartime general, responsible both for holding Japan and for repelling Kim Il-Sung's armies—directed prime minister Yoshida to crack down on *Red Flag* and its editors. Yoshida, who favored banning the Communist Party outright, was happy to oblige. The "Red Purge" deepened and publication of *Red Flag* was suspended until the occupation's end.[37] This shift in SCAP's policies toward the JCP at best postponed, but could not avert, the full-throated use of "blood mixing" for partisan ends.

By February 1952, Japan was preparing for the end of the Allied occupation and also for a new school year. The eldest occupation-born *konketsuji* were coming of school age, setting the stage for renewed debate. In late February, minister of education Amano Teiyū, deputy minister of education Imamura Chūsuke, and other high-ranking officials from Yoshida's government gathered in the House of Representatives. Their task was to discuss with legislators the best means to implement SCAP's mandate to provide nine years of equal education to every schoolboy and girl in a nation beset by straitened budgets.[38] JCP leader Kazahaya Yasoji (1899–1989) seized this opportunity to drag focus from equal education and school funding to *konketsuji* and the uncounted costs of alliance with the United States.[39]

Kazahaya was a professor of law in imperial Japan who suffered forced retirement and repeated arrests for communist activity in the 1930s. Incarcerated again in 1940, Kazahaya, unlike many wartime dissidents, refused to recant and declare his loyalty to the emperor.[40] As a result, he remained in prison until after Japan's surrender, when he reemerged as a tyranny-resisting hero and political activist under SCAP's protection. Kazahaya joined the revived JCP in 1946, where he quickly rose to the post of secretary-general, editor of *Red Flag*, and member of the House of Representatives. By 1949, Kazahaya was renowned as an extraordinarily popular speechmaker and a major force behind the JCP's striking success with the electorate. SCAP officials at the time determined that Kazahaya's "teachings, research, travels and prolific pen stamp him as a qualified leader." Then came the Cominform criticism and Korean War. In July 1950, in a speech carefully watched by SCAP, Kazahaya delivered a blistering rebuke in the Diet to Yoshida's leadership in Japan and his cooperation with the United States. Yoshida claimed that US alignment bolstered Japan's security and prosperity, but if such advantages came at the cost of "American soldiers forever stationed" in Japan, Kazahaya declaimed that what Yoshida and the United States offered was no better than "security within a pigpen."[41]

Yoshida signed *Anpo* the following year. Acrimony between Japan's left on the one side and Yoshida and the United States on the other continued to mount. Historian Hans Martin Krämer has shown that the so-called Red Purge in these latter years of occupation was less systematic in suppressing communists than often assumed, with purge targets often chosen not by SCAP but rather by low-ranking Japanese with their own political, fiscal, or administrative agendas.[42] This reality helps explain why, despite Kazahaya's high-profile antipathy to SCAP by 1950, he retained elected office. Hence he was on hand for public school budget debates in the Diet in February 1952, which he interrupted to remind fellow legislators and bureaucrats of JCP objections to "blood mixing."

"Immediately after the end of the war, many foreign soldiers came, and without delay many *konketsuji* appeared," declared Kazahaya. True to JCP priorities, Kazahaya focused exclusively on "mixed" children born after the war. This foreshortened view, in which "blood mixing" began with defeat, allowed Kazahaya to present the current year of 1952, when "these sorts of people have reached school age," as an unprecedented moment in Japan's history. Never mind that "mixed blood" children had been attending schools in Japan for generations. Like his JCP comrade Ezaki had done in 1950, Kazahaya again demanded to both know the numbers of *konketsuji* born under occupation and what Yoshida's government intended to do about them. Kazahaya did not lay out a platform for handling the vaguely referenced "various problems" he insisted *konketsuji* would present to postwar Japan's educational system. The JCP did not appear to have a policy for educating or otherwise governing *konketsuji*, other than to needle the ruling party about the "problem."

"That question seems unsuited to you, Kazahaya-san." Whether dismayed by the JCP's politicization of a minority of schoolchildren or simply unpersuaded that there was a nuts-and-bolts policy problem to be solved, deputy minister of education Imamura answered by lecturing Kazahaya on the inaptness of his interjection. Kazahaya spoke, Imamura remarked, "as if the number of children occupation soldiers left behind is so colossal as to derange [*kuruwasu*]" the nation's school system. But there was no reason to imagine so vast a number of *konketsuji*. Warming up to his rebuke, Imamura added, "I believe you'll understand if you would please think about this using common sense." Although the number of *konketsuji* born since 1946 was unknown, "we don't think this will rise to several tens of thousands or several hundreds of thousands of cases." If only "several hundred or several thousand" *konketsuji* had been born under occupation, Japan's school system would readily absorb them along with other children coming of school age. Yoshida's cabinet continued to stand by the policy, first articulated to the JCP in February 1950, to educate and rear *konketsuji* identically to other Japanese children. "It amazes me," Imamura added, that a leader of the Communist Party would not understand the need for the whole nation to come together to cover school budgets in a time of economic hardship.[43] The race, blood, or parentage of the children should not matter to a good communist.

To this rebuke, the typically eloquent firebrand Kazahaya offered no rebuttal. Perhaps his heart was not in it. The budget committee returned to its core agenda unimpeded by further digressions about *konketsuji*. One wonders why Kazahaya, hardly a man to shrink from political debate or even violent oppression, fell silent that day when scolded by a deputy minister of education. As an old-guard communist, perhaps he was still more interested in class politics than in politicizing race and "blood mixing." Another factor is audience: If no one is listening, why speak? Kazahaya was outnumbered and nigh isolated in the Budget Committee that day in an increasingly anticommunist Diet. Even legislators and bureaucrats who might have shared Kazahaya's concerns over "mixture" would not have spoken up to reinforce the point when it was first raised by an avowed communist.

By 1952, even once-sympathetic parties and voters had grown mistrustful of the JCP's intentions, its ties to Moscow, and its violent tactics. Ultimately, it was not SCAP but Japanese voters who drove Kazahaya and his colleagues out of office a few months after the occupation's end, when the JCP lost all thirty-five seats it had held in the Diet.[44] Nevertheless, the JCP continued lambasting "the Japanese government's sexual unconditional surrender" to US soldiers in the salacious 1953 bestseller *The Chastity of Japan*. The JCP masked its involvement in production of the book and the movie it inspired, and Japanese audiences were eager to consume its anti-American, anti-mixing message. Although fabricated in pursuit of profits and partisan gain, *The Chastity of Japan* was widely cited as a factual account of Japan's sexual victimization under US occupation for decades to come.[45]

The JCP had taken an early lead in attempting to politicize interracial sex and "blood mixing" for partisan gain, but the JCP's fall from grace did not spell the end of partisan rancor over "blood mixing." On the contrary, remarks by Kazahaya and Ezaki are tame compared to what was to come from members of other parties. The first postwar US ambassador to Japan, Robert Daniel Murphy, warned Washington in 1952 that the policy platforms of all the major opposition parties in Japan had "disquieting overtones... In fact there is a definite ring of hostility in some of it." Only Yoshida's "Liberal Party has not seen fit to adopt even [a] hint of anti-Americanism in its platform."[46] As the JCP faded from the front lines of partisan power struggles in the Diet, Socialists and members of right-wing opposition parties came to the forefront in decrying *Anpo*, American Empire, and "blood mixing."

In fact, only one day after Kazahaya's failed attempt in the Diet to leverage *konketsuji* to embarrass Yoshida's government, councilor Yamashita Gishin, who entered the Diet as an independent, then joined the Japan Socialist Party (JSP), waded more effectively into the fray. Two months before the occupation's end, he fired warning shots from the Diet floor over "these *konketsuji*, or international orphans, or whatever we should call them." Whereas *Red Flag* had claimed that "half" of *konketsuji* were orphans, Yamashita conflated the two categories altogether. This conflation allowed him to present "blood mixing" as a "humanitarian" crisis for which Yoshida's government callously refused to hold the United States responsible. "Making Japan's women bear children and then casting them off... on humanitarian grounds that's something we can't permit. Even if the women who gave birth to them are shameful." Endorsing the leftist politics of contempt toward mothers of *konketsuji*, he insisted that the foreign fathers take the lion's share of blame and full legal custody. "Take them and go home to [America]. Take responsibility and take them with you."

The transcript of Yamashita's comments shows only dashes where I have written, in brackets, "America." SCAP censorship of Japanese presses had long ceased, but on the eve of emancipation, this Diet transcript still bears censorial traces. In theory, Yamashita might have been criticizing any country involved in the occupation for siring and abandoning *konketsuji*. Yet general trends and internal textual evidence point to the United States, an inference confirmed when Yamashita, after a long stream of dash-riddled remarks, finally got the term on the record. In a discussion of jurisdiction in child support suits involving *konketsuji*, he asked, "Can a Japanese court handle that, or does it go through a US military court?"[47]

Yamashita's bombastic demand that US troops decamp Japan and take all "mixed" children with them is revealing in several respects. Yamashita's remarks in the Diet are an early example of what soon became an almost universal tendency to speak of *konketsuji* as if they all had American fathers. In reality, quite a few had English, Australian, Indian, Filipino, Korean, Chinese, or Russian fathers, among other possibilities. Other *konketsuji* had Japanese fathers and foreign mothers; but as during the war, so too in the postwar era, a Japanese man's sovereign prerogative to choose women with whom to couple was seldom politicized and denigrated.

Of occupation-born *konketsuji*, the most numerous besides children of Americans were children of the multiracial British Commonwealth Occupation Force (BCOF). Members of the latter hailed from the United Kingdom, Indian subcontinent, New Zealand, and, most numerously, Australia (figures 5.2 and 5.3). Numbers varied year by year, but at full strength, the BCOF accounted for nearly a quarter of the Allied force in Japan, with forty thousand BCOF soldiers concentrated in southwestern Japan. The fact that the BCOF was not stationed in Tokyo and its environs, and was not party to the *Anpo* treaty, helps explain why Japanese presses and politicians concentrated in Tokyo paid less attention to "mixing" with multiracial Brits.[48] Even Japanese who were well aware of the diverse parentage of *konketsuji* often described them as all fathered by Americans. Yamashita misstated the facts and hyperfocused on Americans as miscegenators because doing so suited his political purpose: to discredit Yoshida's government and elevate his own political profile by tarring *Anpo* with the black brush of "blood mixing."

Looking beyond these partisan motivations brings into focus more comprehensive ideological effects. Sociologist Shimoji Rōrensu Yoshitaka finds that in postwar Japan, "mixed blood" Japanese with Asian roots are often

FIGURE 5.2. On the left: Fumika Clifford, née Fumika Itoh, standing beside her husband, Private John Kenneth Clifford of the British Commonwealth Occupation Forces. The Cliffords pose for this photograph on holiday with other BCOF troops and an unidentified Japanese woman in Miyajima, Japan. Fumika married the Australian private, a veteran of World War II and the Korean War who participated in the Allied occupation of Japan, in 1952. Courtesy of the Australian War Memorial.

Japanized and pass as such; some are even disbelieved when they avow their "mixed" heritage. This homogenization of difference undergirds the false postwar perception that Japanese are all of the same bloodline, all "pure." By contrast, "mixed blood" Japanese who look "different" may be assigned US identities by other Japanese, even when they have no US "blood" ties. The racialization of *konketsuji* as Americans, an identity tainted by association with US violence inflicted on Japan, proceeds regardless of any individual's "roots." So does discrimination on that basis.[49]

Postwar Japanese selectively disavowed their empire and disowned its "mixed blood" offspring when they began to speak of all *konketsuji* as bastards of American Empire. Fixating on *konketsuji* with US paternity tended to support, by sustained omission, an emerging sense that there was no "blood mixing" worth mentioning before defeat. Such willful erasure and performances of selective outrage accumulated into the illusion that the

FIGURE 5.3. Fumika Clifford and her "mixed blood" daughter Mary smile for an Australian passport photograph. Fumika and Mary emigrated from Japan in 1953; after settling in Australia, Fumika and John had a second "mixed blood" child, Julia. In Japan, there was little interest in the stories of Australian-Japanese *konketsuji* or their "mixed blood" families. Courtesy of the Australian War Memorial.

COLD WAR *KONKETSUJI*

Japanese *minzoku* had, until that violent moment of rupture in 1945, been "pure." Americanizing *konketsuji* promoted this temporal and biopolitical mirage and, with it, a righteous sense of racial and sexual victimization at American hands (or American loins).

Yamashita explicitly gendered his complaint when he described "shameful" women who "gave birth to those things" (*sore o umimashita*)—to *konketsuji*.[50] Yamashita used this critical and dehumanizing diction in the same Welfare Committee on which he served alongside Taniguchi Yasaburō, who in 1948 had spearheaded passage and guided enforcement of the Eugenic Protection Law. In the November 1948 committee meeting where Taniguchi instructed the MOW to round up *panpan* and impose abortions on them to prevent degradation of the Japanese *minzoku* (chapter 3), Yamashita voiced no objection.[51] In 1952, Yamashita joined Taniguchi in reiterating

FIGURE 5.4. A Japanese woman, whom Japan Socialist Party representative Yamashita Gishin and like-minded Japanese would label "shameful," walks hand-in-hand with an American soldier down a street near a bilingual hotel. Photograph by Kageyama Kōyō, 1951. Courtesy of the Mead Art Museum, Amherst College. Museum purchase with gift of funds from Scott H. Nagle (Class of 1985) in honor of Samuel C. Morse, Howard M. and Martha P. Mitchell Professor of the History of Art and Asian Languages and Civilizations, and the Richard Templeton (Class of 1931) Photography Fund. Accession No. 2014.65.

that mothers of *konketsuji* were mentally and eugenically inferior specimens. Eugenic and nationalist antipathy toward women who fornicated with the enemy and their "mixed blood" offspring were points on which left-wing Yamashita and right-wing Taniguchi could agree. In 1948, neither Yamashita nor Taniguchi had risked going public, and suffering SCAP's rebuke, to castigate Allied personnel for their role in breeding *konketsuji*. As the occupation ended, Yamashita began doing exactly that—adding that US fathers of *konketsuji* were eugenically inferior, too.[52] By this point, US disapproval of his political utterances meant little, except as a badge of honor for Yamashita to claim as a "humanitarian" leftist daringly denouncing "blood mixing" with US forces.

The most revealing aspect of Yamashita's remarks in the Diet in February 1952 is the total disregard he expressed for how any "mixed blood" child's Japanese family might feel about their child being removed from the country by a foreign army. In demanding that US forces decamp Japan and take "mixed" children with them, Yamashita moved far beyond the more temperate insinuations and complaints voiced by JCP spokesmen in the Diet. The mass removal that Yamashita now endorsed amounted to ethnic cleansing of native-born children of "mixed blood."[53]

While "ethnic cleansing" is sometimes used as a synonym or euphemism for genocidal slaughter, mass killing is better understood as one possible means to the end. Other means of "cleansing" include the expulsion of racialized others and the implementation of reproductive control to breed or weed that other out.[54] In postwar Japan, ethnic cleansing through genocidal slaughter was happily not on the table. But reproductive control to prevent the births of *konketsuji* and mass expulsion of *konketsuji* already born were desiderata endorsed by a growing list of postwar politicians and pundits.

Socialist Party councilor Umezu Kin'ichi likewise demanded in a discussion of what he termed the "tremendous number" and "extreme problem" of *konketsuji*, "Is America likely to take them away or not?" He clearly hoped that America would. To underscore the urgency of mass removal of *konketsuji*, Umezu ominously added that "the black children in particular have become a particular problem [sic]."[55] The "particularity" of black *konketsuji* and the purportedly extraordinary "problem" they posed for Japan was emerging as a kind of cultural common sense. Preexisting anti-Black racism offers one explanation for this trend. Equally important is the fact that focusing on "black" children reenforced the Americanization of *konketsuji*. For as right-wing representative Nagata Ryōichi put it while fulminating over *konketsuji* in the Diet in 1953, "As you know, almost all black people come from America."[56]

By this time, the occupation had ended, and censoring dashes no longer marred legislative transcripts. It was now much easier to denounce "blood mixing" as a perversely American crime perpetrated against a Japanese *minzoku* constructed as otherwise innocent of "blood mixing"—otherwise "pure."

Political independents also advanced their political careers and agendas by decrying "blood mixing." One prominent example is Ichikawa Fusae, the famed prewar suffragette and eugenicist who renounced her pacifism in the 1930s to endorse "the Japanese *minzoku*'s superiority" and right to rule Asia. Ichikawa threw herself into supporting Japan's war effort as leader in the National Spiritual Mobilization campaign, director of the Greater Japan Patriotic Speech Society, and eugenic propagandist boosting Japanese women's "self-consciousness as mothers of the *minzoku*." For her troubles, Japan lost the war and Ichikawa was purged by SCAP—one of only eight women so distinguished.[57] Unchastened and unrepentant, Ichikawa reemerged from forced political retirement at the occupation's end. Ministry of Foreign Affairs Treaty Bureau chief Nishimura Kumao warned US officials in April 1952 that "depurgees feel resentment toward the United States," which must "foreshadow a significant problem in future Japanese relations with the United States."[58] Ichikawa's return to politics would seem a case in point.

In May 1952, Ichikawa published an article decrying "The Problem of Women in 'Independent' Japan: *Panpan* and *Konketsuji*."[59] This headline, featuring "independent" in scare quotes, reflected and promoted doubt and cynicism regarding Japan's liberation from US rule. The subheadline suggested sexual sovereignty and freedom from "blood mixing" were the sine qua non of political independence, which Japan had yet to achieve. Even so, Ichikawa exploited the political and press freedom achieved at the end of April 1952 to voice her bitter critique of *Anpo*. Central to her critique was outrage that Japanese women, whom she had long celebrated and defined as "mothers of the *minzoku*," dared abandon that eugenic and patriotic duty to indulge in sex and "blood mixing" with Americans.

Ichikawa assured her audience that although *konketsuji* were "without sin," they "will without a doubt spark many social problems" in Japan as they grow up. "If things continue like this ... we're on the road to a ruined country." Ichikawa sharply criticized Yoshida and his cabinet, who allegedly lacked "the good faith to try to solve" the problem. Ichikawa insisted that she had the solution, one prong of which was to crack down on *panpan* and criminalize sex work, the actual or imagined profession of "blood mixing" mothers. Although other sex workers should be rehabilitated into nationally approved forms of labor, Ichikawa argued that *panpan* should be ejected from the country altogether. "Make them marry, send them to the United States." In Ichikawa's view, women who slept with Americans thereby forfeited their claim to being Japanese, their right to choose their own husbands, and their right to live in their native land. She essentially wanted to repurpose recent changes in US law, which facilitated immigration of Japanese "war brides" to the United States, to cleanse Japan of an undesirable population: disloyal and dysgenic Japanese women who bred *konketsuji*.[60] Naturally, Ichikawa wanted to round up *konketsuji* and send them to the United States, too. Hers was a call for ethnic cleansing through coercive sexual policing and coerced emigration.[61]

In part on the strength of this vision, Ichikawa was elected to the Diet as an independent in 1953. She held office for almost thirty years. Historian

FIGURE 5.5. An immaculately dressed Japanese bride marries a uniformed US serviceman as snow falls at Heian Shrine in Kyoto, February 7, 1952. Courtesy of *Asahi shinbun*.

Sarah Kovner deems Ichikawa one of the most prominent "women's rights activists known for their interest in eugenics" who was "instrumental in linking what they called the *konketsuji* problem and prostitution in public minds." Ichikawa and other women leading the movement, such as Christian activist Uemura Tamaki and JSP representatives Fujiwara Michiko and Fukuda Masako, tarred "blood mixing" by association with sex work and sex work by association with *konketsuji*. Using such tactics and weaponizing partisan debate over *Anpo* to her own ends, Ichikawa helped effect passage of a Prostitution Prevention Law in 1956. This law criminalized sex work nationwide for the first time in Japan's history.

The antiprostitution movement in Japan long predated the 1950s, but antipathy to women selling or freely granting sex to foreign soldiers and bearing "mixed blood" children changed the political balance of power. A new moral majority emerged in the 1950s as local police, progressive intellectuals, parents' groups, and left-leaning protestors converged to stage book-burnings and other civic campaigns against a "colonial culture" in which young Japanese women abandoned chastity and patriotism to cavort with foreign men."[62] Amid vociferous recrimination toward *panpan* and "blood mixing" under *Anpo*, Ichikawa and her allies saw to it that Japanese women were subjected to unprecedented forms of sexual surveillance and "rehabilitation" toward chastity and national purity.[63]

THE NUMBERS GAME

Ichikawa published her article, which alleged that "white and black *konketsuji* left behind in Japan" by US soldiers number "two hundred thousand," among a flood of similar articles in May 1952. It was the first month in which Japan's modern media operated free of the heavy hand of censorship, whether by imperial censors or by SCAP.[64] Japan's press greeted the end of censorship and occupation by declaring a state of crisis. "As souvenirs of the occupation army, two hundred thousand *konketsuji* have been left behind in Japan."[65] Fathered by US soldiers posted in Japan in the wake of World War II, mothered by women of the defeated nation, "the *konketsuji* born from those unhappy relations are mostly abandoned and end up orphans. In six and a half years, two hundred thousand international orphans have been born."[66] Two years prior, *Red Flag* had left the exact number of *konketsuji* sired and abandoned by Americans in Japan in doubt, even while alleging that the number must be shockingly high. Nonpartisan presses after independence showed fewer scruples, rushing to affix a specific statistic to undergird and inflate the underlying claim. The number "two hundred thousand" and the phrase *konketsuji mondai*, or "mixed-blood children crisis," was suddenly on every tongue, in the pages of every periodical, and bandied about in debates on the Diet floor. The phrase signified to all appearances a crisis in child welfare, a disaster in the national budget, and an injustice of international scope. Most troubling of all, warned one expert, among the two hundred thousand mixed-blood waifs already clogging the alleys and orphanages of Japan, "forty thousand are black."[67]

The highbrow women's magazine *Ladies Review* had hewed to SCAP press controls, eschewing criticism of Allied soldiers and their interracial liaisons until the occupation's end. One April 1952 article had even featured US-Japan romance in a positive light. A first-person piece by Jane Fischer, a white veteran of the US Navy during World War II who proudly married a Japanese man during the occupation, focused on the "power of love" to "overcome national borders" and breed deep bonds between Japanese and Americans.[68]

One month later, such an article celebrating interracial romance between Japanese and Americans would be virtually unprintable, even in the same magazine. A single issue of *Ladies Review* in May 1952 featured five separate articles decrying US servicemen for impregnating Japanese women and abandoning them and their *konketsuji* in Japan.[69] Although deemed "progressive" by media ethnographer Nakao Kaori, the magazine was nonpartisan and could not be accused of trying to bolster the prospects of the JCP.[70] *Ladies Review* was more likely to peddle cosmetics and consumerist aspirations to the transactable good life than communist slogans and proletarian politics. Yet even more than *Red Flag*, *Ladies Review* took a hard turn toward fomenting moral panic over interracial sex and *konketsuji* at the occupation's end. The topic of interracial romance between Japanese *men* and foreign *women* fell from favor to make room for incessant coverage of the more outrageous interracial conjugation of Japanese *women* and foreign *men*.

In one of the magazine's May articles, famed novelist Nogami Yaeko (1885–1985) insisted that the "unavoidable problem" confronting Japan was not so much the relations between "Mr. Occupation" and the "daughters of Japan" as the "'fruit' inevitably born" of such relations. With "an occupation army semipermanently" stationed in the country under *Anpo*, the number of such *konketsuji* would increase every year. *Konketsuji* had "borrowed the wombs of daughters of Japan," but Nogami insisted that such borrowing and birth did not bestow membership in the *minzoku*. "Their fathers are American citizens. As such, more than they're children of Japan, we have to call them children of America."

Nogami distinguished "mixed" children as foreign to Japan by virtue of both their paternity and their racial features. "These little ones have different colored skin, colored eyes, colored hair." Nogami demurred that she was "not expert in the conclusions of race-scientific research" and could not speak definitively on the eugenic quality of *konketsuji*. She made her lack of optimism clear, however, when she dwelled on the "profound problem of black babies" and the mothers she deemed "sad and ashamed" to have born them. Nogami denied that she viewed *konketsuji* with racial contempt "simply because they are not pure." Some of what she wrote reflected a lingering imperial-era consciousness that "mixture" was the norm among the world's leading *minzoku*. Even Hitler's blood, Nogami mused, was of doubtful purity; and she wrote approvingly of Cleopatra as a "mixed blood" queen of old. "But I'm not such an idealist that I'll try to find a little Cleopatra among . . . the two hundred thousand *konketsuji*" sired by US forces in Japan.[71]

Veteran women's rights and left-wing labor activist Tatewaki Sadayo assured any "who feel doubts about this number two hundred thousand" that she had conducted a careful investigation and "was never presented any kind of evidence that could refute it." In the highbrow journal *Kaizō*, she called on her fellow Japanese to rise up and demand a political solution to this crisis: the reform of US immigration law so that *konketsuji* could be removed to the United States.[72] Nogami and Ichikawa had endorsed the same solution. None of these women considered whether *konketsuji* might have Japanese kin who would object to this policy. Nor did they contemplate whether Japanese (rather than US) law might bar de facto alienation and deportation of Japanese children singled out on racial grounds. As we have seen, independents and socialists were already demanding from the Diet floor that the United States take "mixed" children out of Japan. Such calls to ethnic cleansing spread more quickly through a free and uncensored press than they had through more narrow partisan political outlets.

Koya Yoshio, the MOW bureaucrat and leading eugenic opponent of "blood mixing" during the war (chapter 2), had fallen into a state of cautious quiet during the occupation. He protected his government job and prospects for promotion by keeping his anti-mixing convictions out of public view, even as he helped reconstruct Japan's postwar population policy and legal-medical praxis to facilitate systematic eugenic abortion of *konketsuji* (chapter 3). As these efforts succeeded, Koya was promoted to director of Japan's National Institute of Public Health. At the occupation's end, Koya removed his muzzle and reemerged as a vocal opponent of "mixing" alongside his old colleague from the Japan Race Hygiene Association, Nagai Hisomu. They spread their message in speeches nationwide in a peregrinating public health campaign.[73]

Koya also propounded his anti-mixing argument in *Ladies Review*, warning Japanese women of the dysgenic consequences of interracial breeding and detailing the inborn maladies and genetic disharmonies he claimed were common and inevitable in humans of "mixed" racial stock. Although many of Koya's warnings applied to "mixing" with white people, he shone an especially harsh light on "mixing" with Black Americans. During the war, Koya had compared Han Chinese to Jews as dangerously inassimilable through "blood mixing"; now he revived his old anti-Semitic take on "prepotency" while turning it against Black Americans. Koya argued that even a small infusion of Black American "blood" could permanently alter the Japanese genotype, as "that peculiar shape of nose, and lips, and crinkled hair of black people unexpectedly haunts generation after generation, and cannot easily be removed."

Perhaps because he was a career bureaucrat rather than a partisan operative, Koya did not directly criticize *Anpo* or Liberal Party politicians for keeping US forces in Japan. He had little to gain and much to lose by offending such power-holders. Nonetheless, Koya extended his arguments against "mixing" well beyond the eugenic to the political. He warned that as they aged, *konketsuji* might consolidate into a "mixed-blood caste" separate from and hostile to "pure blooded" Japanese. Once *konketsuji* achieved sufficient numbers and united against the majority, it would be too late for countermeasures.

The chief evidence Koya offered for this imminent racial "ruin" was, tellingly, the Haitian Revolution—horrifying tales of which were used by nineteenth-century slaveholders and their supporters to prove Black savagery, terrify whites, and discredit calls for abolition. Koya recounted the Haitian Revolution as a "slaughter of French people" who had been too intimate and liberal with Black people, thereby producing a "mulatto" caste overly insistent on the idea of equality. Koya had no patience for "notional equality" and preferred to keep allegedly lesser peoples in their place. He noted that the Haitian Revolution was "happily put down" without once mentioning that the defeated revolutionaries were enslaved people fighting for their freedom. Koya's discussion of "minority problems" in the contemporary United States likewise presented Black people as troublesome insurgents against dominant whites, with whom he encouraged his Japanese audience to identify. In fomenting fears about the predestined disloyalty of "mixed blood" people in Japan, he even claimed that as malcontents and racial outsiders, *konketsuji* would be susceptible to recruitment by international communism.[74] Ironically, in the early Cold War, *konketsuji* were defined as outsiders and potential enemies of the *minzoku* both by leftists and by anticommunists.

Yoshida's government was caught off guard by the vehemence and volume of bad press over *konketsuji*. Flummoxed by media clamor over "two hundred thousand" children allegedly "orphaned" in Japan by its nominal ally, the United States, and hounded by opposition politicians demanding quantification of *konketsuji*, government representatives in December 1952 could only stammer, "people are saying there are one hundred thousand or two hundred thousand or so, but on that point in answer to your question, we haven't in fact received clear materials at this time."[75]

The MOW rushed to compile statistics. Claims of massive numbers of orphaned *konketsuji* had been so vociferous that in 1952 even conservative government estimates placed them at as much as 20 percent of the total population of Japan's child-welfare institutions. In February 1953, the MOW announced that there were only 482 such *konketsuji* nationwide—a scant 1.68 percent of all children in welfare institutions.[76] Even these 482 were not all orphans. As to the total population of *konketsuji* born of foreign fathers since defeat in the war, in a speech in the House of Councilors, welfare minister Yamagata proudly reported the findings. "The official result is that right now there are 5013 of these *konketsuji* . . . among whom 4205 are white, 714 are black, and the other 94 are mongrels [*zasshu*]."[77] Yamagata's reference to "mongrels," the legislative record notes, met with laughter.

Soon, the MOW completed a more ambitious and labor-intensive study of *konketsuji*. This second study yielded an even lower number: 3490. The scale of the *konketsuji* "crisis" had plummeted toward the vanishing point.

Or that would logically be true, if soaring numbers had been the origin rather than the output of the mass-mediated moral panic. Instead, the precise number of occupation-born *konketsuji*, which had for more than a year been a topic of urgent governmental and popular concern, was now brushed away as beside the point. In response to a detailed report from MOW bureau chief Takada Masami on the survey methods and results that had been so insistently demanded of him and his colleagues in months past, JSP representative Fukuda Masako now replied indifferently, "In any event, *konketsuji* are on the road to increase year by year." Moments later she resumed, as if nothing had changed, her discussion of *konketsuji* as a racial crisis, Liberal Party failure, and abuse of Japan by its nominal ally, the United States. "I want to ask you about countermeasures for these *konketsuji* who continue to increase in numbers. Is it your intention to tolerate the matter in silence?" On behalf of Yoshida's government, Takada replied, "that we could somehow check this trend is not something the government is even considering."[78]

In and outside the Diet, national-purity advocates set aside current numbers of *konketsuji* to emphasize future increase. Their message remained "even one is too many." They also emphasized the question of where and to what race *konketsuji* belonged. The answer remained "not in Japan" and "not Japanese." Literary scholar Itagaki Naoko, who bewailed that after the war, Japan's "entire citizenry lost self-consciousness as a nation and became a sort of prostitute to Americans," met the new numbers with the old solution. "The best path is for America, which respects humanism, to take all the mixed-blood war children out of Japan."[79] These children were now confirmed rarely to be orphans. Nonetheless, their bonds with their mothers and mother country were routinely denied. Foreign censors had found they could not unmake public opinion by fiat, and MOW statisticians found they could not unmake it by numeration. Ethnic cleansing through international exile was widely preferred to welcoming a few thousand *konketsuji* as fellow Japanese. Partisan politicians had no concrete plan for effecting this widely endorsed outcome, but as we will see in chapter 6, some Japanese did build institutions and programs for gathering up *konketsuji* and removing them from the country.

One final word is necessary on the use and misuse of numbers in the postwar debate on *konketsuji*. After 1953, when successive surveys of children born postwar of foreign fathers found evidence of five thousand and then fewer than four thousand such *konketsuji* in Japan, future "increase" became the new numerical certainty cited everywhere. The only party to the debate to take seriously MOW findings that the "mixed" population was on the *decline* rather than on the rise was the US Embassy in Japan. In October 1953, the US Embassy noted that the shrinking number of *konketsuji* between the first survey and the second "may be explained partly by the fact that United States consulates throughout Japan had issued American passports to a total of 2,585 children born of mixed marriages as of December 31, 1952."[80] This was more than half the number of *konketsuji* identified in the initial MOW survey. Imprecise though these figures and their comparison may be, they offer a striking counter to the narrative of "blood mixing" as mass production of orphans.

Far fewer "blood mixers" abandoned their children than was generally claimed. In fact, those looking for evidence that the figure "five thousand" was an undercount had no better source than welfare minister Yamagata's initial report to the Diet, when he noted that MOW surveys excluded *konketsuji* born at foreign hospitals. In other words, they excluded *konketsuji* born under the care of their fathers and their fathers' nations, whether in hospitals overseas or in US or British Commonwealth bases in Japan.[81]

For alarmists in the *konketsuji* debate, the proposition that they were getting exactly what they claimed they wanted—the large-scale emigration of "mixed" children from Japan—was less satisfying than potentially frustrating. The *konketsuji* "crisis" was less a problem than a solution for those seeking means to discredit *Anpo*, the United States, and Yoshida's Liberal Party. Even premier journalist Kanzaki Kiyoshi (no friend to US bases in Japan) attested in 1953 that reportage on *konketsuji* was marked by "sensationalism" and a disregard for fact-checking. Setting aside that supply-side problem, he averred that there was also a demand-side problem in the information ecosphere regarding "blood mixing." In short, "there was definitely a social atmosphere in which everyone wanted to believe the story of two hundred thousand *konketsuji*."[82] That the will to believe was not dispelled by the dissemination of more accurate data in 1953 is made clear by the fact that decades later, one still finds the old misinformation cited anew. For instance, historian Nomoto Sankichi recycles the figure "two hundred thousand" while omitting any discussion of "mixed blood" children who were *not* orphans.[83] Other scholars are more cautious.[84] But in profound and perduring ways, the malign narrative of "blood mixing" established in 1952 continues to stain the US-Japan alliance and distort historical memory and racial identity in Japan.[85]

RIGHT-WING REALIGNMENT

In January 1954, as debates over *panpan* and "blood mixing" continued to roil the Diet, right-wing firebrand Nakasone Yasuhiro (1918–2019) took the podium to explicate opposition to *Anpo* among members of the Democratic Party. Nakasone had served in the Imperial Navy during World War II, when one of his proud accomplishments was to construct a comfort station in Indonesia to foster sex between Japanese servicemen and conscripted sex workers. In that context, interracial sex did not perturb him. After defeat, however, with foreign soldiers pursuing local liaisons with Japanese women, Nakasone took a different stance, utterly uncompromising in its insistence on sexual sovereignty and racial purity. Nakasone won his seat in the House of Representatives in 1947 in a campaign that featured him flying a rising sun flag—banned by SCAP at the time—and wearing a black tie to mourn imperial defeat.[86] At the occupation's end, Nakasone joined the chorus of politicians decrying "blood mixing" and denying that Japan could ever be sovereign, sexually or otherwise, under *Anpo*.

In a plenary session of the House of Representatives, Nakasone insisted that "true independence starts with the removal of the American military." He denounced prime minister Yoshida and other members of the Liberal Party as "loyal subjects of General MacArthur"—as collaborators—who were no longer "Japanese at all." In response to Yoshida and the Liberal Party's argument that the US alliance was in Japan's best economic interest, Nakasone decried to parliamentary applause the "sordid Jewish thinking" that put fiscal problems above "our first duty, which is the return of our sovereignty and protecting the purity of our blood."[87] In a final rhetorical flourish, Nakasone asked: "Can we bear to pass on to our children and grandchildren . . . a Japan overrun with *konketsuji* and their prostitute mothers?"[88]

By the end of the year, Yoshida was forced from power. Yoshida's cabinet was not toppled in 1954, in any simple sense, because of uproar over "blood mixing." But left-wing and right-wing rivals did wield *panpan* and *konketsuji* as symbolic cudgels against Yoshida's government, consistently and to great effect, throughout the early 1950s. Yoshida's ouster cleared the way for consolidation of a government farther to the right, with Hatoyama Ichirō, who had been purged as a militarist during the occupation, and Kishi Nobusuke, who had been imprisoned for three years as a suspected Class A war criminal, taking over the premiership in the late 1950s. This occurred after Yoshida's center-conservative Liberal Party merged in 1955 with the right-wing Democratic Party to form the Liberal Democratic Party (LDP), which has dominated Japanese politics ever since. Much has been written about the rehabilitation of the right and their return to power, and about the simultaneous stabilization of the JSP as the major opposition party in something resembling a two-party system, as the JCP lost its footing in the 1950s. Less remarked upon is the fact that the Cold War was a race war and a sexualized war; so too were partisan politics in Japan.

In 1955, the Cabinet Office conducted a survey in which investigators asked Japanese adults whether their country had become a colony of the United States. Almost half said yes. Another quarter were unsure. This left not even a third of Japanese respondents confident that their country was in fact independent. In the same survey, Japanese adults had a chance to pass judgment on how the Unites States had influenced Japan in the ten years since the end of World War II. Almost half deemed the US influence, on balance, positive, whereas a mere 10 percent decried it as harmful. In other words, even if nearly half of Japanese felt the United States had reduced Japan to colonial or semicolonial status, only one in ten felt the United States had treated Japan badly.[89] Counterintuitive though this might seem, the question of whether Japan had been colonized by the United States and the question of whether Japan benefited from its relationship with the United States were held logically distinct by many Japanese. Japan might be both a colony and a beneficiary. That some Japanese would hold this view, even implicitly, makes a lot of sense given their recent history of "benevolently" colonizing many a foreign land.

For many on Japan's right and left, the public sense that colonization by the United States might not be all bad was either intolerable or inopportune. Partisan nationalists wanted to prove not only that the alleged colonization of their country by Americans was really underway, but also that American Empire was fundamentally destructive. If it was difficult to convince most Japanese that the United States had inflicted material hardship on Japan since the end of the war, they would make a case about hardship of another kind. What some agitators chose to focus on was the concept of harm to the chastity of Japanese women and the "pure blood" of the nation. Partisans had support in this mission from nonpartisan scholar-bureaucrats, such as Koya Yoshio and Koyama Eizō, who reminded postwar readers of the well-established imperial-era fact that "blood mixing" was a universal feature of colonial societies.⁹⁰ The very existence of *konketsuji* was thus citable as evidence of Japan's ongoing colonization by a foreign power.

In this context, even Socialists could celebrate the rise to power of right-wing Kishi over moderate, pro-American proponents of *Anpo* such as Yoshida. Koyama Makoto, an imperial-era politician who returned to the Diet as a Socialist after the occupation, advised Kishi in 1957 of the "heavy responsibility" he bore as prime minister to undo the "damage Japan suffered as a result of the war." Koyama, who had been purged by SCAP for his collusion with the wartime regime, did not charge Kishi, whom SCAP had arrested as a war criminal, with repenting of their shared wartime leadership or the harms they had caused. On the contrary, Koyama clarified that it was not the war, but rather the US alliance, that had caused Japan the most harm: "When we look at postwar conditions, what we feel is most tragic . . . are various incidents born of *Anpo*." Specifically, Koyama complained about "red-line [prostitution] districts popping up and numerous *konketsuji* living in Japan. All the things like this that I see and hear about I truly feel are tragic. I can't bear the sadness. I look at each one of them and my chest constricts, and I think if only there hadn't been that war. I'm sure you, prime minister, feel the same way. So revision of *Anpo* is an absolute necessity."⁹¹ Such resentments, hopes, and expectations about sex, blood, and sovereignty helped fuel Kishi's rise to power. They also fueled his downfall, in 1960, when Kishi exercised his power to ratify a revised *Anpo* in the face of massive nationwide protests. Kishi resigned, having narrowly survived an assassin's knife. Japan's fraught alliance with the United States also survived another day.⁹²

The revised *Anpo* had much more favorable terms for Japan than the original treaty negotiated by Yoshida when Japan was still under occupation. Kishi revoked permission for US troops to intervene in the case of "internal disturbances"—a clause intended but never used as a check against a communist takeover. Kishi also secured a say over US troop movements, a pledge that the United States defend Japan in case of a foreign attack (while making no reciprocal pledge that Japan defend the United States), the right to cancel *Anpo* unilaterally at any time with one year's notice, and assurance of greater economic benefits from its US ally.⁹³ None of these major emendations mollified the opposition, however. For many observes, the equation of *Anpo* to colonization was just too strong. Looking back on the protests, LDP operative Miyazawa Kiichi (1919–2007), who was close to party leaders at the time and secured the post of prime minister in the early 1990s, remarked of the protestors that "they never made it clear in their view what was wrong about *Anpo*." Baffled by why the revised treaty, which he viewed as advantageous to Japan, was so objectionable to huge portions of the populace, Miyazawa opined that "there was so little content behind the protest that nothing was left once the fuss was over. . . . it was an empty protest."[94]

In fact, the *Anpo* protests were less "empty" than overflowing with symbolic resonance. No matter the geopolitical or fiscal benefits, the presence of US troops signified a violation of sovereignty—including sexual sovereignty—and a threat to racial purity. That argument had been made too strongly and too often in the 1950s for Japanese to have forgotten it by 1960. Ultimately, LDP politicians managed this tension by concentrating most US bases and protests against them in a single subordinated prefecture: Okinawa.[95] "Blood mixing" between Japanese women and multiracial Americans remained stigmatized by association with defeat, occupation, and "horizontal collaboration." Yet the LDP successfully exported most of this stigma to Okinawa.[96]

Nakasone Yasuhiro rose to the height of power in the world that *Anpo* built. As LDP prime minister in the 1980s, Nakasone built a chummy relationship with US president Ronald Reagan and tenderly ministered to the US-Japan alliance, which continued to see US troops stationed in Japan. Once in power, Nakasone ceased to decry that alliance as "sordid Jewish thinking." No longer did he privilege the "purity of our blood" over *Anpo* and economic growth. In an era when both Japanese and foreign observers hailed "Japan as Number One" and Nakasone led an economic superpower, the notion that Japanese were a race of victims suffering "colonization" under US boots was no longer as plausible at it once seemed.[97] Much less was it appealing as an LDP campaign slogan.

Despite these economic and ideological turnabouts, Nakasone maintained his "pure blood" pride decades past the backlash against "blood mixing" that he helped foment in the early 1950s. As prime minister in 1986, Nakasone offended the international community by proclaiming that the superior intellectual abilities and economic achievements of the Japanese were thanks to their racial purity, unlike the lower-achieving United States, allegedly dragged down by racial minorities.[98] Nakasone's shift from emphasizing Japan's racial vulnerability in the 1950s to trumpeting Japan's economic and racial superpower status in the 1980s is telling of just how historically contingent the construction of race can be.

Young communist students on the left, young Nakasone on the right, mature Socialists such as Yamashita, and depurged feminist Ichikawa all converged to stoke moral outrage over "blood mixing" in the democratic free-for-all of the early 1950s. In the process, they forged a powerful new weapon in Japanese politics and private life: an ethos of racial purity that would define and discipline the postwar nation, Japanese family, and Japanese women for years to come. Whether opportunistic or born of deep conviction, partisan bickering over *Anpo* as an unprecedented act of imperialist "blood mixing" had real effects in narrowing the acceptable scope of sexual conduct, family formation, and racial identity in Japan. What in the imperial era was called—even celebrated as—"intermarriage," a grassroots practice that could breed eugenic futures and forge interracial union in an utopian empire, was now condemned as "whoring out" the prostrate nation to an amoral enemy empire. In Americanizing *konketsuji* and crafting a narrative of "blood mixing" as imperial aggression *against Japan*, 1950s activists fostered a passion for "pure blood," a norm of racial chastity, and an abiding victimhood nationalism.

Anpo was not destroyed by this outpouring of negative emotion, and for some, destroying *Anpo* was likely never the intent. Regardless, the "mixed" and "mixing" people who had enjoyed some support, in the ideological orthodoxy of the imperial era, lost their cultural claim to "Japaneseness" in the partisan squabbles of the early 1950s. From that point onward, "mixed blood" children and their families were living in a hostile political milieu. Amid widespread endorsement of ethnic cleansing, which certain activists were intent on putting into action, some "mixed" Japanese would find themselves unable to continue living in Japan at all.

Chapter Six

ORPHANS BY DESIGN

Ethnic Cleansing and International
Adoption in the 1950s

One of the first *konketsuji* to attempt to migrate from occupied Japan to the United States was Nagamine Shizue, who appears in the Congressional record in 1946 under the Americanized name Amelia Shidzee (*sic*) Nagamine Toneman. The House Committee on Immigration and Naturalization (CIN) noted the legal barrier that brought her to Congress's attention: "Being half Japanese, she is racially ineligible to citizenship." At the time, US law prohibited immigration by anyone ineligible to naturalize as a citizen, and the 1940 Nationality Act determined eligibility to naturalize on racial (i.e., racist) grounds. To wit, only "white persons, persons of African nativity or descent, and persons who are descendants of races indigenous to the continents of North or South America" could immigrate and become US citizens. In 1943, Chinese were deleted from the list of "races" ineligible to immigrate and naturalize in a gesture of respect for a wartime ally and limited rebuttal to Japanese imperial critiques of US racism. In 1946, wartime allies from India and the Philippines were likewise reclassified as racially eligible to Americanize. The Japanese, however, were still barred at war's end.[1]

What of "mixed blood" people? At twenty-three years old, Nagamine was an imperial-era *konketsuji* longing to depart devastated Japan and enter the United States as part of a new "mixed" family. Congress and the US military took pains to facilitate the immigration and naturalization of "war brides," thereby bolstering the heterosexual sovereignty and patriarchal status of servicemen and veterans who married foreign women while serving overseas.[2] One such deserving veteran was Paul Toneman. Had he been posted to Europe, China, or the Philippines and married a woman there—assuming the woman he married was not "half Japanese"—his legal situation on attempting to return to the United States would have been easier. But Toneman was deployed to Japan, where he met and married Nagamine mere months after the war's end. Unfortunately for this young "mixed" couple, the War Brides Act, which Congress passed in December 1945, contained no provisions to suspend racial bars to immigration and naturalization. US authorities deemed Nagamine "of the half-Japanese race and of the half-South American race." Under the law, the Japanese "half" that was ineligible to enter the US trumped the South American "half" that was eligible. As a *konketsuji*, Nagamine was legally ineligible to become a "war bride."

Daunted but not deterred, the Nagamine-Toneman family petitioned Congress to pass a law of exception that would apply to only one person. A private bill—so termed in contrast to public law designed to apply in every case—could suspend the usual barriers to immigration for a person of Mrs. Nagamine Toneman's "race," licensing her to become a war bride. Members of the House CIN expressed both sympathy and doubt that such a private bill was warranted. On the one hand, "there is considerable merit to the question of permitting a United States citizen to have his wife come to the United States to reside with him." On the other, "any deviation from the naturalization qualifications as far as race is concerned should not be indulged in by way of private bill."[3] Full reconsideration and revision of public law to devise a system adequate to address all cases was preferred. Comprehensive legal reform would take years, however, leaving "mixed" families in the lurch with no promise of relief.

The number of "mixed" families marooned between "races" and nations and the inequitable laws that governed them was destined to increase with every week that US forces remained in Japan. Remain they would, as US forces transitioned from invaders to occupiers, from occupiers to allies, from building beachheads to building permanent outposts. Those biopolitical outposts were built not only in geographic regions of "Asia" but also in "races" of Asia once dismissed as beyond the bounds of American kinship and national interests. In postwar US efforts to forgive the Japanese enemy, reimagine them as allies and kin, and reimagine the United States as more race-blind and nurturing than racist and violent, Americans learned to embrace Japanese "women and children first."[4] Multiracial Japan quickly became ground zero in a grassroots rebellion against the politics of purity on both sides—the national chastity demanded of Japanese women under occupation and the fantasy of racial purity undergirding US laws on immigration, naturalization, and family formation.

To be clear, non-Japanese Americans had formed "mixed" families with Japanese long before the postwar period. After Japan's attack on Pearl Harbor in December 1941, once-thriving "mixed" families on the West Coast of the United States were subject to internment. When white American patriarchs with Japanese or Japanese-American wives and "mixed" children lodged vociferous protests, US authorities began to exempt their "mixed" kin from concentration camps. (White women, by contrast, might enter the camps along with their Japanese husbands and "mixed" children.)[5]

At the height of World War II, white men asserted their sexual sovereignty and right to form and govern their "mixed" families free from federal interference. In the process, they began carving out gendered exceptions to internment that challenged the definition of Japanese as an enemy "race."[6] Such efforts to normalize and win legal protections for "mixed" families intensified amid the new wave of intermarriage and "blood mixing" that accompanied the Allied occupation of Japan and subsequent alliance-building between Japan and the United States.

Thousands of Americans soon demanded to bring interracial sexual and conjugal practice and its living offspring back "home" to the United States. The Nagamine-Toneman family is but one example. In answer to their petition, the House CIN set aside its concerns over legislative consistency and came down in favor of a private bill, which would license Nagamine to become a war bride, settle with her veteran husband in the United States, and beget a new generation of *konketsuji* with birthright citizenship on American soil.[7] A flood of further petitions from American husbands, fiancées, and lovers of Japanese women and from American natural or adoptive fathers of Japanese children exerted constant pressure on US authorities to suspend racialized border controls in the years to come.

The result was a high workload and perduring state of exception. A beleaguered Congress in 1947 passed a public law to suspend racial bars to naturalization and immigration for war brides, if only for thirty days. Afterward, passage of private bills to authorize immigration by Japanese

FIGURE 6.1. Ninety-five US soldiers, sailors, and Marines married Japanese brides at the US consulate in Tokyo on March 19, 1952. Some brought along their "mixed" children. Some had already married in civil or religious ceremonies in Japan, but today they registered as "war brides." Sergeant Harley Kenneth Gray of Oklahoma holds his two-year-old "mixed" child as he fills out the requisite paperwork. Consulate employee Violet Niemiec assists while other "mixed" families wait their turn. AP Photo/Max Desfor.

and "mixed blood" brides resumed.[8] So persistent was demand that race-blind provisions for "war brides" were renewed in 1950 and kept in force almost until the occupation's end in April 1952. "Along with the newly married couples," reported Peter Kalischer from the US consulate in Tokyo, "more than 2,000 children, born out of consulate wedlock, walked, toddled or were carried in to be documented as American citizens."[9] By the time the occupation wound down, thousands of American-Japanese couples had married and begun migrating to the United States with their "mixed blood" children.[10]

Although the story of Japanese war brides is relatively well known, the story of *konketsuji* negotiating similar barriers to entry is lesser known. To be clear, the border did not block all *konketsuji*—not those who could prove "blood ties" to the United States. American "blood" was defined statutorily as follows: children born to an US citizen mother, to the wife of a US citizen (under the legal presumption the citizen was the father), or to a US citizen who acknowledged paternity outside wedlock. All such children were citizens by "right of blood" (jus sanguinis), regardless of where in the world they were born and regardless of their "race" or "mixture."[11] *Konketsuji* with no demonstrable "blood" ties, however, confronted a closed border. Some, like Nagamine, had no kin ties to the United States until she married a US serviceman. Marriage was insufficient to overcome racist border laws and blood-quantum logic. Other *konketsuji* had no US kin until they were adopted or became stepchildren to US citizens. Like matrimony, adoption and step-parentage were insufficient to overcome "blood"-based border laws. Americans therefore flooded Congress with petitions for private bills to admit the children of their Japanese spouses and children they had adopted in Japan. Some of these children were "mixed blood" offspring of Allied fathers who had abandoned them; other were "full blood" Japanese.[12] Regardless, the legal construct of "race" determined their treatment at the border. Put differently, the border rendered such children a separate and unequal race, ineligible to enter the United States without private acts of Congress.

Postwar *konketsuji* thus found themselves in a trans-Pacific double bind. On the one hand, *konketsuji* born out of wedlock to Japanese mothers were legally Japanese with every right to Japanese citizenship. On the other hand, socially, eugenically, and in the bitter partisan politics of early Cold War Japan, these citizen *konketsuji* were defined as undesirable, unwelcome, and foreign in every sense except the statutory. As we have seen (chapter 5), there were widespread calls in the 1950s to remove all such "mixed" children from Japan. The preferred destination was the United States. In that country across the Pacific, these same children were not so venomously politicized. Yet venom was not necessary to block their entry to the United States when prewar statutes had the same effect. Hence the double bind: Rather than being Japanese and American, *konketsuji* could be construed as neither/nor, a newborn people entitled to exist nowhere. Out of these postwar contradictions emerged an activist movement spanning the Pacific to lower racial bars to the migration of *konketsuji* to the United States.

The Japanese Empire had long known that when soldiers and civilians occupy foreign lands, "intermarriage" and "blood mixing" inevitably follow. Japanese authorities once sought to harness such "mixture" to imperial ends, praising intermarriage as patriotic and *konketsuji* as the eugenic offspring of empire. But postimperial Japan plunged into biological defeatism and eugenic and partisan backlash against *konketsuji* and their miscegenating mothers. It was now the United States's turn to deploy hundreds of thousands of soldiers and civilians to a "racially" foreign land and manage the "mixed" fruits of expansion. With its blood quantum logic, statutory and cultural hostility to intermarriage and "miscegenation," and prewar standard of monoracial kinship, the United States seemed ill suited to its new role as imperial hegemon in East Asia. Ironically, as postwar Japanese became increasingly intolerant of "mixing" with Americans and other foreigners, the United States reversed course toward an increased tolerance and even passion for "mixture."

This biopolitical reverse course was driven by many factors, from Cold War geopolitics to domestic race relations. Equally pivotal was the brute fact that, as US representative John Lesinski put it in a meeting of the CIN in May 1945, "the production of children is already rolling along with the Army."[13]

THE OTHER REVERSE COURSE

Because "blood" children of US citizens born anywhere in the world had "blood rights" to immigrate and claim US citizenship, they were not the object of trans-Pacific activism to facilitate the migration of *konketsuji*. Rather, the chief target for this activist-driven Pacific passage were socially orphaned *konketsuji* who would be adopted into US families. Under prewar law, such children had no legal right to immigrate or claim citizenship in the United States. Legal scholar Sara Dillon specifies that "social orphans are children who have come apart from their original families, and who tend to live in state-run or other group care. . . . This term is sometimes objected to because many of the children included in the 'social orphan' category have living parents."[14] As we will see, most *konketsuji* targeted for international adoption in the 1950s did indeed have living kin.

Rendering these *konketsuji* socially kinless and therefore eligible for adoption and emigration was the work of Japan's architects of international adoption, chief among them Sawada Miki (1901–1980). Japanese activists promoted international adoption as the best available solution to the purported "crisis of *konketsuji*" explored in chapter 5.[15] Cleansing Japanese families and bloodlines of *konketsuji* would restore the nation to a fictive racial purity and contrived sense of prewar wholeness. Rendering *konketsuji* kinless was work that could be done within Japan, but crafting mechanisms of international adoption, including legislation that could get *konketsuji* across the border into the United States, required collaboration with US citizens and government agents.

After Japan's government signed the *Anzen hoshō jōyaku* (*Anpo*) security treaty providing for the continued stationing of US troops in Japan, Japanese politicians, pundits, and mass media repeatedly called for US troops to leave the country and take all *konketsuji* with them. The United States military, however, never contemplated effecting the mass removal of "mixed blood" children from Japan. Neither did the military of any other power that had stationed troops in Japan after World War II. Such a scheme seems so unlikely, so legally problematic, that it is hard to resist the conclusion that Japanese calls for mass deportation of *konketsuji* were not serious policy proposals designed to solve a putative crisis in child welfare. They were rhetorical feints aimed at embarrassing the United States and its friends in Japan, discrediting the US-Japan alliance, and unseating the ruling Liberal Party, which had negotiated and signed *Anpo* (chapter 5).

The alliance did not crumble under this rhetorical assault, but strain and embarrassment were keenly felt on both sides of the Pacific. US news media began covering the problem as early as 1948.[16] By the 1950s, US church groups, journalists, diplomats, and legislators had all taken an interest in Japan's so-called *konketsuji* crisis. The "middlebrow imagination" of early Cold War America, theorized by historian Christina Klein, was amply activated by trans-Pacific furor over *konketsuji*.[17] Neither US officials nor the US public were willing to entertain the solution so ardently advanced in Japan: the removal of all US troops along with the children they were blamed for siring. Yet Japanese reports and US media coverage did convince US audiences that the crisis was real and that it was America's crisis to solve. News headlines such as "Children of Conquerors Have No Future in Japan," "How the Stork Adds to the Horrors of War," and "Future Pales for 100,000 Children," made a bold and unmistakable argument that the United States must act urgently to avert a child-welfare catastrophe in Japan.[18] US attention was riveted by reports of Japanese racism toward *konketsuji*, "mixed" children's suffering, and US complicity and capacity to set things right.

Somehow, Cold War Americans wanted to prove that they were not the most racist country on the planet—Japanese and Soviet propaganda to the contrary. What better way to improve America's international standing and self-image than to take in interracial child refugees from racism in a foreign land—especially the land of the former enemy at Pearl Harbor?

However exaggerated and falsified the key "facts" circulated in Japanese protests and international press coverage, they were sufficient to make the mass-mediated "*konketsuji* crisis" a real crisis in US-Japan relations. In the early 1950s, a trans-Pacific consensus emerged that if Americans refused to take steps to relieve Japan of its "unwanted" *konketsuji*, Japanese confidence in US goodwill would be forfeit. Worse yet, Washington's embattled alliance with Japan, a key Cold War outpost in Asia, might crumble. Americans needed to act to secure not only the interests of "mixed blood" children but also the interests of the "free world."

In October 1953, a Congressional Subcommittee on International Operations arrived in Tokyo to survey the scene. US consul general James Pilcher gave the subcommittee a detailed briefing on the *konketsuji* crisis in which he complained of the "misinformation" and "grossly exaggerated" rhetoric that were distorting America's image in Japan. For one thing, there were nowhere near two hundred thousand children orphaned by GIs in Japan, as was widely claimed. Investigations by Japan's Ministry of Welfare (MOW), he clarified, turned up fewer than five hundred "mixed" children in child welfare facilities nationwide. Perhaps ten times as many occupation-born *konketsuji* "live with their relatives, their mothers principally." Thousands more had been taken back to the United States to live with their fathers. In short, a nonnegligible but low number of occupation-born *konketsuji* were orphans, not all of them sired by Americans.[19] Regardless, the MOW's findings never circulated as widely, in Japanese or Western media or politics, as did the more sensational figures.

Pilcher and members of Congress had every reason to believe that Americans were losing the propaganda war. One year before the subcommittee's trip to Tokyo, Washington's favored newspaper, the *Washington Post*, declared of Japan that "100,000 illegitimate babies" were the "pathetic aftermaths of seven years of American occupation."[20] In press reports to come, the numbers kept changing, but bad news kept rolling in. Just weeks before the subcommittee convened, the *Los Angeles Times* broadcast that GIs in Japan had abandoned some seventy-five thousand "Japanese-American war orphans."[21] Months prior, the same paper had recounted "200,000 'occupation orphans,' discarded in Japan mainly by American fathers." Of those *konketsuji*, "many, it is feared, have been caught in the net of child slave-trading."[22] That US servicemen had spawned two hundred thousand child slaves in Japan was an alarming claim, happily unsubstantiated. Alas, international presses trafficked in similar sensational stories. For instance, *Times of India* discounted claims of one hundred thousand or two hundred thousand "Eurasian and Afrasian babies born to Japanese mothers since 1945" only to assert that fifty thousand "would be more accurate."[23]

Some English-language papers did eventually take note of the MOW's careful investigation of the actual numbers and living conditions of *konketsuji*. For instance, the *Boston Globe* in December 1952 ran the headline, "Japan Says Reports of G.I. Parenthood Are Exaggerated." Rather than set the record straight, however, the Associated Press (which was the source of the story) further muddied the waters by announcing that the MOW had counted "less than fifty thousand" GI babies in Japan. Technically correct—five thousand is far fewer than fifty thousand. By failing to cite the actual count, this trusted news outlet left the US reading public with an impression of reproductive wastage in occupied Japan exaggerated by a factor of ten.[24]

Whatever the actual numbers, consul general Pilcher advised Congress that "the Japanese people would probably like to see most of these babies adopted" by Americans. Never mind that 95 percent were not orphans, social or otherwise, but were being raised by their mothers or other close kin. Pilcher assured Congress that the Japanese government was supportive and "Japanese family courts have been very lenient in their adoption proceedings."[25] The disquieting implication was that Japan's authorities authorized foreigners to take *konketsuji* out of the country under conditions that would be deemed legally inadequate for "pure" children.

That implication turns out to be true. The MOW was building a powerful network of civic groups, private charities, national, prefectural, and metropolitan governments, Child Consultation Centers, and welfare officials to find *konketsuji* wherever they were living and push them into channels for international adoption. Government workers were sent to inquire at households with *konketsuji* whether their kin would consider relinquishing them to institutions and international adoption—an inquiry to which "pure" families were not subjected. Regardless of their poverty, family background, or status as orphans, children deemed "unmixed" were not targeted for international adoption in this way. Sociologist Shimoji concludes that the MOW "proactively supported migration, making 'konketsuji,' as adoptees, into 'foreigners' under the law." Once established in the early 1950s, this racially discriminatory pattern has held true ever since. Children come apart from their families in many ways in Japan as elsewhere, but however long and severe that separation, abused, unhoused, or poor but "pure" social orphans are kept in Japan and close to their kin. Only for "mixed" children is adoption by foreigners encouraged.[26]

US officials accepted this emerging dichotomy in the early 1950s rather than attempting to challenge its justice or propriety. It was enough that the Japanese government and public preferred to be rid of *konketsuji*. Pilcher provided Congress with a detailed translation of MOW survey findings on *konketsuji*, careful explanations of adoption proceedings in Japan and relevant US laws, evidence of support for international adoption of such children by US religious and civic groups, and the transcript of a speech by chief justice Kondo Rinji of the Tokyo Family Court, who praised the "many generous American couples [who] have called at my office and expressed their sincere desire to adopt" *konketsuji*.[27]

Thus, the United States stumbled toward international adoption as its preferred solution to the diplomatic black eye known as the "*konketsuji* crisis." In lieu of mass removal, it would be case-by-case removal. To the chagrin of US policymakers, case-by-case removal was never enough to satisfy America's critics in Japan. Yet international adoption could satisfy US audiences that America was living up to its responsibilities, exhibiting moral leadership, and doing something to save what US news outlets and Japanese activists dubbed "Japan's unwanted."[28]

International adoption was a novel concept at the time, and it took years of policy innovation and private experimentation to figure out how it would work. One key moment came in 1952, when Congress passed the Immigration and Nationality Act (INA), abolishing the racial-national bar to Japanese immigration and naturalization. Koreans, who had been Japanese under prewar and wartime law, were likewise freed of the racial bar to immigration. Repeal of that old racist provision in US law was an important plank in the platform of trans-Pacific rapprochement. Rapprochement with all possible allies felt urgently necessary in the wake of the fall of China, North Korea, and Eastern Europe to the expanding communist bloc. The United States, which had begun repealing racist border controls to court international allies in World War II, went even further in repealing racist laws to court non-white allies during the Cold War.[29] Still, immigration remained tightly constrained, as the INA established an annual quota of a mere 185 immigrants from Japan.

President Harry Truman and his allies fought for a more liberal bill. In explaining his decision to veto the INA, Truman pointedly addressed people "of Japanese ancestry, and all our friends throughout the far East." He explained that he delighted in the INA's liberating measures but deplored that it instated a narrow and racialized quota for people "as much as 50 percent Asian." Truman accurately predicted that this new quota system for Asian "races" and "mixes" would compel Congress to adopt further "emergency legislation" to admit additional nonquota migrants, such as *konketsuji*, in the future. He complained that the low quota was "insulting to large numbers of our finest citizens" and "irritating to our allies abroad."[30] Yet rather than risk further delay and possible failure to craft and pass a better law, the State Department secretly recommended that Truman sign the bill. The State Department's recommendation hinged on deference to "the views of our Far Eastern friends" and acute concern over "how strongly the Japanese felt" about the ongoing racist insult of statutory exclusion from the United States. When the Department's advice was leaked, enough of Truman's allies in Congress defected to override his veto.[31] The INA went into effect, allotting Japan a quota of 185 emigrants per year.

Actual immigration proceeded more quickly, as spouses and "blood" children of US citizens immigrated with nonquota status. Under the INA, it was no longer necessary to pass private laws to admit the Japanese wives of US servicemen. Yet even as nonquota migration of "mixed" families soared, the statutory quota remained and was often quoted, at home and abroad, in criticism of a still racist United States. The *Chicago Defender* railed that the INA "Jim Crows . . . Asians."[32] Moscow lost no time in propagandizing exclusion by quota as further evidence of the US imperialists' racial contempt for Asians.[33] Adding to the ongoing headache was the fact that adopted children were not treated equally to "blood" children—under the INA, adoptees were subject to the quota.[34]

Despite these flaws, Japan's government touted the INA as proof of the United States reforming its racist ways and behaving as a true friend to its ally, Japan.[35] In this regard, the State Department had been right and had helped to deliver in the INA exactly what their counterparts in Tokyo had desperately wanted.

During her trip to Tokyo in 1953, congresswoman Katharine St. George asked how the "change in the immigration status of the Japanese [was] received in Japan? Did that make a good impression?" Consul general Pilcher replied, "Extremely well received!" Rarely one to sugarcoat America's challenges or reputation in Japan, Pilcher followed up with an anecdote that demonstrated exactly how little pro-American sentiment was in the atmosphere. US ambassador Robert Daniel Murphy, who oversaw the first tumultuous year of the *Anpo* alliance, had recently delivered a farewell address in Japan in which he attempted to put a positive spin on the past few years of bilateral relations. Yet according to Pilcher, in his speech, Murphy managed to elicit "only 2 points of applause. There was loud and prolonged applause when he made the point that we had removed restrictions against the immigration of Japanese to the United States and against their naturalization." St. George was "very glad to hear it." She and Pilcher were both aware of ongoing critique of the INA in the United States and internationally. Pilcher insisted, however, that the Japanese reactions was overwhelmingly positive: "I have not heard 1 complaint from any Japanese source whatever regarding the small quota. . . . All they wanted was for the restriction to be removed." St. George mused that the INA worked because it "took away a stigma which they had probably always resented for many years [sic]."[36] What Japanese wanted was not so much to emigrate en masse to the United States as to not be insulted by outright denial.

Yet many Japanese did want "mixed blood" children to emigrate en masse. In high-level discussions of *konketsuji*, it became clear that Japanese were not as uniformly uncritical of the INA as Pilcher implied. In the Diet, Democratic party councilor Fukagawa Tamae (1903–1992) lost no time linking the INA to "the problem of *konketsuji*," particularly those "children whose fathers won't do us the courtesy of taking them away." Fukagawa was pleased that "American volunteers" were willing to adopt such children, but she complained that the INA with its low quota stood in the way. Foreign minister Okazaki Katsuo replied with praise for the INA, stating that the United States has "abolished racial discrimination" in immigration law and "repealed distinctions between Orientals and Occidentals." In this attempt to defend his government's allies in Washington and the concessions they had made in the INA, Okazaki coyly overlooked contravening facts: that the INA set far higher quotas for European than Asian countries, and that in continuity with prewar legislation, the INA racialized "mixed blood" people to count them against low Asian quotas using the old familiar blood-quantum logic.[37] Keenly aware of this persisting barrier, Fukagawa urged the foreign minister and prime minister to prevail upon US authorities to revise US immigration law once more. She was not so much advocating race-blind as race-conscious migration policy of a different kind, one that would speed the exit of "mixed" children from Japan. Okazaki promised to look into the matter. But he warned Diet members that it would be difficult for Japan to lobby for such race-conscious legislation when the United States had just renounced race-based immigration controls, in part as a favor to Japan.[38]

Sawada Miki took a similar proposal for race-conscious immigration and legislation directly to the US press and public. Wife of one of Japan's senior diplomats, Sawada Renzō, and eldest daughter of Iwasaki Hisaya, prewar president of the Mitsubishi conglomerate, Sawada Miki was born and raised in wealth and power. She climbed to international fame in her own right in the 1950s when she positioned herself as the world's leading expert on *konketsuji* and their care. Her chief qualification was that in 1948, she founded a residential facility for *konketsuji*, the Elizabeth Saunders Home, on her old family estate in Ōiso, south of Tokyo. Although the Home is usually described as an orphanage, most inmates were not children without parents, but rather children deliberately separated from their parents by people hostile to "mixing." Sawada was one such hostile power.

At the occupation's end in 1952, Sawada made her first of many annual trips to the United States to raise funds for her Home and awareness about "orphaned" *konketsuji*. To redress the "tragedy of the offspring of foreign fathers and Japanese mothers," Sawada urged Americans to embrace international adoption.[39] To drive her message home, she deliberately linked her "humanitarian" mission to Cold War paranoia. *Konketsuji* were "shunned by American immigration and adoption procedure," she warned, creating "a situation the Communists easily turn into propaganda." As she lobbied for a quota for *konketsuji*, Sawada advised readers of the *Washington Post* that "any little bit of humanitarianism on the part of the United States would help" to win the Cold War.[40]

Shortly after Congress passed the INA, Sawada began lobbying for a "separate quota" solely for *konketsuji*. In Washington, Sawada met with the head of the State Department's Bureau of Far Eastern Affairs and seven lawyers in the Immigration and Naturalization Service (INS) to argue for a *konketsuji* quota. Her efforts were followed closely in Japan, where *Yomiuri* news printed a photograph of Sawada holding court with white American men in suits and ties, leaning in to capture her every word.[41] Such was Sawada's stature at home and abroad that members of the Diet educational and welfare committees visited the Saunders Home to observe her program for dealing with people they described as "bearing the handicap called mixed-blood child." By December 1952, Sawada was back in Tokyo giving her testimony and advice to legislators in the Diet. Here, too, Sawada argued not for a larger quota for "pure" Japanese to freely emigrate to the United States, but rather for a special quota only for *konketsuji*.[42]

Sawada complained that securing a private bill for each "mixed" child to be adopted by Americans was "almost impossible."[43] In reality, such procedures, while laborious, were becoming routine. Perhaps the first "mixed" child at Sawada's facility to be granted a visa via private bill was "George Lukes, also known as Hideo Shimizu," born of a Japanese mother and Black American father. According to information passed from the Saunders Home to the INS, after the father repatriated, in retaliation for her affair with a Black soldier, "the mother's parents expelled her from their home and she gradually became insane. She was subsequently taken to an institution for the insane." Thus a black-Japanese child with two living parents and living grandparents was transformed into a social orphan. By 1951, Sawada had taken custody of the boy and matched him to a Black American couple in Tokyo, who adopted George née Hideo with the support of Congress and private legislation.[44] From that point forward, Sawada appears regularly in the Congressional record as she facilitates passage of private bills providing visas to *konketsuji*.[45] By September 1953, Congress had passed 349 private bills to grant visas to Japanese nationals who were otherwise legally ineligible to immigrate and settle in the United States. Many of those visas went to "racially" ineligible children adopted by Americans, often *konketsuji*. Yet Sawada wanted to export *konketsuji* more quickly and at larger scale.

A rising tide of trans-Pacific enthusiasm and legislative fatigue regarding such adoptions led Congress in 1953 to pass two new laws providing visas for orphans on a large scale. Public Law 162 allocated five hundred visas to be used by US military or government personnel stationed overseas when they adopted foreign children. Within three months, more than half of those visas had been claimed by US public servants in Japan. Although open to use around the world, consul general Pilcher expected the remainder of those visas to be used up in Japan as well.[46] The 1953 Refugee Relief Act (RRA) created four thousand more visas for foreign orphans. By 1955, it was clear that a high proportion of those visas, too, were being claimed by Americans adopting in Japan. The *New York Times* emphasized that most such adoptees were *konketsuji*.[47] Needless to say, such child migration is not free but rather is "a type of forced migration, since orphans . . . have no control over whether or where they will be moved."[48] Indeed, "mixed blood" orphans' lack of control and liminal legal rights made them tempting targets for Japanese looking to achieve ethnic cleansing through international adoption.

US public law providing visas for foreign orphans made no distinction between those who were "mixed" and those who were not, but Japanese who spearheaded international adoption definitely did. Both of the 1953 laws providing US visas to foreign orphans were interpreted in Japan as tools to solve the "*konketsuji* crisis" rather than as a means of helping Japanese orphans more generally. This bias is all the more striking when one considers that in 1947, the MOW counted 123,511 orphans and homeless children throughout Japan—victims of war, poverty, displacement, and the inadvertent or deliberate dissolution of kinship. Although US adoption of such children did occur, there was limited enthusiasm in Japan for such a solution to a nationwide crisis in child welfare. Regardless of dire conditions, the vast majority of orphaned and unhoused children were kept in Japan.[49] By contrast, the *konketsuji* minority were targeted for export overseas, even when they did have homes and families. Congress never legislated a quota for *konketsuji* in the 1950s, as Sawada and like-minded Japanese demanded. But deliberately race-blind legislation for international orphans, which was applied in racially specific ways on the ground in Japan, obviated the need.

It has often been said that US international adoption of children from Asia started in Korea. Public Law 162 has repeatedly been mischaracterized as designed to meet demand to adopt by US troops stationed in Korea.[50] In fact, almost all adoptees under that law were from Japan; zero were from Korea. Adoption from Korea did commence under the subsequent RRA, but adoptees from Japan and the Ryukyu Islands still outnumbered them by three to one. By 1953, the majority of US international adoption involved children of formerly excluded Asian "races" and "mixes" (whereas European children had predominated in earlier years), with adoptees from Japan by far the most numerous.[51] Heedless of these early facts, historian Huping Ling sums up the historical consensus as follows: "The transnational transracial adoption of Asian children in the United States began with the adoption of the Korean War orphans."[52]

This misimpression is likely fueled by later developments. As Japan's economy boomed in the late 1950s, the supply of homeless and orphaned children sharply declined. Economic recovery reinforced the already pronounced reluctance in Japan to export "pure" children to be raised by foreign families. And there were never many "mixed" children in Japan available for adoption to begin with—certainly not enough to sustain large-scale international adoption for decades to come. So Americans, who by the mid-1950s had developed both a taste and infrastructure for such adoptions, turned to a new source: postcolonial Korea.

When Korea was a colony, nationalists resisting "fusion" with Japan propounded a *minzoku* consciousness centered on pride in pure Korean blood and decried "mixture" with foreign races—above all the Japanese colonizers. "Blood purity" functioned as a biopolitical form of resistance to imperialism (chapter 1). In the wake of Japan's expulsion and US and Soviet intrusion into the peninsula in 1945, "pure blood," far from fading away, became the dominant vision of the Korean *minzoku* (K. *minjok*), propounded by Korean politicians and race scientists alike.[53] In the transition from empire to Cold War, Japanese and Koreans embraced mimetic norms of "pure blood" under shared geopolitical influences.[54] The main target for exclusion from "blood" ties in this new era of Korean history was no longer the Japanese, but rather Allied forces, predominately Americans, who arrived in Korea in late summer 1945 to dismantle the Japanese Empire and stayed on to fight the Korean War and Cold War. As in Japan, so too in Korea in the late 1940s and 1950s, *konketsuji* born of foreign fathers were repudiated as violations of national chastity and racial purity. Americans responded to the outcry in Korea in the same way they had already responded to the same outcry in Japan: international adoption.[55]

International adoption emerged as a trans-Pacific process engaging all three countries, yet in writing the history of international adoption, Japan has all but been written out. Historian Arissa Oh suggests that Japan "did not seem to demonstrate the same desire to be rid of GI babies" as

Korea and prioritized nondiscrimination and support for the mothers of *konketsuji* over international adoption. Based on this misimpression, Oh concludes that Korea was "the place where organized, systematic international adoption began."[56] Anthropologist Eleana Kim acknowledges that Japanese adoptees preceded Korean adoptees into the United States, only to downplay their significance with the claim that "these first transracial intercountry adoptions did not become the object of media attention."[57] She frames US adoptions of Japanese children as private acts, estranged from biopolitics, which left no significant marks in politics or culture on either side of the Pacific.

In reality, newspapers around the world lavished attention on the *konketsuji* crisis. Japan's Ministry of Foreign Affairs carefully tracked international media coverage.[58] Politicians, presses, and publics in the United States were deeply concerned with Japanese orphans and *konketsuji*—categories too often conflated. Americans frequently touted their responsibility to those children and through them, to the "free world" and US allies in Asia. Japanese presses reciprocated by pouring attention on Americans who provided parental care to Japanese children, whether as "spiritual parents" who offered charitable gifts or as legal parents certified through international adoption.[59] Japanese lavished even more attention on Americans who collectively failed to provide for *konketsuji* and to remove these "unwanted" children from Japan.[60]

In many respects, the story of US adoption from Japan closely resembles the story of adoption from Korea. Yet there was a significant difference in how South Korean versus Japanese government and civil society made use of the newfound US willingness to adopt Asia's "unwanted." From the mid-1950s onward, the South Korean government managed both the specific stigma attached to "mixed" children and generalized economic hardship by encouraging Americans to adopt "pure" and "mixed" children alike. Because Japan was by then enjoying an economic recovery built partly on profits from the Korean War, and because Japan was loathe to surrender "pure" children overseas, the number of US adoptions from Korea soon dwarfed those from Japan.

The Korean adoption boom of the mid- to late-1950s was sustained by a capstone act of legislative reform in the United States. In 1961, Congress concluded the postwar era of experimentation in trans-Pacific kinship and migration by amending the INA to erect permanent legal infrastructure for international adoption. As amended, the INA exempted foreign orphans from national quotas and racial blood-quantum counts. The door was now open to unlimited adoption of previously excluded Asian "races" of children and their conversion to US kin and citizens.[61]

International adoption was a trilateral mechanism developed in the 1950s to manage the biopolitical tension of alliance-building between the United States and both postcolonial Korea and postimperial Japan. The latter countries were in the process of redefining themselves, in the wake of collapse of the Japanese Empire, as racially pure. In this racial-nationalist environment, backlash against Korean and Japanese women's liaisons with multiracial US troops was harsh. International adoption mediated between the reality that "mixture" was ongoing under new Cold War alliances and the sexist and racial-nationalist backlash against that fact. Despite shared racism and hostility to "miscegenation" across the Pacific, that backlash was far stronger in Korea and Japan than in the United States. If not orphans in fact, many *konketsuji* were orphans by design, systematically stripped of kinship by their countrymen and women to make them available for international adoption.

ORPHANING *KONKETSUJI*

No one played a larger role in promoting international adoption and stripping *konketsuji* of kin ties to Japan than did Christian philanthropist Sawada Miki. Japan was awash in more than 123,000 war orphans and other homeless children by the time she founded her Saunders Home in 1948.[62] However numerous they were or severe their needs, the "pure" majority of homeless and kinless children in Japan found no succor at the Saunders Home. The Home was a facility that gathered up *konketsuji* alone, segregating them from other Japanese children and from their families and preparing them for export overseas.

Sawada and her Home became famous in Japan and internationally in no small part because she was a relentless self-promoter. It made a world of difference that Sawada, as a Mitsubishi heiress and diplomat's wife, had savvy, confidence, political connections, and experience in overseas travel and that she was conversant in English. Who else would US journalists interview than the bilingual and peripatetic Sawada Miki? Who else would US church groups and clubs of officers' wives invite to speak about the *konketsuji* crisis and its purported solution: international adoption? No one made herself more accessible, nay inescapable, than Sawada Miki. In 1966, she received an award from the Japanese prime minister; in 1989, she made one list of women who "devoted their lives to love of humanity"; and twenty years later, she was again celebrated in a TV Tokyo documentary for the "paradise" she bestowed upon *konketsuji*.[63] Decades after her death, she continues to enjoy the deference of scholars such as historian Kamita Seiji, who much like earlier generations, tends to take her rendition of events and of her selfless action on behalf of "orphans" at something like face value.[64] Sawada's primary historical role, however, was not that of a humble caregiver for needy children. Rather, she played a leading role in severing *konketsuji* from kin ties in Japan and fostering an ethic and practice of ethnic cleansing.

Sawada's first book, published in 1953, contains the following anecdote. A Japanese woman and her son had recently appeared at the Saunders Home with an infant in their arms. Neither was the parent of that infant and neither had the legal right to dispose of it. They explained their reasons for bringing it to the Home as follows: The infant had been born to the woman's daughter, the man's sister; it was a *konketsuji*; they "don't need it" and the "neighbors don't like it." Sawada took the infant and followed the legal procedures appropriate for an abandoned child, creating a new household registry (household of one) and assigning the infant a new name. Shortly thereafter, the infant's young mother, having learned from her kin what had become of it, arrived to reclaim her baby. Sawada turned the mother away. A few days later, the mother came back to demand her baby once more. At this insistence on maternal rights, Sawada erupted. She berated the young mother, demanding that she "learn shame," and refused to return the baby. Instead, Sawada threatened to involve the police and to lie to them to the mother's detriment. "If you say it's your own child, you'll be detained for abandonment. If you want it at all costs, file a civil suit after you've taken your punishment."[65]

This threat was levied against a naïve young girl with no family to support her and no ready access to legal counsel. It was levied by a matron born into Japan's wealthiest nonroyal family, whose social calendar across her lifetime included birthdays with the emperor, tea with the prime minister, dinner with the Rockefellers, and dancing at Buckingham Palace. The differential in power between the two women was vast. So too was the differential in each woman's moral standing in the eyes of Japanese society. Sawada Miki was a folk hero engaged in "saving" children from unchaste, unfit, miscegenating mothers, whereas the mother was subject to abuse in exactly those terms. This was uneven combat, and Sawada was playing to win. Her threat had its intended effect. The young mother desisted, and her kidnapped child was rendered an orphan.[66] The actions that Sawada so proudly described were baldly duplicitous and plainly illegal. But Sawada recounted the tale in the expectation that 1950s Japanese readers would approve her strong-arm tactics for orphaning *konketsuji* and retaliating against their mothers; and for the most part, it appears they did.

This hostility to kinship presents a paradox, as Sawada's first book is designed as a hymn to "motherly love" (*boseiai*). Indeed, Sawada stakes her postwar claim for public virtue and status in her assumption of the role of "loving mother" to *konketsuji*. Sawada performs a curious dance, insisting that no one, least of all their mothers, wanted *konketsuji* to come into the world. As evidence, she repeatedly insists that *konketsuji* are born of botched abortions or an inability to afford such procedures. Time and again, she describes all her wards as "children who were born uninvited and unloved." At other times, she defines a "mixed" child as "the wages of sin" born to a promiscuous mother.[67]

Yet Sawada also dwells on tales of mothers who love their *konketsuji*, sacrifice for them, and are unwilling to part with them. On its most basic level, Sawada's insistence on "motherly love" works to prove the moral superiority of Japan, embodied in loving women, over the United States, embodied in callous men. Her later books had a different focus, but in 1953, at the peak of the early backlash against "blood mixing" and *Anpo*, Sawada depicted *konketsuji* as overwhelmingly fathered by US soldiers and those soldiers as reprobates and absentees.

"Motherly love" plays a far more subtle and important role in Sawada's first and most famous book than simply elevating Japan over America in a performance of victimhood nationalism. Paradoxically, Sawada deploys "motherly love" to validate the dissolution of Japanese kin ties for *konketsuji*. For if most mothers selflessly love the *konketsuji* they have placed in the Saunders Home, as Sawada claims, then this relinquishment functions as evidence that *konketsuji* are better off institutionalized than with their mothers. Sawada deploys anecdotes and excerpts from her correspondence to make just this point. She cites one Tokyo mother who wrote of how people were so intolerant of her "mixed blood" daughter that she contemplated "jumping into a river holding her and leaving this world together." Both mother and daughter were relieved of their burdens at the Home. Another

ORPHANS BY DESIGN

FIGURE 6.2. Sawada Miki, center, holds a "mixed" child while other social orphans convene in the foreground at the Elizabeth Saunders Home. Photograph by Margaret Bourke-White, 1952.

mother writes from Ibaraki: "For my child's sake I have to put him in your Home. I know very, very well that that's his path to happiness." Still another mother, after surrendering her child to Sawada, declares that "I have no regrets." She knew that *konketsuji* at the Home "are being raised ... wanting for nothing in a flower garden in a dream country, so I'm happy."[68] This Edenesque description, disturbingly divorced from the realities of institutionalized care, was offered by Sawada in stark contrast to carefully selected accounts of the miseries of families who kept and raised their *konketsuji*.

Sawada describes mothers who endured rude clerks when shopping, mothers evicted by their landlords, a mother fired after giving birth to a black *konketsuji*, a pregnant woman whose parents "disown the daughter in front of their ancestors," and other such acts as "the things you would naturally expect to happen." Discrimination, harassment, bullying, unemployment, kinlessness, homelessness—such were the punishments "naturally" inflicted on Japanese woman who "mixed blood" with U.S soldiers and on their children, too. Some of these women contacted Sawada in search of a confidant or advisor, a sensei who could offer expert knowledge and compassion. The specific crises faced by each mother varied, but Sawada took every opportunity to inform a doubtful mother that she and her *konketsuji* would be happier if they never met again. She traveled to Osaka to meet one such mother and "persuade her that for the child's sake, giving up her child now would be the best avenue." Yet the mother resisted. "Though logically she knew I was right, when it came to letting go of a child she had raised to the age of seven, her feelings wouldn't permit it. I had to go home empty-handed."[69]

Often, to smooth the path to relinquishing a child, Sawada counseled mothers to cut ties with the fathers, always on the premise that foreign men were never loyal. Sawada explained her plan to worm her way into one woman's confidence and break her family apart as follows. "I won't tell her now to forget the man, but . . . she must start again. To that end, I'll become her advisor. I'll take her child too." In another case, Sawada exchanged letter after letter with a young mother who was adamant that she wanted to keep her "mixed blood" child and let the father help raise him. Impatiently Sawada insisted, "Give up on that man already! And you know you should, so bring the child to me." After months of what can only be described as bullying, the young mother finally bowed to pressure from Sawada and her disapproving parents and relinquished her son to the Home.[70]

Afterward, the grandmother wrote to Sawada to express her thanks for restoring her daughter's future and family's honor by removing the *konketsuji*. She predicted that her husband, a public official who had utterly rejected his "mixed" grandchild, would overcome his rage and revoke his disownment of their daughter in time. With the grandchild gone, the grandmother had gone to visit her bereaved daughter for the first time since the latter gave birth. "Even my daughter has realized that her behavior till now was extremely bad, and as her parent I'm very happy she's resolved upon a new life." Yet purifying their public life of a *konketsuji* was insufficient to erase him from his mother's heart. "We talked the whole night through, and my daughter's grief at being parted from her boy is powerful. She doesn't have much appetite, she's vacant and depressed with no interest in doing anything." This grandmother's testimony to the trauma inflicted on mothers bereaved of their "mixed" children put Sawada on high alert. There was a real risk this loving mother would come to the Home to recover her child. Within a few days, before the grieving mother had a chance to act, Sawada gave her baby to an adoptive couple to "raise him into a fine American citizen."[71]

Sawada tended not to tell such tales to US journalists. One brief reference to Sawada's efforts to recruit "mixed" children from resistant mothers did appear in the *Los Angeles Times* in 1967, nearly twenty years after Sawada began collecting and exporting *konketsuji*. Even then, neither journalist Don Shannon nor Sawada admitted that she was as willing to kidnap children as to "rescue" them when abandoned.[72] In Japan, by contrast, from the very start, Sawada publicly reveled in destroying bonds between Japanese mothers and "mixed" children. Her fame and influence were built on publicizing such activity.

Legally, mothers who entrusted their children to residential childcare facilities in Japan, including the Saunders Home, maintained parental rights, including the right to visit, the right to reclaim the child, and the right to approve or disapprove any potential adoption.[73] Sawada, however, did her utmost to discourage mothers from exercising those rights and to block every effort to maintain familial bonds. Sawada insisted that her wards call her "Mama" and that they be told "absolutely nothing about their mothers and fathers." In 1951, Sawada published a long list of complaints about mothers who interfered with her plan by visiting their children, providing gifts or food, or (worst of all) taking them back to live at home again.[74] By 1952, Sawada instituted a strict "no visitation" policy. It is remarkable that Sawada was able to violate legal standards for rights of parents and care of children so openly. Sawada's immunity from the law owed something to her social stature, no doubt, but was sustained by hostile public sentiment toward *konketsuji* and their mothers.

Apparently, it was Sawada who created and spread the mythical figure of "two hundred thousand" *konketsuji* born and abandoned by the occupiers in Japan. Long after this number was discredited, she continued to inflate the count to one hundred thousand in overseas wires and fundraising campaigns.[75] According to one of Sawada's biographers, Robert Fish, "Her ability to convince both major and minor American newspapers to reproduce her story (in one almost quoting entirely from her fundraising brochure) verged on public relations genius."[76] That Americans relied on Sawada

Miki as a source of both "facts" and moral guidance does much to explain the absurdly high numbers of *konketsuji* reported in the US press and the persistent conflation of *konketsuji* with orphans whose only hope, news reports alleged, lay in being adopted and becoming foreigners to Japan.

News audiences in Atlanta and Cleveland were advised, citing Sawada, that "there is no future in this island country" of Japan for *konketsuji*. Audiences across the United States were told that such children were categorically "unwanted." The *Los Angeles Times* reported that Sawada took in "abandoned babies," not babies and older children whom she deliberately separated from their grieving mothers.[77] In paperwork filed with Congress, too, Sawada misrepresented the facts, describing each intended adoptee as "abandoned by [the] father and found unwanted by the mother."[78] Sawada, usually portrayed as giving her all to save masses of "unwanted" children from dark fates, was in fact at the very heart of constituting *konketsuji* as a numerically unprecedented national crisis, as racially other, and as kinless and in need of international adoption.

As soon as Sawada founded her Home in 1948, she started sowing these seeds through direct mail campaigns to US and European audiences and interviews with US correspondent in Tokyo, Darryl Berrigan.[79] Berrigan was an important outlet for Sawada in these early years, given that Supreme Commander for the Allied Powers (SCAP) censorship was still in effect in Japan and that SCAP permitted few Japanese to travel overseas, delaying Sawada's blitz on US media, lobbying in Washington, and in-person public speaking campaign to summer 1952. Berrigan began laying the groundwork for Sawada years earlier, when Japan was still under occupation. In 1948, in what appears to be the first "*konketsuji* crisis" style of report to US audiences, Berrigan alleged something he could not prove: that Japanese mothers do not want their *konketsuji* and "usually attempt to hide the child's paternity or kill or abandon it." Berrigan duly quoted colonel Crawford Sams on SCAP's decision to treat *konketsuji* like any other Japanese. Sams furthered argued, drawing on imperial precedents, that "Japanese are not a race" but rather a "mixture," and that "there've been Eurasians in Japan for many years. They've not been a problem at all." Berrigan undercut Sams's case for integration by citing at greater length Sawada Miki and like-minded Japanese activists who promoted a more pessimistic outlook on *konketsuji*. "We want to keep them separated from the pure Japanese ... and, if possible, send them back to the United States and Britain."[80] The idea that *konketsuji* could be sent "back" to foreign countries, as if they were immigrants rather than native born Japanese, speaks volumes about the racial borderlines being drawn through "mixed" bodies.

As SCAP censorship waned in the final years of occupation, the first incendiary reports appeared in Japanese presses defining *konketsuji* as a burgeoning national crisis. From the postcensored article in the centrist journal *Flag* in 1949 to the uncensored report in the communist organ *Red Flag* in 1950 (chapter 5), these early reports drew heavily on information from Sawada and her facility in Ōiso. Reporter and critic Kanzaki Kiyoshi complained in 1953 that "Japan's journalists became utter slaves to the broadcasts from Ōiso, and spread the story of 200,000 *konketsuji*" that Sawada fed them. Beyond the "sensationalism of journalism," which prioritized selling copy above confirming the facts, Kanzaki also blamed the success of Sawada's misinformation campaign on the "social atmosphere in which everyone wanted to believe the story of 200,000 *konketsuji*."[81] Kanzaki denounced this collective will to misinform and misbelieve in the aftermath of the emergence of amply disconfirming evidence, when repeated MOW studies found only a few thousand *konketsuji* nationwide. Nevertheless, the record was never quite set straight. The rest, as they say, is history.

By her own account of her confrontations with SCAP in 1948, Sawada was perhaps the first person to demand that the US military remove all *konketsuji* from Japan. Nullification of matrilineal bonds with *konketsuji* was more an advantage than a drawback to this plan. In the absence of such a policy of ethnic cleansing enforced by an occupying power, the Saunders Home provided Sawada a smaller-scale venue for excising *konketsuji* from kinship and country. On occasions when Japanese inquired about adopting a "mixed" child from the Home, Sawada refused.[82] Over thirty years of operation, sixteen hundred *konketsuji* passed through the Home; none was ever adopted in Japan. Roughly eight hundred were dispatched overseas, principally as adoptees to the United States.[83]

Sawada also established a labor colony in Brazil so that *konketsuji* could migrate there as they matured. She started planning the Brazilian colony as soon as she established the Home, knowing that Americans would not adopt all her wards. Brazil had long been a preferred site of emigration from Japan, particularly after Canada and the United States shut their doors to Japanese immigrants at the turn of the twentieth century.[84]

As an imperial diplomat's wife during the war, Sawada had attended a sending-off ceremony for a group of war orphans dispatched by the MOW to Brazil. Sawada admitted it was not clear whether those orphans migrated "as adopted children or as laborers." The distinction may indeed be moot. As historian Tsuchiya Atsushi observes, Japan's "foster parent system was often administered for the aim of employing children's labor power."[85] The wartime exportation of war orphans was a useful model for Sawada, but there would be no ambiguity over labor versus kinship in her emigration plan, as she made no effort to find adoptive families for *konketsuji* in Brazil.

Sawada secured an untouched swath of Amazonian jungle for her wards to clear and convert into a segregated settlement and a profit-turning plantation. Dubious of this plan, the Brazilian government rejected a number of the *konketsuji* Sawada dispatched as "unsuitable for agricultural labor." The "mixed blood" teenagers who made it to Sawada's plantation proved unwilling to endure the hard conditions there. The settlement collapsed within a few years of its launch in the early 1960s as all but one *konketsuji* left for other farms or prowled from city to city scrounging work in bars, looking for ways to feed and house themselves, learning Portuguese, and building community as best they could. As in so many things *konketsuji*, a hierarchy of race more finely divided than "non-Japanese" was at work in the Brazilian plantation plan. Sawada began planning it upon taking in her first black *konketsuji*, selecting him for tropical labor before he was two years old.[86]

In 1952, Takasaki Setsuko, a member of the board at the Saunders Home, published a widely read book titled *Konketsuji*. Within a year, her book was remade as a movie under the same title by left-wing filmmaker Sekigawa Hideo, shortly before he released the equally political film *Hiroshima*. A commotion commenced in the Diet when teachers in Yamaguchi showed *Konketsuji* to elementary school children in what was decried as "red education" aimed at "planting anti-foreign thought in innocent children."[87] Neither Takasaki nor Sawada were "reds" by any stretch of the imagination, but the easy conversion of their conservative Christian narrative about *konketsuji* into left-wing propaganda is further testimony to the convergence of the right and left in postwar Japan in lionizing national chastity and demonizing "blood mixing."

The success of Takasaki's book, and the movie based on it, elevated her to a position of lasting influence in Japanese public discourse. She was perhaps second only to Sawada as a propagandist for exporting "mixed" children, especially black-Japanese children, overseas. Takasaki grossly exaggerated the numbers of such *konketsuji*, alleging that forty thousand black children had been born in Japan since 1945. She upbraided Japan's government for failing to arrest this alleged reproductive disaster, and she amplified the sense of crisis by insisting that black *konketsuji* were generally born of rape. "Their violence overflows," she wrote of Black GIs, "and this is how black Japanese are born, mutated *konketsuji* with crinkled hair and skin the color of pale ink." Whatever the circumstances of their conception, the fact that "so many *konketsuji* of Negro and Anglo-Saxon lineage have been born, are now being born, and will be born in the future too" was "a new experience for Japan, like a thunderclap from a clear sky."[88] Takasaki presented "blood mixing" as a novel and extreme situation demanding a novel and extreme solution: international adoption.

Takasaki's book *Konketsuji* sold well and was promoted as an accurate record of the titular problem by diverse opinion leaders. One was left-leaning reporter Kanzaki Kiyoshi, a prominent opponent of US bases and prostitution in Japan. Kanzaki only later realized, to his chagrin, that the record on *konketsuji* was being systematically distorted by such spokeswomen for the Saunders Home. Other promoters of Takasaki's book were less inclined to recant: prize-winning fiction writer Hirabayashi Taiko, also active in the antibase movement; literary scholar Itagaki Naoko; and the scientific journal *Heredity*.[89]

The editors of *Heredity* published a series of studies of *konketsuji* after the war that defined them as dysgenic and non-Japanese. Many such race-scientific studies were in fact conducted on inmates at the Saunders Home.[90] Sawada Miki admitted that parents would probably not approve of subjecting their children to such research, but she rationalized doing so by speculating that such was God's plan. Since "healthy children" could not fill the need, she quipped, God must have placed dysgenic *konketsuji* on earth to help train doctors.[91]

Whatever God's intentions, Sawada and Takasaki's success in shaping the scholarly and popular narrative about the *konketsuji* is indisputable. Latter-day scholars continue to cite Takasaki's book as factual.[92] This lasting reverence for a dubious source is all the more remarkable given that Takasaki admits that the book contains "some fiction," and that what is not overt fiction is a mélange of reportage, untruths, and negrophobia.[93] Some of the enduring and uncritical citation of Takasaki and Sawada may be explained by what anthropologist John Russell describes as Japan's "denial" regarding domestic racism toward Black people.[94] Worse even than denial, such citation reflects the extent to which anti-Black racism is naturalized and approved.

In 2000, the city of Yokohama published an official history that cites Takasaki without qualms or qualification. Takasaki discussed the city of Yokahama at length, noting that her Yokohama neighbor's "mixed" child inspired her to start writing *Konketsuji*.[95] Five decades later, the authors of the city's official history cite Takasaki and follow her lead in depicting "mixed" children as a shock to the postwar system. In terms that mirrored her own, they wrote: "Whether they were of Anglo-Saxon or Negro descent, the prospect that mixed-blood children would be born and live their lives in Japan was something that had not even been imagined until then."[96]

How can we make sense of this claim, so dismissive of the long transwar history of "mixing" in Japan? Yokohama was one of the first of new Japanese ports opened to foreigners in the 1850s (figure 6.3). In the preceding centuries, Dutch, Chinese, and other foreign traders had been confined to encamping and "mixing blood" in the southerly port of Nagasaki.[97] From the 1850s onward, Yokohama and similar ports were designed and built with both international trade and interracial sex in mind. Brothels for foreign men and the practice of intermarriage were built into treaty-port life from the beginning. Hence by the early twentieth century, Yokohama was the home turf of many "mixed blood" children. "Mixed" celebrities, such as film star Egawa Ureo (1902–1970) and author Hirano Imao (1900–1986), emerged from this milieu and climbed to fame in Japan's imperial era.

Yet rather than attend to such realities and document the "mixed" celebrities and society born of the first century of mixed life in this vibrant port town, the City of Yokohama chose to repeat misinformation from Takasaki Setsuko. The official history of Yokohama reiterates her fantastic claim that before defeat in World War II, no one had imagined "mixed blood" children of white or black parentage could be born and live their lives in Japan. In such ways, the postwar myth that "blood mixing" was a novelty and threat to Japan under occupation and *Anpo* is consolidated and perpetuated in the twenty-first century.

In the face of such protestations of novelty and "crisis" and bald denial that they had even existed in the imperial era, "mixed blood" adults such as Egawa and Hirano recalled that "there were quite a lot of us" in port towns like Yokohama early in the twentieth century. In 1953, these "mixed" adults founded the 1953 Society to raise awareness of the long history of "mixed blood" Japanese. Because they were already famous, these "mixed" adults could grab the microphone to rebut their erasure, reminding any

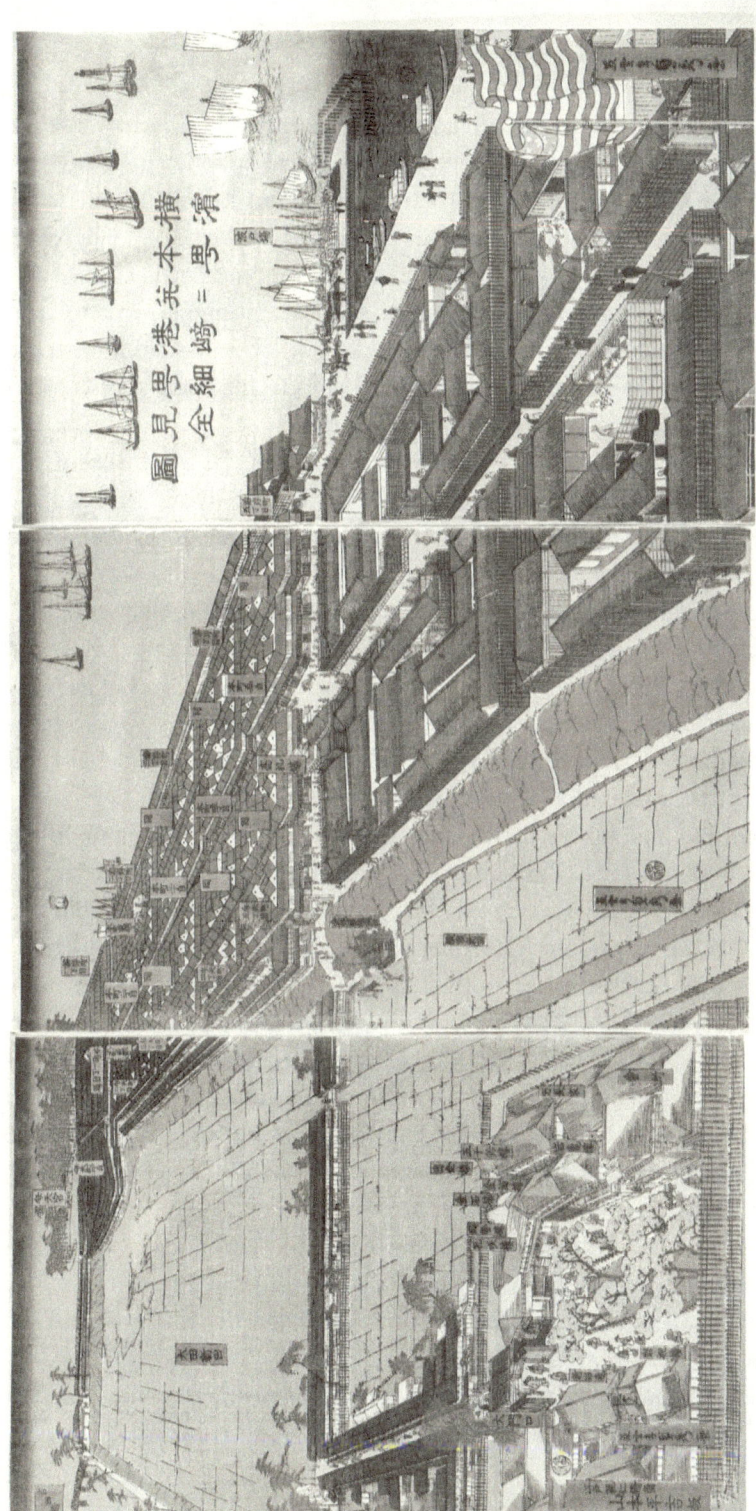

FIGURE 6.3. This woodblock print shows the port of Yokohama in 1860. The US flag is pictured flying in the bottom right, opposite the Miyozaki sex district pictured in the bottom left. Interracial sex with Americans is already vividly imagined, planned for, and profited from at the city's founding. "Mixed blood" children, however, were not made the target of nationwide outcry until ninety years later. "Detailed Print of Yokohama Honchō and the Miyozaki District," Utagawa (Gountei) Sadahide, 1860. Courtesy of the Metropolitan Museum of Art.

audience they could muster that Japan had been multiracial for many years. In this and other ways, they strove to shield *konketsuji* and their mothers from a rising tide of disinformation, discrimination, and exclusion.

Hirano publicly repudiated Sawada's methods at the Saunders Home, protesting that she treated *konketsuji* "like trash" she had to clean up. Resisting international adoption as the cleaning solution, Hirano labored to keep *konketsuji* in the country and in the care of their oft-maligned mothers—mothers like his own. He also promoted domestic adoption and adopted "mixed" children.[98] In 1967, Hirano published a history of "blood mixing" in Japan stretching back into the seventeenth century. He insisted that "*konketsuji* were living" in Japan then and "they'll go on living" in Japan. He challenged his fellow Japanese to abandon "racial prejudice" and embrace their "mixed" conationals.[99]

It was a tough sell. The voices of "mixed" adults arguing that "mixture" and inclusion were a proud part of Japan's heritage tended to be swamped by the voices of people such as Sawada Miki and other advocates of postimperial purity. An indifferent or hostile majority of "Japanese" were refashioning themselves as pure precisely by marginalizing "mixed" people and forgetting their own "mixed" history.

Takashi Fujitani argues that a transwar methodology "allows us to see 1945 as a junction for exchanges among the empires that had been at war with each other."[100] *Konketsuji* put into circulation through new circuits of international adoption were one such object of exchange. Junctions between empire circa 1945 are both ideological and embodied, as the shifting fates of "mixed" and "mixing" families goes to show.

After World War II, the United States struggled to shake off its white-supremacist roots and redefine itself as "universal-imperial" rather than as "particular-national." Postimperial Japan moved in the opposite direction, renouncing universalist ambitions in favor of nationalistic particularism.[101] This nationalist particularism was rooted in racial and eugenic thought. It entailed racist and sexist hostility to "mixing" and a politics of forgetting that Japan had always been "mixed" and always would be. In reality, neither country on opposite sides of the Pacific has a monopoly on "mixture," on backlash against border-crossing women and their children, or on the forgetfulness that undergirds nations and empires. We are all still living in a world of uncertain biopolitical borders and mixed-up nationalistic amnesia.

Afterword

RACE AND THE MYTH OF "ABSENT NATIONALISM" IN POSTWAR JAPAN

Historian Maruyama Masao (1914–1996) achieved a rare degree of fame and public influence in 1946, just months after Japan's surrender in World War II, when he began publicly to reconceive the history and future of Japanese nationalism. Such was the impact of his ideas, not only in the immediate postwar moment but also for decades to come, that Maruyama was said to have appeared "'like a comet' . . . to illuminate the devastated intellectual landscape."[1] The pattern of light and shadow that Maruyama's ideas cast over that postwar landscape are too widely studied to require detailed exposition. But one of his assertions merits careful consideration in light of the "crisis of mixed-blood children" that erupted in Japanese politics and presses in 1952. For in the aftermath of defeat and surrender, Maruyama declared "nationalism nonexistent"[2] in Japan.

The reality is that nationalism in Japan never went away. Yet Maruyama's formulation of "nationalism nonexistent" (*nashonarizumu fuzai*) has proven persistent and persuasive. Historian Tsuda Michio confirms that Maruyama's thesis of non-nationalism has become the "greatest common denominator" among many theorists of postwar Japan. Although critics asserted that nationalism had not so much vanished as gone dormant in the wake of defeat, Tsuda correctly notes that this perspective is but a few steps removed from Maruyama's initial formulation.[3]

In the same vein, sociologist John Lie has theorized a postwar "nullity of Japaneseness." In a discussion that draws heavily on Maruyama's oeuvre, Lie asserts that "the dominant discourses in the 1950s negated or nullified the idea of Japan and emphasized instead the shortcomings that had led to the fiasco of militarism and ultranationalism." Lie's analysis of "monoethnic ideology" in Japan is generally excellent. But in his terse discussion of the early postwar years, one detects a crucial slippage. Lie projects Maruyama's own fierce critique of "the shortcomings that had led to the fiasco of militarism and ultranationalism" onto everyone around him as a consensus position that would negate any positive sense of Japaneseness among postwar Japanese.[4] Anthropologist Harumi Befu makes a similar misstep when he claims that "a few examples" of utterances by early postwar leftists and liberals such as Maruyama "will suffice" to prove that Japanese people rejected everything Japanese during the Allied occupation and for roughly twenty years after defeat. In the place of Japaneseness, people in postwar Japan allegedly embraced the West and the United States in particular.[5]

Analyses like these entirely overlook victimhood nationalism, the scientific nationalism documented by Hiromi Mizuno, and the "anti-American nationalism" of Japan's early postwar left, documented in detail by Oguma Eiji and Hasegawa Kenji.[6] This is the same left responsible for the attack on "traditional Japan" that scholars such as Befu and Lie highlight as a pivotal postwar force, only to equate that antitraditionalist stance with a rejection of all things Japanese and adulation of all things foreign. The fact that left-leaning Japanese rejected certain elements of "tradition," above all the emperor system and militarism, tells us not that they were rejecting the nation but that they were rejecting its former failed leadership. They were engaging in antistate nationalism, salvaging *minzoku* from the ruins of empire and a failed state so as to reestablish nationalism on what seemed to them more solid ground.

In key respects, their efforts resemble those of South Korean activists in the 1980s who redeployed nationalism against an authoritarian state to undermine dictatorship and elevate "we the people" as moral and political sovereigns.[7] Yet unlike Korean democratic activists in the 1980, Japanese liberals and leftists theorized and mobilized antistate nationalism only after domestic dictatorship had been toppled by foreign armies in 1945.

The paradox of early postwar antistate nationalism is that it fostered both pro- and antiforeign sentiment, depending on political context. Initially

AFTERWORD

after Japan's government surrendered, left-leaning Japanese hailed Allied forces as liberators. By the early 1950s, however, as the Cold War heated up, they repudiated as imperialists the Americans who had formerly been liberators. From the 1950s onward, antistate nationalism converged with anti-American nationalism as left-wing nationalists aimed to salvage the "people" from the damage sustained under decades of imperialism—first Japanese and now American.

Who were these "people" the postwar nationalists sought to save? Not an endlessly "mixed" and "mixing" people, but rather a people sharply bounded against foreign others, including former colonial peoples. Of the postwar rebirth as independent nation-states of Japan and Korea, constitutional scholars Chaihark Hahm and Sung Ho Kim note that "founding periods are times when the boundary of 'We the People' undergoes redefinition, sometimes quite radically. They are also times when calls for absolute autonomy, understood as a categorical rejection of all external others, are made most vehemently, precisely because the boundary lines that define the people [are] unsettled."[8] Tolerance for "mixed" and "mixing" people hit an all-time low in both countries in this historical context. Japan's early postwar "We the People" rejected multiethnicity and multiraciality *both* as undesired remnants of a failed empire *and* as injuries inflicted by an American empire on a victimized nation unable to secure its sexual borders.

The rapid postwar transition from a nationalism centered on the military and emperor to a nationalism arrayed against them suggests that the emperor and state had not been the sine qua non of nationalism in Japan to begin with. During the war, the emperor was already competing for primacy as the glue that held the empire together with "blood" as the evolutionary and spiritual essence of the *minzoku*. For nationalists, the emperor had been a useful symbol to rally around, but only one among many; when he ceased to be useful after defeat 1945, left-wing and liberal nationalists were quick to displace him. In rejecting the emperor, they did not reject the nation.

With the new constitution enacted in 1947 and a democratic ethos ascendant, Japanese were transformed from subjects (*shinmin*) to citizens (*kokumin*). In this new milieu, Japan's postwar right, which retained the emperor as a symbol of Japanese unity and uniqueness, nonetheless fully embraced "blood" as a primary value and measure of *minzoku*. This despite the fact in the heyday of empire, imperialization (*kōminka*) made loyalty to the emperor the only requirement for becoming Japanese. In the postwar era, however, such voluntary or coerced attainment of Japaneseness by people of foreign "blood" was rejected by the right as well as left in favor of a closed racial community. The result was that the emperor took a few forced steps back while "blood" took center stage in conceptions of Japanese identity. "Blood talk" fortified Japaneseness against potentially dangerous outsiders and internal others, ranging from formerly colonized Koreans to colonizing Americans and their widely despised offspring, *konketsuji*.[9]

As the emperor and empire moved from the center of Japanese discourse, blood and birth became central to an unprecedented degree. Tropes of racial chastity and "pure blood" signified in the postwar era, much as the emperor had done in the past, a long and glorious tradition of Japaneseness. The alleged continuity of "pure" bloodlines in Japan projected the postwar *minzoku* back into the incalculably distant past, rendering Japan eternal and nigh immortal. Despite the pain and ignominy of slaughter, defeat, and occupation, and despite reforms forced from above and outside the *minzoku* by authorities in the Supreme Commander for the Allied Powers (SCAP), the symbolism of blood rendered the *minzoku* not new but ancient, not changeable but constant, not subject to foreign influence but innately self-contained and eternally perduring. Japan was a race and territory in which neither foreigner nor half-breed could stake a claim. Except when they did: by force of arms, alliance, interracial sex, and "mixed" childbirth.

It was a time to test loyalties. It was a moment when all Japanese were called upon to decide who they were and where they stood. For some, the early postwar was a time of cosmopolitanism, of embracing the foreigner figuratively or literally. Some Japanese dared to forge fresh life out of the DNA of defeat, making babies and families with occupying soldiers. In the eyes of many other Japanese, such "horizontal collaboration" was unforgivable. The Allied soldier remained an intruder if not an enemy. If an American soldier must be invited in, it was only to keep him from destroying the country by force of superior arms; if his presence must be tolerated, it was only grudgingly; his "mixed" children and Japanese consorts need not be tolerated at all. Ressentiment focused on military and sexual intrusion into the *minzoku* persisted from the early occupation, with its racially targeted campaigns of eugenic abortion and infanticide, into the birthing pains of a contested US-Japan alliance in the 1950s. When the United States retained bases in Japan after the occupation's end in 1952, "liberated" Japanese began using their new freedoms of association and the press to bewail the continued "colonial" presence of their enemy-turned-ally, the United States. A moral panic erupted over *konketsuji* born of that alliance.

A people that had so thoroughly abandoned nationalism, as many scholars claim, would not have protested sexual and military colonization by the United States so bitterly. They would not have decried "*panpan* politics" and demanded "Yankee go home!" in the early 1950s or continued to protest *Anpo* in huge numbers in 1960. Neither would they have protested so strongly the peopling of Japan with "mixed blood" children fathered by men of foreign "races" and defined by postwar logic as genetically foreign, despite their native birth. Fujitani argues that far from being psychologically shattered and politically denationalized after defeat—a collective blank slate devoid of national identity—"elements in the 'Japanese' population who began to regain confidence in themselves as a superior and homogeneous race unleashed a renewed wave of brutality and exploitation against discriminated populations such as Okinawans, ethnic Koreans, and poor women who had been pressured or lured into prostitution." We can add "blood mixing" women and *konketsuji* to the list of minorities against whom an emerging postwar majority discriminated in the process of reconstituting themselves as a "superior and homogenous race."[10]

It appears that even Maruyama did not believe the lesson so many scholars have learned from him: that nationalism was "nonexistent" in postwar Japan. In 1951, he explained that "it would not be quite right to say that the old nationalism has either died out or qualitatively changed. It would be more precise to say that it had vanished from the political surface only to be inlaid at the social base in an atomized form."[11] Far from being convinced that nationalism had perished with the imploding empire, Maruyama saw "atoms" of nationalism scattered across the Japanese islands like radiation. Animating his postwar writings is a palpable fear that someone would gather those atoms together and again engineer them into a weapon of mass destruction.

Tsuda Michio suggests that when Maruyama spoke of "nationalism nonexistent" he really only had educated liberals and leftists like himself in mind. Populist nationalism and the masses were another matter.[12] Yet Maruyama clearly perceived that Japan's left was as susceptible to the radiation sickness of nationalism as anyone else. In 1947 and 1948, the Japan

Communist Party and Marxist intellectuals began proclaiming themselves the vanguard of a "new nationalism" dedicated to the *minzoku* and divested of its old fealty to the emperor and state. In 1951, Maruyama cautioned these leftists that they might be "bewitched" by that old pseudo-scientific term, *minzoku*. If leftists abandoned themselves to enthusiasm for the *minzoku*, Maruyama warned, their "new nationalism will inevitably turn harshly towards reaction and probably revert" to the old fascist mode.[13] Nevertheless, the left doubled down on defending a blood-based *minzoku* amid anti-American struggle.[14]

Fulmination over "blood mixing" proved central to this "new nationalism" centered on the *minzoku*. Although members of the Japan Communist Party were early leaders in this anti-mixing discourse, in the early 1950s, Socialists, right-wing conservatives, and mainstream media eagerly joined complainants on the far left in denouncing foreign enemies and domestic traitors in racialized and sexualized terms. As Maruyama feared, Japanese nationalism was neither gone nor particularly new.

From the imperial era to the Cold War, Japanese nationalists incessantly emphasized their "blood" identity and debated the eugenic and political value of "blood mixing." Japanese men's interracial sexual conduct was more often naturalized or even celebrated, whereas "blood mixing" by Japanese women often sparked anxiety and vituperation. These sexual politics are on dramatic display in the reversal of value assigned to "blood mixing" from largely positive in the imperial era to largely negative in the context of defeat. What did not change is that racism and sexism remained indispensable to Japanese nationhood. The postwar repudiation of *konketsuji* reveals the structuring force of racism and sexual sovereignty in Japanese nationalism.

The moral panic over "blood mixing" with Americans in the early 1950s caused considerable embarrassment to the reigning Liberal Party and its friends in Washington. The US-Japan alliance survived the assault, but in the course of partisan squabbling and media frenzy, considerable harm was done to the "mixed" and "mixing" minority in Japan. Their very Japaneseness was called into question by a rising chorus favoring ethnic cleansing of *konketsuji*, sometimes along with their Japanese mothers, who were repudiated as unfit to live in Japan. Better to expel them to the United States or Brazil.

Nationalists in the democratic 1950s proved no more tolerant of ideological or sexual deviation than wartime nationalists had been. Just as in the empire, so too in a postwar liberal democracy, nationalists felt entitled to treat women as fertile territory to be possessed, guarded, and cultivated or culled as national resources. Japanese women were still expected to perform sex and reproduction for national and eugenic ends and endured public shaming and worse for failure to conform. Some of these women even had their children stripped from them and consigned to orphanages or sent overseas to purify Japan of the "mixed" fruits of their sexual deviance.

The presumption of absent nationalism in postwar Japan leads some scholars to conclude that "the late 1960s" saw the rise of a "new nationalism," which offered for the first time since defeat a "usable narrative of Japanese identity and uniqueness."[15] This usable narrative came in the form of a mass-mediated *Nihonjinron*, a contemporaneous term that literally means "theory of the Japanese people." *Nihonjinron* celebrated Japan as distinct for its racial, cultural, and linguistic homogeneity. Moreover, in an era of vibrant economic growth, *Nihonjinron* attributed the postwar nation's prowess to the "fact" of its racial singularity. A profusion of self-congratulatory nationalistic rhetoric offered exclusivist and essentialized explanations for why the *minzoku* of Japan was so wealthy. Certainly the new prosperity gave Japanese something new to talk about, and it rapidly became a focus of national pride. Yet neither the economic focus nor the celebration of racial homogeneity in the "new nationalism" of the 1960s was truly new.[16]

Rather than inventing sanguinary nationalism from scratch, *Nihonjinron* proponents recycled received wisdom about "blood" and "purity" from their younger days in the 1950s. Some of the luminaries of late twentieth-century *Nihonjinron*, such as right-wing politician Nakasone Yasuhiro, had in fact cut their teeth in the *konketsuji* crisis years before. Other *Nihonjinron* ideologues had grown up in that intellectual milieu, which naturalized obsession with Japanese "blood" as the unifying essence of a nation that must be defended and held apart from outsiders. Once mass prosperity dawned, *Nihonjinron* activists revised the old familiar "blood talk," updating the early 1950s tone of panic in favor of fiscal pride and racial swagger suited to an affluent era. All in all, very little in late twentieth-century *Nihonjinron*, aside from prosperity itself, would have been unfamiliar to early 1950s Japanese.

Japanese in the late twentieth century felt a declining sense of urgency over being "colonized" by the United States. The Liberal Democratic Party (LDP) managed tensions over *Anpo* by concentrating most US bases and protests against them in a single subordinated prefecture: Okinawa.[17] It is now Okinawa where controversies over interracial sex with Americans are most intense.[18] As Japan's economy boomed and the containment of controversy over *Anpo* to Okinawa bore fruit, Japan seemed more and more like an equal partner in the *Anpo* alliance.[19] In much of the country, the hated and feared specter of "'America' as militarized violence" faded from the daily lives of most Japanese. Japanese public opinion toward the United States took a hit every time the United States went to war (in Vietnam, in Iraq) but, overall, favor toward the United States was high.[20] The alliance was working. It helped that memories of the war were fading and that younger generations of Japanese were raised amidst plenty in a world far safer than their parents and grandparents had known.

For leaders like Nakasone, so proud of Japan's "blood," a little "mixing" in Okinawa might seem a low price to pay for riches exceeding the wildest dreams of previous generations of Japanese, cheap security with US support, and an economic superpower status envied around the world. At the peak of his power in the 1980s, the Japanese economy grew so large and rose so far that it seemed poised to eclipse the world. Despite this fact, right-wing politician and "vulgar" racist Ishihara Shintarō complained in a book read around the world that Japan still could not "say no" to the United States.[21] Yet many on both sides of the Pacific had begun to feel that, far from being a colony of the United States, Japan was the stronger of the two.

Perhaps it was the United States that could no longer "say no" to Japan. The strategic imbrication and economic intimacy born of *Anpo* was too central to the American way of politics and way of life. Starting in the occupation, when Washington determined to succor Japan into the capitalist camp in the Cold War, Washington has made economic concessions to Japan in exchange for access to bases. Cash for bases remained the modus operandi undergirding *Anpo* to the end of the century, as Washington tolerated protectionist policies in Japan while throwing open US markets to Japanese manufacturers. President Ronald Reagan's strategy in East Asia depended on *Anpo* and a close working relationship with prime minister Nakasone, that formerly fiery enemy of "blood mixing" with Americans he had insisted were reducing his country to colonial status. By 1985, the US trade deficit with Japan was the largest ever documented between two countries. Japanese economic and security policies reported to be at odds with US interests came in for blistering critique in the United States, especially by Democrats in election years.[22]

AFTERWORD

The 1980s thus brought *Anpo* in for a level of vituperation not seen since its first decade on the world stage, 1951–1960. But this time, it was not Japanese but rather Americans bemoaning that the alliance left them vulnerable, not even sovereign, in an unfair global confrontation with an arrogant and intrusive foreign "race." These debates in the 1980s and early 1990s ushered in a new era of "yellow peril" in US politics and culture. Eminent political columnist Theodore White suggested that Japanese were the real victors in World War II. Some Americans spoke of a new, fiscal Pearl Harbor. Media outlets warned of a resurgent Japanese empire bent on conquering the world with the power of yen. Racist rhetoric and hate crimes against Asian Americans spiked. As Japanese firms bought up land, buildings, factories, and companies in the United States, some decried these maneuvers as threats to US sovereignty and independence. One US governor complained that "we are forming a type of colonial relationship with Japan." This time, Japan was the superrich and predatory colonizer, the United States depleted and on the defensive.[23]

As had been true in Japan in the 1950s and early 1960s, so too in United States in the 1980s and early 1990s, partisan politicians out of power often took the lead in smearing the US-Japan alliance as an offense against national sovereignty. They alleged that the party in power (Liberal, LDP, or Republican) refused to act on behalf of the beleaguered people because powerholders in Tokyo and Washington were more invested in their alliance than in than welfare of the people. In both cases, mass media stirred up moral panic and racialized resentment to boost readership, viewership, and ad sales. In both 1950s–60s Japan and 1980s America, the principle parties out of power were liberal and left-leaning, whereas Cold War conservatives safeguarded the US-Japan alliance from often racist recrimination. History does repeat itself, although it is never exactly the same.

It was in this heated context that prime minister Nakasone added insult to injured US pride, declaring that Japanese preeminence over the United States was thanks to the purity of the Japanese "race." Nakasone deemed Japan happily almost free of minorities and "mixture," whereas Americans were burdened, their prosperity dampened, by an overabundance of the same. Some Japanese were embarrassed by these remarks and did not agree.[24] But Nakasone's controversial comments reflected a deep conviction held by many on both sides of the Pacific that the Japanese are a "race" unlike any other in the world. Historian Michael Heale suggests that for Americans overawed by Japanese accomplishments at the time, "the suspicion that they were some kind of master race could not be so easily shrugged off." Yet despite the prevalence of bilateral and mutually reinforcing racisms, Heale finds Americans largely unswayed by the economic and racial nationalism propounded by Reagan-era Democrats hoping to win elections by painting Japanese as a dangerous race of yen-drunk imperialists. Instead, Americans emerged from the moral panic with a positive view of Japan and of Japan's economic influence on the United States.[25]

The parallel to 1950s Japan is striking. Partisan and mass media clamor alleged that Americans were a dangerous race bent on colonizing and debasing the "blood and soil" of Japan. Yet sociologist Yoshimi Shunya finds that the "majority of Japanese" credited their prosperity after World War II to the United States and embraced a generally positive view of the country.[26] In both cases, despite the racial-nationalist brouhaha fomented by partisan politicians and commercial presses in 1950s Japan and 1980s America, the alliance endured.

As we have seen, Japanese leftists under US occupation proclaimed themselves at the forefront of a "new nationalism," laden though this "novelty" was with inherited notions of "blood," sexual sovereignty, and racial rivalry with Americans. Ever since, declarations of a "new nationalism" rising like a sun over Japan recur with regularity. In 1966, an editorial in the liberal *Asahi shinbun* similarly proclaimed that the time had come for a "new Japanese nationalism" (*atarashii Nihon nashonarizumu*). In 1969, *Asahi* confirmed the newness of its nationalism by emphasizing its utter distinctiveness from the "narrow-minded, self-righteous nationalism" that had ended in the debacle of World War II. Then in the 1980s, Nakasone, the conservative prime minister, announced yet another dawn of a glorious "new nationalism."[27] Foreign observers, too, are party to this false narrative, hailing the twenty-first-century "rebirth of Japanese nationalism" after its supposed demise in 1945.[28] One cannot escape a feeling of déjà vu. It does not seem that nationalism in Japan will stop being "new" anytime soon.

Recurrent denial that proper nationalism predates one's own nationalistic utterance paradoxically appears to be one of the defining features of postwar Japanese nationalist discourse. Disavowal of prior nationalism serves a number of useful ends. It allows one to deny that one's nationalism is a received value. Rather than a hand-me-down from the past, uncritically accepted and blindly parroted, nationalism is thereby rendered something freely chosen and intelligently crafted. Innovation and voluntarism are particularly important values for progressives, liberals, and leftists eager to distance themselves from the discredited "ultranationalism" of the imperial past.

But the right, too, has something to gain in constructing all of Japanese experience from the end of the war to the present as barren of proper nationalism. In doing so, the right can affirm that it is introducing something new and sorely needed, a patriotism tailored to the times. Such right-wing patriotism can conveniently combine narratives of national strength rooted in "blood" with victimization by foreign "races" while exploiting "traditional" gender roles to naturalize its message and soften its image.[29] Whoever thus invents or revives Japanese nationalism gets to be a national hero, at least among his or her own partisans. Needless to say, not all announcements of nationalist recrudescence are made in a positive vein, particularly about a nationalism that differs from one's party line.

It is time to put decisively to rest the notion that Japanese nationalism is in any way absent or underdeveloped. The corollary claim is that the star of a new nationalism is just now lighting up the horizon. This too is a notion, exhausted from constant repetition, that we must finally put to rest. Japanese nationalism with all its apparent discontinuities has followed much the same course as nationalism in any other country. According to historian Frank Tipton, since "Japanese nationhood" debuted on the world stage in the nineteenth century, it evolved "from a state-centered instrument of a modernising elite ... to an identity contested among leaders," both military and democratic, "who aimed to mobilize larger masses of people in the 1920s and 1930s, and finally to a diffuse debate over the 'essence' of Japanese culture in the decades after the Second World War."[30] As agents and power-holders in the domestic debate changed along with Japan's geopolitical situation, nationalism was reconfigured time and again, always with sex at the center. Rather than developing new ideas, postwar nationalists reshuffled the deck, and the value of economy versus military, emperor versus blood, shifts as each new hand is dealt and different players take their turns at calling trump. The deck is little changed from all the wear, and hardly anyone wants to walk away from the game. The blood sport of nationalism remains a popular pastime, in Japan as in most of the modern world.

Arguably, the most significant shift in postwar nationalism was that it sanctified "pure blood." Racial purity could be achieved only by asserting sexual sovereignty and imposing eugenic limits on reproduction. Yet even "pure blood" was not a new idea, but rather a notion debated and transformed over the course of imperial conquest and failure to fuse many peoples into one. At the peak of imperial expansion and global war, Japanese tended to explain both their successes and their failures with reference to "blood." Biological pride in Japan's "mixed blood" explained Japan's supposedly distinct ability to fuse countless races into one harmonious empire. Yet when Chinese defied the Japanese attempt to conquer and absorb them, biological defeatists began revising the old script, redescribing the Japanese "race" as existentially imperiled by "blood mixture" with a racialized Han Chinese enemy.

Postwar racial nationalism was built on these imperial precedents. After Japan's surrender and retreat from the continent, the sense of military and reproductive threat from China faded, only to be supplanted by a new "blood" enemy: the United States. Even as the military surrendered, Japanese patriots demanded that Japanese women remain sexually resistant, sexually pure.

Meanwhile, Japan plunged back into the bitter electoral politics typical of democratic life. Among party politicians out of power, the once-marginal ideal of "pure blood" became suddenly fashionable, because suddenly useful, in partisan power struggles against the dominant Liberal Party with its pro-American platform. The timing and direction of this shift toward purity set the pendulum of racial-nationalist discourse in Japan swinging in the opposite direction of the United States, which attempted to build a multiracial Cold War coalition in the same era.

This exclusionary ethos and "blood" identity, forged in ruins of Japanese Empire, persists in the twenty-first century.[31] Despite the everyday reality of "mixture" and diversity in Japan, the nationalistic rhetoric of "blood" that sparked the "*konketsuji* crisis" in the 1950s, which in turn spawned the "pure" and "homogenous" *minzoku* celebrated in *Nihonjinron*, is still alive and thriving in Japan today.[32] This postwar rise of "pure blood" nationalism speaks less to the essential or peculiar nature of Japan than it does to the historically contingent nature of race, nation, and nationalism everywhere.

NOTES

All Japanese-language books were published in Tokyo unless otherwise noted.

INTRODUCTION

1. On the sovereign "right to make live," see Takashi Fujitani, *Race for Empire: Koreans as Japanese and Japanese as Americans During World War II* (Berkeley: University of California Press, 2011), chap. 1; and Michel Foucault, *The History of Sexuality*, vol. 1, *An Introduction*, trans. Robert Hurley (New York: Vintage, 1990), esp. part 5.
2. Oguma Eiji, *Genealogy of "Japanese" Self-Images*, trans. David Askew (Melbourne: Trans Pacific, 2002); and Oguma Eiji, *The Boundaries of "the Japanese,"* 2 vols., trans. Leonie R. Stickland (Balwyn North, Australia: Trans Pacific, 2014–2017). See also Masataka Endo, *The State Construction of "Japaneseness": The Household Registration System in Japan and Beyond* (Balwyn North, Victoria: Trans Pacific, 2019); and Shimoji Rōrensu Yoshitaka, *"Konketsu" to "Nihonjin": Hāfu, daburu, mikkusu no shakaishi* ["Mixed blood" and "Japanese": a social history of halves, doubles, and mixes] (Seidosha, 2018).
3. Barbara K. Fields and Karen E. Fields, *Racecraft: The Soul of Inequality in American Life* (New York: Verso, 2012), 4.
4. Shimoji, *"Konketsu" to "Nihonjin,"* 68.
5. SCAP refers both to the commander himself and to the occupation administration in its entirety. When MacArthur was relieved of command by president Harry Truman in April 1951, the title of Supreme Commander passed to US Army general Matthew Ridgway.
6. Kanō Mikiyo, "'Konketsuji' mondai to tan'itsu minzoku shinwa no seisei" [The "mixed-blood children" crisis and generation of the myth of the homogenous

INTRODUCTION

nation], in Okuda Akiko et al., *Senryō to sei: seisaku, jittai, hyōshō* [Sex and occupation: policy, reality, representation] (Inpakuto shuppankai, 2007); and Oguma, *Genealogy of "Japanese" Self-Images*.

7. See Amy Stanley, *Selling Women: Prostitution, Markets, and the Household in Early Modern Japan* (Berkeley: University of California Press, 2012); and Yoshiaki Yoshimi, *Comfort Women: Sexual Slavery in the Japanese Military during World War II*, trans. Suzanne O'Brien (New York: Columbia University Press, 2000).
8. Sarah C. Kovner, *Occupying Power: Sex Workers and Servicemen in Postwar Japan* (Stanford, CA: Stanford University Press, 2012); and Lori Watt, *When Empire Comes Home: Repatriation and Reintegration in Postwar Japan* (Cambridge, MA: Harvard University Asia Center, 2009), chap. 3.
9. Matsubara Yōko, "Hikiagesha iryō ni okeru jinkō ninshin chuzetsu" [Artificially induced abortion in the medical care for repatriates], in *Jendā to nama seiji* [Gender and the politics of life], ed. Tsuboi Hideto (Kyoto: Rinsen shoten, 2019), 37–79.
10. Kovner, *Occupying Power*; see also Chazono Toshimi, *Mō hitotsu no senryō: sekkusu to iu kontakuto zōn kara* [The other occupation: from the contact zone of sex] (Inpakuto, 2018); and Michael Molasky, *The American Occupation of Japan and Okinawa: Literature and Memory* (New York: Routledge, 1999).
11. Iris Wigger, *The "Black Horror on the Rhine": Intersections of Race, Nation, Gender and Class in 1920s Germany* (London: Palgrave Macmillan, 2017).
12. Stargardt, "Wartime Occupation by Germany: Food and Sex," in *The Cambridge History of the Second World War*, vol. 2, ed. Richard Bosworth and Joseph Maiolo (Cambridge: Cambridge University Press, 2015), 408; see also Kjersti Ericsson and Eva Simonsen, eds., *Children of World War II: The Hidden Enemy Legacy* (New York: Oxford University Press, 2005).
13. Oguma, *Genealogy of "Japanese" Self-Images* and *Boundaries of "the Japanese."*
14. See Mark E. Caprio, *Japanese Assimilation Policies in Colonial Korea, 1910–1945* (Seattle: University of Washington Press, 2009); Sayaka Chatani, *Nation-Empire: Ideology and Rural Youth Mobilization in Japan and its Colonies* (Ithaca, NY: Cornell University Press, 2018); Leo Ching, *Becoming "Japanese": Colonial Taiwan and the Politics of Identity Formation* (Berkeley: University of California Press, 2001); and Jun Uchida, *Brokers of Empire: Japanese Settler Colonialism in Korea, 1876–1945* (Cambridge, MA: Harvard University Press, 2001).
15. Fujitani, *Race for Empire*.
16. Benedict Anderson, *Imagined Communities: Reflections on the Origin and Spread of Nationalism* (London: Verso, 2006), 7.
17. Naoki Sakai, "Imperial Nationalism and the Comparative Perspective," *Positions: East Asia Cultures Critique* 17, no. 1 (2009): 188.
18. Ishiwara Kanji, "Sekai sensō-kan" [Outlook on world war] (1939), in *Ishiwara Kanji shiryō* [Ishiwara Kanji documents], vol. 2, ed. Tsunoda Jun (Hara shobō, 1967–68), 303–304.
19. Sakai, "Imperial Nationalism," 175.
20. Max Ward, "Crisis Ideology and the Articulation of Fascism in Interwar Japan: The 1938 Thought-War Symposium," *Japan Forum* 26, no. 4 (2014): 473–77.
21. Naoki Sakai, *The End of Pax Americana: The Loss of Empire and Hikikomori Nationalism* (Durham, NC: Duke University Press, 2022), 31.

1. IN PRAISE OF "MIXED BLOOD"

22. On "blood talk," see Jennifer Robertson, "Blood Talks: Eugenic Modernity and the Creation of New Japanese," *History and Anthropology* 13, no. 3 (2002): 191–216.
23. Ministry of Welfare, *Yamato minzoku o chūkaku to suru sekai seisaku no kentō* [Investigation of global policy with the *Yamato minzoku* as the nucleus], vol. 3 (Kōseisho kenkyūjo, jinkō minzokubu, 1943), 2747. John Dower characterizes this multivolume *Investigation* as expressing "the rationale behind policies that were actually adopted toward other races" during the war. See John Dower, *War without Mercy: Race and Power in the Pacific War* (New York: Pantheon, 1986), 263. Oguma Eiji criticizes this argument on the grounds that Dower never addresses the "contradiction" between the segregationist goals outlined in the *Investigation* and actual imperial policies promoting intermarriage and assimilation. Oguma, *Genealogy of "Japanese" Self-Images*, 383n32. *Investigation* can be understood as one expression of the late-war reaction against pro-mixing ideology and practice among MOW officials such as Koya Yoshio (detailed in chapter 2).
24. On population policy, see Fujime Yuki, *Sei no rekishigaku: kōshō seido, dataizai taisei kara baishun bōshihō, yūsei hogohō taisei e* [The history of sex: from the public prostitution system and criminal abortion law to the Prostitution Prevention Law and Eugenic Protection Law system] (Fuji shuppan, 1997); Aya Homei, *Science for Governing Japan's Population* (Cambridge: Cambridge University Press, 2023); Sujin Lee, *Wombs of Empire: Population Discourses and Biopolitics in Modern Japan* (Stanford, CA: Stanford University Press, 2023), and Sidney Xu Lu, *The Making of Japanese Settler Colonialism: Malthusianism and Trans-Pacific Migration, 1868–1961* (Cambridge: Cambridge University Press, 2019).
25. On debates over the translation of *minzoku* and the false dichotomy sometimes drawn between "ethnicity" and "race," see Koichi Iwabuchi and Yasuko Takezawa, "Rethinking Race and Racism in and from Japan," *Japanese Studies* 25, no. 1 (2015): 1–3; Yuko Kawai, *A Transnational Critique of Japaneseness: Cultural Nationalism, Racism, and Multiculturalism in Japan* (Lanham, MD: Lexington, 2020), 8–13; Oguma, *Boundaries of "the Japanese,"* 9–14; and Sakai, "Imperial Nationalism," 183–89.
26. Noriaki Hoshino, "Racial Contacts Across the Pacific and the Creation of *Minzoku* in the Japanese Empire," *Inter-Asia Cultural Studies* 17, no. 2 (2016): 186–205.
27. Dower, *War Without Mercy*, 296–97.
28. Dower, *War Without Mercy*.
29. US Army Forces, Pacific, General Headquarters, CCD, "Code for Japanese Press" (September 21, 1945), in Gordon W. Prange Collection, McKeldin Library, University of Maryland at College Park (hereafter Prange), accessed February 28, 2013, http://www.lib.umd.edu/binaries/content/gallery/public/prange/about-us/censordocs_presscode.jpg.

1. IN PRAISE OF "MIXED BLOOD"

1. Jennifer Robertson, "Hemato-Nationalism: The Past, Present, and Future of 'Japanese Blood,'" *Medical Anthropology* 31 (2012): 99–101.
2. Paul D. Barclay, "Cultural Brokerage and Interethnic Marriage in Colonial Taiwan: Japanese Subalterns and Their Aborigine Wives, 1895–1930," *Journal of Asian Studies* 64, no. 2 (May 2005), 325 et passim. See also Kirsten Ziomek, *Lost Histories:*

1. IN PRAISE OF "MIXED BLOOD"

Recovering the Lives of Japan's Colonial Peoples (Cambridge, MA: Harvard University Asia Center, 2019), 196–223.
3. Oguma Eiji, *Genealogy of "Japanese" Self-Images*, trans. David Askew (Melbourne: Trans Pacific, 2002).
4. Mark Peattie, *Nan'yō: The Rise and Fall of the Japanese in Micronesia, 1885–1945* (Honolulu: University of Hawai'i Press, 1988), 125, 160–61, 208–209, 338n25; and Ziomek, *Lost Histories*, 256.
5. Peattie, *Nan'yō*, 218. Historian David Ambaras explores the "sexualized geopolitics" and "imperialist Japanese male subjectivity" of Andō's wartime travel writing in *Japan's Imperial Underworlds: Intimate Encounters at the Borders of Empire* (Cambridge: Cambridge University Press, 2018), 164–65.
6. Ziomek, *Lost Histories*, 284.
7. Eguchi Tamezō, "Nan'yō ni okeru konketsuji" [Mixed-blood children in the South Seas], *Nihon iji shinpō* [Japan medical news] no. 1008 (January 1942): 51.
8. Oguma, *Genealogy of "Japanese" Self-Images*, 207.
9. Jennifer Robertson, *Takarazuka: Sexual Politics and Popular Culture in Modern Japan* (Berkeley: University of California Press, 1998), chap. 3; Miriam Silverberg, *Erotic Grotesque Nonsense: The Mass Culture of Japanese Modern Times* (Berkeley: University of California Press, 2006), 79–80; Chikako Nagayama, "The Flux of Domesticity and the Exotic in a Wartime Melodrama," *Signs* 34, no. 2 (Winter 2009): 369–95; Takashi Fujitani, *Race for Empire: Koreans as Japanese and Japanese as Americans During World War II* (Berkeley: University of California Press, 2011), 299–374; and Ziomek, *Lost Histories*, 197–223.
10. Sabine Frühstück, *Playing War: Children and the Paradoxes of Modern Militarism in Japan* (Oakland: University of California Press, 2017), 116–46.
11. Ijichi Susumu, "Kōateki konketsuron" [Blood mixing for the development of Asia], *Kaizō* [Reconstruction] 21 (March 1939): 83.
12. Oguma Eiji, *The Boundaries of "the Japanese,"* vol. 1, trans. Leonie R. Stickland (Balwyn North, Australia: Trans Pacific, 2014), 9–14.
13. Sidney Xu Lu, *The Making of Japanese Settler Colonialism: Malthusianism and Trans-Pacific Migration, 1868–1961* (Cambridge: Cambridge University Press, 2019). See also Eiichiro Azuma, *In Search of Our Frontier: Japanese America and Settler Colonialism in the Construction of Japan's Borderless Empire* (Oakland: University of California Press, 2019); and Aya Homei, *Science for Governing Japan's Population* (Cambridge: Cambridge University Press, 2023), 92–129.
14. Ijichi, "Kōateki konketsuron," 84.
15. Azuma, *In Search of Our Frontier*; Emer O'Dwyer, *Significant Soil: Settler Colonialism and Japan's Urban Empire in Manchuria* (Cambridge, MA: Harvard University Asia Center, 2015); Lu, *Making of Japanese Settler*, esp. part 3; and Louise Young, *Japan's Total Empire: Manchuria and the Culture of Wartime Imperialism* (Berkeley: University of California Press, 1998).
16. On pan-Asianism, see Eri Hotta, *Pan-Asianism and Japan's War, 1931–1945* (New York: Palgrave Macmillan, 2007); Sven Saaler and Christopher W. A. Szpilman, eds., *Pan-Asianism: A Documentary History*, 2 vols. (Lanham, MD: Rowman and Littlefield, 2011); and Torsten Weber, *Embracing "Asia" in China and Japan: Asianism Discourse and the Contest for Hegemony, 1912–1933* (Cham, Switzerland: Palgrave Macmillan, 2018).

1. IN PRAISE OF "MIXED BLOOD"

17. Ijichi, "Kōateki konketsuron," 85–86.
18. Osa Shizue, "Kindai Nihon no jinshu/jinshukaron to 'kokusai kekkon' gensetsu no hen'yō" [Modern Japanese theories of race and racialization and transformation in the discourse of "international marriage"], *Jinbun gakuhō* [Humanities review] no. 114 (2019): 171–86.
19. Ijichi, "Kōateki konketsuron," 86.
20. Ijichi, "Kōateki konketsuron," 87-88.
21. Gregory J. Kasza, *The State and Mass Media in Japan, 1918–1945* (Berkeley: University of California Press, 1993), 169–72; on press control violations and punishments, see 225–31.
22. Ijichi, "Kōateki konketsuron," 87-88.
23. *Diplomatic Revue* suspended publication on the brink of Japanese defeat, only to be reborn as a monthly periodical in the 1950s. After a century of shaping public opinion on foreigners and foreign affairs, the journal ceased publication in 1998.
24. See Nanba Monkichi, "Daitōa sensō to jinshu sensen" [Racial battle lines and the Greater East Asia War], *Gaikō jihō* [Diplomatic revue] no. 893 (February 15, 1942): 22–34; "Minzoku no kōbō to jinkō mondai" [Population problems and the rise and fall of *minzoku*], *Gaikō jihō* [Diplomatic revue] no. 805 (June 15, 1938): 57–77; and "Shina minzoku ishiki to Tōa renmei" [Chinese *minzoku* consciousness and East Asian alliance], *Gaikō jihō* [Diplomatic revue] no. 863 (November 15, 1940): 89–103.
25. Nanba Monkichi, "Minzokuteki yūgō no kihon mondai: gengo, konketsu, ijū" [Fundamental problems in racial fusion: language, blood mixing, migration], *Gaikō jihō* [Diplomatic revue] no. 800 (April 1, 1938): 72–83.
26. On Gobineau's reception in twentieth-century German race science, see Robert Proctor, "From *Anthropologie* to *Rassenkunde* in the German Anthropological Tradition," in *Bones, Bodies, and Behavior: Essays on Biological Anthropology*, ed. George W. Stocking, Jr. (Madison: University of Wisconsin Press, 1988), 138–79.
27. Nanba, "Minzokuteki yūgō," 81–83.
28. Nanba, "Minzokuteki yūgō," 86.
29. Ijichi, "Kōateki konketsuron," 88.
30. Nanba, "Minzokuteki yūgō," 85–86.
31. Oguma, *Genealogy of "Japanese" Self-Images*, 265.
32. Watsuji Tetsurō, "Kodai Nihonjin no konketsu jōtai" [The state of blood mixing among ancient Japanese] (1917), in *Watsuji Tetsurō Nihon kodai bunka-ron shūsei* [Watsuji Tetsurō's collected works on Japan's ancient culture] (Shoshi shinsui, 2012), 279–82.
33. Cited in Oguma, *Genealogy of "Japanese" Self-Images*, 162–66, 169–70.
34. Yi Jonson, "'Naisen kekkon' no kodomotachi: naichijin to Chōsenjin no hazama de" [The children of 'interior-Korea marriage': at the interstices of inlanders and Koreans], *Rekishi hyōron* [Historical journal] no. 815 (2018): 47–48.
35. There is no way to quantify *konketsuji* or "mixed" relations, and the pursuit of such numbers risks reifying an ideological construct as a human type. But for a careful study along these lines, see Yi, "'Naisen kekkon.'" See also Masataka Endo, *The State Construction of "Japaneseness": The Household Registration System in Japan and Beyond* (Balwyn North, Victoria: Trans Pacific Press, 2019), chap. 4; and Eika Tai, "The Discourse of Intermarriage in Colonial Taiwan," *Journal of Japanese Studies* 40, no. 1 (Winter 2014): 87–116.

36. Oguma, *Genealogy of "Japanese" Self-Images*, 208–16.
37. Fujitani, *Race for Empire*, 239–74; Suzuki Yūko, *Jūgun ianfu, naisen kekkon* [Military comfort women and Japan-Korea intermarriage] (Miraisha, 1992), 78–87; and Yi, "'Naisen kekkon,'" 48–54.
38. Yi, "'Naisen kekkon,'" 49.
39. See Jaehwan Hyun, "Blood Purity and Scientific Independence: Blood Science and Postcolonial Struggles in Korea, 1926–1975," *Science in Context* (2019): 239–60; Hyun, "Racializing *Chōsenjin*: Science and Biological Speculations in Colonial Korea," *East Asian Science, Technology, and Society* 13, no. 4 (December 2019): 489–510; Gi-Wook Shin, *Ethnic Nationalism in Korea: Genealogy, Politics, and Legacy* (Stanford, CA: Stanford University Press, 2006); and Vladimir Tikhonov, *Modern Korea and Its Others: Perceptions of the Neighbouring Countries and Korean Modernity* (New York: Routledge, 2016), chap. 6.
40. Park Chan-seung, "Yi Kwang-su and the Endorsement of State Power," *Seoul Journal of Korean Studies* 19, no. 1 (December 2006): 179.
41. Fujitani, *Race for Empire*, 28.
42. Kurashima did not cite any specific anthropologists, but Taniguchi Konen was one who described Japanese in northern Kyushu and western Honshu as having "body length identical with Koreans," whereas in eastern and northern Honshu, Japanese "have the most Ainu body length." Taniguchi presented this internal diversity in constitutions as evidence of divergent ancestry among "mixed blood" Japanese. Taniguchi Konen, *Tōyō minzoku to taishitsu* [Eastern races and bodily constitutions] (Sangabō, 1942), 34.
43. Kurashima Itaru, *Zenshin suru Chōsen* [Korea on the march] (Keijō: Chōsen sōtokufu jōhōka [Government-General of Korea Information Bureau], 1942), 11–12; and Oguma, *Genealogy of "Japanese" Self-Images*, 211–13.
44. Ueda Tatsuo, *Sumera Chōsen* [The Emperor's Korea] (Nihon seinen bunka kyōkai, 1943), 36, 45, 63–65, 70–72.
45. Ueda, *Sumera Chōsen*, 120.
46. On Korean soldiers in the Japanese military, see Fujitani, *Race for Empire*, 239–386; and Brandon Palmer, *Fighting for the Enemy: Koreans in Japan's War, 1937–1945* (Seattle: University of Washington Press, 2013).
47. Ueda, *Sumera Chōsen*, 3, 120–126.
48. Ueda, *Sumera Chōsen*, 3, 293.
49. Sayaka Chatani, *Nation-Empire: Ideology and Rural Youth Mobilization in Japan and Its Colonies* (Ithaca, NY: Cornell University Press, 2018).
50. Ueda, *Sumera Chōsen*, 122–25, 130.
51. Ueda, *Sumera Chōsen*, 125.
52. On *kokutai*, see Bitō Masahide, *Nihon no kokkashugi: "kokutai" shisō no keisei* [Japanese statism: the formation of "*kokutai*" thought] (Iwanami shoten, 2014); John Person, *Arbiters of Patriotism: Right-Wing Scholars in Imperial Japan* (Honolulu: University of Hawai'i Press, 2020); and Max Ward, *Thought Crime: Ideology and State Power in Interwar Japan* (Durham, NC: Duke University Press, 2019).
53. Palmer, *Fighting for the Enemy*, 27–28, 104–106.
54. See Chatani, *Nation-Empire: Ideology and Rural Youth*.
55. Mizushima Haruo, "Nihon minzoku no kōsei to konketsu mondai" [Japanese race formation and the problem of blood mixing] (1), *Yūseigaku* [Eugenics] no. 220 (June 1942): 7.

1. IN PRAISE OF "MIXED BLOOD"

56. The organization, still in existence today, has operated under the name Japanese Society for Hygiene [Nihon eisei gakkai] since 1949. "Enkaku: eiseigaku no hajimari" [History: the beginnings of hygiene], accessed February 16, 2021, http://www.nihon-eisei.org/about_jsh/history.
57. Ishiwara Fusao and Satō Hifumi, "Nikka konketsu jidō no igakuteki chōsa" [Medical survey of Japanese-Chinese mixed-blood children], *Minzoku eisei* [Race hygiene] 9, no. 3 (August 1941): 162–65. I discuss Ishiwara and Satō's critique of the political values of "mixed blood" families further in chapter 2.
58. On contact zones, see Chazono Toshimi, *Mō hitotsu no senryō: sekkusu to iu kontakuto zōn kara* [The other occupation: from the contact zone of sex] (Inpakuto, 2018); and Mary Louise Pratt, *Imperial Eyes: Travel Writing and Transculturation* (New York: Routledge, 1992).
59. On hybrid vigor, see Lisa Onaga, "More Than Metamorphosis: The Silkworm Experiments of Toyama Kametarō and His Cultivation of Genetic Thought in Japan's Sericulture Practices, 1894–1918," in *New Perspectives on the History of Life Sciences and Agriculture*, ed. Denise Phillips and Sharon Kingsland (New York: Springer, 2015), 415–37; and Kori A. Graves, *A War Born Family: African American Adoption in the Wake of the Korean War* (New York: New York University Press, 2020), 189–205.
60. Miyake Katsuo and Mizushima Haruo, "Naisen konketsu mondai" [The problem of blood mixing between the interior and Korea], in *Jinkō seisaku to kokudo keikaku* [Population policy and territorial planning], ed. Jinkō mondai kenkyūkai [Center for research on population problems], *Jinkō mondai shiryō* [Population problems materials] no. 51 (Jinkō mondai kenkyūkai, 1942), 20–21.
61. Miyake Katsuo, "Naisen konketsuji no shintai hatsuiku ni tsuite: konketsuji no minzoku-seibutsugakuteki kenkyū" [On the corporeal development of naichi-Korean mixed-blood children: racial-biological research on blood mixing], *Jinkō mondai* [Population problems] 6, no. 2 (1943): 105–54.
62. Miyake, "Naisen konketsuji," 150.
63. See Jeremy Yellen, *The Greater East Asia Co-Prosperity Sphere: When Total Empire Met Total War* (Ithaca, NY: Cornell University Press, 2019).
64. On research and policymaking regarding populations in the Sphere, see Homei, *Science for Governing*, 134–72.
65. See Jon Alfred Mjöen, "Race-Crossing and Glands: Some Human Hybrids and Their Parent Stocks," *Eugenics Review* 23, no. 1 (1931): 32.
66. Mizushima, "Nihon minzoku no kōsei" (1), 7; and Mizushima Haruo, "Nihon minzoku no kōsei to konketsu mondai [The formation of the Japanese race and the problem of blood mixing]" (2), *Yūseigaku* [Eugenics] no. 221 (July 1942): 3.
67. Mizushima, "Nihon minzoku no kōsei" (1), 6; and Mizushima, "Nihon minzoku no kōsei" (2), 3–5.
68. Mizushima, "Nihon minzoku no kōsei" (1), 6; and Mizushima, "Nihon minzoku no kōsei" (2), 5.
69. Yi, "'Naisen kekkon,'" 53–54.
70. Taniguchi, *Tōyō minzoku*, 94–96, 103.
71. Taniguchi, *Tōyō minzoku*, 83, 105.
72. Taniguchi, *Tōyō minzoku*, 97, 105.
73. Taniguchi, *Tōyō minzoku*, 83, 20, 104–5.

1. IN PRAISE OF "MIXED BLOOD"

74. Taniguchi Konen, "Konketsu no mondai" [The problem of blood mixing], *Yūseigaku* no. 229 (1943): 17–19. This and other Japanese-language publications gloss the pronunciation of Taniguchi's given name as Konen, but in European languages, the name is sometimes transliterated as Toratoshi. See e.g. Hyun, "Racializing *Chōsenjin*," 494.
75. Hirano Yoshitarō and Kiyono Kenji, *Taiheiyō no minzoku = seijigaku* [Pacific races = politics] (Nihon hyōronsha, 1942), 482. See also Kiyono Kenji, *Sumatora kenkyū* [Research on Sumatra] (Kawade shobō, 1943), 583–84.
76. Taniguchi, *Tōyō minzoku*, 20, 95–98, 104.
77. Taniguchi Konen, "Nihon rettō minzoku-ron" [On race in the Japanese archipelago], in *Nihon rettō hen* [Compilation on the Japanese archipelago], ed. Honda Masaji (Yamagabō, 1944), 378–88.
78. John Dower, "Throwing Off Asia II: Woodblock Prints of the Sino-Japanese War," *Visualizing Cultures*, accessed August 26, 2023, https://visualizingcultures.mit.edu/throwing_off_asia_01/pdf/toa2_essay.pdf.
79. On popular culture and the construction of Japaneseness via invasion of the continent during the 1890s, see Saya Makito, *The Sino-Japanese War and the Birth of Japanese Nationalism* (Tokyo: International House of Japan, 2011).
80. Benjamin Uchiyama, *Japan's Carnival War: Mass Culture on the Home Front, 1937–1945* (New York: Cambridge University Press, 2019), 23–66.
81. Stephen Mackinnon, *Wuhan, 1938: War, Refugees, and the Making of Modern China* (Berkeley: University of California Press, 2008), 2.
82. This and other negatives from the "Wuhan Lullaby" series sourced from the Nihon shashin hozon sentā [Center for the preservation of Japanese photographs].
83. Frühstück, *Playing War*, 137.
84. Dower, "Throwing Off Asia II."
85. Julia Adeney Thomas, "Japan's War Without Pictures: Normalizing Fascism," in *Visualizing Fascism: The Twentieth-Century Rise of the Global Right*, ed. Julia Adeney Thomas and Geoff Eley (Durham, NC: Duke University Press, 2020), 168. See also Kari Shepherdson-Scott, "Entertaining War: Spectacle and the Great 'Capture of Wuhan' Battle Panorama of 1939," *Art Bulletin* 100, no. 4 (December 2018): 81–105.
86. See Theodore F. Cook, Jr., "Making 'Soldiers': The Imperial Army and the Japanese Man in Meiji Society and State," in *Gendering Modern Japanese History*, ed. Barbara Molony and Kathleen Uno (Cambridge, MA: Harvard University Press, 2005), 259–94; Shizuko Koyama, *Ryōsai Kenbo: The Educational Ideal of Good Wife, Wise Mother in Modern Japan*, trans. Stephen Filler (Leiden: Brill, 2012); and Kathleen Uno, *Passages to Modernity: Motherhood, Childhood, and Social Reform in Early Twentieth-Century Japan* (Honolulu: University of Hawai'i Press, 1999), 19–46.
87. Wakakuwa Midori, *Sensō ga tsukuru josei zō* [The image of woman forged in war] (Chikuma shobō, 1995), 120–231. See also Sawayama Mikako, "'Kindai kazoku' ni okeru otoko: otto to shite, chichi to shite" [Man in the "modern family": as husband, as father], in *Danseishi* [History of men], vol. 2, *Modanizumu kara sōryokusen e* [From modernism to total war], ed. Abe Tsunehisa et al. (Nihon keizai hyōronsha, 2006), 17–56; and Akiko Takenaka, *Yasukuni Shrine: History, Memory, and Japan's Unending Postwar* (Honolulu: University of Hawai'i Press, 2015), 74–130.
88. Cited in Oguma, *Genealogy of "Japanese" Self Images*, 121–23, 165.
89. Shimizu Yuichirō, "Kokusaku gurafu 'Shashin shūhō' no enkaku to gaiyō" [History and outline of government graphic *Photographic Weekly*], in *Senji Nihon no*

1. IN PRAISE OF "MIXED BLOOD"

kokumin ishiki: kokusaku gurafu 'Shashin shūhō' to sono jidai [People's consciousness in wartime Japan: government graphic *Photographic Weekly* and its time], ed. Tamai Kiyoshi (Keiō gijuku daigaku shuppankai, 2008), 1–2.

90. Tsuruoka Satoshi, "'Shashin shūhō' ni miru Higashi Ajia-kan" [The view of East Asia seen in *Photographic Weekly*], in *Senji Nihon*, ed. Tamai, 298–99.
91. Kanō Mikiyo, "Nihon no sensō puropaganda to jendā: *Shashin shūhō* no 'Daitōa kyōeiken' 'kichiku Bei-Ei' hyōshō o chūshin ni" [Japan's war propaganda and gender: on the representation of 'Greater East Asian Co-Prosperity Sphere' and 'Anglo-American demon-beasts' in *Photographic Weekly*], *Keiwa gakuen daigaku jinbun shakai kagaku kenkyūjo nenpō* [Annual report of Keiwa Liberal Arts Research Center], vol. 6 (2008), 11.
92. "Wuhan komori-uta" [Wuhan lullaby], *Shashin shūhō* [Photographic weekly] no. 47, January 11, 1939, 5.
93. See Tsuchiya Atsushi, *"Sensō koji" o ikiru: raifu sutōrī, chinmoku, katari no rekishi shakaigaku* [Living as a "war orphan": the historical sociology of life stories, silence, and narrative] (Seikyūsha, 2021).
94. "Wuhan komori-uta," 4.
95. "Haha no kuni e mukerarenu jū" [Rifle he can't turn toward his mother's country], *Asahi shinbun*, February 24, 1940, evening edition, p. 2.
96. Frühstück, *Playing War*, 116–46.
97. "Konketsuji ga jūgun shinan" [Mixed-blood child applies for military service], *Asahi shinbun*, February 26, 1932, evening edition, p. 2.
98. "Konketsu no senshōhei" [Mixed-blood war-wounded soldier], *Asahi shinbun*, July 5, 1939, evening edition, p. 2; and Jirō Higuchi, "Henry Spencer Palmer, 1838–93," in *Britain and Japan: Biographical Portraits*, vol. 4, ed. Hugh Cortazzi (London: Japan Library, 2002), 198–212.
99. W. Puck Brecher, *Honored and Dishonored Guests: Westerners in Wartime Japan* (Cambridge, MA: Harvard University Asia Center, 2017).
100. "Kensetsusen ni konketsu josei" [Mixed-blood woman in the war for construction], *Asahi shinbun*, April 30, 1942, morning edition, p. 3.
101. See "Gaijin senmon no *konketsu* kaitō Keijō de torawaru" [Mysterious *mixed-blood* thief targeting foreigners arrested in Keijō], *Asahi shinbun*, August 15, 1935, evening edition, p. 2 (emphasis in original); "Hentai seiyoku no jigoku ni ochita konketsuji" [Mixed-blood child descended into hell of sexual deviance], *Asahi shinbun*, August 17, 1933, morning edition, p. 11; and "Kankōkyaku o arasu konketsu no sagikan" [Mixed-blood scammer devastates tourists], *Asahi shinbun*, December 27, 1939, morning edition, p. 11.
102. "Genjūmin ni naritaya" [Turned indigenous], *Asahi shinbun*, January 15, 1943, evening edition, p. 2. On the racial and broader politics of the occupation, see Ethan Mark, *Japan's Occupation of Java in the Second World War* (London: Bloomsbury, 2018).
103. "Jawa konketsujin ni keikoku," *Asahi shinbun*, January 13, 1943, morning edition, p. 2.
104. Murata Takaharu, "Kyōiku ni yoru mindo kōjō" [Raising the cultural level through education], *Asahi shinbun*, October 15, 1942, morning edition, p. 1.
105. Emma Jinhua Teng, *Eurasian: Mixed Identities in the United States, China, and Hong Kong, 1842–1943* (Berkeley: University of California Press, 2013), 249.

106. A. Carly Buxton, *Unthinking Collaboration: American Nisei in Transwar Japan* (Honolulu: University of Hawai'i Press, 2022). See also Azuma, *In Search of Our Frontier*, 242–60.
107. Leo Ching, *Becoming "Japanese": Colonial Taiwan and the Politics of Identity Formation* (Berkeley: University of California Press, 2001); and Seiji Shirane, *Imperial Gateway: Colonial Taiwan and Japan's Expansion in South China and Southeast Asia, 1895–1945* (Ithaca, NY: Cornell University Press, 2022).
108. Emma Teng, "On Not Looking Chinese: Does 'Mixed Race' Decenter the Han from Chineseness?," in *Critical Han Studies: The History, Representation, and Identity of China's Majority*, ed. Thomas S. Mullaney et al. (Berkeley: University of California Press, 2012), 72.

2. BIOLOGIZING DEFEAT

1. Hattori Satoshi with Edward J. Drea, "Japanese Operations from July to December 1937," in *The Battle for China: Essays on the Military History of the Sino-Japanese War of 1937–1945*, ed. Mark Peattie et al. (Stanford, CA: Stanford University Press, 2011), 159.
2. Stephen Mackinnon, *Wuhan, 1938: War, Refugees, and the Making of Modern China* (Berkeley: University of California Press, 2008), 2.
3. Edward Drea and Hans van de Ven, "An Overview of Major Military Campaigns During the Sino-Japanese War, 1937–1945," in *The Battle for China: Essays on the Military History of the Sino-Japanese War of 1937–1945*, ed. Mark Peattie et al. (Stanford, CA: Stanford University Press, 2011), 32–39.
4. Yoshiaki Yoshimi, *Grassroots Fascism: The War Experience of the Japanese People*, trans. Ethan Mark (New York: Columbia University Press, 2015), 87.
5. On the Sphere, see Jeremy Yellen, *The Greater East Asia Co-Prosperity Sphere: When Total Empire Met Total War* (Ithaca, NY: Cornell University Press, 2019).
6. Yoshimi, *Grassroots Fascism*, 55; and Louise Young, "Ideologies of Difference and the Turn to Atrocity: Japan's War on China," in *A World at Total War: Global Conflict and the Politics of Destruction, 1937–1945*, ed. Roger Chickering et al. (Cambridge: Cambridge University Press, 2005), 343–47.
7. See Drea and van de Ven, "Overview of Major Military Campaigns," 42–46; Eri Hotta, *Japan 1941: Countdown to Infamy* (New York: Knopf, 2013); and Saburō Ienaga, *The Pacific War: 1931–1945* (New York: Pantheon, 1978).
8. Takashi Fujitani, *Race for Empire: Koreans as Japanese and Japanese as Americans During World War II* (Berkeley: University of California Press, 2011).
9. Sakurai Hyōgorō, "Shokumin seisaku to Nisshi konketsu no haigeki" [Colonial policy and the rejection of Japanese-Chinese blood mixing], *Gaichi hyōron* [Colonial review] (March 1940): 87.
10. Kirsten Ziomek, *Lost Histories: Recovering the Lives of Japan's Colonial Peoples* (Cambridge, MA: Harvard University Asia Center, 2019), 284.
11. Sakurai, "Shokumin seisaku," 87.
12. Banno Junji, *Democracy in Pre-War Japan: Concepts of Government, 1871–1937, Collected Essays*, trans. Andrew Fraser (New York: Routledge, 2001), 117–44.

2. BIOLOGIZING DEFEAT

13. "The Ambassador in Japan (Grew) to the Secretary of State," in United States Department of State, *Foreign Relations of the United States: Diplomatic Papers, 1937*, vol. 3, *The Far East* (Washington, DC: US Government Printing Office, 1954), 30.
14. Mayumi Itoh, *The Hatoyama Dynasty: Japanese Political Leadership Through the Generations* (New York: Palgrave Macmillan, 2003), 67–70.
15. For biographical details on Sakurai, see Osawa Koji, "Biruma no dokuritsu to busshari hōsen: Sakurai Hyōgorō ga kōsōshita Daitōa-ji" [Burmese independence and transfer of Buddha's ashes: the Greater East Asia Temple planned by Sakurai Hyōgorō], in *Shūkyō kara miru sensō* [War from the perspective of religion], ed. Sensō shakaigaku kenkyūkai (Mizuki shorin, 2019), 64–82.
16. See chapter 1 and Oguma Eiji, *Genealogy of "Japanese" Self-Images*, trans. David Askew (Melbourne: Trans Pacific, 2002), 208–16.
17. Sakurai, "Shokumin seisaku," 87–88.
18. Osawa, "Biruma," 68–69.
19. Sakurai, "Shokumin seisaku," 84–85.
20. Takagi Tomosaburō, "Minzoku no masatsu izon seiri jidai" [The era of adjustment of dependence on conflict between *minzoku*], *Gaikō jihō* [Revue diplomatique] no. 813 (October 15, 1938): 61–67.
21. Noriaki Hoshino, "Racial Contacts across the Pacific and the Creation of *Minzoku* in the Japanese Empire," *Inter-Asia Cultural Studies* 17, no. 2 (2016): 186–205.
22. Takagi, "Minzoku no masatsu," 63.
23. Takagi, "Minzoku no masatsu," 66–67.
24. Takagi Tomosaburō, "Nisshi no minzokuteki taisho" [Diametrical opposition between Japanese and Chinese minzoku], *Gaikō jihō* [Revue diplomatique] No. 801 (April 15, 1938): 88.
25. Takagi, "Nisshi," 88–91.
26. Thomas S. Mullaney, ed., *Critical Han Studies: The History, Representation, and Identity of China's Majority* (Berkeley: University of California Press, 2012).
27. Tsou Jung [Zou Rong], *The Revolutionary Army: A Chinese Nationalist Tract of 1903*, trans. John Lust (Paris: Mouton, 1968), 108; see also Kai-wing Chow, "Imagining Boundaries of Blood: Zhang Binglin and the Invention of the Han 'Race' in Modern China," in *The Construction of Racial Identities in China and Japan*, ed. Frank Dikötter (Honolulu: University of Hawai'i Press, 1997), 34–52.
28. James Leibold, "Searching for Han: Early Twentieth-Century Narratives of Chinese Origins and Development," in *Critical Han Studies*, 210–233.
29. Kutsuna Shōa, "Shukō Tanmin no taishitsu" [Constitution of the Pearl River Tanka people], in *Jinkō, minzoku, kokudo: kigen nisen-roppyaku-nen kinen dai-yon-kai jinkō mondai zenkoku kyōgikai hōkokusho* [Population, race, territory: report of the fourth convention of the All-Country Conference on Population Problems on the 2600th anniversary of the empire's founding], ed. Foundation-Institute for Research on Population Problems [Zaidan-hōjin jinkō mondai kenkyūkai] (FRPP), Jinkō mondai shiryō [Population problems documents] 43, no. 1 (FRPP, 1941), 211–12. Seiji Shirane details relations between colonial Taiwan and Japanese-occupied south China in *Imperial Gateway: Colonial Taiwan and Japan's Expansion in South China and Southeast Asia, 1895–1945* (Ithaca, NY: Cornell University Press, 2022), 103–59.

2. BIOLOGIZING DEFEAT

30. Huei-Ying Kuo, "Learning from the South: Japan's Racial Construction of the Southern Chinese, 1895–1941," in *Race and Racism in Modern East Asia*, vol. 2, *Interactions, Nationalism, Gender and Lineage*, ed. Rotem Kowner and Walter Demel (Leiden: Brill, 2015), 152, 172–73.
31. Takagi, "Nisshi," 87–91.
32. See "Hisshō no jishin" [Confidence in certain victory], *Dōmei sekai shūhō* [Allied world bulletin] 26, no. 17 (July 7, 1945): 2.
33. Simon Avenell, *Asia and Postwar Japan: Deimperialization, Civic Activism, and National Identity* (Cambridge, MA: Harvard University Asia Center, 2022), 9–13, 104.
34. Sakurai, "Shokumin seisaku," 84–85.
35. Nanba Monkichi, "Shina minzoku ishiki to Tōa renmei" [Chinese *minzoku* consciousness and East Asian alliance], *Gaikō jihō* [Revue diplomatique] no. 863 (November 1940): 91, 99–100.
36. Nanba, "Shina minzoku," 90.
37. Aya Homei, *Science for Governing Japan's Population* (Cambridge: Cambridge University Press, 2023), 115–17; and Sugita Naho et al., "Zaidan hōjin jinkō mondai kenkyūkai no gaiyō" [Overview of the Foundation-Institute for Research on Population Problems], Kokuritsu shakai hoshō, jinkō mondai kenkyūjo [National Institute of Population and Social Security Research], working paper series no. 41 (2020), 3–5.
38. "Keika gaiyō" [Overview of course of events], in *Jinkō, minzoku, kokudo*, 2.
39. Ishiwara Fusao, "Nisshi konketsu jidō no igakuteki chōsa" [Medical survey of Japanese-Chinese mixed-blood children], in *Jinkō, minzoku, kokudo*, 209–211. See also Ishiwara Fusao and Satō Hifumi, "Nikka konketsu jidō no igakuteki chōsa" [Medical survey of Japanese-Chinese mixed-blood children], *Minzoku eisei* [Race hygiene] Vol. 9.3 (August 1941): 162–165.
40. Ueno Chizuko, *Nationalism and Gender*, trans. Beverley Yamamoto (Melbourne: Trans Pacific, 2004), 46, 48.
41. Ishiwara, "Nisshi konketsu," 210–11.
42. Ishiwara, "Nisshi konketsu," 211; and Ishiwara and Satō, "Nikka konketsu," 164.
43. The RHA changed its name to *Nihon minzoku eisei kyōkai* in 1935. On the RHA, see Matsubara Yōko, "Minzoku yūsei hogohōan to Nihon no yūseihō no keifu" [The *minzoku* eugenic protection bills and the genealogy of Japan's eugenic laws], *Kagakushi kenkyū* [History of science] 36 (1997): 42–50; Suzuki Zenji, *Nihon no yūseigaku: sono shisō to undō no kiseki* [Japanese eugenics: traces of the idea and movement] (Sankyō shuppan, 1983), 143–191; and Yokoyama Takashi, *Nihon ga yūsei shakai ni naru made: kagaku keimō, media, seishoku no seiji* [Until Japan is a eugenic society: scientific enlightenment, media, and the politics of reproduction] (Keisō shobō, 2015), 153–298.
44. On the wartime MOW, see Fujino Yutaka, *Kōseishō no tanjō: iryō wa fashizumu o ikani suishinshita ka* [The birth of the Ministry of Welfare: how did medicine drive fascism?] (Kyoto: Kamogawa shuppan, 2003); Gregory James Kasza, *One World of Welfare: Japan in Comparative Perspective* (Ithaca, NY: Cornell University Press, 2006), 36–41; and Benjamin Uchiyama, *Japan's Carnival War: Mass Culture on the Home Front, 1937–1945* (New York: Cambridge University Press, 2019), 67–104.
45. Mizuno Hiromi, *Science for the Empire: Scientific Nationalism in Modern Japan* (Stanford, CA: Stanford University Press, 2009), 1–70.
46. Homei, *Science for Governing*, 199.

2. BIOLOGIZING DEFEAT

47. Sakurai, "Shokumin seisaku," 85–87.
48. Koya Yoshio, *Minzoku mondai o megurite* [On the problem of race] (Kyoto: Jinbun shoin, 1935), 19.
49. See also Koyama Eizō, *Minzoku to jinkō no riron* [Race and population theory] (Hata shoten, 1941), 35.
50. Koya Yoshio, *Kokudo, jinkō, ketsueki* [Territory, population, blood] (Asahi shinbunsha, 1941), 120.
51. Koya, *Kokudo*, 120–26.
52. Koya, *Minzoku mondai*, 16–19; and *Kokudo*, 128–31.
53. Koya Yoshio, Komai Taku, Taniguchi Konen, and Ōyuki Yoshio, "Minzoku konketsu no zehiron" [The pros and cons of racial blood mixing], *Nihon iji shinpō* [Japan medical news] no. 961 (February 1, 1941), 584.
54. See Koya Yoshio, "Konketsu no mondai" [The blood mixing problem], in *Minzoku kagaku kenkyū* [Research in race science] no. 1, ed. Hayashi Haruo and Koya Yoshio (Asakura shoten, 1943), 165; Koya, *Minzoku mondai*, 19; and Koya Yoshio, "Konketsu monogatari: sekaiteki ni mita konketsuji mondai" [Story of blood mixing: the problem of mixed-blood children seen globally], *Fujin kōron* [Ladies review] 39, no. 4 (1953), 165.
55. Koya et al., "Minzoku konketsu," 584. Koya makes the same categorical distinction in "Konketsu no mondai," 165.
56. Koya Yoshio, "Konketsu no mondai," 166 (emphasis mine).
57. Yoshiaki Yoshimi, *Comfort Women: Sexual Slavery in the Japanese Military During World War II*, trans. Suzanne O'Brien (New York: Columbia University Press, 2000).
58. Koya, *Minzoku mondai*, 13–15.
59. Koya et al., "Minzoku konketsu," 584–85.
60. Komai Taku, *Nihonjin o shutoshita ningen no iden* [Human genetics centered on the Japanese] (Sōgensha, 1942), 298.
61. Koya et al, "Minzoku konketsu," 586–89.
62. Koya et al., "Minzoku konketsu," 591–92.
63. Koya et al, "Minzoku konketsu," 589–90.
64. Moriyoshi Yoshiaki, *Yamato minzoku no zenshin* [Advance of the Yamato people] (Kokusai hankyō renmei, 1942), 1–2, 116–38.
65. On Nagai and the RHA, see Katō Shūichi, *"Ren'ai kekkon" wa nani o motarashita ka: sei dōtoku to yūsei shisō no hyakunenkan* [What did "love marriage" bring about? a century of sexual morals and eugenic thought] (Chikuma shinsho, 2004), 179–88, 206–10; Matsubara, "Minzoku yūsei hogohōan"; Suzuki, *Nihon no yūseigaku*, 144–67; and Yokoyama, *Nihon ga yūsei shakai ni naru made*, 153–271.
66. Nagai Hisomu, "Minzoku no konketsu ni tsuite" [On Blood Mixing Between Minzoku], *Minzoku eisei* [Race hygiene] 2, no. 4 (1933): 395–96.
67. Sakano Tōru, *Teikoku Nihon to jinruigakusha: 1884–1952* [Anthropologists and imperial Japan: 1884–1952] (Keisō shobō, 2005), 204–10.
68. Eika Tai, "The Discourse of Intermarriage in Colonial Taiwan," *Journal of Japanese Studies* 40, no. 1 (Winter 2014): 110–11.
69. Juliette Chung, "Struggle for National Survival: Eugenics in the Second Sino-Japanese War and Population Policies," in *Trans-Pacific Relations: America, Europe, and Asia in the Twentieth Century*, ed. Richard Jensen, Jon Davidann, and Yoneyuki Sugita (Westport, CT: Praeger, 2003), 67.

2. BIOLOGIZING DEFEAT

70. Nagai, "Minzoku no konketsu," 395–96.
71. Nagai Hisomu, *Yūseigaku gairon* [Introduction to eugenics], vol. 1 (Yūzankaku, 1936), 3, 209.
72. Tai, "Discourse of Intermarriage."
73. Chung, "Struggle for National Survival," 74–78.
74. Nagai Hisomu, "Chūgoku ni okeru minzoku ketsueki no kōryū" [Mingling of blood between races in China], *Nihon iji shinpō* [Japan medical news] 1058 (1943): 8–9.
75. Chung, "Struggle for National Survival," 66–78; John Dower, *War Without Mercy: Race and Power in the Pacific War* (New York: Pantheon, 1986), 203–290; Tessa Morris-Suzuki, "Debating Racial Science in Wartime Japan," *Osiris*, 2nd ser., vol. 13 (1998): 362; Jennifer Robertson, "Biopower: Blood, Kinship, and Eugenic Marriage," in *A Companion to the Anthropology of Japan*, ed. Jennifer Robertson (Oxford: Blackwell, 2005), 339; and Sakano, *Teikoku Nihon*, 204–10.
76. Oguma, *Genealogy*, 290, 296–97.

3. FROM NO ABORTION TO PROABORTION

1. John Dower, *War Without Mercy: Race and Power in the Pacific War* (New York: Pantheon, 1986), 311.
2. Nicholas Stargardt, "Wartime Occupation by Germany: Food and Sex," in *The Cambridge History of the Second World War*, vol. 2, ed. Richard Bosworth and Joseph Maiolo (Cambridge: Cambridge University Press, 2015), 408; see also Kjersti Ericsson and Eva Simonsen eds., *Children of World War II: The Hidden Enemy Legacy* (New York: Oxford University Press, 2005).
3. Shimojima Tetsurō, *Higyō no seishatachi: shūdan jiketsu Saipan kara Manshū e* [The living dead: group suicide from Saipan to Manchuria] (Iwanami shoten, 2012), 33, 115–17, 276–69. See also Haruko Taya Cook and Theodore F. Cook, Jr., *Japan at War: An Oral History* (New York: New Press, 1992), 363–66.
4. Haruko Taya Cook, "Women's Deaths as a Weapon of War in Japan's 'Final Battle,'" in *Gendering Modern Japanese History*, ed. Barbara Molony and Kathleen Uno (Cambridge, MA: Harvard University Press, 2005), 326–56; and Donald Keene, *So Lovely a Country Will Never Perish: Wartime Diaries of Japanese Writers* (New York: Columbia University Press, 2010), 6–7.
5. Norma Field, *In the Realm of a Dying Emperor* (New York: Pantheon, 1999), 59; Shimojima, *Higyō no seishatachi*, 13, 27–29.
6. David C. Earhart, *Certain Victory: Images of World War II in the Japanese Media* (London: M.E. Sharpe, 2008), 355–71; Heiwa hakubutsukan o tsukurukai [Association for creating a peace museum], ed., *Kami no sensō dentan: bōryaku senden-bira wa kataru* [The paper propaganda war: propaganda policy posters tell the tale] (Emīrusha, 1990), 49–50; and Shimojima, *Higyō no seishatachi*, 17–18, 26–28, 276–78.
7. Cook and Cook, *Japan at War*, 360–62; and Field, *In the Realm*, 57–59.
8. Shimojima, *Higyō no seishatachi*, 17, 26, 118–122 (emphasis in original).
9. Dower, *War Without Mercy*, 299.
10. Andrew Barshay, *The Gods Left First: The Captivity and Repatriation of Japanese POWs in Northeast Asia, 1945–1956* (Berkeley: University of California Press, 2013);

3. FROM NO ABORTION TO PROABORTION

and Sherzod Muminov, *Eleven Winters of Discontent: The Siberian Internment and the Making of a New Japan* (Cambridge, MA: Harvard University Press, 2022).
11. Shimojima, *Higyō no seishatachi*, 322–406.
12. Russian women, too, were vulnerable to sexual violence by men in Soviet uniform. Eliot Borenstein, *Men Without Women: Masculinity and Revolution in Russian Fiction, 1917–1929* (Durham, NC: Duke University Press, 2000), 58–68; Jeffrey Burds, "Sexual Violence in Europe in World War II, 1939–1945," *Politics and Society* 37, no. 1 (2009): 35–73; and Barbara Alpern Engel, "The Womanly Face of War: Soviet Women Remember World War II," in *Women and War in the Twentieth Century: Enlisted With or Without Consent*, ed. Nicole Ann Dombrowski (New York: Garland, 1999), 138–59.
13. Cook and Cook, *Japan at War*, 490. See also Shimojima, *Higyō no seishatachi*, 322–406.
14. Kozy Kazuko Amemiya, "The Road to Pro-Choice Ideology: A Social History of the Contest Between the State and Individuals Over Abortion" (PhD diss., University of California, San Diego, 1993), 161–62; Katō Kiyofumi, *Kaigai hikiage no kenkyū: bōkyakusareta "Dai Nihon teikoku"* [Research on overseas repatriation: the "Great Japanese empire" consigned to oblivion] (Iwanami shoten, 2020), 136–39; Matsubara Yōko, "Hikiagesha iryō ni okeru jinkō ninshin chuzetsu" [Artificially induced abortion in medical care for repatriates], in *Jendā to nama seiji* [Gender and the politics of life], ed. Tsuboi Hideto (Kyoto: Rinsen shoten, 2019), 48, 62; and Lori Watt, *When Empire Comes Home: Repatriation and Reintegration in Postwar Japan* (Cambridge, MA: Harvard University Asia Center, 2009), 109.
15. See the remarks of Okamoto Yoshito, Shūgiin zaigai dōhō hikiage mondai ni kansuru tokubetsu iinkai seigan oyobi chinjō ni kansuru shōiinkai [House of Representatives, Subcommittee on Petitions and Appeals of the Special Committee on the Crisis of Repatriating Our Compatriots Overseas], no. 1 (August 27, 1948).
16. Hamano Kikuo et al., "Kokuritsu byōin no hassoku o kaikoshite" [Recalling the inauguration of the National Medical Services], *Iryō: Kokuritsu iryō gakkaishi* [Journal of the National Medical Services] 9, no. 12 (December 1955): 83.
17. Louise Young, "Ideologies of Difference and the Turn to Atrocity: Japan's War on China," in *A World at Total War: Global Conflict and the Politics of Destruction, 1937–1945*, ed. Roger Chickering et al. (Cambridge: Cambridge University Press, 2005), 339–51.
18. See also Fujime Yuki, *Sei no rekishigaku: kōshō seido, dataizai taisei kara baishun bōshihō, yūsei hogohō taisei e* [The history of sex: from the public prostitution system and criminal abortion law to the Prostitution Prevention Law and Eugenic Protection Law system] (Fuji shuppan, 1997), 358.
19. Watt, *When Empire Comes Home*, 112.
20. Matsubara, "Hikiagesha," 56–57, 60–61. For more on VD control under occupation, see Hirai Kazuko, *Nihon senryō to jendā: beigun/baibaishun to Nihon joseitachi* [Gender and the occupation of Japan: US military/prostitution and Japanese women] (Yūshisha, 2014), 71–97; Izuoka Manabu, "Karikomi to seibyōin: sengo Kanagawa no sei seisaku [Round-ups and VD clinics: postwar Kanagawa's sex policies], in Okuda Akiko et al., *Senryō to sei: seisaku, jittai, hyōshō* [Occupation and sex: policy, reality, and representation] (Inpakuto shuppankai, 2007), 119–46; Sarah C. Kovner, *Occupying Power: Sex Workers and Servicemen in Postwar Japan*

3. FROM NO ABORTION TO PROABORTION

(Stanford, CA: Stanford University Press, 2012); Robert Kramm, *Sanitized Sex: Regulating Prostitution, Venereal Disease, and Intimacy in Occupied Japan, 1945–1952* (Oakland: University of California Press, 2017); and Okuda Akiko, "GHQ no sei seisaku: seibyō kanri ka kin'yoku seisaku ka" [GHQ's sex policy: venereal disease control or anti-lust policy?], in *Senryō to sei*, 13–44.

21. Matsubara, "Hikiagesha," 60.
22. Kramm, *Sanitized Sex*, 40. Michael Molasky makes a similar argument in *The American Occupation of Japan and Okinawa: Literature and Memory* (New York: Routledge, 1999).
23. Atina Grossman, "A Question of Silence: The Rape of German Women by Soviet Occupation Soldiers," in *Women and War*, 167–74.
24. Kamitsubo Takashi, *Mizuko no fu: dokyumento hikiage koji to onnatachi* [Record of lost children: documentation of repatriate orphans and women] (Shakai shishōsha, [1979] 1993), 180; Katō, *Kaigai hikiage*, 135–38; Matsubara, "Hikiagesha," 48–49; and Watt, *When Empire Comes Home*, 71. Miriam Kingsberg Kadia chronicles Izumi and his closest colleagues' careers, without delving into their (anti-)reproductive activism, in *Into the Field: Human Scientists of Transwar Japan* (Stanford, CA: Stanford University Press, 2019).
25. Kamitsubo, *Mizuko*, 171–73; Matsubara, "Hikiagesha," 41–43, 48; and SCAP, Government Section, *Political Reorientation of Japan: September 1945 to September 1948* [hereafter *PRJ*], vol. 2 (Washington, DC: US Government Printing Office, 1949), 742. On the Patriotic Women's Association, see also Lee Pennington, *Casualties of History: Wounded Japanese Servicemen and the Second World War* (Ithaca, NY: Cornell University Press, 2015), chap. 1.
26. Matsubara, "Hikiagesha," 64–66; Ogino Miho, *Kazoku keikaku e no michi: kindai Nihon no seishoku o meguru seiji* [The road to family planning: the politics of reproduction in modern Japan] (Iwanami shoten, 2008), 142–51; and Tessa Morris-Suzuki, *Borderline Japan: Foreigners and Frontier Controls in the Postwar Era* (Cambridge: Cambridge University Press, 2011), 52–71.
27. *PRJ*, 2: 479–89. On the Tokyo war crimes trial, see John Dower, *Embracing Defeat: Japan in the Wake of World War II* (New York: W. W. Norton, 1999), 443–84.
28. See chapter 2; Koyama Eizō, *Nanpō kensetsu to minzoku jinkō seisaku* [Constructing the South Pacific and racial population policy] (Dainihon shuppan, 1944), 587–645; Tessa Morris-Suzuki, "Debating Racial Science in Wartime Japan," *Osiris*, 2nd ser., vol. 13 (1998): 363–75; and Morris-Suzuki, "Ethnic Engineering: Scientific Racism and Public Opinion Surveys in Midcentury Japan," *Positions: East Asia Cultures Critique* 8, no. 2 (Fall 2000): 499–529.
29. Cabinet Meeting Minutes, 3/8/1946; File Unit March 8, 1946; Notes on Cabinet Meetings Files, 1945–1953; Matthew J. Connelly Papers, 1945–1953, Collection HST-MJC; Harry S. Truman Library.
30. Matsubara, "Hikiagesha," 64–67; and Aiko Takeuchi-Demirci, *Contraceptive Diplomacy: Reproductive Politics and Imperial Ambitions in the United States and Japan* (Stanford, CA: Stanford University Press, 2018), 117–150.
31. Cited in Watt, *When Empire Comes Home*, 119.
32. Amemiya, "Road to Pro-Choice Ideology," 162; Matsubara, "Hikiagesha," 50, 55, 60–63; and Watt, *When Empire Comes Home*, 114–15.
33. Matsubara, "Hikiagesha," 63.

3. FROM NO ABORTION TO PROABORTION

34. Matsubara, "Hikiagesha," 44–45, 54, 63–64.
35. Matsubara, "Hikiagesha," 44, 54–55.
36. Shūgiin seikatsu hogohōan iinkai [House of Representatives, Livelihood Protection Bill Committee], no. 8 (August 6, 1946).
37. Matsubara, "Hikiagesha," 55–56; and Shūgiin seikatsu hogohōan iinkai.
38. Cited in Kamitsubo, *Mizuko*, 175–77.
39. Kamitsubo, *Mizuko*, 176; and Matsubara, "Hikiagesha," 50.
40. Amemiya, "Road to Pro-Choice Ideology," 164.
41. Kamitsubo, *Mizuko*, 167–68.
42. Kamitsubo, *Mizuko*, 178–81.
43. Watt, *When Empire Comes Home*, 119–20.
44. Kamitsubo, *Mizuko*, 179–80, 231–33.
45. Watt, *When Empire Comes Home*, 20.
46. Shūgiin zaigai dōhō, no. 1.
47. Shimojima, *Higyō no seishatachi*, 17, 26, 118–122 (emphasis in original).
48. Takemae Eiji, *Inside GHQ: The Allied Occupation of Japan and Its Legacy*, trans. Robert Ricketts and Sebastian Swann (New York: Continuum, 2002), 126, 131.
49. Dower, *Embracing Defeat*, 45, 90–103, 115; Katō, *Kaigai hikiage*; Tsuchiya Atsushi, "*Sensō koji*" *o ikiru: raifu sutōrī, chinmoku, katari no rekishi shakaigaku* [Living as a "war orphan": the historical sociology of life stories, silence, and narrative] (Seikyūsha, 2021); and Watt, *When Empire Comes Home*.
50. For an account of amenorrhea during the war, see Nosaka Akiyuki, "American *Hijiki*," trans. Jay Rubin, in *Contemporary Japanese Literature: An Anthology of Fiction, Film, and Other Writing since 1945*, ed. Howard Hibbett (New York: Knopf, 1977), 453.
51. William R. LaFleur, *Liquid Life: Abortion and Buddhism in Japan* (Princeton, NJ: Princeton University Press, 1992), 128.
52. Aya Homei, *Science for Governing Japan's Population* (Cambridge: Cambridge University Press, 2023), chaps. 3–4; Sujin Lee, *Wombs of Empire: Population Discourses and Biopolitics in Modern Japan* (Stanford, CA: Stanford University Press, 2023); Ogino, *Kazoku keikaku*, 1–140; and Wakakuwa Midori, *Sensō ga tsukuru josei zō* [The image of women forged in war] (Chikuma shobō, 1995), 66–71.
53. Ochiai Emiko, "Modern Japan Through the Eyes of an Old Midwife: From an Oral Life History to Social History," trans. Mio Neuse, in *Gender and Japanese History*, vol. 1, ed. Wakita Haruko et al. (Osaka: Osaka University Press, 1999), 273–77.
54. Nagai Hisomu, *Minzoku no unmei: Nihon kokumin ni uttau* [The fate of the race: I appeal to the people of Japan] (Muramatsu shoten, 1948).
55. Matsubara Yōko, "The Enactment of Japan's Sterilization Laws in the 1940s: A Prelude to Postwar Eugenic Policy," *Historia Scientiarum* 8, no. 2 (1998): 192–94; Sumiko Otsubo, "Engendering Eugenics: Feminists and Marriage Restriction Legislation in the 1920s," in *Gendering Modern Japanese History*, 244; and Hiroko Takeda, *The Political Economy of Reproduction in Japan: Between Nation-State and Everyday Life* (New York: RoutledgeCurzon, 2005), 82–85, 107, 131, 202–3.
56. Haruhiro Fukui, "Postwar Politics, 1945–1973," in *The Cambridge History of Japan*, vol. 6, *The Twentieth Century*, ed. Peter Duus (New York: Cambridge University Press, 2005), 159–62.
57. Sally Ann Hastings, "Women Legislators in the Postwar Diet," in *Re-Imaging Japanese Women*, ed. Anne E. Imamura (Berkeley: University of California Press, 1996),

271–300; US Department of State, "Analysis of the 1946 Japanese General Election," Office of Research and Intelligence, no. 3492 (Washington, DC, May 15, 1946), B-109.
58. Shūgiin seigan iinkai [House of Representatives, Petition Committee], no. 6 (August 7, 1946).
59. On ob-gyns as a powerful special interest group in the postwar Diet, see Tiana Norgren, *Abortion Before Birth Control: The Politics of Reproduction in Postwar Japan* (Princeton, NJ: Princeton University Press, 2001).
60. Shūgiin kōsei iinkai [House of Representatives, Welfare Committee], no. 35 (December 1, 1947).
61. Matsubara, "Enactment of Japan's Sterilization Laws," 192–94.
62. On Taniguchi's career, see Norgren, *Abortion Before Birth Control*; and Yokoyama Takashi, *Nihon ga yūsei shakai ni naru made: kagaku keimō, media, seishoku no seiji* [Until Japan is a eugenic society: scientific enlightenment, media, and the politics of reproduction] (Keisō shobō, 2015), chap. 8.
63. Shūgiin kōsei iinkai [House of Representatives, Welfare Committee], no. 14 (June 24, 1948).
64. On the frequency of rape in occupied Japan, see Kovner, *Occupying Power*, 50–56.
65. Sangiin honkaigi [House of Councilors Plenary Session], no. 52 (June 23, 1948); and Yūsei hogohōan [Eugenic Protection Bill], in *Sei to seishoku no jinken mondai shiryō shūsei* [The problem of human rights in sex and reproduction source collection], vol. 25, ed. Ogino Miho et al. (Fuji shuppan, 2002), 203–10.
66. Amemiya, "Road to Pro-Choice Ideology," 164n27.
67. Taniguchi Yasaburō and Fukuda Masako, *Yūsei hogohō kaisetsu* [Explanation of the Eugenic Protection Law] (Kenshinsha, 1948), 3, 35.
68. House of Representatives, Hōritsu dai-hyakugojūroku-gō [Law 156] (July 13, 1948), Yūsei hogohō [Eugenic Protection Law].
69. Abe Yūkichi, *Yūsei hogohō to ninshin chūzetsu* [The Eugenic Protection Law and abortion] (Jiji tsūhinsha, 1948), 24, 65; and Sangiin kōsei iinkai [House of Councilors, Welfare Committee], no. 14 (June 22, 1948).
70. Tina Marie Campt, *Other Germans: Black Germans and the Politics of Race, Gender, and Memory in the Third Reich* (Ann Arbor: University of Michigan Press, 2004), 63–80; Robert Proctor, *Racial Hygiene: Medicine Under the Nazis* (Cambridge, MA: Harvard University Press, 1988), 96, 107–14.
71. Grossman, "Question of Silence," 167–74.
72. Matsubara Yōko, "Chūzetsu kisei kanwa to yūsei seisaku kyōka: Yūsei hogohō saikō" [Loosening abortion regulations and strengthening eugenic policies: Rethinking the Eugenic Protection Law], *Shisō* [Thought] no. 886 (1998): 116–36; and "The Enactment of Japan's Sterilization Laws in the 1940s: A Prelude to Postwar Eugenic Policy," *Historia Scientiarum* 8, no. 2 (1998): 187–201. See also Aya Homei, *Science for Governing Japan's Population* (Cambridge: Cambridge University Press, 2023); and Ogino Miho, "From Natalism to Family Planning: Population Policy in Wartime and the Post-War Period," trans. Leonie Stickland, in *Gender, Nation and State in Modern Japan*, ed. Andrea Germer et al. (New York: Routledge, 2014), 198–211.
73. On popular and political responses to *panpan*, see Chazono Toshimi, *Mō hitotsu no senryō: sekkusu to iu kontakuto zōn kara* [The other occupation: from the contact zone of sex] (Inpakuto, 2018); and Kovner, *Occupying Power*.

4. SEX, CENSORSHIP, AND SCAP

74. Sangiin kōsei iinkai [House of Councilors, Welfare Committee], no. 2 (November 11, 1948).
75. Taniguchi Yasaburō et al., "Ninshin chūzetsu to jutai chōsetsu: zadankai" [Abortion and birth control: round-table talk], *Fujin kōron* [Ladies review] 38, no. 7 (1952): 141.
76. Ogino, *Kazoku keikaku*, 174–75.
77. Shūgiin naikaku iinkai [House of Representatives, Cabinet Committee], no. 26 (March 31, 1959).
78. Nagai Hōji, "Gomen nasai: Konketsuji no shomondai" [Sorry: mixed-blood children problems], *6/3 kyōshitsu* [6/3 classroom] 6, no. 10 (1952): 55–59.
79. Itagaki Naoko, "Konketsuji no ryōshin" [Mixed-blood children's parents], *Kaizō* [Reconstruction] 34, no. 3 (1953): 163.
80. Takagi Masataka, "Nishi Doitsu no onnatachi" [West German women], *Fujin kōron* [Ladies review] 38, no. 7 (1952): 81.
81. Sawada Miki et al., "Keredomo konketsuji wa . . . sodatte yuku: zadankai" [Nonetheless, mixed-blood children . . . are growing up: round-table talk], *Fujin kōron* [Ladies review] 38, no. 7 (1952): 50.

4. SEX, CENSORSHIP, AND SCAP

1. Nihon Teikōku Kenpō [Constitution of the Empire of Japan] (1889), article III.
2. See Naoko Shibusawa, *America's Geisha Ally: Reimagining the Japanese Enemy* (Cambridge, MA: Harvard University Press, 2006); and Lisa Yoneyama, *Hiroshima Traces: Time, Space, and the Dialectics of Memory* (Berkeley: University of California Press, 1999), chap. 6.
3. Yoshikuni Igarashi, *Bodies of Memory: Narratives of War in Postwar Japanese Culture, 1945–1970* (Princeton, NJ: Princeton University Press, 2000), 31. The contentious photograph is still reproduced widely, including in John Dower, *Embracing Defeat: Japan in the Wake of World War II* (New York: W.W. Norton, 1999), 294.
4. "Further Steps Toward Freedom of Press and Speech" (September 27, 1945), in SCAP, Government Section, *Political Reorientation of Japan: September 1945 to September 1948*, vol. 2 (hereafter *PRJ*) (Washington, DC: US Government Printing Office, 1949), 462; and Toshio Nishi, *Unconditional Democracy: Education and Politics in Occupied Japan, 1945–1952* (Stanford, CA: Hoover Institution, 1982), 90–91.
5. Donald Keene, *So Lovely a Country Will Never Perish: Wartime Diaries of Japanese Writers* (New York: Columbia University Press, 2010), 106–8, 113–16, 126.
6. Takami Jun, entry dated August 16, 1945, *Takami Jun nikki* [Diaries of Takami Jun], vol. 5 (Tokyo: Keisō shobō, 1965), 15–16.
7. Cited in Keene, *So Lovely a Country*, 128.
8. "Civil Liberties" (September 10, 1945), in *PRJ*, 460; Dower, *Embracing Defeat*, 65–85; and Yui Daizaburō, "Democracy from the Ruins: The First Seven Weeks of the Occupation in Japan," *Hitotsubashi Journal of Social Studies* 19 (1987): 37–45.
9. Nakano Shigeharu, "Sokkuri sono mama" [Exactly like before], *Kaizō* [Reconstruction] 27, no. 3 (March 1946), cited in Jonathan E. Abel, *Redacted: The Archives of Censorship in Transwar Japan* (Berkeley: University of California Press, 2012), 202–3.

4. SEX, CENSORSHIP, AND SCAP

10. Nishi, *Unconditional Democracy*, 87–88.
11. "Civil Liberties," 460.
12. US Army Forces, Pacific, General Headquarters, CCD, "Code for Japanese Press" (September 21, 1945), in Gordon W. Prange Collection, McKeldin Library, University of Maryland at College Park (hereafter Prange), accessed February 28, 2013, http://www.lib.umd.edu/binaries/content/gallery/public/prange/about-us/censordocs_presscode.jpg.
13. For an example of SCAP suppressing "criticism of Russian soldiers," see Dan Tokusaburō, "Akagun shinchū" [Red army occupation], *Sekai hyōron* [World review] 3 (October 1948), and related censorship documents, in Prange, S765.
14. Sarah C. Kovner, *Occupying Power: Sex Workers and Servicemen in Postwar Japan*. (Stanford, CA: Stanford University Press, 2012), 49–50; Robert Kramm, *Sanitized Sex: Regulating Prostitution, Venereal Disease, and Intimacy in Occupied Japan, 1945–1952* (Oakland: University of California Press, 2017), 29–35; and Barak Kushner, *The Thought War: Japanese Imperial Propaganda* (Honolulu: University of Hawai'i Press, 2006), 171–77.
15. Yamada Fūtarō, *Senchūha fusen nikki* [Anti-war diary of the war generation] (Tokyo: Kōdansha, 2002), 508–9.
16. Yamada seemed to approve of every Japanese person who resolved to die rather than submit to a foreign power, although he himself resolved to live on for the sake of "new Japan." Keene, *So Lovely a Country*, 116–17.
17. Keene, *So Lovely a Country*, 149.
18. On the "liberation" of Japanese women under occupation, see Dower, *Embracing Defeat*, 346–404; and Mire Koikari, *Pedagogy of Democracy: Feminism and the Cold War in the US Occupation of Japan* (Philadelphia: Temple University Press, 2008).
19. Okuda Akiko, "GHQ no sei seisaku: seibyō kanri ka kin'yoku seisaku ka" [GHQ's sex policy: venereal disease control or anti-lust policy?], in Okuda Akiko et al., *Senryō to sei: seisaku, jittai, hyōshō* [Occupation and sex: policy, reality, and representation] (Inpakuto shuppankai, 2007), 13–44.
20. Keene, *So Lovely a Country*, 149, 163.
21. Jay Rubin, "From Wholesomeness to Decadence: The Censorship of Literature Under the Allied Occupation," *Journal of Japanese Studies* 11, no. 1 (1985): 92.
22. Cited in Nishi, *Unconditional Democracy*, 105.
23. Kanō Mikiyo, "'Konketsuji' mondai to tan'itsu minzoku shinwa no seisei" [The 'mixed-blood children' crisis and generation of the myth of the homogenous nation], in *Senryō to sei*, 219.
24. See Rachel F. Moran, *Interracial Intimacy: The Regulation of Race and Romance* (Chicago: University of Chicago Press, 2001), 76–100.
25. "Konketsu no sutego" [Abandoned mixed-blood child], *Nihon keizai shinbun* [Japan economic news], August 9, 1947, in Prange, 47-loc-0535.
26. CCD, "Code for Japanese Press."
27. Kanō, "'Konketsuji' mondai," 219.
28. Yukiko Koshiro, *Trans-Pacific Racisms and the US Occupation of Japan* (New York: Columbia University Press, 1999), 62; see also Yuko Kawai, *Transnational Critique of Japaneseness: Cultural Nationalism, Racism, and Multiculturalism in Japan* (Lanham, MD: Lexington, 2020), 20.

4. SEX, CENSORSHIP, AND SCAP

29. On censorship and publication regarding the atomic bombs, see Rubin, "Wholesomeness to Decadence," 88–91.
30. Okazaki Ayanori, "Minzoku no junketsu to konketsu kekkon" [The pure blood of nations and blood mixing marriages], *Seikei shunjū* [Annals of politics and economics] 1, no. 6 (June 1946): 9–12, in Prange, S465.
31. Okazaki Ayanori, *Kumon no jinkō* [Population anguish] (Ginza shoten, 1946), 1–2, 170–78, in Prange, HQ-0196.
32. "Junketsu" [Pure blood], *Shin'ai* [True love] 2, no. 5 (May 1947): 27, in Prange, S1269.
33. Etō Jun, *Closed Linguistic Space: Censorship by the Occupation Forces and Postwar Japan*, trans. Japan Institute of International Affairs (Tokyo: Japan Publishing Industry Foundation for Culture, 2020), 152–53; and Rubin, "Wholesomeness to Decadence," 97–100.
34. Hiromi Mizuno argues that few scientists reflected critically, much less publicly repented, of their promotion of imperialism or complicity in militarism after defeat in *Science for the Empire: Scientific Nationalism in Modern Japan* (Stanford, CA: Stanford University Press, 2009), 173–84.
35. Kiyono Kenji, *Nihon minzoku seiseiron* [Theory of Japanese race formation] (Nihon hyōronsha, 1946), 1–2, 67, 108–111, in Prange, GN-0023.
36. Kiyono, *Nihon minzoku seiseiron*, 4.
37. Imamura Yutaka and Ikeda Jirō, "Kiyono hakushi no Nihon jinshuron ni kansuru gigi" [Doubts about Dr. Kiyono's Japanese race theory], *Minzokugaku kenkyū* [Raciological research] 14, no. 4 (1950): 317. This journal, published by the Nihon minzoku gakkai since 1935, changed its name (and that of the umbrella organization) to *Bunka jinruigaku* [Cultural anthropology] in 2004; it is still published today. Whatever the latter-day developments, I disagree with moves to identify *minzokugaku* with "cultural anthropology" from the start. Many practitioners in the transwar era were practicing physical anthropology and overt race science rather than deracialized cultural studies. On the origins of *minzokugaku* as a field, see Sakano Tōru, *Teikoku Nihon to jinruigakusha: 1884–1952* [Anthropologists and imperial Japan: 1884–1952] (Keisō shobō, 2005), 403–54.
38. Robert Hellyer, *Defining Engagement: Japan and Global Contexts, 1640–1868* (Cambridge, MA: Harvard University Asia Center, 2009), 39 et passim.
39. Miriam Kingsberg Kadia, *Into the Field: Human Scientists of Transwar Japan* (Stanford, CA: Stanford University Press, 2019), 122.
40. Kadia, *Into the Field*, 128.
41. "Tsushima wa Nihon nari: junsui no Yamato minzoku" [Tsushima is Japan: the pure Yamato *minzoku*], *Yomiuri shinbun*, July 29, 1950, p. 3.
42. Hasebe Kotondo, "Nihon minzoku wa konketsu minzoku de nai" [The Japanese *minzoku* is not a mixed-blood *minzoku*], *Kagaku sekai* [World of science] 23, no. 1 (January 1, 1948): 18–22, in Prange, K70.
43. Arnaud Nanta, "Physical Anthropology and the Reconstruction of Japanese Identity in Postcolonial Japan," *Social Science Japan Journal* 11, no. 1 (2008): 31–32.
44. Kevin Doak, *A History of Nationalism in Modern Japan: Placing the People* (Boston: Brill, 2007), 156.
45. Koyama Eizō, *Shakaigaku gairon* [Introduction to sociology] (Yūzankaku, 1948), 63, 65.

46. Kudō Tokuyasu et al., "Hakujin oyobi kokujin to Nihon fujin to no konketsu taiji" [Mixed-blood fetuses of Japanese women and whites or blacks], *Igaku to seibutsugaku* [Medicine and biology] 10, no. 3 (1947): 179–81, in Prange, I74.
47. Shōji Tadashi, "Konketsuji no keishitsu iden" [The phenogenetics of mixed-blood children], *Iden* [Heredity] 3, no. 1 (1949): 21–23; and Shōji Tadashi, "Aoi me no konketsuji" [A blue-eyed mixed-blood child], *Iden* [Heredity] 3, no. 5 (1949): 22. CCD passed both without examination; see Prange, I55.
48. Shōji, "Konketsuji no keishitsu," 21.
49. Since 1958, Iwakuni has played host to US Marine Corps and Japanese Self Defense forces. US Marine Corps, "Marine Corps Station Iwakuni, Japan," accessed March 15, 2014, http://www.mcasiwakuni.marines.mil/History.aspx.
50. Shōji Tadashi, "Taiwan banzoku (Taiyaru-zoku) seitai no kotsuban keisoku" [Pelvic measurements of the bodies of Taiwanese savage tribes (Atayal tribe)], *Taiwan igaku kaishi* [Journal of the Taiwan Medical Association] 32 (June 1933): 847–51; and Shōji Tadashi and Takeo Uhei, "Taiwan banzoku no gekkei ni tsuite" [On the menstruation of Taiwanese savage tribes]," *Taiwan igaku kaishi* [Journal of the Taiwan Medical Association] 32 (January 1933): 701–7.
51. Yuki Terazawa, "Racializing Bodies Through Science in Meiji Japan: The Rise of Race-Based Research in Gynecology," in *Building a Modern Japan: Science, Technology, and Medicine in the Meiji Era and Beyond*, ed. Morris Low (New York: Palgrave Macmillan, 2005), 83–102. On raciological research in colonial Taiwan, see Sakano, *Teikoku Nihon*, 227–94.
52. See also Mizuno, *Science for the Empire*.
53. Kadia, *Into the Field*; Nanta, "Physical Anthropology"; and Sakano, *Teikoku Nihon*, 469–92.
54. The number of US troops in Japan varied widely, from a peak of more than four hundred thousand in late 1945 to a low of just over one hundred thousand in 1948. At their peak, British Commonwealth Occupation Forces made up one-quarter of the Allied garrison. Takemae Eiji, *Inside GHQ: The Allied Occupation of Japan and Its Legacy*, trans. Robert Ricketts and Sebastian Swann (New York: Continuum, 2002), 126, 131.
55. Shōji, "Aoi me no konketsuji," 22. The Japanese Society of Breeding (Nihon ikushu gakkai) first met in 1915. Five years later, it was renamed the Genetics Society of Japan (Nihon iden gakkai). After a brief interruption in the crisis year of 1945, the society resumed its activities and indeed expanded them with its new journal, *Heredity* (*Iden*), in 1947. By 1956, the Genetics Society had more than one thousand members at sixteen different branches nationwide. Taku Komai, "Genetics of Japan, Past and Present," *Science*, n.s., vol. 123, no. 3202 (May 11, 1956): 825. *Heredity* and the Genetics Society remain prominent today.
56. Shōji, "Aoi me no konketsuji," 22.
57. Shōji, "Konketsuji no keishitsu," 22.
58. C. D. Darlington, "The Genetic Component of Language," *Heredity* 1, no. 3 (1947): 273.
59. Egawa Ureo et al., "Konketsuji ni umarete: zadankai" [Born a mixed-blood child: round-table talk], *Bungei shunjū* [Annals of literature] 31, no. 4 (1953): 239.
60. Shimoji Rōrensu Yoshitaka, *"Konketsu" to "Nihonjin": Hāfu, daburu, mikkusu no shakaishi* ["Mixed blood" and "Japanese": a social history of halves, doubles, and mixes] (Seidosha, 2018), 287–90.

5. COLD WAR *KONKETSUJI*

61. Nagai Hisomu, *Minzoku no unmei: Nihon kokumin ni uttau* [The fate of the race: I appeal to the people of Japan] (Muramatsu shoten, 1948), 3–4, 13.
62. Nagai, *Minzoku no unmei*, 82, 101; and John Dower, *War Without Mercy: Race and Power in the Pacific War* (New York: Pantheon Books, 1986), 311 et passim.
63. Nagai, *Minzoku no unmei*, 5–6, 82.
64. Sumiko Otsubo, "Engendering Eugenics: Feminists and Marriage Restriction Legislation in the 1920s," in *Gendering Modern Japanese History*, ed. Barbara Molony and Kathleen Uno (Cambridge, MA: Harvard University Press, 2005), 244.
65. Nagai Hisomu, *Kekkon dokuhon* [Marriage guidebook] (Shunjūsha, 1939).
66. Nagai Hisomu, *Shin kekkon dokuhon* [New marriage guidebook] (Izumo shobō, 1949), 319–23. Emphasis mine.
67. Nagai Hisomu, *Yūseigaku gairon* [Introduction to eugenics], vol. 1 (Yūzankaku, 1936), 209.
68. Nagai, *Shin kekkon dokuhon*, 319–20.
69. "Sodachiyuku konketsuji: akiraka ni otoru chinō, shakaisei," *Yomiuri shinbun*, morning edition, November 25, 1952, p. 5.
70. Ishiwara Fusao, "Konketsuji no chinō oyobi gakuryoku tesuto no seiseki ni tsuite (II)" [On the results of tests of mental and academic ability among mixed-blood children (II)], *Jinruigaku zasshi* [Journal of anthropology] 77, no. 4 (August 1969): 1–7.
71. Ishiwara Fusao, "Konketsuji no kenkyū wa dō natte iru ka" [How is research on mixed-blood children progressing?] *Iden* [Heredity] 6, no. 11 (1952): 45–48.
72. See e.g. Ishiwara, "Konketsuji no kenkyū wa dō natte iru ka (I)" [How is research on mixed-blood children progressing? (I)], *Iden* [Heredity] 7, no. 1 (1953): 27–28; and Ministry of Welfare, *Konketsu oyobi imin ni yoru Nihon minzoku tai'i no eikyō ni tsuite* [Anthropometric influences of emigration and blood mixture on Japanese race], Jinkō mondai kenkyūjo kenkyū shiryō [Research materials of the Institute for research on population problems (IRPP)], no. 97 (IRPP, 1954).
73. Ministry of Education, *Konketsuji shidō shiryō* [Materials on the instruction of mixed-race children] (Monbushō, 1960), 149.
74. Hiromu Nagahara, *Tokyo Boogie-Woogie: Japan's Pop Era and Its Discontents* (Cambridge, MA: Harvard University Press, 2017), 153–88.

5. COLD WAR *KONKETSUJI*

1. On treaty negotiations, see Jennifer M. Miller, *Cold War Democracy: The United States and Japan* (Cambridge, MA: Harvard University Press, 2019), 114–54.
2. Kenji Hasegawa, *Student Radicalism and the Formation of Postwar Japan* (Singapore: Palgrave Macmillan, 2019), 3–4.
3. "Security Treaty Between the United States and Japan" (September 8, 1951), in US Department of State, *American Foreign Policy 1950–55: Basic Documents*, vol. 1 (Washington, DC: US Government Printing Office, 1957), 885–86.
4. Chris Ames, "Crossfire Couples: Marginality and Agency Among Okinawan Women in Relationships with US Military Men," in *Over There: Living with the US Military Empire from World War Two to the Present*, ed. Maria Höhn and Seungsook Moon (Durham, NC: Duke University Press, 2010), 176–202; Annmaria Shimabuku, "Securing Okinawa for Miscegenation: Gender and Trans-Pacific Empire of the United States and Japan," in *Trans-Pacific Imagination: Rethinking*

Boundary, Culture and Society, ed. Naoki Sakai and Hyun-Joo Yoo (Singapore: World Scientific, 2012), 107–139; and Uezato Kazumi, *Amerajian: mō hitotsu no Okinawa* [Amerasian: Another Okinawa] (Kyoto: Kamogawa shuppan, 1998).

5. John Swenson-Wright, *Unequal Allies? United States Security and Alliance Policy toward Japan, 1945–1960* (Stanford, CA: Stanford University Press, 2005), 7.
6. Joseph Stalin, "Stalin's Message to Japan," *Far Eastern Survey* 21, no. 4 (February 27, 1952): 39; and "US Analyzes Comments by U.S.S.R. for Effecting Japanese Peace Treaty," *Department of State Bulletin* 24, no. 621 (May 28, 1951): 858.
7. Harada Katsumasa et al., eds., *Shōwa nimannichi no zenkiroku* [Shōwa day by day] (Kōdansha, 1989), 249–50; and Hasegawa, *Student Radicalism*, 110.
8. "Rioting Japanese Reds Tee Off on the Yankees," *Life* 32, no. 19 (May 12, 1952): 24–29.
9. See Miller, *Cold War Democracy*.
10. Nick Kapur, *Japan at the Crossroads: Conflict and Compromise After Anpo* (Cambridge, MA: Harvard University Press, 2018).
11. Kanō Mikiyo, "'Konketsuji' mondai to tan'itsu minzoku shinwa no seisei" [The 'mixed-blood children' crisis and generation of the myth of the homogenous nation], in Okuda Akiko et al., *Senryō to sei: seisaku, jittai, hyōshō* [Occupation and sex: policy, reality, and representation] (Inpakuto shuppankai, 2007), 213–60.
12. See John Dower, *Empire and Aftermath: Yoshida Shigeru and the Japanese Experience, 1878–1954* (Cambridge, MA: Council on East Asian Studies, 1988), 305–495; Bert Edström, "Japan's Foreign Policy and the Yoshida Legacy Revisited," in *Turning Points in Japanese History*, ed. Bert Edström (New York: Routledge, 2002), 215–31; Kapur, *Japan at the Crossroads*; and Miller, *Cold War Democracy*.
13. Stanley Cohen, *Folk Devils and Moral Panics: The Creation of the Mods and Rockers* (1972; repr., New York: Routledge, 2002).
14. John Dower, *Embracing Defeat: Japan in the Wake of World War II* (New York: W.W. Norton, 1999), 26; and Yoshida Shigeru, *Yoshida Shigeru: The Last Meiji Man*, trans. Yoshida Ken'ichi and Hiroshi Nara (Lanham, MD: Rowman and Littlefield, 2007), 185.
15. Yoshida, *Yoshida Shigeru*, 183.
16. See Dower, *Embracing Defeat*, 65–86, 225–76; and J. Victor Koschmann, *Revolution and Subjectivity in Postwar Japan* (Chicago: University of Chicago Press, 1996), 203–30.
17. Hasegawa, *Student Radicalism*, 76.
18. Koschmann, *Revolution and Subjectivity*, 220–22.
19. Kim Donggil, "Stalin's Korean U-Turn: The USSR's Evolving Security Strategy and the Origins of the Korean War," *Seoul Journal of Korean Studies* 24, no. 1 (June 2011): 89–114.
20. Oguma Eiji, *"Minshū" to "aikoku": sengo Nihon no nashonarizumu to kōkyōsei* ["People" and "patriotism": nationalism and communalism in postwar Japan] (Shin'yōsha, 2002), 280–81.
21. Hasegawa, *Student Radicalism*, 73.
22. Hasegawa, *Student Radicalism*, 10, 73–76. On male sexual entitlement and misogyny in Japan's postwar leftist student movement, see also Chelsea Szendi Schieder, *Coed Revolution: The Female Student in the Japanese New Left* (Durham, NC: Duke University Press, 2021).

5. COLD WAR KONKETSUJI

23. Christopher Gerteis, *Gender Struggles: Wage-Earning Women and Male-Dominated Unions in Postwar Japan* (Cambridge, MA: Harvard University Asia Center, 2009), 47–50, 58–63.
24. Simon Avenell, *Asia and Postwar Japan: Deimperialization, Civic Activism, and National Identity* (Cambridge, MA: Harvard University Asia Center, 2022), 45–47, 75; and Naoyuki Umemori, "Appropriating Defeat: Japan, America, and Eto Jun's Historical Reconciliations," in *Inherited Responsibility and Historical Reconciliation in East Asia*, ed. Jun-Hyeok Kwak and Melissa Noble (New York: Routledge, 2013), 142. On victimhood nationalism, see also Jie-Hyun Lim, *Global Easts: Remembering, Imagining, Mobilizing* (New York: Columbia University Press, 2022), chap. 1; and James Orr, *The Victim as Hero: Ideologies of Peace and National Identity in Postwar Japan* (Honolulu: University of Hawai'i Press, 2001).
25. Fujioka Tsuyoshi, *Ruisenko-shugi wa naze shutsugenshitaka: seibutsugaku no benshōhōka no seika to zasetsu* [Why did Lysenkoism appear? Fruits and frustrations of dialectical biology] (Gakujutsu shuppankai, 2010), 199–218.
26. "Itamashii hansū wa sutego" [A heartbreaking half are abandoned], *Akahata* [Red flag], January 29, 1950, p. 2.
27. National Security Council 13/2, "Recommendations w/r/t US Policy Toward Japan," in US Department of State, *Foreign Relations of the United States, 1948*, vol. 6 (Washington, DC: US Government Printing Office, 1974), 859.
28. Jay Rubin, "From Wholesomeness to Decadence: The Censorship of Literature Under the Allied Occupation," *Journal of Japanese Studies* 11, no. 1 (1985), 84–85.
29. Hara Momoyo, "Konketsuji no kojitachi: Erizabesu Sandāzu Hōmu" [Mixed-blood orphans: the Elizabeth Saunders Home], *Hata* [Flag] 16, no. 2 (May 1, 1949): 15. See censors' remarks in Gordon W. Prange Collection, McKeldin Library, University of Maryland at College Park, H268.
30. Elsewhere, however, Etō admits that "an unspoken agreement among the Japanese censors" could "sabotage" SCAP aims. Etō Jun, *Closed Linguistic Space: Censorship by the Occupation Forces and Postwar Japan*, trans. Japan Institute of International Affairs (Tokyo: Japan Publishing Industry Foundation for Culture, 2020), 170, 193. On Etō's postwar political project, see Jonathan Abel, *Redacted: The Archives of Censorship in Transwar Japan* (Berkeley: University of California Press, 2012), 1–15; and Umemori, "Appropriating Defeat, 123–44.
31. Rubin, "Wholesomeness to Decadence," 85n43.
32. "Itamashii hansū wa sutego," 2.
33. Ezaki Kazuharu, "Konketsuji ni taisuru shitsumon shuisho" [Gist of questions regarding mixed-blood children], Seventh Diet, question 51 (February 1950); and Yoneyuki Sugita, "A Paradox: The Red Purge Has Made Japan a Law-Abiding Nation," *East Asia: An International Quarterly* 38, no. 4 (2021), 359.
34. Kanō, "'Konketsuji' mondai," 217–20.
35. Sawada Miki, *Konketsuji no haha: Erizabesu Sandāzu Hōmu* [Mother to mixed-blood children: the Elizabeth Saunders Home] (Mainichi shinbunsha, 1953), 30–33.
36. Shimoji Rōrensu Yoshitaka discusses the inquiry, but not the political context, in *"Konketsu" to "Nihonjin": Hāfu, daburu, mikkusu no shakaishi* ["Mixed blood" and "Japanese": a social history of halves, doubles, and mixes] (Seidosha, 2018), 72–74.
37. Sugita, "Paradox," 364–66. On anti-communism, see also Yoshida, *Yoshida Shigeru*, 144–48, 172–96.

38. On educational reform and backlash under SCAP and after, see Toshio Nishi, *Unconditional Democracy: Education and Politics in Occupied Japan, 1945–1952* (Stanford, CA: Hoover Institution, 1982); and Julia C. Bullock, *Coeds Ruining the Nation: Women, Education, and Social Change in Postwar Japanese Media* (Ann Arbor: University of Michigan Press, 2019).
39. Shūgiin yosan iinkai [House of Representatives, Budget Committee], Daisan bunkakai [Third breakout session], no. 1 (February 20, 1952).
40. On the incarceration and "rehabilitation" of thought criminals in late-imperial Japan, see Max M. Ward, *Thought Crime: Ideology and State Power in Interwar Japan* (Durham, NC: Duke University Press, 2019).
41. "Kazahaya, Yasoji," Biographical File, 1945–1952; Records of Allied Operational and Occupation Headquarters, World War II, 1907–1966, RG 331; National Archives at College Park; and Shūgiin honkaigi [House of Representatives, Plenary Session] No. 5 (July 17, 1950).
42. Hans Martin Krämer, "Just Who Reversed the Course? The Red Purge in Higher Education during the Occupation of Japan," *Social Science Japan Journal* 8, no. 1 (2005): 1–18. In "Paradox," Sugita also argues that SCAP sometimes restrained Japanese conservatives from going farther in suppressing communists.
43. Shūgiin yosan iinkai, Daisan bunkakai, no. 1.
44. Hasegawa, *Student Radicalism*, 115.
45. Michael Molasky, *The American Occupation of Japan and Okinawa: Literature and Memory* (New York: Routledge, 1999), 116–23.
46. US Department of State, *FRUS, 1952–1954: China and Japan*, vol. 14, part 2 (Washington, DC: US Government Printing Office, 1985), 1330.
47. Sangiin kōsei iinkai [House of Councilors, Welfare Committee], no. 8 (February 21, 1952).
48. Takemae Eiji, *Inside GHQ: The Allied Occupation of Japan and Its Legacy*, trans. Robert Ricketts and Sebastian Swann (New York: Continuum, 2002), 131. On *konketsuji* sired by men of the BCOF, see Walter Hamilton, *Children of the Occupation: Japan's Untold Story* (2012; repr., New Brunswick, NJ: Rutgers University Press, 2013).
49. Shimoji, "Konketsu" to "Nihonjin," 52, 271–84.
50. Sangiin kōsei iinkai, no. 8.
51. Sangiin kōsei iinkai [House of Councilors, Welfare Committee], no. 2 (November 11, 1948).
52. Sangiin kōsei iinkai [House of Councilors, Welfare Committee], no. 1 (December 6, 1952).
53. Sangiin kōsei iinkai, no. 8.
54. See J. Otto Pohl, *Ethnic Cleansing in the U.S.S.R, 1937–1949* (Westport, CT: Greenwood, 1999); and Heather Rae, *State Identities and the Homogenisation of Peoples* (New York: Cambridge University Press, 2002).
55. Sangiin un'ei iinkai [House of Councilors, Steering Committee], no. 66 (July 7, 1952).
56. Shūgiin yosan iinkai [House of Representatives, Budget Committee], no. 26 (February 20, 1953).
57. Barbara Molony, "From 'Mothers of Humanity' to 'Assisting the Emperor': Gendered Belonging in the Wartime Rhetoric of Feminist Ichikawa Fusae," *Pacific Historical Review* 80, no. 1 (2011): 1–27; Suzuki Yūko, *Feminizumu to sensō: Fujin*

5. COLD WAR *KONKETSUJI*

undōka no sensō kyōryoku [Feminism and war: war collaboration in the women's movement] (Marujusha, 1986), 129; and Chizuko Ueno, *Nationalism and Gender*, trans. Beverley Yamamoto (Melbourne: Trans Pacific, 2004), 22–45.

58. US Department of State, *FRUS, 1952–1954*, 1250.
59. Ichikawa Fusae, "'Dokuritsu' Nihon no fujin mondai: panpan to konketsuji mondai no kaiketsu o" ["Independent" Japan's problem with women: how to solve the *panpan* and *konketsuji* crisis], *Tōyō keizai shinpō* [Eastern economic news] (May 1952): 51–55.
60. Arissa H. Oh, "Japanese War Brides and the Normalization of Family Unification After World War II," in *A Nation of Immigrants Reconsidered: US Society in an Age of Restriction, 1924–1965*, ed. Maddalena Marinari, Madeline Y. Hsu, and Maria Cristina Garcia (Urbana: University of Illinois Press, 2019), 231–39. See also Susan Zeiger, *Entangling Alliances: Foreign War Brides and American Soldiers in the Twentieth Century* (New York: New York University Press, 2010).
61. Ichikawa, "'Dokuritsu' Nihon no fujin mondai."
62. Hiromu Nagahara, *Tokyo Boogie-Woogie: Japan's Pop Era and Its Discontents* (Cambridge, MA: Harvard University Press, 2017), 153–188.
63. Sarah C. Kovner, *Occupying Power: Sex Workers and Servicemen in Postwar Japan* (Stanford, CA: Stanford University Press, 2012), 68–69 et passim.
64. Jonathan Abel aptly notes that press freedom is never absolute in *Redacted*, 2, 13. "Obscenity" is still subject to interdiction by Japanese authorities. See Ann Sherif, *Japan's Cold War: Media, Literature, and the Law* (New York: Columbia University Press, 2009), 54–84.
65. Takagi Masataka, "Nishi Doitsu no onnatachi" [The women of West Germany], *Fujin kōron* [Ladies review] 38, no. 7 (1952): 81.
66. Uemura Tamaki, "Ridgway fujin e: panpan ni atarashii michi o hiraku tame ni wa" [To Mrs. Ridgway: to open a new path for *panpan*], *Fujin kōron* [Ladies review] 38, no. 5 (1952), 38.
67. Takasaki Setsuko, *Konketsuji* [Mixed-blood children] (Dōkōsha isobe shobō, 1952), 16. With less precision but equal alarm, Hotta Yoshie asserted "there must be several tens of thousands" of black *konketsuji*. Hotta Yoshie, "Wareware no unmei" [Our fate], *Fujin kōron* [Ladies review] 38, no. 5 (1952), 125.
68. Jane Fischer, "Kokkyō o koete musubareta watashitachi" [We who are bound together across national borders], *Fujin kōron* [Ladies review] 38, no. 4 (1952): 145–47.
69. Hotta, "Wareware no unmei"; Koyanagi Ayako, "Kono ko ga kawaisō desu" [This pitiable child], *Fujin kōron* [Ladies review] 38, no. 5 (1952): 112–14; Nogami Yaeko, "Konketsuji o kōfuku na michi e" [Toward a happy road for mixed-blood children], *Fujin kōron* [Ladies review] 38, no. 5 (1952): 28–35; Uemura, "Ridgway fujin e"; and Yamakawa Sayoko, "Konketsu no aiji o idaite" [Holding a mixed-blood child], *Fujin kōron* [Ladies review] 38, no. 5 (1952): 108–11.
70. Nakao Kaori, *"Shinpoteki shufu" o ikiru: sengo Fujin kōron no esunogurafī* [Living as a "progressive woman": ethnography of postwar *Ladies Review*] (Sakuhinsha, 2009).
71. Nogami, "Konketsuji o kōfuku," 32–34.
72. Tatewaki Sadayo, "Mibōjin to konketsuji: sensō to chūryū no sanbutsu" [Widows and mixed-blood children: products of war and occupation], *Kaizō* [Reconstruction] 33, no. 11 (1952), 186–87.

73. "Kiken na kyōiku no waku: sodachiyuku konketsuji" [Dangerous framework for education: mixed-blood children who are growing up], *Yomiuri shinbun*, morning edition, November 26, 1952, p. 5.
74. Koya Yoshio, "Konketsu monogatari: sekaiteki ni mita konketsuji mondai" [The story of blood mixing: the problem of mixed-blood children seen globally], *Fujin kōron* [Ladies review] 39, no. 4 (1953): 164–69.
75. Sangiin monbu iinkai [House of Councilors, Educational Committee], no. 8 (December 9, 1952).
76. Sangiin kōsei iinkai, no. 8; and Shūgiin gaimu iinkai [House of Representatives, Committee on Foreign Affairs], no. 21 (February 28, 1953).
77. Sangiin honkaigi [House of Councilors, plenary session], no. 20 (February 2, 1953).
78. Shūgiin gaimu iinkai, no. 21.
79. Itagaki Naoko, "Konketsuji no ryōshin" [Parents of mixed-blood children], *Kaizō* [Reconstruction] 34, no. 3 (1953): 163–64.
80. US House of Representatives, *Report on United States Embassy, Consular Service, and United States Information Agency Operations in Japan* (Washington, DC: US Government Printing Office, 1955), 34.
81. Sangiin honkaigi, no. 20.
82. Kanzaki Kiyoshi, "Shiro to kuro: nichibei konketsuji no chōsa hōkoku" [White and black: report on survey of Japanese-American mixed-blood children], *Fujin kōron* [Ladies review] 39, no. 3 (1953), 128.
83. Nomoto Sankichi, *Kodomokan no sengoshi* [Views of children: a postwar history] (Gendai shokan, 1999), 64–77.
84. See Kanō, "'Konketsuji' mondai," 224; and Shimoji, *"Konketsu" to "Nihonjin,"* 72–87.
85. See also Kristin Roebuck, "Orphans by Design: 'Mixed-Blood' Children, Child Welfare, and Racial Nationalism in Postwar Japan," *Japanese Studies* 36 (2016): 191–212.
86. Norimitsu Onishi, "Yasuhiro Nakasone, Assertive Prime Minister of Japan, Dies at 101," *New York Times* (November 28, 2019).
87. Interestingly, although the United States was well known for its Jewish population, Japanese sounding the alarm about "blood mixing" with Americans almost never voiced concern over "Jewish" blood entering Japan. *Konketsuji* sired by Americans were almost always labeled either "black" or "white," to the exclusion of all other racial possibilities.
88. Shūgiin honkaigi [House of Representatives, plenary session], no. 7 (January 29, 1954).
89. Naikakufu seifu kōhōshitsu [Cabinet Office, Public Relations Room], "Kokusai mondai ni kansuru yoron chōsa" [Opinion poll on international issues], June 1955, http://survey.gov-online.go.jp/s30/S30-06-30-02.html.
90. Koya, "Konketsu monogatari"; and Koyama Eizō, "Shokumin shakaigaku to konketsu genshō" [Colonial sociology and the phenomenon of blood mixing], in *Shakaigaku no shomondai: Takata sensei koki shukuga ronbunshū* [Problems in sociology: essays in honor of Takata Sensei's seventieth birthday], ed. Takata Yasuma (Yūhikaku, 1954), 409–33.
91. Shūgiin yosan iinkai [House of Representatives, Budget Committee], no. 12 (March 4, 1957).

6. ORPHANS BY DESIGN

92. Kapur, *Japan at the Crossroads*, 1–74.
93. Kapur, *Japan at the Crossroads*, 18.
94. Mikuriya Takashi and Nakamura Takafusa eds., *Politics and Power in 20th-Century Japan: The Reminiscences of Miyazawa Kiichi* (New York: Bloomsbury, 2015), 134–35.
95. Sarah Kovner, "The Soundproofed Superpower: American Bases and Japanese Communities, 1945–1972," *Journal of Asian Studies* 75, no. 1 (February 2016): 87–109.
96. See Ames, "Crossfire Couples," 176–202; and Annmaria Shimabuku, *Alegal: Biopolitics and the Unintelligibility of Okinawan Life* (New York: Fordham University Press, 2019).
97. Ezra F. Vogel, *Japan as Number One: Lessons for America* (New York: Harper and Row, 1980).
98. Ezra Bowen, "Nakasone's World-Class Blunder," *Time*, June 24, 2001.

6. ORPHANS BY DESIGN

1. Mae Ngai, *Impossible Subjects: Illegal Aliens and the Making of Modern America* (Princeton, NJ: Princeton University Press, 2004), 233; and Public Law 79–483 Chapter 534, 79 Congress 60 Stat. (1946), 416.
2. Susan Zeiger, *Entangling Alliances: Foreign War Brides and American Soldiers in the Twentieth Century* (New York: New York University Press, 2010), 71–202.
3. "Relief of Amelia S. N. Toneman," *US Congressional Serial Set* (1946): 1–2.
4. Naoko Shibusawa, *America's Geisha Ally: Reimagining the Japanese Enemy* (Cambridge, MA: Harvard University Press, 2006), 13–53.
5. Jennifer Ann Ho, *Racial Ambiguity in Asian American Culture* (London: Rutgers University Press, 2015), 22–43.
6. See also Takashi Fujitani, *Race for Empire: Koreans as Japanese and Japanese as Americans During World War II* (Berkeley: University of California Press, 2011), 125–236.
7. "Relief of Amelia S. N. Toneman"; and *Congressional Record*, vol. 92, no. 7 (1946), 8217.
8. See "Relief of Denise Simeon Boutant," *US Congressional Serial Set* (1949): 1–4; and *Congressional Record*, vol. 95, no. 8 (1949), 11106.
9. Peter Kalischer, "Madame Butterfly's Children," *Collier's*, September 20, 1952, 17.
10. Arissa Oh, "Japanese War Brides and the Normalization of Family Unification After World War II," in *A Nation of Immigrants Reconsidered: US Society in an Age of Restriction, 1924–1965*, ed. Maddalena Marinari, Madeline Y. Hsu, and Maria Cristina Garcia (Urbana: University of Illinois Press, 2019), 235–36.
11. Kristin Collins, "Illegitimate Borders: Jus Sanguinis Citizenship and the Legal Construction of Family, Race and Nation," *Yale Law Journal* 123 (2014): 2134–235; and Ian Haney-López, *White by Law: The Legal Construction of Race* (New York: New York University Press, 2006).
12. See "Relief of Teiko Horikawa and Yoshiko Horikawa," *US Congressional Serial Set* (1949): 1–4; "Relief of Betsy Sullivan," *US Congressional Serial Set* (1950): 1–3; and "Relief of George Lukes," *US Congressional Serial Set* (1951): 1–2.
13. US House, CIN, 79 Cong., hearing, May 16, 1945, 29.

14. Sara Dillon, "Time for a Truth-Based Policy: Humanitarian Access to Children Living Without Family Care," *Florida Journal of International Law* 27, no. 1 (January 2015): 33–34.
15. See also Kristin Roebuck, "Orphans by Design: 'Mixed-Blood' Children, Child Welfare, and Racial Nationalism in Postwar Japan," *Japanese Studies* 36 (2016): 191–212.
16. Darrell Berrigan, "Japan's Occupation Babies," *Saturday Evening Post*, June 19, 1948, p. 24–25, 117–18.
17. Christina Klein, *Cold War Orientalism: Asia in the Middlebrow Imagination, 1945–1961* (Berkeley: University of California Press, 2003).
18. Dorothee Pattee, "Future Pales for 100,000 Children," *Washington Post*, October 5, 1952, p. 78; Milton A. Smith, "Children of Conquerors Have No Future in Japan," *Atlanta Daily World*, December 30, 1950, p. 6; Milton A. Smith, "Babes of Tan Yanks Unwanted in Japan," *Cleveland Call and Post*, January 13, 1951, p. 1A, 3A.
19. US House, Committee on Government Operations, *United States Embassy, Consular Service, and United States Information Agency Operations in Japan*, Hearing (October 7 and 9, 1953), 27. Of "mixed blood" children born before the occupation began or being raised by their foreign fathers, the MOW studies took no note.
20. Pattee, "Future Pales."
21. "Japanese-American War Orphan Discussion Set," *Los Angeles Times*, May 31, 1953, p. A14.
22. Sydney Brookes, "200,000 Set as Orphans of Occupation," *Los Angeles Times*, June 5, 1952, p. 14.
23. Hessell Tiltman, "Occupation Babies: Japan Faces New Social Problem," *Times of India*, July 3, 1952, p. 6.
24. "Japan Says Reports of G.I. Parenthood Are Exaggerated," *Daily Boston Globe*, December 23, 1952, p. 3.
25. US House, *United States Embassy*, 27.
26. Kathryn E. Goldfarb, "Parental Rights and the Temporality of Attachment: Law, Kinship, and Child Welfare in Japan," *Positions: Asia Critique* 29, no. 3 (2021): 569–93; Kerry O'Halloran, *The Politics of Adoption: International Perspectives on Law, Policy, and Practice* (Dordrecht: Springer Netherlands, 2015), 651–52; and Shimoji Rōrensu Yoshitaka, *"Konketsu" to "Nihonjin": Hāfu, daburu, mikkusu no shakaishi* ["Mixed blood" and "Japanese": a social history of halves, doubles, and mixes] (Seidosha, 2018), 88–92.
27. US House, *United States Embassy*, 27–50.
28. See Smith, "Babes of Tan Yanks Unwanted"; and Milton A. Smith "Woman Assisting Japan's Unwanted," *Los Angeles Times*, November 24, 1952, p. 19.
29. Mary L. Dudziak, *Cold War Civil Rights: Race and the Image of American Democracy* (Princeton, NJ: Princeton University Press, 2011); see also Ngai, *Impossible Subjects*, 238–40.
30. Press release of June 25, 1952, McCarran-Walters Bill, General Files 1945–1953, President's Secretary's Files (Truman Administration), HST-PSF, Harry S. Truman Library (HSTL).
31. Memorandum of Conversation with Secretary of State Dean Acheson, Senator William Benton, and Ben Hill Brown, 7/18/1952; Memoranda of Conversations File, 1949–1953: July 1952; Secretary of State Files, 1945–1972; Dean Acheson Papers, 1928–1972; Collection HST-DA, HSTL.

6. ORPHANS BY DESIGN

32. Ethel Payne, "How US Makes Enemies Abroad," *Chicago Defender*, February 6, 1954, p. 9.
33. Yukiko Koshiro, *Trans-Pacific Racisms and the US Occupation of Japan* (New York: Columbia University Press, 1999), 148.
34. US House, *United States Embassy*, 44.
35. See e.g. Okazaki Katsuo's remarks in Sangiin yosan iinkai [House of Councilors, Budget Committee], no. 15 (March 9, 1953).
36. US House, *United States Embassy*, 54.
37. Ngai, *Impossible Subjects*, 238–40.
38. Sangiin yosan iinkai, no. 15.
39. Smith, "Woman Assisting Japan's Unwanted," 19.
40. Pattee, "Future Pales."
41. "Kaigai tanpo" [Overseas shortwave], *Yomiuri shinbun*, evening edition, September 6, 1952, p. 2.
42. Sangiin kōsei iinkai [House of Councilors, Welfare Committee], Boshi fukushi ni kansuru shōiinkai [Subcommittee on mother-child welfare], no. 1 (December 6, 1952); and Tayama Shigeru, "Erizabesu Sandāzu Hōmu no konketsuji yōiku" [Upbringing of mixed-blood children in the Elizabeth Saunders Home], *Refarensu* [Reference] (1953): 48–49.
43. Smith, "Woman Assisting Japan's Unwanted," 19.
44. "Relief of George Lukes," passed as Private Law No. 82–289. For more on the Black American relationship to international adoption in the 1950s, see Kori A. Graves, *A War Born Family: African American Adoption in the Wake of the Korean War* (New York: New York University Press, 2020).
45. See "Relief of Joyce J. Johnson," *US Congressional Serial Set* (1951): 1–4, enacted as Private Law No. 82–380; "Relief of Gregory Joseph Coles," *US Congressional Serial Set* (1951): 1–2, passed as Private Law No. 82–503; "Relief of Eugene Kline," *US Congressional Serial Set* (1952): 1–4, enacted as Private Law No. 82–578; "Relief of Robert Wendell Tadlock," *US Congressional Serial Set* (1951): 1–3, enacted as Private Law No. 82–637; "Relief of Steve Emery Sobanski," *US Congressional Serial Set* (1953): 1–4, enacted as Private Law No. 83–4; "Relief of Norma Jean Whitten (Naneyo Suzuki)," *US Congressional Serial Set* (1953): 1–6, enacted as Private Law No. 83–67; "Relief of Gary M. Stevens (Kazuo Omiya)," *US Congressional Serial Set* (1953): 1–6, enacted as Private Law No. 83–58.
46. US House, *United States Embassy*, 21.
47. "Orphans from Japan Getting Homes in US," *New York Times*, January 10, 1955: 20; US House, Committee on the Judiciary, *Third Semiannual Report of the Administrator of the Refugee Relief Act of 1953, as Amended* (Washington, DC: US Government Printing Office, 1955), 9.
48. Richard H. Weil, "International Adoption: The Quiet Migration," *International Migration Review* 18, no. 2 (1984): 277.
49. Shimoji, *"Konketsu" to "Nihonjin,"* 91; Tsuchiya Atsushi, *"Sensō koji" o ikiru: raifu sutōri, chinmoku, katari no rekishi shakaigaku* [Living as a "war orphan": the historical sociology of life stories, silence, and narrative] (Seikyūsha, 2021), 14–19 et passim.
50. Richard R. Carlson, "Transnational Adoption of Children," *Tulsa Law Journal* 23, no. 3 (Spring 1988), 328; Kirsten Lovelock, "Intercountry Adoption as a Migratory Practice: A Comparative Analysis of Intercountry Adoption and Immigration

Policy and Practice in the United States, Canada and New Zealand in the Post W.W.II Period," *International Migration Review* 34, no. 3 (Fall 2000): 912.
51. Weil, "International Adoption," 280–81.
52. Huping Ling, *Asian American History* (New Brunswick, NJ: Rutgers University Press, 2023), 196.
53. Jaehwan Hyun, "Blood Purity and Scientific Independence: Blood Science and Postcolonial Struggles in Korea, 1926–1975," *Science in Context* (2019): 239–60; and Gi-Wook Shin, *Ethnic Nationalism in Korea: Genealogy, Politics, and Legacy* (Stanford, CA: Stanford University Press, 2006).
54. Kristin Roebuck, "Science Without Borders? The Contested Science of 'Race Mixing' circa World War II in Japan, East Asia, and the West," in *Who Is the Asianist? The Politics of Representation in Asian Studies*, ed. Will Bridges et al. (Ann Arbor, MI: Association for Asian Studies, 2022), 109–124.
55. Arissa Oh, *To Save the Children of Korea: The Cold War Origins of International Adoption* (Stanford, CA: Stanford University Press, 2015).
56. Oh, *Save the Children*, 2, 7.
57. Eleana J. Kim, *Adopted Territory: Transnational Korean Adoptees and the Politics of Belonging* (Durham, NC: Duke University Press, 2010), 46.
58. Examples abound in "Honpōjin to shogaikokujin tono konketsuji mondai" [The problem of mixed-blood children of our nationals and foreigners of various countries], I'6005, I'-0146, Diplomatic Archives of the Ministry of Foreign Affairs of Japan.
59. Tsuchiya, "Sensō koji," 44–55.
60. Roebuck, "Orphans by Design."
61. Oh, *Save the Children*, 150.
62. Tsuchiya, "Sensō koji," 14–19.
63. Setouchi Harumi, *Jinruiai ni sasageta shōgai: jinbutsu kindai joseishi* [Lives devoted to love of humanity: history of the lives of modern women] (Kōdansha, 1989), 245; *Tonneru no mukō wa bokura no rakuen datta* [Beyond the tunnel was our paradise], TV Tokyo, December 28, 2009; Robert A. Fish, "The Heiress and the Love Children: Sawada Miki and the Elizabeth Saunders Home for Mixed-Blood Orphans" (PhD diss., University of Hawai'i, 2002), 9, 220; and "Oiso Orphanage Founder Mrs. Miki Sawada Dies," *Japan Times*, May 13, 1980, p. 2.
64. Kamita Seiji, *"Konketsuji" no sengoshi* [The postwar history of "mixed blood children"] (Seikyūsha, 2018).
65. On Sawada's life as an international socialite and diplomat's wife, see Fish, "Heiress and the Love Children," 5; Naraoka Sōchi, "Sawada Renzō/Miki to Iwasaki-ka, Shōwa tennō" [Sawada Renzō/Miki and the Iwasaki family, Shōwa emperor] (1–3), *Hōgaku ronsō* [Kyoto Law Review] 169–70 (2011); and Sawada Miki, *Kuroi hada to shiroi kokoro: Sandāzu Hōmu e no michi* [Black skin and white heart: road to the Saunders Home] (Nihon keizai shinbunsha, 1963), 89–154.
66. Sawada Miki, *Konketsuji no haha: Erizabesu Sandāzu Hōmu* [Mother to mixed-blood children: the Elizabeth Saunders Home] (Mainichi shinbunsha, 1953), 66–67.
67. Sawada, *Kuroi hada*, 316; Sawada, *Konketsuji no haha*, 62, 90–91, 104.
68. Sawada, *Konketsuji no haha*, 115–18, 121–34.
69. Sawada, *Konketsuji no haha*, 76, 88, 104, 131–32.
70. Sawada, *Konketsuji no haha*, 49–50, 90, 118–119, 141.

6. ORPHANS BY DESIGN

71. Sawada, *Konketsuji no haha*, 105–13.
72. Don Shannon, "Mixed-Blood Children in Japan Find Haven," *Los Angeles Times*, February 6, 1967: 10.
73. See Goldfarb, "Parental Rights."
74. Matsushita Shizuko [likely Sawada writing under an alias], "Konketsuji o sodatete" [Raising mixed-blood children], *Fujin kōron* [Ladies review] 37, no. 12 (1951): 77.
75. Kanzaki Kiyoshi, "Shiro to kuro: nichibei konketsuji no chōsa hōkoku" [White and black: survey report on Japanese-American mixed-blood children], *Fujin kōron* [Ladies review] 39, no. 3 (1953), 128.
76. Fish, "Heiress and the Love Children," 208.
77. See "Babies Deserted by GI Dads Cared for by Tokyo Woman," *Los Angeles Times*, September 26, 1954, p. C8; Pattee, "Future Pales"; Smith, "Babes of Tan Yanks Unwanted," 1A; Smith, "Children of Conquerors Have No Future."
78. "Relief of Gregory Joseph," 2; "Relief of Norma Jean," 3; "Relief of Steve Emery," 3; "Relief of Robert Wendell," 3.
79. Fish, "Heiress and the Love Children," 208–12.
80. Berrigan, "Japan's Occupation Babies," 24, 118; see also Fish, "Heiress and the Love Children," 195–99.
81. Kanzaki, "Shiro to kuro," 128.
82. Sawada, *Konketsuji no haha*, 169–70; and Sawada, *Kuroi hada*, 174–175.
83. "Erizabesu Sandāzu Hōmu: umi o wattata happyakujin" [Elizabeth Saunders Home: eight hundred who crossed the ocean], *Shūkan bunshun* [Bunshun weekly] 20, no. 27 (July 6, 1978): 143.
84. Sidney Xu Lu, *The Making of Japanese Settler Colonialism: Malthusianism and Trans-Pacific Migration, 1868–1961* (Cambridge: Cambridge University Press, 2019).
85. Tsuchiya, "Sensō koji," 128.
86. Sawada, *Kuroi hada*, 241–45, 306–7; and "Erizabesu Sandāzu Hōmu: umi o wattata," 142–43.
87. Shūgiin yosan iinkai [House of Representatives, Budget Committee], no. 13 (July 2, 1953).
88. Takasaki Setsuko, *Konketsuji* [Mixed-blood children] (Dōkōsha isobe shobō, 1952), 16, 19–20, 22.
89. Hirabayashi Taiko, "Jo" [Introduction] to Takasaki, *Konketsuji*, 1–2; Kanzaki Kiyoshi, "Hashigaki" [Foreword] to Takasaki, *Konketsuji*, 3–5; Itagaki Naoko, "Konketsuji no ryōshin" [Parents of mixed-blood children], *Kaizō* [Reconstruction] 34, no. 3 (1953): 163; and "Konketsuji" [Mixed-blood children], *Iden* [Heredity] 6, no. 12 (1952): 10–11.
90. See e.g. Ishiwara Fusao, "Konketsuji no kenkyū wa dō natte iru ka" [How is research on mixed-blood children progressing?] *Iden* [Heredity] 6, no. 11 (1952): 45–48; and Ishiwara Fusao, "Konketsuji no kenkyū wa dō natte iru ka (I)" [How is research on mixed-blood children progressing? (I)], *Iden* [Heredity] 7, no. 1 (1953): 25–29.
91. Sawada, *Konketsuji no haha*, 196; Sawada, *Kuroi hada*, 298–99.
92. See Kamita, *"Konketsuji" no sengoshi*, 28–35, 69, 100; and Nomoto Sankichi, *Kodomokan no sengoshi* [Views of children: a postwar history] (Gendai shokan, 1999), 54–55.
93. Takasaki, *Konketsuji*, 271; see also Roebuck, "Orphans by Design."
94. John G. Russell, "Narratives of Denial: Racial Chauvinism and the Black Other in Japan," *Japan Quarterly* 38, no. 4 (1991): 416–28.

95. Takasaki, *Konketsuji*, 4 et passim.
96. Yokohama-shi sōmukyoku shishi henshū-shitsu [City of Yokohama, General Affairs Bureau, Municipal History Editing Room], ed., *Yokohama shishi* [History of Yokohama] II, vol. 2, part 2 (Yokohama: Yokohama-shi, 2000), 642–43.
97. On interracial liaisons in early modern Japan, see Gary Leupp, *Interracial Intimacy in Japan: Western Men and Japanese Women, 1543–1900* (New York: Continuum, 2003); and Amy Stanley, *Selling Women: Prostitution, Markets, and the Household in Early Modern Japan* (Berkeley: University of California Press, 2012), 72–100. On "blood mixing" in imperial-era Yokohama, see W. Puck Brecher, "Eurasians and Racial Capital in a 'Race War,'" in *Defamiliarizing Japan's Asia-Pacific War*, ed. Brecher and Michael Myers (Honolulu: University of Hawai'i Press, 2019), 209–21; and Yamazaki Yōko, *Onnatachi no andāguraundo: sengo Yokohama no hikari to yami* [Women's underground: postwar Yokohama's light and dark] (Akishobō, 2019), 48–86.
98. Egawa Ureo et al., "Konketsuji ni umarete: zadankai" [Born a mixed-blood child: round-table talk], *Bungei shunjū* [Annals of literature] 31, no. 4 (1953): 233, 240; Hirano Imao, "Konketsuji mondai" [The mixed-blood children problem], in *Senryōka no jidai: shashin kiroku* [Occupation era: photographic records], ed. Nihon kindaishi kenkyūkai (Nihon bukkueisu, 2010), 8–11; "Mushin ni utau konketsuji" [Innocently singing mixed-blood children], *Yomiuri shinbun*, April 8, 1953, p. 6; and Shimoji, *"Konketsu" to "Nihonjin,"* 123–25.
99. Hirano Imao, *Remi no hahatachi* [Remy's mothers] (Kyoto: Shirakawa shoin, 1967), 238.
100. Takashi Fujitani, "Afterword: Transwar as Method," in *Transwar Asia: Ideology, Practices, and Institutions, 1920–1960*, ed. Reto Hofmann and Max Ward (London: Bloomsbury, 2022), 201.
101. See Benedict Anderson, *Imagined Communities: Reflections on the Origin and Spread of Nationalism* (London: Verso, 2006), 85; and Naoki Sakai, "Imperial Nationalism and the Comparative Perspective," *Positions: East Asia Cultures Critique* 17, no. 1 (2009): 159–205.

AFTERWORD

1. Andrew E. Barshay, "Imagining Democracy in Postwar Japan: Reflections on Maruyama Masao and Modernism," *Journal of Japanese Studies* 18, no. 2 (1992): 387. See also Masao Maruyama, *Thought and Behavior in Modern Japanese Politics*, ed. Ivan Morris (New York: Oxford University Press, 1963), 1–24.
2. Maruyama Masao et al, *Gendai Nihon no kakushin shisō* [Progressive thought in contemporary Japan] (Kawade shobō shinsha, 1966), 13.
3. Tsuda Michio, *Zōho Nihon nashonarizumu ron* [Theories of Japanese nationalism, revised edition] (Fukumura shuppan, 1973), 19–20.
4. John Lie, *Multiethnic Japan* (Cambridge, MA: Harvard University Press, 2001), 128–30.
5. Harumi Befu, *Hegemony of Homogeneity: An Anthropological Analysis of Nihonjinron*, (Melbourne: Trans Pacific, 2001), 135–39. A similar argument appears in Kosaku Yoshino, *Cultural Nationalism in Contemporary Japan: A Sociological Enquiry* (New York: Routledge, 1992), 32–36.

AFTERWORD

6. Kenji Hasegawa, *Student Radicalism and the Formation of Postwar Japan* (Singapore: Palgrave Macmillan, 2019); Hiromi Mizuno, *Science for the Empire: Scientific Nationalism in Modern Japan* (Stanford, CA: Stanford University Press, 2009), 173–88; and Oguma Eiji, *"Minshū" to "aikoku": sengo Nihon no nashonarizumu to kōkyōsei* ["People" and "patriotism": nationalism and communalism in postwar Japan] (Shin'yōsha, 2002), 15. See also Oguma Eiji, *Genealogy of "Japanese" Self-Images*, trans. David Askew (Melbourne: Trans Pacific, 2002), 308–12.
7. Jungmin Seo, "Using the Enemy's Vocabularies: Rethinking the Origins of Student Anti-State Nationalism in 1980s Korea," *Review of Korean Studies* 12, no. 3 (2009): 125–46.
8. Chaihark Hahm and Sung Ho Kim, *Making We the People: Democratic Constitutional Founding in Postwar Japan and South Korea* (New York: Cambridge University Press, 2015), 31.
9. On "blood talk," see Jennifer Robertson, "Blood Talks: Eugenic Modernity and the Creation of New Japanese," *History and Anthropology* 13, no. 3 (2002): 191–216.
10. Takasahi Fujitani, "Afterword: Transwar as Method," in *Transwar Asia: Ideology, Practices, and Institutions, 1920–1960*, ed. Reto Hofmann and Max Ward (London: Bloomsbury, 2022), 197.
11. Maruyama, *Thought and Behavior*, 151.
12. Tsuda, *Nihon nashonarizumu*, 19–20.
13. Curtis Anderson Gayle, "Progressive Representations of the Nation: Early Post-War Japan and Beyond," *Social Science Japan Journal* 4, no. 1 (2001): 13.
14. See also Simon Avenell, *Asia and Postwar Japan: Deimperialization, Civic Activism, and National Identity* (Cambridge, MA: Harvard University Asia Center, 2022), chap. 1; and Curtis Anderson Gayle, *Marxist History and Postwar Japanese Nationalism* (New York: RoutledgeCurzon, 2003).
15. Lie, *Multiethnic Japan*, 128–31. Oguma Eiji also suggests the 1960s as the point when praise of Japan as a "homogenous nation" became a frequent feature of Japanese discourse in *Genealogy*, 316. See also Befu, *Hegemony of Homogeneity*, 139–40; and Yoshino, *Cultural Nationalism*, 162–84.
16. See Sheldon Garon, "Saving for 'My Own Good and the Good of the Nation': Economic Nationalism in Modern Japan," in *Nation and Nationalism in Japan*, ed. Sandra Wilson (New York: RoutledgeCurzon, 2002), 97–113.
17. Sarah Kovner, "The Soundproofed Superpower: American Bases and Japanese Communities, 1945–1972," *Journal of Asian Studies* 75, no. 1 (February 2016): 87–109.
18. See Chris Ames, "Crossfire Couples: Marginality and Agency Among Okinawan Women in Relationships with US Military Men," in *Over There: Living with the US Military Empire from World War Two to the Present*, ed. Maria Höhn and Seungsook Moon (Durham, NC: Duke University Press, 2010), 176–202; and Annmaria Shimabuku, *Alegal: Biopolitics and the Unintelligibility of Okinawan Life* (New York: Fordham University Press, 2019).
19. Nick Kapur, *Japan at the Crossroads: Conflict and Compromise After Anpo* (Cambridge, MA: Harvard University Press, 2018), 35–74.
20. Yoshimi Shunya, *Shinbei to hanbei: sengo Nihon no seijiteki muishiki* [Pro-American and anti-American: postwar Japan's political unconscious] (Iwanami shoten, 2007), 10–16.

AFTERWORD

21. Shintaro Ishihara, *The Japan That Can Say No*, trans. Frank Baldwin (New York: Simon and Schuster, 1991). For an example of Ishihara's racism, see Shintaro Ishihara, "Nihon yo uchinaru boei o" [Japan! Defend yourself from internal enemies], *Sankei shinbun*, May 8, 2001, p. 1.
22. M. J. Heale, "Anatomy of a Scare: Yellow Peril Politics in America, 1980–1993," *Journal of American Studies* 43, no. 1 (2009): 24, 27.
23. Heale, "Anatomy of a Scare," 23–38. For the opposite point of view positing Japan as perpetual colony, see Gavan McCormack, *Client State: Japan in the American Embrace* (New York: Verso, 2007).
24. Ezra Bowen, "Nakasone's World-Class Blunder," *Time*, June 24, 2001.
25. Heale, "Anatomy of a Scare," 31–33, 39.
26. Yoshimi, *Shinbei to hanbei*, 13.
27. Shun'ichi Takekawa, "Forging Nationalism from Pacifism and Internationalism: A Study of *Asahi* and *Yomiuri*'s New Year's Day Editorials, 1953–2005," *Social Science Japan Journal* 10, no. 1 (2007): 60, 66.
28. Eugene A. Matthews, "Japan's New Nationalism," *Foreign Affairs* 82, no. 6 (2003): 75–76.
29. See Jackie Kim-Wachutka, "When Women Perform Hate Speech: Gender, Patriotism, and Social Empowerment in Japan," *Asia-Pacific Journal: Japan Focus* 17, no. 1 (June 1, 2015): 1–26.
30. Frank B. Tipton, "Japanese Nationalism in Comparative Perspective," in *Nation and Nationalism in Japan*, ed. Sandra Wilson (New York: RoutledgeCurzon, 2002), 147.
31. Jennifer Robertson, "Hemato-nationalism: The Past, Present, and Future of 'Japanese Blood,'" *Medical Anthropology* 31 (2012): 93.
32. Shimoji Rōrensu Yoshitaka, *"Konketsu" to "Nihonjin": Hāfu, daburu, mikkusu no shakaishi* ["Mixed blood" and "Japanese": a social history of halves, doubles, and mixes] (Seidosha, 2018).

BIBLIOGRAPHY

JAPANESE-LANGUAGE NEWSPAPERS

Akahata
Asahi shinbun
Dōmei sekai shūhō
Mainichi shinbun
Nihon keizai shinbun
Sankei shinbun
Yomiuri shinbun

ENGLISH-LANGUAGE NEWSPAPERS

Atlanta Daily World
Chicago Defender
Cleveland Call and Post
Daily Boston Globe
Japan Times
Los Angeles Times
Times of India
Washington Post

ARCHIVES AND LIBRARIES

Australian War Memorial
Congress.gov (for federal legislative information)

BIBLIOGRAPHY

Diplomatic Archives of the Ministry of Foreign Affairs of Japan
Gordon W. Prange Collection, McKeldin Library, University of Maryland at College Park
Harry S. Truman Library
Japan Center for Photographic Preservation (Nihon shashin hozon sentā)
National Archives and Records Administration, College Park, MD
National Diet Library, Tokyo
Proceedings of the Imperial Diet (https://teikokugikai-i.ndl.go.jp/#/)
Proceedings of the National Diet (https://kokkai.ndl.go.jp/#/)

WORKS CITED

All Japanese-language books were published in Tokyo unless otherwise noted.

Abe Yūkichi. *Yūsei hogohō to ninshin chūzetsu* [Eugenic Protection Law and abortion]. Jiji tsūhinsha, 1948.

Abel, Jonathan E. *Redacted: The Archives of Censorship in Transwar Japan.* Berkeley: University of California Press, 2012.

Ambaras, David. *Japan's Imperial Underworlds: Intimate Encounters at the Borders of Empire.* Cambridge: Cambridge University Press, 2018.

Amemiya, Kozy Kazuko. "The Road to Pro-Choice Ideology: A Social History of the Contest Between the State and Individuals Over Abortion." PhD diss., University of California, San Diego, 1993.

Ames, Chris. "Crossfire Couples: Marginality and Agency Among Okinawan Women in Relationships with US Military Men." In *Over There: Living with the US Military Empire from World War Two to the Present*, ed. Maria Höhn and Seungsook Moon, 176–202. Durham, NC: Duke University Press, 2010.

Anderson, Benedict. *Imagined Communities: Reflections on the Origin and Spread of Nationalism.* London: Verso, 2006.

Avenell, Simon. *Asia and Postwar Japan: Deimperialization, Civic Activism, and National Identity.* Cambridge, MA: Harvard University Asia Center, 2022.

Azuma, Eiichiro. *In Search of Our Frontier: Japanese American Settler Colonialism in the Construction of Japan's Borderless Empire.* Oakland: University of California Press, 2019.

Banno Junji. *Democracy in Pre-War Japan: Concepts of Government, 1871–1937, Collected Essays.* Trans. Andrew Fraser. New York: Routledge, 2001.

Barclay, Paul D. "Cultural Brokerage and Interethnic Marriage in Colonial Taiwan: Japanese Subalterns and Their Aborigine Wives, 1895–1930." *Journal of Asian Studies* 64, no. 2 (May 2005): 323–60.

Befu, Harumi. *Hegemony of Homogeneity: An Anthropological Analysis of Nihonjinron.* Melbourne: Trans Pacific, 2001.

Barshay, Andrew. *The Gods Left First: The Captivity and Repatriation of Japanese POWs in Northeast Asia, 1945–1956.* Berkeley: University of California Press, 2013.

Barshay, Andrew. "Imagining Democracy in Postwar Japan: Reflections on Maruyama Masao and Modernism." *Journal of Japanese Studies* 18, no. 2 (1992): 365–406.

Berrigan, Darrell. "Japan's Occupation Babies." *Saturday Evening Post*, June 19, 1948, p. 24–25, 117–18.

BIBLIOGRAPHY

Bitō Masahide. *Nihon no kokkashugi: "kokutai" shisō no keisei* [Japanese statism: the formation of "kokutai" thought]. Iwanami shoten, 2014.
Borenstein, Eliot. *Men Without Women: Masculinity and Revolution in Russian Fiction, 1917–1929*. Durham, NC: Duke University Press, 2000.
Bowen, Ezra. "Nakasone's World-Class Blunder." *Time*, June 24, 2001.
Burds, Jeffrey. "Sexual Violence in Europe in World War II, 1939–1945." *Politics and Society* 37, no. 1 (March 2009): 35–73.
Brecher, W. Puck. "Eurasians and Racial Capital in a 'Race War.'" In *Defamiliarizing Japan's Asia-Pacific War*, ed. W. Puck Brecher and Michael Myers, 207–26. Honolulu: University of Hawai'i Press, 2019.
Brecher, W. Puck. *Honored and Dishonored Guests: Westerners in Wartime Japan*. Cambridge, MA: Harvard University Asia Center, 2017.
Bullock, Julia C. *Coeds Ruining the Nation: Women, Education, and Social Change in Postwar Japanese Media*. Ann Arbor: University of Michigan Press, 2019.
Buxton, A. Carly. *Unthinking Collaboration: American Nisei in Transwar Japan*. Honolulu: University of Hawai'i Press, 2022.
Campt, Tina Marie. *Other Germans: Black Germans and the Politics of Race, Gender, and Memory in the Third Reich*. Ann Arbor: University of Michigan Press, 2004.
Caprio, Mark. *Japanese Assimilation Policies in Colonial Korea, 1910–1945*. Seattle: University of Washington Press, 2009.
Carlson, Richard R. "Transnational Adoption of Children." *Tulsa Law Journal* 23, no. 3 (Spring 1988): 317–77.
Chatani, Sayaka. *Nation-Empire: Ideology and Rural Youth Mobilization in Japan and Its Colonies*. Ithaca, NY: Cornell University Press, 2018.
Chazono Toshimi. *Mō hitotsu no senryō: sekkusu to iu kontakuto zōn kara* [The other occupation: from the contact zone of sex]. Inpakuto, 2018.
Ching, Leo. *Becoming "Japanese": Colonial Taiwan and the Politics of Identity Formation*. Berkeley: University of California Press, 2001.
Chow, Kai-wing. "Imagining Boundaries of Blood: Zhang Binglin and the Invention of the Han 'Race' in Modern China." In *The Construction of Racial Identities in China and Japan*, ed. Frank Dikötter, 34–52. Honolulu: University of Hawai'i Press, 1997.
Chung, Juliette. "Struggle for National Survival: Eugenics in the Second Sino-Japanese War and Population Policies." In *Trans-Pacific Relations: America, Europe, and Asia in the Twentieth Century*, ed. Richard Jensen, Jon Davidann, and Yoneyuki Sugita, 63–90. Westport, CT: Praeger, 2003.
Cohen, Stanley. *Folk Devils and Moral Panics: The Creation of the Mods and Rockers*. 3rd ed. New York: Routledge, 2002.
Collins, Kristin. "Illegitimate Borders: Jus Sanguinis Citizenship and the Legal Construction of Family, Race and Nation." *Yale Law Journal* 123 (2014): 2134–235.
Cook, Haruko Taya. "Women's Deaths as a Weapon of War in Japan's 'Final Battle.'" In *Gendering Modern Japanese History*, ed. Barbara Molony and Kathleen Uno, 326–56. Cambridge, MA: Harvard University Press, 2005.
Cook, Haruko Taya, and Theodore F. Cook. *Japan at War: An Oral History*. New York: New Press, 1992.
Cook, Theodore F., Jr. "Making 'Soldiers': The Imperial Army and the Japanese Man in Meiji Society and State." In *Gendering Modern Japanese History*, ed. Barbara Molony and Kathleen Uno, 259–94. Cambridge, MA: Harvard University Press, 2005.

Darlington, C. D. "The Genetic Component of Language." *Heredity* 1, no. 3 (December 1947): 269–86.

Dillon, Sara. "Time for a Truth-Based Policy: Humanitarian Access to Children Living Without Family Care." *Florida Journal of International Law* 27, no. 1 (January 2015): 23–64.

Doak, Kevin. *A History of Nationalism in Modern Japan: Placing the People*. Boston: Brill, 2007.

Dower, John. *Embracing Defeat: Japan in the Wake of World War II*. New York: W. W. Norton, 1999.

Dower, John. *Empire and Aftermath: Yoshida Shigeru and the Japanese Experience, 1878–1954*. Cambridge, MA: Council on East Asian Studies, 1988.

Dower, John. "Throwing Off Asia II: Woodblock Prints of the Sino-Japanese War." Accessed August 26, 2023. https://visualizingcultures.mit.edu/throwing_off_asia_01/pdf/toa2_essay.pdf.

Dower, John. *War Without Mercy: Race and Power in the Pacific War*. New York: Pantheon, 1986.

Drea, Edward, and Hans van de Ven. "An Overview of Major Military Campaigns During the Sino-Japanese War, 1937–1945." In *The Battle for China: Essays on the Military History of the Sino-Japanese War of 1937–1945*, ed. Mark Peattie et al., 39–46. Stanford, CA: Stanford University Press, 2011.

Dudziak, Mary L. *Cold War Civil Rights: Race and the Image of American Democracy*. Princeton, NJ: Princeton University Press, 2011.

Earhart, David C. *Certain Victory: Images of World War II in the Japanese Media*. London: M.E. Sharpe, 2008.

Egawa Ureo et al. "Konketsuji ni umarete: zadankai" [Born a mixed-blood child: roundtable talk]. *Bungei shunjū* [Annals of literature] 31, no. 4 (1953): 232–40.

Endo, Masataka. *The State Construction of 'Japaneseness': The Household Registration System in Japan and Beyond*. Balwyn North, Victoria: Trans Pacific, 2019.

Engel, Barbara Alpern. "The Womanly Face of War: Soviet Women Remember World War II." In *Women and War in the Twentieth Century: Enlisted With or Without Consent*, ed. Nicole Ann Dombrowski, 138–59. New York: Garland, 1999.

Edström, Bert. "Japan's Foreign Policy and the Yoshida Legacy Revisited." In *Turning Points in Japanese History*, ed. Bert Edström, 215–31. New York: Routledge, 2002.

Eguchi Tamezō. "Nan'yō ni okeru konketsuji" [Mixed-blood children in the South Seas]. *Nihon iji shinpō* [Japan medical news] no. 1008 (January 1942): 51.

Ericsson, Kjersti, and Eva Simonsen, eds. *Children of World War II: The Hidden Enemy Legacy*. New York: Oxford University Press, 2005.

"Erizabesu Sandāzu Hōmu: umi o wattata happyakujin" [Elizabeth Saunders Home: eight hundred who crossed the ocean]. *Shūkan bunshun* [Bunshun weekly] 20, no. 27 (July 6, 1978): 138–43.

Etō Jun. *Closed Linguistic Space: Censorship by the Occupation Forces and Postwar Japan*. Trans. Japan Institute of International Affairs. Tokyo: Japan Publishing Industry Foundation for Culture, 2020.

Field, Norma. *In the Realm of a Dying Emperor*. New York: Pantheon, 1999.

Fields, Barbara, and Karen Fields. *Racecraft: The Soul of Inequality in American Life*. New York: Verso, 2012.

Fischer, Jane. "Kokkyō o koete musubareta watashitachi" [We who are bound together across national borders]. *Fujin kōron* [Ladies review] 38, no. 4 (April 1952): 145–47.

BIBLIOGRAPHY

Fish, Robert A. "The Heiress and the Love Children: Sawada Miki and the Elizabeth Saunders Home for Mixed-Blood Orphans." PhD diss., University of Hawai'i, 2002.

Foucault, Michel. *The History of Sexuality.* Vol. 1, *An Introduction*, trans. Robert Hurley. New York: Vintage, 1990.

Foundation-Institute for Research on Population Problems [Zaidan-hōjin jinkō mondai kenkyūkai] (FRPP), ed. *Jinkō, minzoku, kokudo: kigen nisen-roppyaku-nen kinen dai-yon-kai jinkō mondai zenkoku kyōgikai hōkokusho* [Population, race, territory: report of the fourth convention of the All-Country Conference on Population Problems on the 2600th anniversary of the empire's founding]. Jinkō mondai shiryō [Population problems documents] 43, no. 1. FRPP, 1941.

Frühstück, Sabine. *Playing War: Children and the Paradoxes of Modern Militarism in Japan.* Oakland: University of California Press, 2017.

Fujime Yuki. *Sei no rekishigaku: kōshō seido, dataizai taisei kara baishun bōshihō, yūsei hogohō taisei e* [The history of sex: from the public prostitution system and criminal abortion law to the Prostitution Prevention Law and Eugenic Protection Law system]. Fuji shuppan, 1997.

Fujino Yutaka. *Kōseishō no tanjō: iryō wa fashizumu o ikani suishinshita ka* [Birth of the Ministry of Welfare: how did medicine drive fascism?]. Kyoto: Kamogawa shuppan, 2003.

Fujioka Tsuyoshi. *Ruisenko-shugi wa naze shutsugenshitaka: seibutsugaku no benshōhōka no seika to zasetsu* [Why did Lysenkoism appear? Fruits and frustrations of dialectical biology]. Gakujutsu shuppankai, 2010.

Fujitani, Takashi. "Afterword: Transwar as Method." In *Transwar Asia: Ideology, Practices, and Institutions, 1920–1960*, ed. Reto Hofmann and Max Ward, 195–204. London: Bloomsbury, 2022.

Fujitani, Takashi. *Race for Empire: Koreans as Japanese and Japanese as Americans During World War II.* Berkeley: University of California Press, 2011.

Fukui, Haruhiro. "Postwar Politics, 1945–1973." In *The Cambridge History of Japan.* Vol. 6, *The Twentieth Century*, ed. Peter Duus, 154–214. New York: Cambridge University Press, 2005.

Garon, Sheldon. "Saving for 'My Own Good and the Good of the Nation': Economic Nationalism in Modern Japan." In *Nation and Nationalism in Japan*, ed. Sandra Wilson, 97–113. New York: RoutledgeCurzon, 2002.

Gayle, Curtis Anderson. *Marxist History and Postwar Japanese Nationalism.* New York: RoutledgeCurzon, 2003.

Gayle, Curtis Anderson. "Progressive Representations of the Nation: Early Post-War Japan and Beyond." *Social Science Japan Journal* 4, no. 1 (2001): 1–19.

Gerteis, Christopher. *Gender Struggles: Wage-Earning Women and Male-Dominated Unions in Postwar Japan.* Cambridge, MA: Harvard University Asia Center, 2009.

Goldfarb, Kathryn E. "Parental Rights and the Temporality of Attachment: Law, Kinship, and Child Welfare in Japan." *Positions: Asia Critique* 29, no. 3 (2021): 469–93.

Graves, Kori A. *A War Born Family: African American Adoption in the Wake of the Korean War.* New York: New York University Press, 2020.

Grossman, Atina. "A Question of Silence: The Rape of German Women by Soviet Occupation Soldiers." In *Women and War in the Twentieth Century: Enlisted With or Without Consent*, ed. Nicole Ann Dombrowski, 162–83. New York: Garland, 1999.

Hahm, Chaihark, and Sung Ho Kim. *Making We the People: Democratic Constitutional Founding in Postwar Japan and South Korea.* New York: Cambridge University Press, 2015.

Hamano Kikuo et al. "Kokuritsu byōin no hassoku o kaikoshite" [Recalling the inauguration of the National Medical Services]. *Iryō: Kokuritsu iryō gakkaishi* [Journal of the National Medical Services] 9, no. 12 (December 1955): 76–91.

Hamilton, Walter. *Children of the Occupation: Japan's Untold Story.* 2012. Reprint, New Brunswick, NJ: Rutgers University Press, 2013.

Haney-López, Ian. *White by Law: The Legal Construction of Race.* New York: New York University Press, 2006.

Hara Momoyo. "Konketsuji no kojitachi: Erizabesu Sandāzu Hōmu" [Mixed-blood orphans: the Elizabeth Saunders Home]. *Hata* [Flag] 16, no. 2 (May 1, 1949): 14–21, 30.

Harada Katsumasa et al., eds. *Shōwa nimannichi no zenkiroku* [Shōwa day by day]. Kōdansha, 1989.

Hasebe Kotondo. "Nihon minzoku wa konketsu minzoku de nai" [The Japanese *minzoku* is not a mixed-blood *minzoku*]. *Kagaku sekai* [World of science] 23, no. 1 (January 1, 1948): 18–22.

Hasegawa, Kenji. *Student Radicalism and the Formation of Postwar Japan.* Singapore: Palgrave Macmillan, 2019.

Hastings, Sally Ann. "Women Legislators in the Postwar Diet." In *Re-Imaging Japanese Women*, ed. Anne E. Imamura, 271–300. Berkeley: University of California Press, 1996.

Hattori Satoshi with Edward J. Drea. "Japanese Operations from July to December 1937." In *The Battle for China: Essays on the Military History of the Sino-Japanese War of 1937–1945*, ed. Mark Peattie et al., 159–80. Stanford, CA: Stanford University Press, 2011.

Heale, M. J. "Anatomy of a Scare: Yellow Peril Politics in America, 1980–1993," *Journal of American Studies* 43, no. 1 (2009): 19–47.

Heiwa hakubutsukan o tsukurukai [Association for creating a peace museum], ed. *Kami no sensō dentan: bōryaku senden-bira wa kataru* [The paper propaganda war: propaganda policy posters tell the tale]. Emīrusha, 1990.

Hellyer, Robert. *Defining Engagement: Japan and Global Contexts, 1640–1868.* Cambridge, MA: Harvard University Asia Center, 2009.

Higuchi, Jirō. "Henry Spencer Palmer, 1838–93." In Vol. 4 of *Britain and Japan: Biographical Portraits*, ed. Hugh Cortazzi, 198–212. London: Japan Library, 2002.

Hirabayashi Taiko. "Jo" [Introduction] to *Konketsuji* [Mixed-blood children], by Takasaki Setsuko. Dōkōsha isobe shobō, 1952.

Hirai Kazuko. *Nihon senryō to jendā: beigun/baibaishun to Nihon joseitachi* [Gender and the occupation of Japan: US military/prostitution and Japanese women]. Yūshisha, 2014.

Hirano Imao. "Konketsuji mondai" [The mixed-blood children problem]. In *Senryōka no jidai: shashin kiroku* [Occupation era: photographic records], ed. Nihon kindaishi kenkyūkai [Modern Japan research association], 8–11. Nihon bukkueisu, 2010.

Hirano Imao. *Remi no hahatachi* [Remy's mothers]. Kyoto: Shirakawa shoin, 1967.

Hirano Yoshitarō and Kiyono Kenji. *Taiheiyō no minzoku = seijigaku* [Pacific races = politics]. Nihon hyōronsha, 1942.

Ho, Jennifer Ann. *Racial Ambiguity in Asian American Culture.* London: Rutgers University Press, 2015.

BIBLIOGRAPHY

Homei, Aya. *Science for Governing Japan's Population*. Cambridge: Cambridge University Press, 2023.
Hoshino, Noriaki. "Racial Contacts Across the Pacific and the Creation of *Minzoku* in the Japanese Empire." *Inter-Asia Cultural Studies* 17, no. 2 (2016): 186–205.
Hotta, Eri. *Japan 1941: Countdown to Infamy*. New York: Knopf, 2013.
Hotta, Eri. *Pan-Asianiam and Japan's War, 1931–1945*. New York: Palgrave Macmillan, 2007.
Hotta Yoshie. "Wareware no unmei" [Our fate]. *Fujin kōron* [Ladies review] 38, no. 5 (1952): 120–29.
Hyun, Jaehwan. "Blood Purity and Scientific Independence: Blood Science and Postcolonial Struggles in Korea, 1926–1975." *Science in Context* (2019): 239–60.
Hyun, Jaehwan. "Racializing *Chōsenjin*: Science and Biological Speculations in Colonial Korea." *East Asian Science, Technology, and Society* 13, no. 4 (2019): 489–510.
Ichikawa Fusae. "'Dokuritsu' Nihon no fujin mondai: panpan to konketsuji mondai no kaiketsu o" ["Independent" Japan's problem with women: how to solve the *panpan* and *konketsuji* problem]. *Tōyō keizai shinpō* [Eastern economic news] (May 1952): 51–55.
Ienaga, Saburō. *The Pacific War: 1931–1945*. New York: Pantheon, 1978.
Igarashi, Yoshikuni. *Bodies of Memory: Narratives of War in Postwar Japanese Culture, 1945–1970*. Princeton, NJ: Princeton University Press, 2000.
Ijichi Susumu. "Kōateki konketsuron" [Blood mixing for the development of Asia]. *Kaizō* [Reconstruction] 21 (March 1939): 83–84.
Imamura Yutaka and Ikeda Jirō. "Kiyono hakushi no Nihon jinshuron ni kansuru gigi" [Doubts about Dr. Kiyono's Japanese race theory.] *Minzokugaku kenkyū* [Raciological research] 14, no. 4 (1950): 311–18.
Ishihara, Shintaro. *The Japan That Can Say No*. Trans. Frank Baldwin. New York: Simon and Schuster, 1991.
Ishiwara Fusao. "Konketsuji no kenkyū wa dō natte iru ka" [How is research on mixed-blood children progressing?] *Iden* [Heredity] 6, no. 11 (1952): 45–48.
Ishiwara Fusao. "Konketsuji no kenkyū wa dō natte iru ka (I)" [How is research on mixed-blood children progressing? (I)]. *Iden* [Heredity] 7, no. 1 (1953): 25–29.
Ishiwara Fusao. "Konketsuji no chinō oyobi gakuryoku tesuto no seiseki ni tsuite (II)" [On the results of tests of mental and academic ability among mixed-blood children (II)]. *Jinruigaku zasshi* [Journal of anthropology] 77, no. 4 (August 1969): 1–7.
Ishiwara Fusao. "Nisshi konketsu jidō no igakuteki chōsa" [Medical survey of Japanese-Chinese mixed-blood children]. In *Jinkō, minzoku, kokudo: kigen nisen-roppyaku-nen kinen dai-yon-kai jinkō mondai zenkoku kyōgikai hōkokusho* [Population, race, territory: report of the fourth convention of the All-Country Conference on Population Problems on the 2600th anniversary of the empire's founding], 209–11. FRPP, 1941.
Ishiwara Fusao and Satō Hifumi. "Nikka konketsu jidō no igakuteki chōsa" [Medical survey of Japanese-Chinese mixed-blood children]. *Minzoku eisei* [Race hygiene] 9, no. 3 (1941): 162–65.
Ishiwara Kanji. *Ishiwara Kanji shiryō* [Ishiwara Kanji documents]. 2 vols. Ed. Tsunoda Jun. Hara shobō, 1967–68.
Itagaki Naoko. "Konketsuji no ryōshin" [Mixed-blood children's parents]. *Kaizō* [Reconstruction] 34, no. 3 (1953): 162–64.
Itoh, Mayumi. *The Hatoyama Dynasty: Japanese Political Leadership Through the Generations*. New York: Palgrave Macmillan, 2003.

BIBLIOGRAPHY

Iwabuchi Koichi and Yasuko Takezawa. "Rethinking Race and Racism in and from Japan." *Japanese Studies* 25, no. 1 (2015): 1–3.

Izuoka Manabu. "Karikomi to seibyōin: sengo Kanagawa no sei seisaku" [Round-ups and VD clinics: postwar Kanagawa's sex policies]. In Okuda Akiko et al., *Senryō to sei: seisaku, jittai, hyōshō* [Occupation and sex: policy, reality, and representation], 119–46. Inpakuto shuppankai, 2007.

Japanese Society for Hygiene [Nihon eisei gakkai]. "Enkaku: eiseigaku no hajimari" [History: the beginnings of hygiene]. Accessed February 16, 2021. http://www.nihon-eisei.org/about_jsh/history.

"Junketsu" [Pure blood]. *Shin'ai* [True love] 2, no. 5 (May 1947): 27.

Kadia, Miriam Kingsberg. *Into the Field: Human Scientists of Transwar Japan*. Stanford, CA: Stanford University Press, 2019.

Kalischer, Peter. "Madame Butterfly's Children." *Collier's*, September 20, 1952, p. 15–18.

Kamita Seiji. *"Konketsuji" no sengoshi* [The postwar history of "mixed blood children"]. Seikyūsha, 2018.

Kamitsubo Takashi. *Mizuko no fu: dokyumento hikiage koji to onnatachi* [Record of lost children: documentary on repatriate orphans and women]. 1979. Reprint, Shakai shishōsha, 1993.

Kanō Mikiyo. "'Konketsuji' mondai to tan'itsu minzoku shinwa no seisei" [The "mixed-blood children" crisis and generation of the myth of the homogenous nation]. In Okuda Akiko et al., *Senryō to sei: seisaku, jittai, hyōshō* [Occupation and sex: policy, reality, and representation], 213–60. Inpakuto shuppankai, 2007.

Kanō Mikiyo. "Nihon no sensō puropaganda to jendā: *Shashin shūhō* no 'Daitōa kyōeiken' 'kichiku Bei-Ei' hyōshō o chūshin ni" [Japan's war propaganda and gender: on the representation of "Greater East Asian Co-Prosperity Sphere" and "Anglo-American demon-beasts" in *Photographic Weekly*]. *Keiwa gakuen daigaku jinbun shakai kagaku kenkyūjo nenpō* [Annual report of Keiwa Liberal Arts Research Center] 6 (2008): 1–11.

Kanzaki Kiyoshi. "Hashigaki" [Foreword] to *Konketsuji* [Mixed-blood children], by Takasaki Setsuko. Dōkōsha isobe shobō, 1952.

Kanzaki Kiyoshi. "Shiro to kuro: nichibei konketsuji no chōsa hōkoku" [White and black: report on survey of Japanese-American mixed-blood children]. *Fujin kōron* [Ladies review] 39, no. 3 (1953): 128–39.

Kapur, Nick. *Japan at the Crossroads: Conflict and Compromise After Anpo*. Cambridge, MA: Harvard University Press, 2018.

Kasza, Gregory J. *One World of Welfare: Japan in Comparative Perspective*. Ithaca, NY: Cornell University Press, 2006.

Kasza, Gregory J. *The State and Mass Media in Japan, 1918–1945*. Berkeley: University of California Press, 1993.

Katō Kiyofumi. *Kaigai hikiage no kenkyū: bōkyakusareta "Dai Nihon teikoku"* [Research on overseas repatriation: the "Great Japanese empire" consigned to oblivion]. Iwanami shoten, 2020.

Katō Shūichi. *"Ren'ai kekkon" wa nani o motarashita ka: seidōtoku to yūsei shisō no hyakunenkan* [What did "love marriage" bring about? One hundred years of sexual morals and eugenic thought]. Chikuma shinsho, 2004.

Kawai, Yuko. *A Transnational Critique of Japaneseness: Cultural Nationalism, Racism, and Multiculturalism in Japan*. Lanham, MD: Lexington, 2020.

BIBLIOGRAPHY

Keene, Donald, *So Lovely a Country Will Never Perish: Wartime Diaries of Japanese Writers*. New York: Columbia University Press, 2010.
Kim, Donggil. "Stalin's Korean U-Turn: The U.S.S.R.'s Evolving Security Strategy and the Origins of the Korean War." *Seoul Journal of Korean Studies* 24, no. 1 (June 2011): 89–114.
Kim, Eleana J. *Adopted Territory: Transnational Korean Adoptees and the Politics of Belonging*. Durham, NC: Duke University Press, 2010.
Kim-Wachutka, Jackie. "When Women Perform Hate Speech: Gender, Patriotism, and Social Empowerment in Japan." *Asia-Pacific Journal: Japan Focus* 17, no. 1 (June 1, 2015): 1–26.
Kiyono Kenji. *Nihon minzoku seiseiron* [Theory of Japanese race formation]. Nihon hyōronsha, 1946.
Kiyono Kenji. *Sumatora kenkyū* [Sumatra research]. Kawade shobō, 1943.
Klein, Christina. *Cold War Orientalism: Asia in the Middlebrow Imagination, 1945–1961*. Berkeley: University of California Press, 2003.
Koikari, Mire. *Pedagogy of Democracy: Feminism and the Cold War in the US Occupation of Japan*. Philadelphia: Temple University Press, 2008.
Komai, Taku. "Genetics of Japan, Past and Present." *Science*, n.s., vol. 123, no. 3202 (May 11, 1956): 823–26.
Komai, Taku. *Nihonjin o shutoshita ningen no iden* [Human genetics centered on the Japanese]. Sōgensha, 1942.
"Konketsuji" [Mixed-blood children]. *Iden* [Heredity] 6, no. 12 (1952): 10–11.
Koschmann, J. Victor. *Revolution and Subjectivity in Postwar Japan*. Chicago: University of Chicago Press, 1996.
Koshiro, Yukiko. *Trans-Pacific Racisms and the US Occupation of Japan*. New York: Columbia University Press, 1999.
Kovner, Sarah C. *Occupying Power: Sex Workers and Servicemen in Postwar Japan*. Stanford, CA: Stanford University Press, 2012.
Kovner, Sarah C. "The Soundproofed Superpower: American Bases and Japanese Communities, 1945–1972." *Journal of Asian Studies* 75, no. 1 (February 2016): 87–109.
Koya Yoshio. *Kokudo, jinkō, ketsueki* [Territory, population, blood]. Asahi shinbunsha, 1941.
Koya Yoshio. "Konketsu monogatari: sekaiteki ni mita konketsuji mondai" [The story of blood mixing: the problem of mixed-blood children seen globally]. *Fujin kōron* [Ladies review] 39, no. 4 (1953): 164–69.
Koya Yoshio. "Konketsu no mondai" [The blood-mixing problem]. In *Minzoku kagaku kenkyū* [Research in race science], no. 1, ed. Hayashi Haruo and Koya Yoshio, 165–170. Asakura shoten, 1943.
Koya Yoshio. *Minzoku mondai o megurite* [On the problem of race]. Kyoto: Jinbun shoin, 1935.
Koya Yoshio, Komai Taku, Taniguchi Konen, and Ōyuki Yoshio. "Minzoku konketsu no zehiron" [The pros and cons of racial blood-mixing]. *Nihon iji shinpō* [Japan medical news] no. 961 (February 1, 1941): 584–92.
Koyama Eizō. *Minzoku to jinkō no riron* [Race and population theory]. Hata shoten, 1941.
Koyama Eizō. *Nanpō kensetsu to minzoku jinkō seisaku* [Constructing the South Pacific and racial population policy]. Dainihon shuppan, 1944.
Koyama Eizō. *Shakaigaku gairon* [Introduction to sociology]. Yūzankaku, 1948.

Koyama Eizō. "Shokumin shakaigaku to konketsu genshō" [Colonial sociology and the phenomenon of blood-mixing]. In *Shakaigaku no shomondai: Takata sensei koki shukuga ronbunshū* [Problems in sociology: essays in honor of Takata Sensei's seventieth birthday], ed. Takata Yasuma, 409–33. Yūhikaku, 1954.

Koyama, Shizuko. *Ryōsai Kenbo: The Educational Ideal of Good Wife, Wise Mother in Modern Japan*. Trans. Stephen Filler. Leiden: Brill, 2012.

Koyanagi Ayako. "Kono ko ga kawaisō desu" [This pitiable child]. *Fujin kōron* [Ladies review] 38, no. 5 (1952): 112–14.

Krämer, Hans Martin. "Just Who Reversed the Course? The Red Purge in Higher Education During the Occupation of Japan." *Social Science Japan Journal* 8, no. 1 (2005): 1–18.

Kramm, Robert. *Sanitized Sex: Regulating Prostitution, Venereal Disease, and Intimacy in Occupied Japan, 1945–1952*. Oakland: University of California Press, 2017.

Kudō Tokuyasu et al. "Hakujin oyobi kokujin to Nihon fujin to no konketsu taiji" [Mixed-blood fetuses of Japanese women and whites or blacks]. *Igaku to seibutsugaku* [Medicine and biology] 10, no. 3 (1947): 179–81.

Kuo, Huei-Ying. "Learning from the South: Japan's Racial Construction of the Southern Chinese, 1895–1941." In *Race and Racism in Modern East Asia*. Vol. 2, *Interactions, Nationalism, Gender and Lineage*, ed. Rotem Kowner and Walter Demel, 151–77. Leiden: Brill, 2015.

Kurashima Itaru. *Zenshin suru Chōsen* [Korea on the march]. Keijō: Chōsen sōtokufu jōhōka [Government-General of Korea Information Bureau], 1942.

Kushner, Barak. *The Thought War: Japanese Imperial Propaganda*. Honolulu: University of Hawai'i Press, 2007.

Kutsuna Shōa. "Shukō Tanmin no taishitsu" [Constitution of the Pearl River Tanka people]. In *Jinkō, minzoku, kokudo: kigen nisen-roppyaku-nen kinen dai-yon-kai jinkō mondai zenkoku kyōgikai hōkokusho* [Population, race, territory: report of the fourth convention of the All-Country Conference on Population Problems on the 2600th anniversary of the empire's founding], 211–12. FRPP, 1941.

LaFleur, William R. *Liquid Life: Abortion and Buddhism in Japan*. Princeton, NJ: Princeton University Press, 1992.

Lee, Sujin. *Wombs of Empire: Population Discourses and Biopolitics in Modern Japan*. Stanford, CA: Stanford University Press, 2023.

Leibold, James. "Searching for Han: Early Twentieth-Century Narratives of Chinese Origins and Development." In *Critical Han Studies: The History, Representation, and Identity of China's Majority*, ed. Thomas Mullaney et al., 210–33. Berkeley: University of California Press, 2012.

Leupp, Gary. *Interracial Intimacy in Japan: Western Men and Japanese Women, 1543–1900*. New York: Continuum, 2003.

Lie, John. *Multiethnic Japan*. Cambridge, MA: Harvard University Press, 2001.

Lim, Jie-Hyun. *Global Easts: Remembering, Imagining, Mobilizing*. New York: Columbia University Press, 2022.

Ling, Huping. *Asian American History*. New Brunswick, NJ: Rutgers University Press, 2023.

Lovelock, Kirsten. "Intercountry Adoption as a Migratory Practice: A Comparative Analysis of Intercountry Adoption and Immigration Policy and Practice in the United States, Canada and New Zealand in the Post WWII Period." *International Migration Review* 34, no. 3 (2000): 907–49.

BIBLIOGRAPHY

Lu, Sidney Xu. *The Making of Japanese Settler Colonialism: Malthusianism and Trans-Pacific Migration, 1868–1961*. Cambridge: Cambridge University Press, 2019.
Mackinnon, Stephen. "The Defense of the Central Yangtze." In *The Battle for China: Essays on the Military History of the Sino-Japanese War of 1937–1945*, ed. Mark Peattie et al., 181–206. Stanford, CA: Stanford University Press, 2011.
Mackinnon, Stephen. *Wuhan, 1938: War, Refugees, and the Making of Modern China*. Berkeley: University of California Press, 2008.
Mark, Ethan. *Japan's Occupation of Java in the Second World War*. London: Bloomsbury, 2018.
Maruyama, Masao. *Thought and Behavior in Modern Japanese Politics*. Ed. Ivan Morris. New York: Oxford University Press, 1963.
Maruyama Masao et al. *Gendai Nihon no kakushin shisō* [Progressive thought in contemporary Japan]. Kawade shobō shinsha, 1966.
Matsubara Yōko. "Chūzetsu kisei kanwa to yūsei seisaku kyōka: Yūsei hogohō saikō" [Loosening abortion regulations and strengthening eugenic policies: Rethinking the Eugenic Protection Law]. *Shisō* [Thought] no. 886 (1998): 116–36.
Matsubara Yōko. "The Enactment of Japan's Sterilization Laws in the 1940s: A Prelude to Postwar Eugenic Policy." *Historia Scientiarum* 8, no. 2 (1998): 187–201.
Matsubara Yōko. "Hikiagesha iryō ni okeru jinkō ninshin chuzetsu" [Artificially induced abortion in the medical care for repatriates]. In *Jendā to nama seiji* [Gender and the politics of life], ed. Tsuboi Hideto, 37–79. Kyoto: Rinsen shoten, 2019.
Matsubara Yōko. "Minzoku yūsei hogohōan to Nihon no yūseihō no keifu" [The *minzoku* eugenic protection bills and the genealogy of Japan's eugenic laws]. *Kagakushi kenkyū* [History of science] 36 (1997): 42–50.
Matsushita Shizuko. "Konketsuji o sodatete" [Raising mixed-blood children]. *Fujin kōron* [Ladies review] 37, no. 12 (1951): 76–79.
Matthews, Eugene A. "Japan's New Nationalism." *Foreign Affairs* 82, no. 6 (2003): 74–90.
McCormack, Gavan. *Client State: Japan in the American Embrace*. London: Verso, 2007.
Mikuriya Takashi and Nakamura Takafusa, eds. *Politics and Power in 20th-Century Japan: The Reminiscences of Miyazawa Kiichi*. New York: Bloomsbury, 2015.
Miller, Jennifer M. *Cold War Democracy: The United States and Japan*. Cambridge, MA: Harvard University Press, 2019.
Ministry of Education. *Konketsuji shidō shiryō* [Materials on the instruction of mixed-race children]. Monbushō, 1960.
Ministry of Welfare. Boshika [Mother-and-child section]. *Kenmin daiippo* [First step toward a healthy people]. Dainihon gageki, 1942.
Ministry of Welfare. *Konketsu oyobi imin ni yoru Nihon minzoku tai'i no eikyō ni tsuite* [Anthropometric influences of emigration and blood mixture on Japanese race]. Jinkō mondai kenkyūjo kenkyū shiryō [Research materials of the Institute for research on population problems (IRPP)], no. 97. IRPP, 1954.
Ministry of Welfare. *Yamato minzoku o chūkaku to suru sekai seisaku no kentō* [Investigation of global policy with the *Yamato minzoku* as the nucleus]. 3 vols. Kōseisho kenkyūjo, jinkō minzokubu, 1943.
Miyake Katsuo. "Naisen konketsuji no shintai hatsuiku ni tsuite: konketsuji no minzoku-seibutsugakuteki kenkyū" [On the corporeal development of naichi-Korean mixed-blood children: racial-biological research on blood mixing]. *Jinkō mondai* [Population problems] 6, no. 2 (1943): 105–54.

Miyake Katsuo and Haruo Mizushima. "Naisen konketsu mondai" [The problem of blood mixing between the interior and Korea]. In *Jinkōseisaku to kokudo keikaku* [Population policy and territorial planning], ed. Jinkō mondai kenkyūkai [Center for research on population problems], 20–21. Jinkō mondai shiryō [Population problems materials] no. 51. Jinkō mondai kenkyūkai, 1942.

Mizuno, Hiromi. *Science for the Empire: Scientific Nationalism in Modern Japan*. Stanford, CA: Stanford University Press, 2009.

Mizushima Haruo. "Nihon minzoku no kōsei to minzoku no mondai (1)" [The formation of the Japanese race and the problem of blood mixing (1)]. *Yūseigaku* [Eugenics] no. 220 (June 1942): 2–7.

Mizushima Haruo. "Nihon minzoku no kōsei to konketsu mondai (2)" [The formation of the Japanese race and the problem of blood mixing (2)]. *Yūseigaku* [Eugenics] no. 221 (1942): 2–6.

Mjöen, Jon Alfred. "Race-Crossing and Glands: Some Human Hybrids and Their Parent Stocks." *Eugenics Review* 23, no. 1 (1931): 31–40.

Molasky, Michael. *The American Occupation of Japan and Okinawa: Literature and Memory*. New York: Routledge, 1999.

Molony, Barbara. "From 'Mothers of Humanity' to 'Assisting the Emperor': Gendered Belonging in the Wartime Rhetoric of Feminist Ichikawa Fusae." *Pacific Historical Review* 80, no. 1 (2011): 1–27.

Moran, Rachel F. *Interracial Intimacy: The Regulation of Race and Romance*. Chicago: University of Chicago Press, 2001.

Moriyoshi Yoshiaki. *Yamato minzoku no zenshin* [Advance of the Yamato people]. Kokusai hankyō renmei, 1942.

Morris-Suzuki, Tessa. *Borderline Japan: Foreigners and Frontier Controls in the Postwar Era*. New York: Cambridge University Press, 2011.

Morris-Suzuki, Tessa. "Debating Racial Science in Wartime Japan." *Osiris*, 2nd ser., vol. 13 (1998): 354–75.

Morris-Suzuki, Tessa. "Ethnic Engineering: Scientific Racism and Public Opinion Surveys in Midcentury Japan." *Positions: East Asia Cultures Critique* 8, no. 2 (Fall 2000): 499–529.

Mullaney, Thomas, et al., ed. *Critical Han Studies: The History, Representation, and Identity of China's Majority*. Berkeley: University of California Press, 2012.

Muminov, Sherzod. *Eleven Winters of Discontent: The Siberian Internment and the Making of a New Japan*. Cambridge, MA: Harvard University Press, 2022.

Nagahara, Hiromu. *Tokyo Boogie-Woogie: Japan's Pop Era and Its Discontents*. Cambridge, MA: Harvard University Press, 2017.

Nagai Hisomu. "Chūgoku ni okeru minzoku ketsueki no kōryū" [Mingling of blood between races in China]. *Nihon iji shinpō* [Japan medical news] no. 1058 (1943): 6–9.

Nagai Hisomu. *Kekkon dokuhon* [Guidebook to marriage]. Shunjūsha, 1939.

Nagai Hisomu. "Minzoku no konketsu ni tsuite." *Minzoku eisei* [Race hygiene] 2, no. 4 (1933): 395–96.

Nagai Hisomu. *Minzoku no unmei: Nihon kokumin ni uttau* [The fate of the race: I appeal to the people of Japan]. Muramatsu shoten, 1948.

Nagai Hisomu. *Shin kekkon dokuhon* [The new guidebook to marriage]. Izumo shobō, 1949.

Nagai Hisomu. *Yūseigaku gairon* [Introduction to eugenics]. Vol. 1. Yūzankaku, 1936.

BIBLIOGRAPHY

Nagai Hōji. "Gomen nasai: Konketsuji no shomondai" [Sorry: mixed-blood children problems]. *6/3 kyōshitsu* [6/3 classroom] 6, no. 10 (1952): 55–59.
Nagayama, Chikako. "The Flux of Domesticity and the Exotic in a Wartime Melodrama." *Signs* 34, no. 2 (Winter 2009): 369–95.
Naikakufu seifu kōhōshitsu [Cabinet Office, Public Relations Room]. "Kokusai mondai ni kansuru yoron chōsa" [Opinion poll on international issues]. June 1955. http://survey.gov-online.go.jp/s30/S30-06-30-02.html.
Nakao Kaori. *"Shinpoteki shufu" o ikiru: sengo Fujin kōron no esunogurafī* [Living as a "progressive woman": ethnography of postwar *Ladies Review*]. Sakuhinsha, 2009.
Nanba Monkichi. "Daitōa sensō to jinshu sensen" [Racial battle lines and the Greater East Asia War]. *Gaikō jihō* [Diplomatic revue] no. 893 (February 15, 1942): 22–34.
Nanba Monkichi. "Minzoku no kōbō to jinkō mondai" [Population problems and the rise and fall of *minzoku*]. *Gaikō jihō* [Diplomatic revue] no. 805 (June 15, 1938): 57–77.
Nanba Monkichi. "Minzokuteki yūgō no kihon mondai: gengo, konketsu, ijū" [Fundamental problems in national fusion: language, blood mixing, emigration]. *Gaikō jihō* [Diplomatic revue] no. 800 (April 1, 1938): 72–86.
Nanba Monkichi. "Shina minzoku ishiki to Tōa renmei" [Chinese *minzoku* consciousness and East Asian alliance]. *Gaikō jihō* [Diplomatic revue] no. 863 (November 15, 1940): 89–103.
Nanta, Arnaud. "Physical Anthropology and the Reconstruction of Japanese Identity in Postcolonial Japan." *Social Science Japan Journal* 11, no. 1 (2008): 29–47.
Naraoka Sōchi. "Sawada Renzō/Miki to Iwasaki-ka, Shōwa tennō" [Sawada Renzō/Miki and the Iwasaki family, Shōwa emperor (1–3)]. *Hōgaku ronsō* [Kyoto Law Review] 169–70 (2011).
Ngai, Mae. *Impossible Subjects: Illegal Aliens and the Making of Modern America*. Princeton, NJ: Princeton University Press, 2004.
Nishi, Toshio. *Unconditional Democracy: Education and Politics in Occupied Japan, 1945–1952*. Stanford, CA: Hoover Institution, 1982.
Nogami Yaeko. "Konketsuji o kōfuku na michi e" [Toward a happy road for mixed-blood children]. *Fujin kōron* [Ladies review] 38, no. 5 (1952): 28–35.
Nomoto Sankichi. *Kodomokan no sengoshi* [Views of children: a postwar history]. Gendai shokan, 1999.
Norgren, Christiana A. E. *Abortion Before Birth Control: The Politics of Reproduction in Postwar Japan*. Princeton, NJ: Princeton University Press, 2001.
Nosaka, Akiyuki. "American *Hijiki*," trans. Jay Rubin. In *Contemporary Japanese Literature: An Anthology of Fiction, Film, and Other Writing since 1945*, ed. Howard Hibbett, 436–68. New York: Knopf, 1977.
Ochiai Emiko. "Modern Japan Through the Eyes of an Old Midwife: From an Oral Life History to Social History," trans. Mio Neuse. In Vol. 1 of *Gender and Japanese History*, ed. Wakita Haruko et al., 235–96. Osaka: Osaka University Press, 1999.
O'Dwyer, Emer. *Significant Soil: Settler Colonialism and Japan's Urban Empire in Manchuria*. Cambridge, MA: Harvard University Asia Center, 2015.
Ogino Miho. "From Natalism to Family Planning: Population Policy in Wartime and the Post-War Period," trans. Leonie Stickland. In *Gender, Nation and State in Modern Japan*, ed. Andrea Germer et al., 198–211. New York: Routledge, 2014.

Ogino Miho. *Kazoku keikaku e no michi: kindai Nihon no seishoku o meguru seiji* [The road to family planning: the politics of reproduction in modern Japan]. Iwanami shoten, 2008.

Ogino Miho et al., eds. *Sei to seishoku no jinken mondai shiryō shūsei* [The problem of human rights in sex and reproduction source collection]. Vol. 25. Fuji shuppan, 2002.

Oguma, Eiji. *The Boundaries of "the Japanese."* 2 vols. Trans. Leonie R. Stickland. Balwyn North, Australia: Trans Pacific, 2014 and 2017.

Oguma, Eiji. *Genealogy of "Japanese" Self-Images*. Trans. David Askew. Melbourne: Trans Pacific, 2002.

Oguma, Eiji. *"Minshū" to "aikoku": sengo Nihon no nashonarizumu to kōkyōsei* ["People" and "patriotism": nationalism and communalism in postwar Japan]. Shin'yōsha, 2002.

Oh, Arissa H. *To Save the Children of Korea: The Cold War Origins of International Adoption*. Stanford, CA: Stanford University Press, 2015.

Oh, Arissa H. "Japanese War Brides and the Normalization of Family Unification After World War II." In *A Nation of Immigrants Reconsidered: US Society in an Age of Restriction, 1924–1965*, ed. Maddalena Marinari, Madeline Y. Hsu, and Maria Cristina Garcia, 231–54. Urbana: University of Illinois Press, 2019.

O'Halloran, Kerry. *The Politics of Adoption: International Perspectives on Law, Policy, and Practice*. Dordrecht: Springer Netherlands, 2015.

Okazaki Ayanori [aka Okazaki Fuminori]. *Kumon no jinkō* [Population anguish]. Ginza shoten, 1946.

Okazaki Ayanori. "Minzoku no junketsu to konketsu kekkon" [The pure blood of nations and blood-mixing marriages]. *Seikei shunjū* [Annals of politics and economy] 1, no. 6 (1946): 9–12.

Okuda Akiko. "GHQ no sei seisaku: seibyō kanri ka kin'yoku seisaku ka" [GHQ's sex policy: venereal disease control or anti-lust policy?] In Okuda Akiko et al., *Senryō to sei: seisaku, jittai, hyōshō* [Occupation and sex: policy, reality, and representation], 13–44. Inpakuto shuppankai, 2007.

Okuda Akiko et al. *Senryō to sei: seisaku, jittai, hyōshō* [Occupation and sex: policy, reality, and representation]. Inpakuto shuppankai, 2007.

Onaga, Lisa, "More Than Metamorphosis: The Silkworm Experiments of Toyama Kametarō and His Cultivation of Genetic Thought in Japan's Sericulture Practices, 1894–1918." In *New Perspectives on the History of Life Sciences and Agriculture*, ed. Denise Phillips and Sharon Kingsland, 415–437. New York: Springer, 2015.

Orr, James. *The Victim as Hero: Ideologies of Peace and National Identity in Postwar Japan*. Honolulu: University of Hawai'i Press, 2001.

Osa Shizue. "Kindai Nihon no jinshu/jinshukaron to 'kokusai kekkon' gensetsu no hen'yō" [Modern Japanese theories of race and racialization and transformation in the discourse of "international marriage"]. *Jinbun gakuhō* [Humanities review] no. 114 (2019): 171–186.

Osawa Koji. "Biruma no dokuritsu to busshari hōsen: Sakurai Hyōgorō ga kōsōshita Daitōa-ji" [Burmese independence and transfer of Buddha's ashes: the Greater East Asia Temple planned by Sakurai Hyōgorō]. In *Shūkyō kara miru sensō* [War from the perspective of religion], ed. Sensō shakaigaku kenkyūkai, 64–82. Mizuki shorin, 2019.

Otsubo, Sumiko. "Engendering Eugenics: Feminists and Marriage Restriction Legislation in the 1920s." In *Gendering Modern Japanese History*, ed. Barbara Molony and Kathleen Uno, 225–56. Cambridge, MA: Harvard University Press, 2005.

Otsubo, Sumiko and James R. Bartholomew. "Eugenics in Japan: Some Ironies of Modernity, 1883–1945." *Science in Context* 11, nos. 3–4 (January 1998): 545–65.
Palmer, Brandon. *Fighting for the Enemy: Koreans in Japan's War, 1937–1945*. Seattle: University of Washington Press, 2013.
Park, Chan-seung. "Yi Kwang-su and the Endorsement of State Power." *Seoul Journal of Korean Studies* 19, no. 1 (December 2006): 161–89.
Peattie, Mark. *Ishiwara Kanji and Japan's Confrontation with the West*. Princeton, NJ: Princeton University Press, 1975.
Peattie, Mark. *Nan'yō: The Rise and Fall of the Japanese in Micronesia, 1885–1945*. Honolulu: University of Hawai'i Press, 1988.
Peattie, Mark, et al., eds. *The Battle for China: Essays on the Military History of the Sino-Japanese War of 1937–1945*. Stanford, CA: Stanford University Press, 2011.
Pennington, Lee. *Casualties of History: Wounded Japanese Servicemen and the Second World War*. Ithaca, NY: Cornell University Press, 2015.
Person, John. *Arbiters of Patriotism: Right-Wing Scholars in Imperial Japan*. Honolulu: University of Hawai'i Press, 2020.
Pohl, J. Otto. *Ethnic Cleansing in the U.S.S.R., 1937–1949*. Westport, CT: Greenwood, 1999.
Pratt, Mary Louise, *Imperial Eyes: Travel Writing and Transculturation*. New York: Routledge, 1992.
Proctor, Robert. "From *Anthropologie* to *Rassenkunde* in the German Anthropological Tradition." In *Bones, Bodies, and Behavior: Essay on Biological Anthropology*, ed. George W. Stocking Jr., 138–79. Madison: University of Wisconsin Press, 1988.
Proctor, Robert. *Racial Hygiene: Medicine Under the Nazis*. Cambridge, MA: Harvard University Press, 1988.
Rae, Heather. *State Identities and the Homogenisation of Peoples*. New York: Cambridge University Press, 2002.
"Rioting Japanese Reds Tee Off on the Yankees." *Life* 32, no. 19 (May 12, 1952): 24–29.
Robertson, Jennifer. "Biopower: Blood, Kinship, and Eugenic Marriage." In *A Companion to the Anthropology of Japan*, ed. Jennifer Robertson, 329–54. Oxford: Blackwell, 2005.
Robertson, Jennifer. "Blood Talks: Eugenic Modernity and the Creation of New Japanese." *History and Anthropology* 13, no. 3 (2002): 191–216.
Robertson, Jennifer. "Hemato-Nationalism: The Past, Present, and Future of 'Japanese Blood.'" *Medical Anthropology* 31 (2012): 93–112.
Robertson, Jennifer. *Takarazuka: Sexual Politics and Popular Culture in Modern Japan*. Berkeley: University of California Press, 1998.
Roebuck, Kristin. "Orphans by Design: 'Mixed-Blood' Children, Child Welfare, and Racial Nationalism in Postwar Japan." *Japanese Studies* 36 (2016): 191–212.
Roebuck, Kristin. "Science Without Borders? The Contested Science of 'Race Mixing' circa World War II in Japan, East Asia, and the West." In *Who Is the Asianist? The Politics of Representation in Asian Studies*, ed. Will Bridges et al., 109–24. Ann Arbor, MI: Association for Asian Studies, 2022.
Rubin, Jay. "From Wholesomeness to Decadence: The Censorship of Literature Under the Allied Occupation," *Journal of Japanese Studies* 11, no. 1 (1985): 71–103.
Russell, John G. "Narratives of Denial: Racial Chauvinism and the Black Other in Japan." *Japan Quarterly* 38, no. 4 (1991): 416–28.

Saaler, Sven, and Christopher W. A. Szpilman. "Imperial Nationalism and the Comparative Perspective." *Positions: East Asia Cultures Critique* 17, no. 1 (2009): 159–205.
Saaler, Sven, and Christopher W. A. Szpilman, eds. *Pan-Asianiam: A Documentary History*. 2 vols. Lanham, MD: Rowman and Littlefield, 2011.
Sakai, Naoki. *The End of Pax Americana: The Loss of Empire and Hikikomori Nationalism*. Durham, NC: Duke University Press, 2022.
Sakai, Naoki. "Imperial Nationalism and the Comparative Perspective." *Positions: East Asia Cultures Critique* 17, no. 1 (2009): 159–205.
Sakano Tōru. "Konketsu to tekiō nōryoku: Nihon ni okeru jinshu kenkyū 1930–1970 nendai" [Blood mixing and adaptability: race science in Japan, 1930s–1970s]. In *Jinshu no hyōshō to shakaiteki riariti* [Racial representations and social realities], ed. Takezawa Yasuko, 188–215. Iwanami shoten, 2009.
Sakano Tōru. *Teikoku Nihon to jinruigakusha: 1884–1952* [Anthropologists and imperial Japan: 1884–1952]. Keisō shobō, 2005.
Sakurai Hyōgorō. "Shokumin seisaku to Nisshi konketsu no haigeki" [Colonial policy and the rejection of Japanese-Chinese blood mixing]. *Gaichi hyōron* [Colonial review] (March 1940): 84–89.
Sawada Miki. *Konketsuji no haha: Erizabesu Sandāzu Hōmu* [Mother to mixed-race children: the Elizabeth Saunders Home]. Mainichi shinbunsha, 1953.
Sawada Miki. *Kuroi hada to shiroi kokoro: Sandāzu Hōmu e no michi* [Black skin and white heart: road to the Saunders Home]. Nihon keizai shinbunsha, 1963.
Sawada Miki et al. "Keredomo konketsuji wa . . . sodatte yuku: zadankai" [Nonetheless, mixed-blood children . . . are growing up: round-table talk]. *Fujin kōron* [Ladies review] 38, no. 7 (1952): 50–57.
Sawayama Mikako. "'Kindai kazoku' ni okeru otoko: otto to shite, chichi to shite" [Man in the "modern family": as husband, as father]. In *Danseishi* [History of men]. Vol. 2, *Modanizumu kara sōryokusen e* [From modernism to total war], ed. Abe Tsunehisa et al., 17–56. Nihon keizai hyōronsha, 2006.
Saya, Makito. *The Sino-Japanese War and the Birth of Japanese Nationalism*. Tokyo: International House of Japan, 2011.
Schieder, Chelsea Szendi. *Coed Revolution: The Female Student in the Japanese New Left*. Durham, NC: Duke University Press, 2021.
Seo, Jungmin. "Using the Enemy's Vocabularies: Rethinking the Origins of Student Anti-State Nationalism in 1980s Korea." *Review of Korean Studies* 12, no. 3 (2009): 125–46.
Setouchi Harumi. *Jinruiai ni sasageta shōgai: jinbutsu kindai joseishi* [Lives devoted to love of humanity: history of the lives of modern women]. Kōdansha, 1989.
Shepherdson-Scott, Kari. "Entertaining War: Spectacle and the Great 'Capture of Wuhan' Battle Panorama of 1939." *Art Bulletin* 100, no. 4 (December 2018): 81–105.
Sherif, Ann. *Japan's Cold War: Media, Literature, and the Law*. New York: Columbia University Press, 2009.
Shibusawa, Naoko. *America's Geisha Ally: Reimagining the Japanese Enemy*. Cambridge, MA: Harvard University Press, 2006.
Shimabuku, Annmaria. *Alegal: Biopolitics and the Unintelligibility of Okinawan Life*. New York: Fordham University Press, 2019.
Shimabuku, Annmaria. "Securing Okinawa for Miscegenation: Gender and Trans-Pacific Empire of the United States and Japan." In *Trans-Pacific Imagination:*

Rethinking Boundary, Culture and Society, ed. Naoki Sakai and Hyun-Joo Yoo, 107–39. Singapore: World Scientific, 2012.

Shimizu Yuichirō. "Kokusaku gurafu 'Shashin shūhō' no enkaku to gaiyō" [History and outline of government graphic *Photographic Weekly*]. In *Senji Nihon no kokumin ishiki: kokusaku gurafu 'Shashin shūhō' to sono jidai* [People's consciousness in wartime Japan: government graphic *Photographic Weekly* and its time], ed. Tamai Kiyoshi, 1–48. Keiō gijuku daigaku shuppankai, 2008.

Shimoji Rōrensu Yoshitaka. *"Konketsu" to "Nihonjin": Hāfu, daburu, mikkusu no shakaishi* ["Mixed blood" and "Japanese": a social history of halves, doubles, and mixes]. Seidosha, 2018.

Shimojima Tetsurō. *Higyō no seishatachi: shūdan jiketsu Saipan kara Manshū e* [The living dead: group suicide from Saipan to Manchuria]. Iwanami shoten, 2012.

Shin, Gi-Wook. *Ethnic Nationalism in Korea: Genealogy, Politics, and Legacy*. Stanford, CA: Stanford University Press, 2006.

Shirane, Seiji. *Imperial Gateway: Colonial Taiwan and Japan's Expansion in South China and Southeast Asia, 1895–1945*. Ithaca, NY: Cornell University Press, 2022.

Shōji Tadashi. "Aoi me no konketsuji" [A blue-eyed mixed-blood child]. *Iden* [Heredity] 3, no. 5 (May 1949): 22.

Shōji Tadashi. "Konketsuji no keishitsu iden" [The phenogenetics of mixed-blood children]. *Iden* [Heredity] 3, no. 1 (January 1949): 21–23.

Shōji Tadashi. "Taiwan banzoku (Taiyaru-zoku) seitai no kotsuban keisoku" [Pelvic measurements of the bodies of Taiwanese savage tribes (Atayal tribe)]. *Taiwan igaku kaishi* [Journal of the Taiwan Medical Association] 32 (June 1933): 847–51.

Shōji Tadashi and Takeo Uhei. "Taiwan banzoku no gekkei ni tsuite" [On the menstruation of Taiwanese savage tribes]. *Taiwan igaku kaishi* [Journal of the Taiwan Medical Association] 32 (January 1933): 701–7.

Silverberg, Miriam. *Erotic Grotesque Nonsense: The Mass Culture of Japanese Modern Times*. Berkeley: University of California Press, 2006.

Stalin, Joseph. "Stalin's Message to Japan." *Far Eastern Survey* 21, no. 4 (February 27, 1952): 39.

Stanley, Amy. *Selling Women: Prostitution, Markets, and the Household in Early Modern Japan*. Berkeley: University of California Press, 2012.

Stargardt, Nicholas. "Wartime Occupation by Germany: Food and Sex." In Vol. 2 of *The Cambridge History of the Second World War*, ed. Richard Bosworth and Joseph Maiolo, 385–411. Cambridge: Cambridge University Press, 2015.

Sugita Naho et al. "Zaidan-hōjin jinkō mondai kenkyūkai no gaiyō" [Overview of the Foundation Institute for Research on Population Problems]. Kokuritsu shakai hoshō, jinkō mondai kenkyūjo [National Institute of Population and Social Security Research]. Working Paper Series No. 41 (2020): 1–14.

Sugita, Yoneyuki. "A Paradox: The Red Purge Has Made Japan a Law-Abiding Nation." *East Asia: An International Quarterly* 38, no. 4 (2021): 353–71.

Supreme Commander of the Allied Powers, Government Section. *Political Reorientation of Japan: September 1945 to September 1948*. Vol. 2. Washington, DC: US Government Printing Office, 1949.

Suzuki Yūko. *Feminizumu to sensō: Fujin undōka no sensō kyōryoku* [Feminism and war: war collaboration in the women's movement]. Marujusha, 1986.

BIBLIOGRAPHY

Suzuki Yūko. *Jūgun ianfu, naisen kekkon* [Military comfort women and Japan-Korea intermarriage]. Miraisha, 1992.
Suzuki Zenji. *Nihon no yūseigaku: sono shisō to undō no kiseki* [Eugenics in Japan: traces of the idea and movement]. Sankyō shuppan, 1983.
Swenson-Wright, John. *Unequal Allies? United States Security and Alliance Policy Toward Japan, 1945–1960.* Stanford, CA: Stanford University Press, 2005.
Tai, Eika. "The Discourse of Intermarriage in Colonial Taiwan." *Journal of Japanese Studies* 40, no. 1 (2014): 87–116.
Takagi Masataka. "Nishi Doitsu no onnatachi" [West German women]. *Fujin kōron* [Ladies review] 38, no. 7 (1952): 78–81.
Takagi Tomosaburō. "Minzoku no masatsu izon seiri jidai" [The era of adjustment of dependence on conflict between minzoku]. *Gaikō jihō* [Revue diplomatique] no. 813 (October 15, 1938): 61–67.
Takagi Tomosaburō. "Nisshi no minzokuteki taisho" [Diametrical opposition between Japanese and Chinese *minzoku*]. *Gaikō jihō* [Revue diplomatique] no. 801 (April 15, 1938): 87–91.
Takami Jun. *Takami Jun nikki* [Diaries of Takami Jun]. Vol. 5. Keisō shobō, 1965.
Takasaki Setsuko. *Konketsuji* [Mixed-blood children]. Dōkōsha isobe shobō, 1952.
Takeda, Hiroko. *The Political Economy of Reproduction in Japan: Between Nation-State and Everyday Life.* New York: RoutledgeCurzon, 2005.
Takekawa, Shun'ichi. "Forging Nationalism from Pacifism and Internationalism: A Study of *Asahi* and *Yomiuri*'s New Year's Day Editorials, 1953–2005." *Social Science Japan Journal* 10, no. 1 (2007): 59–80.
Takemae Eiji. *Inside GHQ: The Allied Occupation of Japan and Its Legacy.* Trans. Robert Ricketts and Sebastian Swann. New York: Continuum, 2002.
Takenaka, Akiko. *Yasukuni Shrine: History, Memory, and Japan's Unending Postwar.* Honolulu: University of Hawai'i Press, 2015.
Takeuchi-Demirci, Aiko. *Contraceptive Diplomacy: Reproductive Politics and Imperial Ambitions in the United States and Japan.* Stanford, CA: Stanford University Press, 2018.
Tamai Kiyoshi, ed. *Senji Nihon no kokumin ishiki: kokusaku gurafu 'Shashin shūhō' to sono jidai* [People's consciousness in wartime Japan: government graphic *Photographic Weekly* and its time]. Keiō gijuku daigaku shuppankai, 2008.
Taniguchi Konen [aka Taniguchi Toratoshi]. *Tōyō minzoku to taishitsu* [Eastern races and bodily constitutions]. Sangabō, 1942.
Taniguchi Konen. "Konketsu no mondai" [The problem of blood mixing]. *Yūseigaku* [Eugenics] no. 229 (1943): 17–19.
Taniguchi Konen. "Nihon rettō minzoku-ron" [On race in the Japanese archipelago]. In *Nihon rettō hen* [Japanese archipelago compilation], ed. Honda Masaji, 378–88. Yamagabō, 1944.
Taniguchi Yasuburō et al. "Ninshin chūzetsu to jutai chōsetsu: zadankai" [Abortion and birth control: round-table talk]. *Fujin kōron* [Ladies review] 38, no. 7 (1952): 136–41.
Taniguchi Yasuburō and Fukuda Masako. *Yūsei hogohō kaisetsu* [Explanation of the Eugenic Protection Law]. Kenshinsha, 1948.
Tatewaki Sadayo. "Mibōjin to konketsuji: sensō to chūryū no sanbutsu" [Widows and mixed-blood children: products of war and occupation]. *Kaizō* [Reconstruction] 33, no. 11 (1952): 184–87.

BIBLIOGRAPHY

Tayama Shigeru. "Erizabesu Sandāzu Hōmu no konketsuji yōiku" [Upbringing of mixed-blood children in the Elizabeth Saunders Home]. *Refarensu* [Reference] (1953): 48–49.
Teng, Emma J. *Eurasian: Mixed Identities in the United States, China, and Hong Kong, 1842–1943*. Berkeley: University of California Press, 2013.
Teng, Emma J. "On Not Looking Chinese: Does 'Mixed Race' Decenter the Han from Chineseness?" In *Critical Han Studies: The History, Representation, and Identity of China's Majority*, ed. Thomas Mullaney et al., 45–71. Berkeley: University of California Press, 2012.
Terazawa, Yuki. "Racializing Bodies Through Science in Meiji Japan: The Rise of Race-Based Research in Gynecology." In *Building a Modern Japan: Science, Technology, and Medicine in the Meiji Era and Beyond*, ed. Morris Low, 83–102. New York: Palgrave Macmillan, 2005.
Thomas, Julia Adeney. "Japan's War Without Pictures: Normalizing Fascism." In *Visualizing Fascism: The Twentieth-Century Rise of the Global Right*, ed. Julia Adeney Thomas and Geoff Eley. Durham, NC: Duke University Press, 2020.
Tikhonov, Vladimir. *Modern Korea and Its Others: Perceptions of the Neighbouring Countries and Korean Modernity*. New York: Routledge, 2016.
Tipton, Frank B. "Japanese Nationalism in Comparative Perspective." In *Nation and Nationalism in Japan*, ed. Sandra Wilson, 146–62. New York: RoutledgeCurzon, 2002.
Tonneru no mukō wa bokura no rakuen datta [Beyond the tunnel was our paradise]. TV Tokyo. December 28, 2009.
Tsou Jung [Zou Rong]. *The Revolutionary Army: A Chinese Nationalist Tract of 1903*. Trans. John Lust. Paris: Mouton, 1968.
Tsuchiya Atsushi. *"Sensō koji" o ikiru: raifu sutōrī, chinmoku, katari no rekishi shakaigaku* [Living as a "war orphan": the historical sociology of life stories, silence, and narrative]. Seikyūsha, 2021.
Tsuda Michio. *Zōho Nihon nashonarizumu ron* [Theories of Japanese nationalism, revised edition]. Fukumura shuppan, 1973.
Tsuruoka Satoshi. "'Shashin shūhō' ni miru Higashi Ajia-kan" [The view of East Asia seen in *Photographic Weekly*]. In *Senji Nihon no kokumin ishiki: kokusaku gurafu 'Shashin shūhō' to sono jidai* [People's consciousness in wartime Japan: government graphic *Photographic Weekly* and its time], ed. Tamai Kiyoshi, 295–332. Keiō gijuku daigaku shuppankai, 2008.
Uchida, Jun. *Brokers of Empire: Japanese Settler Colonialism in Korea, 1876–1945*. Cambridge, MA: Harvard University Press, 2001.
Uchiyama, Benjamin. *Japan's Carnival War: Mass Culture on the Home Front, 1937–1945*. New York: Cambridge University Press, 2019.
Ueda Tatsuo. *Sumera Chōsen* [The Emperor's Korea]. Nihon seinen bunka kyōkai, 1943.
Uemura Tamaki. "Ridgway fujin e: panpan ni atarashii michi o hiraku tame ni wa" [To Mrs. Ridgway: to open a new path for *panpan*]. *Fujin kōron* [Ladies review] 38, no. 5 (1952): 36–40.
Ueno, Chizuko. *Nationalism and Gender*. Trans. Beverley Yamamoto. Melbourne: Trans Pacific, 2004.
Uezato Kazumi. *Amerajian: mō hitotsu no Okinawa* [Amerasian: Another Okinawa]. Kyoto: Kamogawa shuppan, 1998.

Umemori, Naoyuki. "Appropriating Defeat: Japan, America, and Eto Jun's Historical Reconciliations." In *Inherited Responsibility and Historical Reconciliation in East Asia*, ed. Jun-Hyeok Kwak and Melissa Noble, 123–44. New York: Routledge, 2013.

United States Department of State. *American Foreign Policy 1950–55: Basic Documents*. Vol. 1. Washington, DC: US Government Printing Office, 1957.

United States Department of State. *Foreign Relations of the United States: Diplomatic Papers, 1937*. Vol. 3, *The Far East*. Washington, DC: US Government Printing Office, 1954.

United States Department of State. *Foreign Relations of the United States, 1948*. Vol. 6. Washington, DC: US Government Printing Office, 1974.

United States Department of State. *Foreign Relations of the United States, 1952–1954: China and Japan*. Vol. 14, Part 2. Washington, DC: US Government Printing Office, 1985.

United States Department of State. "Analysis of the 1946 Japanese General Election." Office of Research and Intelligence no. 3492. Washington, DC, May 15, 1946.

United States House of Representatives. Committee on Government Operations. *Report on United States Embassy, Consular Service, and United States Information Agency Operations in Japan*. Washington, DC: US Government Printing Office, 1955.

United States House of Representatives. Committee on Immigration and Naturalization. Hearing, 79 Cong., May 16, 1945.

United States House of Representatives. Committee on the Judiciary. *Third Semiannual Report of the Administrator of the Refugee Relief Act of 1953, as Amended*. Washington, DC: US Government Printing Office, 1955.

United States Marine Corps. "Marine Corps Station Iwakuni, Japan." Accessed March 15, 2014. http://www.mcasiwakuni.marines.mil/History.aspx.

Uno, Kathleen. *Passages to Modernity: Motherhood, Childhood, and Social Reform in Early Twentieth-Century Japan*. Honolulu: University of Hawai'i Press, 1999.

"US Analyzes Comments by U.S.S.R. for Effecting Japanese Peace Treaty." *Department of State Bulletin* 24, no. 621 (May 28, 1951): 852–58.

Vogel, Ezra F. *Japan as Number One: Lessons for America*. New York: Harper and Row, 1980.

Watsuji Tetsurō. "Kodai Nihonjin no konketsu jōtai" [The state of blood mixing among ancient Japanese] (1917). In *Watsuji Tetsurō Nihon kodai bunka-ron shūsei* [Watsuji Tetsurō's collected works on Japan's ancient culture] Shoshi shinsui, 2012.

Wakakuwa Midori. *Sensō ga tsukuru josei zō* [Image of women forged in war]. Chikuma shobō, 1995.

Ward, Max. "Crisis Ideology and the Articulation of Fascism in Interwar Japan: The 1938 Thought-War Symposium." *Japan Forum* 26, no. 4 (2014): 462–85.

Ward, Max. *Thought Crime: Ideology and State Power in Interwar Japan*. Durham, NC: Duke University Press, 2019.

Watt, Lori. *When Empire Comes Home: Repatriation and Reintegration in Postwar Japan*. Cambridge, MA: Harvard University Asia Center, 2009.

Weber, Torsten. *Embracing "Asia" in China and Japan: Asianism Discourse and the Contest for Hegemony, 1912–1933*." Cham, Switzerland: Palgrave Macmillan, 2018.

Weil, Richard H. "International Adoption: The Quiet Migration." *International Migration Review* 18, no. 2 (1984): 276–93.

Wigger, Iris. *The "Black Horror on the Rhine": Intersections of Race, Nation, Gender and Class in 1920s Germany*. London: Palgrave Macmillan, 2017.

BIBLIOGRAPHY

Wilson, Sandra, ed. *Nation and Nationalism in Japan*. New York: RoutledgeCurzon, 2002.
"Wuhan komori-uta" [Wuhan lullaby]. *Shashin shūhō* [Photographic weekly], no. 47. January 11, 1939, p. 4–5.
Yamada Fūtarō. *Senchūha fusen nikki* [Anti-war diary of the war generation]. Kōdansha, 2002.
Yamakawa Sayoko. "Konketsu no aiji o idaite" [Holding a mixed-blood child]. *Fujin kōron* [Ladies review] 38, no. 5 (1952): 108–111.
Yamazaki Yōko. *Onnatachi no andāguraundo: sengo Yokohama no hikari to yami* [Women's underground: postwar Yokohama's light and dark]. Akishobō, 2019.
Yellen, Jeremy. *The Greater East Asia Co-Prosperity Sphere: When Total Empire Met Total War*. Ithaca, NY: Cornell University Press, 2019.
Yi Jonson. "'Naisen kekkon' no kodomotachi: naichijin to Chōsenjin no hazama de" [The children of "interior-Korea marriage": at the interstices of inlanders and Koreans]. *Rekishi hyōron* [Historical journal] no. 815 (2018): 42–55.
Yokohama-shi sōmukyoku shishi henshū-shitsu [City of Yokohama, General Affairs Bureau, Municipal History Editing Room], ed. *Yokohama shishi* II [History of the city of Yokohama II]. Vol. 2, Part 2. Yokohama: Yokohama-shi, 2000.
Yokoyama Takashi. *Nihon ga yūsei shakai ni naru made: kagaku keimō, media, seishoku no seiji* [Until Japan is a eugenic society: scientific enlightenment, media, and the politics of reproduction]. Keisō shobō, 2015.
Yoneyama, Lisa. *Hiroshima Traces: Time, Space, and the Dialectics of Memory*. Berkeley: University of California Press, 1999.
Yoshida Shigeru. *Yoshida Shigeru: The Last Meiji Man*. Trans. Yoshida Ken'ichi and Hiroshi Nara. Lanham, MD: Rowman and Littlefield, 2007.
Yoshimi Shunya. *Shinbei to hanbei: sengo Nihon no seijiteki muishiki* [Pro-American and anti-American: postwar Japan's political unconscious]. Iwanami shoten, 2007.
Yoshimi, Yoshiaki. *Comfort Women: Sexual Slavery in the Japanese Military During World War II*. Trans. Suzanne O'Brien. New York: Columbia University Press, 2000.
Yoshimi, Yoshiaki. *Grassroots Fascism: The War Experience of the Japanese People*. Trans. Ethan Mark. New York: Columbia University Press, 2015.
Yoshino, Kosaku. *Cultural Nationalism in Contemporary Japan: A Sociological Enquiry*. New York: Routledge, 1992.
Young, Louise. "Ideologies of Difference and the Turn to Atrocity: Japan's War on China." In *A World at Total War: Global Conflict and the Politics of Destruction, 1937–1945*, ed. Roger Chickering et al., 343–47. Cambridge: Cambridge University Press, 2005.
Young, Louise. *Japan's Total Empire: Manchuria and the Culture of Wartime Imperialism*. Berkeley: University of California Press, 1998.
Yui Daizaburō. "Democracy from the Ruins: The First Seven Weeks of the Occupation in Japan." *Hitotsubashi Journal of Social Studies* 19 (1987): 31–45.
Zeiger, Susan. *Entangling Alliances: Foreign War Brides and American Soldiers in the Twentieth Century*. New York: New York University Press, 2010.
Ziomek, Kirsten. *Lost Histories: Recovering the Lives of Japan's Colonial Peoples*. Cambridge, MA: Harvard University Asia Center, 2019.

INDEX

abandoned children: in China, 44–50, 45, 46, 48, 50, 54–55, 55; in Japan, 54, 129–30, 160–64, 167–168, 175–76, 181; numbers of, 179, 194–95, 209–11; Sawada Miki and, 200, 205–11; in US news reports, 193–95, 209–10
"Abandoned Mixed-Blood Child" (article), 129
Abe Toshio, 103
abortion, 9, 11, 73, 108; coerced, 103, 107–8, 120–22, 140; criminalized, 96, 117–18; decriminalization, 16, 101–2, 110, 115; eugenic, 108, 113, 117–22, 171, 178, 220; Eugenic Protection Law and, 6, 16, 93, 117–22; fatal to mother, 105–6; in Germany, 119; husband's permission for, 118–19; illegal, 93, 96, 101–7; of *konketsuji*, 93, 98–99, 101–7, 120–22, 139–40, 171, 178; *panpan* and, 120, 171; rape and, 96, 98, 116, 118. *See also* infanticide
adoption, 3–4; battlefield, 44–56, 45, 46, 48, 50, 55; ethnic cleansing and, 192–93, 195–96, 198– 205, 209–13, 216; as forced migration, 201; in imperial Japan, 7, 14, 19–20, 28, 44–57; from Korea, 201–4; Sawada Miki and, 192–93, 199–201, 204–13, 207, 216; US international, 16–17, 189–213, 216, 259n44
Aikoku fujinkai. *See* Patriotic Women's Association
Ainu, 2, 35, 234n42
Akahata. *See* Red Flag
All-Country Conference on Population Problems, 68, 72–77
alliance, US-Japan. *See* Anpo
Allied forces, 220; in Korea, 93–95, 156, 202; racism among, 92, 129, 133; sexual violence and, 92–97, 104–6, 108, 116, 118, 127; in World War II, 41, 89, 92–96, 156, 187
Allied occupation of Japan, 5–6, 11, 14, 92–135; Cold War and, 156–67; end of, 120–22, 130, 130–31, 149–154, 161–62, 164–67, 172–79, 218–20; fraternization and, 6, 16, 92–93, 120–21, 127–29, 152, 158–60, 169, 171, 171–75; *konketsuji* and, 92–93, 97–98, 101–8, 111–14, 116–22, 127, 129–34, 137–43, 149–50, 158–81, 170, 171–80, 189–96, 190, 199–216, 207, 221; race science and, 132–50. *See also* BCOF; SCAP
Amaterasu, 27

INDEX

Americanization: of Japan, 144–45, 218; of *konketsuji*, 156, 168–73, 186
Anderson, Benedict, 7–8
Andō Sakan, 19
Anpo (Security Treaty Between the United States and Japan, 1951), 5–6, 13–14, 16, 151–55, 221–26; *konketsuji* and, 16–17, 150, 165–86, 192–96, 198–204, 206, 214–16, 221–22; LDP and, 184–85, 223–24; protests of, 16, 151–55, *154*, 184–85, 221–25; revision of, 184–85; text of, 152; US legal reform and, 16–17, 188–93, 197–204
anti-American. *See* nationalism, anti-American
anti-Blackness. *See* racism, anti-Black
anti-Semitism. *See* racism, anti-Semitic
Aryan "race," 25, 67, 72, 75
Ashida Hitoshi, 101–2, 116
atomic bombs, 131, 212, 221
Australia: Japanese migration to, *170*; *konketsuji* and, 140–41, 168, *170*, 254n48; in Korean War, 169; occupying Japan, 140–41, 168–70, *169*; race in, 129, 133; in World War II, 9, *10*, 62, 169
autogenocide, 94–95. *See also* genocide

baby boom, 11, 110
Baishun bōshihō. See Prostitution Prevention Law
Barclay, Paul, 18–19
battlefield adoption, 44–56, *45*, *46*, *48*, *50*, *55*
BCOF. *See* British Commonwealth Occupation Force
Beijing (Peking), China: Japanese capture of, 87; Nagai in, 87–89
Berrigan, Darryl, 210–11
biologizing defeat, 60, 112, 133, 141–47, 192; JCP and, 160–61; war on China and, 15, 69–72, 79–82, 84–85, 87–91, 145, 152, 228
birth control, 9, 11, 73, 100, 110–12, 115–17, 121
Black Americans, 86, 148, 173, 178–79, *190*, 213; as adoptive parents, 200, 259n44; as "blood mixers," 149, 172–73, 175–76, 178–79, *190*, 200, 212–13; sexual violence and, 213
black *konketsuji*, 172–73, 175–79, 200, 207–8, *207*, 212–14, 256n87; Ishiwara Fusao on, 149; Koya on, 178–79; Nagai on, 86–87, 148–49; Nogami on, 177; numbers of, 176, 179–80, 212, 255n67
Black race, 42, 66, 86, 143. *See also* racism, anti-Black
"blood mixing" (*konketsu*), xiii, 2–17; *Anpo* and, 16–17, 150, 165–86, 192–96, 198–204, 206, 214–16, 221–22; in imperial Japan, anti-, 38, 60–66, 68, 70–72, 74–82, 84–93, 100; in imperial Japan, pro-, 18–60, 63, 67–68, 72–74, 82–85, 132–36, 192; 97, 139, 141–50, 171–75, 177–79, 191–92, 215, 228; in occupied Japan, 92–93, 97–98, 101–8, 111–14, 116–22, 127–34, 137–43, 149–50, 158–81, *170*, 171–80, 189–96, *190*, 199–216, *207*, 221; in Okinawa, 185, 223–24; as race suicide, 63, 79–81, 88–89, 146. *See also konketsuji*, "pure blood"; race science
blood purity. *See* "pure blood"
"blood talk," 8–9, 138–39, 220, 223, 231n22. *See also* Robertson, Jennifer
Bloody May Day, 153–54, *154*
Boas, Franz, 25, 38–39
boseiai (motherly love), 206
Bourke-White, Margaret, *208*
Brazil: Japanese emigration to, 211–12, 222
brides, war. *See* war brides
brides' schools (*hanayome gakkō*), 22
Britain, 15, 34, 38, 41, 57–59, 62–63, 72, 108
British Commonwealth Occupation Force (BCOF), 108, 140–41, 168–70, *169*, 181, 210, 250n54, 254n48; racism and, 129, 133
brothels, 19, 75, 214, *215*. *See also* comfort stations

Cabinet Information Bureau (CIB), 48–56, *48*, *50*, *55*
caste, mixed-blood, 178

INDEX

CCD. *See* Civil Censorship Detachment
censorship, 4–5; atomic bombs and, 131; Berrigan and, 210; CCD and, 126–39, 149, 161–62; end of, 120–21, *130*, 131, 149–50, 173, 175–76, 177, 180; Etō on, 162, 253n30; Higashikuni and, 113, 122, 125; Hirohito and, *124*, 125; JCP and, 160–62, 164; Kanō on, 130, 132; Nishi on, 126; in occupied Japan, 16, 116–17, 120, 122–39, *124*, 141, 147, 161–64, 168, 210–11, 248n13, 253n30; postcensorship, 161–62, 211; Sams and, 163–64; Sawada Miki and, 210–11; Takami and, 125–26, 128.
chastity, 37, 50, 75, 183; abortion and, 15, 93, 107–8, 121–22; CCD and, 133; infanticide and, 107–8; kidnapping and, 205–6; killings, 94–96, 108; in Korea, 202; leftists and, 128, 158–60, 167, 175, 212; of men, 11, 64, 80–81; patriotic, 93, 107–8, 127–28, 175, 220; population policy and, 75; Prostitution Prevention Law and, 174–75; racial, 15–16, 64, 80–81, 97, 121–22, 127, 133, 150, 156, 158–60, 183, 187, 189, 205–6, 212, 220; Sawada Miki and, 205–6, 212; sexual violence and, 93–97; Takami and, 128; women's suffrage and, 128
Chastity of Japan, The (book), 167
chastity suicide, 15, 93–95, 107–8, 127
Chiang Kai-shek, 61, 72, 156
child abandonment. *See* abandoned children
Child Consultation Centers, 195–96
child labor, 212
China: "blood mixing" and, 23–25, 31–32, 63–66, 69–73, 79–90, 93, 96–97, 145, 152, 228; Cold War and, 156–58; nationalism in, 24, 61, 68–69, 72, 75–76; People's Republic of, 157–60; Qing dynasty, 44–45, 68–69, 88; Republic of, 68. *See also* First Sino-Japanese War; Second Sino-Japanese War
Chinese: children, 44–50, *45*, *46*, *48*, *50*, *54–56*, *55*; fathers and patriarchy, 37, 47, 54, 73–76; Hakka, 69; Han, 2, 15, 60, 63, 68–71, 86–90, 228; *konketsuji*, 36–37, 56–59, 84, 73–77, 82, 149; migrants to Japan, 73–74; migrants to US, 187; Tanka, 68–69. *See also* racism, anti-Chinese
Christianity, 7, 51; in Japan, 175, 204, 212–13
CIB. *See* Cabinet Information Bureau
Civil Censorship Detachment (CCD), 126–39, 149, 161–62
civil liberties, SCAP and, 113, 125–26, 156
Clifford, Fumika, *169*, *170*
Clifford, John Kenneth, *169*
Cold War, 4–6, 11–14, 16–17, 111–12, 16–17, 150–56; China and, 156–57; international adoption and, 16–17, 189–213, 216, 259n44; JCP and, 153–67, 172, 176, 221–22; Korean War and, 157, 165, 202–4; occupied Japan and, 156–68; 193–94; Soviet Union and, 13, 95, 133, 151, 153, 156–61, 194; US legal reform and, 16–17, 188–93, 197–204. *See also* Anpo
collaboration: "horizontal," 6–7, 14, 22, 93, 158, 185, 220; with Japanese empire, 22, 29–35, 56–57, 59; with US empire, 156–58, 163, 182
colonial medicine, 140–41
comfort stations, 6, 75, 95; Nakasone and, 182
Cominform criticism, 157–61, 165
communism, 13, 99, 212. *See also* Japan Communist Party
concubines, 3, 7
Congress. *See* United States, Congress
Constitution of Eastern Races, The (Taniguchi), 41
contraception. *See* birth control
criminals, *konketsuji* as, 57–58
Czechoslovakia, 66

Democratic Party, Japan: abortion and, 115–17; *Anpo* and, 182; international adoption and, 198; merger into LDP, 183
Democratic Party, United States, 224–26. *See also* Truman, Harry

Department of State, US, 65, 167, 197–98, 200
Diplomatic Revue (*Gaikō jihō*, journal), 24–25, 28, 233n23
discrimination: against American(ized) *konketsuji*, 168–69; gender, 4, 7, 19, 22–23, 28–29, 63–64, 80–82, 189, 227; against "mixed blood" people, 39–40, 57–58, 168–69, 187–93, 195–96, 198–204, 213–16; against mothers of *konketsuji*, 6, 74–76, 80, 174, 195, 200, 205–9, 215–16, 221; against Okinawa, 185, 221, 223–24; against sex workers, 182, 221. *See also* chastity; *panpan*; racism; sexual sovereignty
disease, 95, 99, 109; eugenics and, 38, 86, 118–19, 148; *konketsuji* and, 38, 42, 97, 148–50; venereal 97–99, 101–3, 120. *See also* mental disability
dishonor. *See* shame
Doak, Kevin, 138
dominant genes. *See* neo-Mendelism
"Doubts About Dr. Kiyono's Theory of the Japanese Race" (article), 136
Dower, John, 44–45, 92, 146–47, 231n23
Dutch Empire: "blood mixing" and, 39, 43, 57–59, 214; war with Japan, 38–39, 41, 57–59, 62–63

education: brides' schools and, 22; chastity suicide and, 95; elementary, 21, 36, 105, 212; Japanese language and, 35; JCP and, 157, 164–66; of *konketsuji*, 36, 43, 73, 76, 164–66, 200; Korea and, 31, 33, 35, 105–6; medical, 35–36, 77, 86–87, 96, 98, 106, 145; Ministry of, 53, 164–66; Ministry of Welfare and, 51–52, *51*, *52*, 114; "red," 212; textbooks, 90, 106, 144
Egawa Ureo, 214, 216
Elizabeth Saunders Home, 199–200, 204–13, *207*; Hirano Imao on, 216
emasculation, 123–25, 140–41, 147
emigration. *See* migration
emperor: Hirohito, 27, 107, 123–25, *124*; Jinmu, 25–27, 35; leftists and, 164, 218–19, 222; loyalty to, 34, 74, 84, 125, 138–39, 164, 219; nationalism and, 218–20, 222, 227; Sawada Miki and, 205; SCAP and, 123–25, *124*, 138–39, 156, 164
Emperor's Korea, The (Ueda), 31–35
endogamy, 3, 138
epilepsy, 118–19
EPL. *See* Eugenic Protection Law
ethnic cleansing: abortion as, 96–98, 101–8, 120–22, 171; definition, 172; forced emigration as, 167–68, 172, 174, 177, 180, 191, 193, 220; Hattori and, 103; Hirano Imao and, 216; Ichikawa and, 112–13, 173–75, 186; infanticide as, 106–8; international adoption as, 192–93, 195–96, 198– 205, 209–13, 216; Itagaki and, 180; of *konketsuji*, 96–98, 101–8, 112–13, 119–122, 167–68, 171–75, 177, 180, 186, 191–205, 209–14, 216, 222; Korea and, 201–04; Nazi Germany and, 22, 82, 97, 119; Nogami and, 177; of *panpan*, 120, 171, 174; Sawada Miki and, 192–93, 199–201, 204–5, 209–13, 216; sterilization as, 119–120; Takasaki and, 213–14; Taniguchi Yasaburō and, 120–21, 171–72; Tatewaki and, 177; Yamashita and, 167–68, 171–72, 186. *See also* genocide
ethnic nation, as translation for *minzoku*, 12–13, 231n25
Etō Jun, 159, 162, 253n30
Eugenic Protection Bill (1947), 115–17
Eugenic Protection Law (*Yūsei hogohō*, EPL, 1948), 6, 16, 93, 117–20, 171
eugenics (*yūseigaku*), 3–4, 6–8, 11–13, 15–16, 18, 20, 222–23; abortion and, 108, 112–22, 171, 178, 220; All-Country Conference on Population Problems and, 72–77; birth control and, 110–12, 115–16; "blood mixing" favored, 20, 24–26, 35–44, 60, 63, 67–68, 73–74, 82–86, 132–36, 192; "blood mixing" opposed, 38, 60, 63, 65–66, 68, 70–72, 77–82, 84–85, 87–91, 93, 139, 141–50, 171–75, 177–79, 191–92, 215, 228; class and, 37, 70, 73–77, 86, 116, 146; disease and, 38, 86, 118–19, 148;

INDEX

eugenic marriage, 37, 86, 112, 147–48; family system and, 74–77; Japanese law and, 6, 93, 114–20; JCP and, 161; Konoe and, 73; MOW and, 15–16, 73, 77, 99–101, 112, 114, 171; Nazi law and, 119; *panpan* and, 120–22, 171–75; sterilization and, 112, 115–16, 119–21; Soviet Union and, 161

Europeans: as "blood mixers," 19, 57–58, 67, 79, 139, 141, 143, 146, 148; as colonizers, 19, 39–40, 53, 57–59; ethnic cleansing and, 22, 82, 97; as inferior to Japanese, 41, 135; international adoption and, 202, 210; in Japan, 57, 139, 141, 146, 214–16; as racists, 22, 38–41, 53, 82, 84, 129, 133, 135, 143; as scientists, 38–39, 41, 143, 148; US immigration law and, 188, 199, 202; World War I and, 6, 66; World War II and, 6–7, 22, 57–58, 66–67, 93–97, 135

euthanasia, 106–7. *See also* infanticide

evolution, 9, 13, 42, 66–67, 70–71, 79–81, 83, 87–88, 135–39, 147–48, 219

extinction, racial, 88, 146

Ezaki Kazuharu, 162–63, 165, 167

family-state, 7, 19, 27, 53, 62

family system, 75, 77, 81; household registry, 28–29, 205

Fate of the Race, The (Nagai), 146

feeblemindedness (*seishin hakujaku*), 118–120, 122, 149–50

First Sino-Japanese War, 18, 44–47, *45*, *46*; adoption and, 44–47, *45*, *46*

Fischer, Jane, 176

Flag (Hata, magazine), 161–62

food supply, 95–96, 100, 105, 107–10, *109*, 115–16

Foundation-Institute for Research on Population Problems, 72–73

Frühstück, Sabine, 49, 56

Fujin kōron. *See Ladies Review*

Fujitani, Takashi, 7, 30, 63, 216, 221

Fujiwara Michiko, 175

Fukagawa Tamae, 198–99

Fukuda Masako: Eugenic Protection Law and, 115–18, 121; at Futsukaichi Sanatorium, 117; *konketsuji* and, 117, 121, 175, 180; prostitution and, 175

Futsukaichi Sanatorium, 98–99, 101–2, 104–7, *105*, 117

Filipinos. *See* Philippines

gaichi (exterior), 28. *See also naichi*

Gaikō jihō. *See Diplomatic Revue*

genes and genetics, 3, 15, 30, 32, 37–39, 41–44, 47, 63, 71–74, 76–89, 119, 131, 139, 141–49, 161, 178, 220–21

Genetics Society of Japan (*Nihon iden gakkai*), 141, 144, 250n55

genius, 70, 83, 120, 148

genocide, 47, 101–2, 172; auto-, 94–95; Nazi Germany and, 22, 82; SCAP and, 100. *See also* ethnic cleansing

Germany: abortion in, 97; ethnic cleansing and, 22, 82, 97; Japanese critiques of, 25, 67, 84; Japanese praise of, 71–72, 82; as "mixed blood," 67, 177; Nazi, 22, 25, 66–76, 71–72, 75, 82, 119; occupied, 6–7, 97; as "pure," 71–72; World War I and, 6, 19; World War II and, 95

German-Americans, 38, 56

Gobineau, Arthur de, 25

gods: Christian, 51, 213; Japanese, 26–27; people compared to, 51, 126

Greater East Asian Co-Prosperity Sphere, 37, 38, 40, 43, 62, 66, 73, 89–90, 125, 135; and gender, 54

Grew, Joseph C., 65

gynecological exams, 102–4, 120

hāfu. *See* "half"

haiku, 143

Haitian Revolution, 178–79

Hakata, Japan, 98–99, 101, 104–5, 107

"half" (*hāfu*) Japanese, 4, 187–88

hanayome gakkō (brides' schools), 22

Han Chinese, 2, 15, 60, 63, 68–71, 87–90, 228. *See also* racism, anti-Chinese

Hara Momoyo, 161–62

Hasebe Kotondo, 137–38

Hashizume Hiroshi, 106–7

Hattori Iwakichi, 103
Heale, Michael, 224–25
heterosexual reproduction, 3, 44, 47, 50, 187–88. *See also* homosocial reproduction
Higashikuni Naruhiko, 113, 123, 125
Higuchi Kaneo, 57
Higuchi Seizaburō, 44, *45*, *46*, 49
Hiraizumi Kiyoshi, 94
Hirano Imao, 143–44, 214, 216
Hirano Yoshitarō, 43
Hirohito, 27, 123–25, *124*
Hiroshima (Sekigawa), 212
Hitler, Adolf, 22, 71–72, 84, 177
homelessness, 96, 105, 107, 109, *109*, 115, 208; children and, 201–2, 204
homosocial reproduction, 3; battlefield adoption and, 44–56, *45*, *46*, *48*, *50*, *55*. *See also* heterosexual reproduction
Hong Kong, 38, 58
honor: of family, 105–6, 208; of fathers, 75; of mothers, 81. *See also* shame
honorable death, 94, 108. *See also* chastity suicide
"horizontal collaboration," 6–7, 14, 22, 93, 158, 185, 220
Hoshino, Noriaki, 13, 67
household registry, 28–29, 205
housing. *See* homelessness

Ichikawa Fusae, 112–13, 173–75, 177, 186
Ide Kawata, 69
Ijichi Susumu, 21–27
Ikeda Jirō, 136–137
"illegal" pregnancies, 101–6, 116, 118
"illegitimate" children, 7, 12, 74–76, 81–82, 93, 169, 190–91, 194
Imamura Chūsuke, 164, 166
Imamura Yutaka, 136–37
immigration. *See* migration
Immigration and Nationality Act (INA, 1952), 196–99, 203–4
Immigration and Naturalization Service (INS), 200
imperialism, 1, 8–12; British, 38, 41, 59, 62–63, 72; Dutch, 38–39, 41, 43, 57–59, 62–63; Japanese, 2, 4–5, 7–15, *10*, 18–35, 39–65, 69, 72, 78–92, 111, 123–25, 136, 139, 143–45; US, 6, 16–17, 72, 150–59, 167, 169, 175, 183–85, 216, 219, 220–21, 223–26
imperialization (*kōminka*), 84, 87, 219–220
Imperial Rule Assistance Association (*Taisei yokusankai*), 65, 100
INA. *See* Immigration and Nationality Act
Indigenous peoples: in Americas, 187; in Taiwan, 2, 7, 18–19, 140
Indonesia, *10*, 38–39, 43, 66, 57–59, 182
infanticide, 93, 106–8, 220
inferiority, blood mixing and, 148–50
INS. *See* Immigration and Naturalization Service
Institute for Research on Population Problems, 132
intelligence: of Chinese, 23, 70; class and, 70, 116; of *konketsuji*, 36–38, 73–74, 79, 83, 86, 142–45, 147–50; of Mongolians or Mongoloids, 23, 38; superiority of Japanese, 23, 65–66, 120, 135, 185. *See also* feeblemindedness
intermarriage. *See* "blood mixing"
international adoption. *See* adoption
internment: in imperial Japan, 58; in US, 189
Introduction to Eugenics (Nagai), 86
Ishihara Shintarō, 224
Ishiwara Fusao, postwar research on *konketsuji*, 149; wartime research on *konketsuji*, 36–37, 73–77, 81, 132
Ishiwara Kanji, 8
Itagaki Naoko, 121, 180, 213
Iwakuni, Japan, 139–141, 250n49
Izumi Seiichi, 98–99, 137, 244n24

Japan Communist Party (JCP): as anti-American, 153–54, 157–58; Cominform criticism, 157–61, 165; electoral politics and, 162–67, 183; eugenics and, 161; Japanese empire's suppression of, 156, 158, 165; on *konketsuji*, 159–67, 172, 176; on *minzoku*, 157–59, 221–22; as pro-American, 156–58, 164; *Red Flag*,

INDEX

160–63; Red Purge, 164–65, 254n42; SCAP and, 156–67; Soviet Union and, 157–58; Yoshida and, 156, 163–66. *See also* Zengakuren

Japanese Americans, 187–92, *190*, 197; internment of, 189; in Japan, 59. *See also* migration, Japanese to US; migration, *konketsuji* to US

Japanese Imperial Army, 21, 56–57, 87, 93; comfort stations and, 75, 95; democratic collapse and, 65; disbanded, 98–100; family and, 44–56, *45*, *46*, *48*, *50*, *55*, 75, 81–82; in First Sino-Japanese War, 44–47, *45*, *46*; *konketsuji* and, 56–58, 75, 81–82; Koreans and, 29–30, 32; sexual violence and, 75, 82, 95–96; surrendered, 97, 107; in World War II, 60–63, 65, 87, 93–97. *See also* Kwantung Army

Japanese Imperial Navy, 93, 100, 107, 140; comfort stations and, 182; disbanded, 98–100; family and, 51, 75; Nakasone and, 182; surrendered, 97, 107

Japanese language. *See* kokugo

Japanism, 29–30, 33

Japanization, 30, 84; genetic, 41–42; of postwar *konketsuji*, 168–69

Japan Race Hygiene Association. *See* Race Hygiene Association

Japan Socialist Party (JSP), 167, 175, 180, 183. *See also* Socialists

Java. *See* Indonesia

JCP. *See* Japan Communist Party

"jeep girls," 151–52

Jews, 22, 25, 38, 66, 82, 256n87. *See also* racism, anti-Semitic

Jim Crow, 197

Jinmu, 25–27, 35

junketsu. *See* "pure blood"

jus sanguinis, 190–92, 197

Kageyama Kōyō, *171*
Kalischer, Peter, 190
Kamitsubo Takashi, 106
Kanemitsu Tsuneo, 73
Kanō Mikiyo, 5, 54, 130, 132, 155

Kanzaki Kiyoshi, 181, 211, 213
Katō Shizue, 110–3, 114–16, 121
Kazahaya Yasoji, 164–67
Keijō Imperial University, 33, 98
kidnapping, 205–6, 209
Kishi Nobusuke, 182, 184
Kiyono Kenji, 39, 43, 134–38
kokugo (national language, i.e. Japanese), 143; *konketsuji* and, 143–44; Koreans and, 35; as Mendelian recessive trait, 143–45
kokutai (body politic), 34–35, 40
Komai Taku, 77, 82–83
kōminka. *See* imperialization
konketsu. *See* "blood mixing"
konketsuji (mixed-blood child), xiii, 2–17, *170*, *190*, *207*; abortion of, 93, 98–99, 101–7, 120–22, 139–40, 171, 178; adoption of, 16–17, 189–213, 216, 259n44; as adults, 43, 56–59, 143–44, 148, 187–89, 214–17; Americanization of, 156, 168–73, 186144–45, 218; Australian, 140–41, 168, *170*, 254n48; black-Japanese, 149, 172–73, 175–79, 200, 207–8, *207*, 212–14, 256n87; black-white, 86–87, 148–49; as criminals, 57–58; "crisis," 107–8, 175–86, 192–96, 201, 203–4, 210–15, 217, 223, 228; ethnic cleansing of, 96–98, 101–8, 112–13, 119–122, 167–68, 171–75, 177, 180, 186, 191–205, 209–14, 216, 222; Eurasian, 38–39, 58; Euro-American, 56; Filipino, 43, 58, 141, 161, 168; Indonesian, 57–58; infanticide of, 93, 106–8, 220; Japanese-Korean, 36–38; Japanese language and, 142–43; JCP on, 159–76; Jewish, 256n87; Korean-American, 202–4; migration to Brazil, 211–12, 222; migration to China, 58, 76; migration to US, 16–17, 181, 186–204, *190*, 210–11, 223; numbers of, politicized, 160, 163, 175–77, 179–81, 194–95, 209, 211; numbers of, verified, 179, 181, 194–95, 201; as orphans, 160–63, 167, 175–76, 179–81, 192–95, 199–213, *207*; racism toward, 6, 12, 14–17, 38–40, 79, 182,

konketsuji (mixed-blood child) (*continued*) 187–92, 193–94, 198–200, 210–14, 216; Sino-Japanese, 36–37, 56–57, 73–77, 81–82, 149; Sino-Korean, 32; United States and, 6, 16–17, 86–87, 92–95, 108, 129–32, 141–46, 150–52, 155–56, 158–204, *190*, 206, 208–13, 216, 221–22; white-Japanese, 57, 106–7, 143–44, 148–50, 179, *190*, *207*, 213–14, 256n87. *See also* "blood mixing"; eugenics; "pure blood"; race science
Konketsuji (Sekigawa), 212
Konketsuji (Takasaki), 212–14
Konoe Fumimaro, 61–63, 65, 73
Korea, 28; Japanese annexation of, 2, 7, 29; March First Movement in, 29; nationalism in, 29, 202, 218–19; North, 157, 159, 164, 197; royal family of, 27, 124; South, 201–4, 218–19; US and Soviet invasions of, 93–94, 95–97, 156, 202. *See also* Korean War
Koreans: intermarriage and, 29, 66, 78, 83, 85, 124; international adoption of, 201–4; as Japanese, 2, 29, 30, 35, 59, 63, 68–69, 85, 196; Japanese surnames for, 30; *konketsuji*, Japanese-Korean, 36–38; *konketsuji*, Korean-American, 202–4; *konketsuji*, Sino-Korean, 32; as *minzoku* (minjok), 29–35, 202, 204; as "mixed blood," 29–35, 41, 136; in postwar Japan, 99, 138, 146, 219; as "pure," 29, 33–34, 202–4; US immigration and naturalization law regarding, 196, 201–4
Korean War, 157, 165, 202–3; BCOF and, *169*; international adoption and, 202–4
Korea on the March (Kurashima), 30–31
Koyama Eizō, 100, 138–39, 183–84
Koyama Makoto, 184
Koya Yoshio: on Black people, 178–79; on "blood mixing" (imperial era), 77–83, 85, 89, 100, 133, 148–49, 231n23; on "blood mixing" (postwar), 177–79, 183; on Chinese people, 79–83, 89; Eugenic Protection Law and, 112, 114, 120; on Japanese women, 77–78; on Jews, 82, 178
Kramm, Robert, 97
Kubushiro Ochimi, 97
Kurashima Itaru, 30–31, 234n42
Kwantung Army, 8, 20, 29; democratic collapse and, 65
Kyushu Imperial University, 35, 101

Ladies Review (*Fujin kōron*, magazine), 122, 176–178
language. *See* kokugo
Law to Prevent Hereditarily Diseased Offspring (*Gesetz zur Verhütung erbkranken Nachwuchses*, 1933), 119
LDP. *See* Liberal Democratic Party
lèse majesté, 125
Liberal Democratic Party (LDP), 183–85, 223–25
Liberal Party, 121, 155, 167, 178, 180–83, 193, 222, 225, 228; and JCP, 163; merger into LDP, 183. *See also* Yoshida Shigeru
liberalism, 33, 82
Lie, John, 218
Lysenkoism, 161

MacArthur, Douglas, 5, 123–25, *124*, 153, 164, 182, 229n5
Maizuru, Japan, 99, 102–3, 107
Malaysia, *10*, 39, 83, 135
male-male kinship. *See* homosocial reproduction
Malthus, Thomas, 110
Malthusian theory, 21, 110–11
Manchukuo, 8, 20, 22–25, 29, 33, 35, 43, 64–65, 77; Korea and, 31–32; Koya on, 80; Nagai on, 85, 88; Soviet invasion of, 93–97, 108
Manchus, 68, 88
March First Movement, 27, 29
Marriage Guidebook (Nagai), 147
Maruyama Masao, 217–18, 221–22
Marxism: anti-Semitism and, 82; birth control and, 110–11; Hirano Yoshitarō and, 43; Koya on, 82; nationalism and,

222; SCAP and, 156; suppression of, 111, 125; Takami and, 125
masculinity, 11, 20–23, 30, 45, 128, 152; emasculation, 123–25, 140–41, 147. *See also* homosocial reproduction; patriarchy
May Day. *See* Bloody May Day
Mendelism. *See* neo-Mendelism
menstruation, 110, 140–41
mental disability: "blood mixing" and, 38, 79, 141–45, 148–50, 172; Eugenic Protection Law and, 118–21; feeblemindedness, 118–120, 122, 149–50; language acquisition and, 141–45; Nazi law and, 119
Micronesia, 19
midwives, 111
migration, 3; African to US, 187; barbarian into China, 70; Chinese from Japan, 99; Chinese to Japan, 73–74; Chinese to US, 187; ethnic cleansing and, 167–68, 172, 174, 177, 180, 191, 193, 220; European to Japan, 57; European to US, 199, 202; Filipino to US, 187–88; between *gaichi* and *naichi*, 8, 18, 27–29, 33, 37; imperial family and, 25–27, 35; Indian to US, 187; international adoption and, 16–17, 189–213, 216; to and from Japan during World War II, 8–12, *10*, 42–43; Japanese to Australia, *170*; Japanese to Brazil, 211–12, 222; Japanese to Canada, 211; Japanese to China and Manchuria, 22–24, 26, 37, 75–76, 79–82, 87–89, 96, 125; Japanese to Korea, 27–29, 96; Japanese to *Nan'yō*, 19, 37, 43, 94; Japanese to Taiwan, 18–19, 28–29, 87, 140; Japanese to US, 174, 187, 189–92, *190*, 196–98; *konketsuji* to Brazil, 211–12, 222; *konketsuji* to China, 58, 76; *konketsuji* to US, 16–17, 181, 186–204, *190*, 210–11, 223; Korean from Japan, 99; Korean to Japan, 28–29, 33, 37; Korean to US, 33, 196, 201–4; labor mobilization and, 8, 37; *Nisei* to Japan, 59; North and South American to US, 187; repatriates to Japan, 95–99, 101–8,

111, 114; war as stimulating, 8, 11. *See also* Immigration and Nationality Act; adoption, international; war brides
Minami Jirō, 29
Ministry of Education, 53, 164–66
Ministry of Foreign Affairs, 173, 197–99, 203, 259n35
Ministry of Justice, 121
Ministry of Welfare (MOW): abortion and, 118; international adoption and, 195–96, 211–12; Kanemitsu and, 73; Koya and, 77, 83, 112, 177–78; Koyama and, 138; occupation era, 15–16, 93, 97–104, 106–7, 111–12, 114, 117, 120, 132–33, 163, 178, 201; Okazaki and, 132–33; Sams and, 163; SCAP and, 99–102, 163; studies on *konketsuji*, 149–50, 163, 179–81, 194–96; wartime, 9, *10*, 15, 51–52, *51*, *52*, 73, 77, 111, 133, 211–12, 231n23
Minseitō, 63–65
minzoku (race / nation), definitions and translation of, 12–13, 21, 66–67, 231n25; German, 66; Han, 68–71, 86–89; JCP and, 157–59, 162; Korean, 29–35, 202, 204, 218, 219; national independence (*minzoku dokuritsu*), 33–34, 66–67, 146; Yamato, 7, 9, 29, 37, 43–44, 64–65, 84, 133, 136–37. *See also* nationalism; "pure blood"
minzoku eisei (race hygiene). *See* eugenics
minzokugaku, 249n37
miscarriage: "artificial," 101–2, 107; "managing," 106
"mixed blood" adults, 43, 56–59, 143–44, 148, 187–89, 214–17
"mixed blood" child. *See konketsuji*
mixing. *See* "blood mixing"
Miyake Katsuo, 36–38, 73, 132
Mizuno, Hiromi, 77, 218, 249n34
Mizushima Haruo, 35–41, 73
Mjöen, Jon Alfred, 38
Mobile Relief Union, 96, 98
Mongolia, 23–24, 64, 88
Mongolian Empire, 88

Mongolians, 39, 88, 135. *See also* racism, anti-Mongolian
monoethnic ideology, 218
moral panic, 97, 103, 150, 156, 176–81, 221–22, 225–26
Moriyoshi Yoshiaki, 84–85
"motherly love" (*boseiai*), 206
MOW. *See* Ministry of Welfare
Mughal Empire, 88
Murphy, Robert Daniel, 198

Nagai Hisomu, 85–89, 90, 112, 119–20, 145–49
Nagamine, Amelia Shizue, 187–89
Nagasaki, Japan, 214
naichi (interior), 28–29, 32, 34–35, 37, 57, 60, 107, 114, 120
Nakano Shigeharu, 125–26
Nakasone Yasuhiro, 182, 185–86, 223, 224, 225, 226
Nanba Monkichi, 24–27, 72
Nan'yō (South Seas), 2, 19–20, 94–95, 108
Nashimoto Masako, 27, 124
National Eugenics Law (1940), 96, 115, 119
nationalism, xiii–xiv, 1–9, 30, 66–67, 138–39, 216; anti-American, 122, 151–186, 154, 218–26, 228; antistate, 218–19, 225; biolinguistic, 142–45; Chinese, 24, 61, 68–69, 72, 76; emperor and, 25–26, 31, 33–35, 85, 138–39, 218–20, 222, 227; gendered, 6, 93–99, 103–8, 111, 119–23, 127–28, 133, 141, 145, 151–52, 155–56, 158–63, 167–77, 180, 182, 184–89, 212, 220–24, 227–28; among *konketsuji*, 39–40, 75–77, 143, 216; Korean, 29–30, 33–34, 202, 204, 218; leftwing, 151–67, 171–75, 177, 180, 183–86, 212, 218–22, 225–27; new, 222–27; *Nihonjinron* and, 223, 228; nonexistent, 217–18, 221–23, 227; racial, 12–14, 17, 67–68, 92–95, 114, 119–22, 133–39, 142–50, 155–93, 202, 204, 212–16, 219–28; rightwing, 159, 177–79, 182–86, 212, 220–27; scientific, 77, 78, 140, 218, 249n34; victimhood, 14, 159, 161, 167, 171, 185–86, 206, 218–19, 225–28

Nationality Act (1940), 187
National Spiritual Mobilization campaign, 173
natural selection, 79–80, 83, 148
navy. *See* Japanese Imperial Navy
Nazi Germany. *See* Germany, Nazi
Negritos, 41
neo-Mendelism, 3–4, 15, 38, 41–42, 47, 63, 79–82, 84–85, 89, 143–45, 148, 161
Netherlands. *See* Dutch Empire
New Caledonia, 43
New Committee for Population Countermeasures, 112–15, 120
New Guinea, 9, 10, 38–39
New Marriage Guidebook (Nagai), 147–48
newspapers: Chinese, 157; Indian, 195; Japanese, 56–58, 60, 94, 97, 121, 123–27, 124, 129–30, 130, 137, 149, 151, 162, 174, 200, 226; US, 193–97, 199, 201, 209–11; worldwide, 203. *See also* Red Flag (*Akahata*)
NHK (Nihon hōsō kyōkai, Japan Broadcasting Corporation), 77, 129, 132
Nihon iden gakkai. *See* Genetics Society of Japan
Nihonjinron (theory of the Japanese people), 223, 228
Ninigi, 26
Nishi, Toshio, 126
Nishimura Fumiko, 106–7
Nogami Yaeko, 176–77
Nordic supremacy, 38, 43–44, 119
North Korea, 157, 159, 164, 197

obstetrician-gynecologists (ob-gyns), 115, 117, 139–40, 141
obstetrics, 102–6, 105
occupation. *See* Allied occupation of Japan
Ogata Gekkō, 45–47, 46
Oguma Eiji, 5, 7, 89–90, 157, 218
Oh, Arissa, 202–3
Okazaki Ayanori, 132–34, 138, 140
Okazaki Fuminori. *See* Okazaki Ayanori
Okazaki Katsuo, 198–99

INDEX

Okinawa: assimilation as Japanese, 2, 7, 33, 35; battle of, 93–95, 108, 127; "blood mixing" in, 185, 223–24; chastity suicide in, 93–95, 108, 127; discrimination against, 185, 221; international adoption and, 201; US bases in, 185, 221, 223–24

Ōkuninushi, 27

orphans, 12; Chinese, 44–56, 45, 46, 48, 50, 55; Japanese, 54, 62, 109, 195–96, 200–202, 211–12; *konketsuji* as, 160–63, 167, 175–76, 179–81, 192–95, 199–213, 207; Korean, 201–4; numbers of, politicized, 160, 163, 175–77, 179–81, 194–95, 209, 211; numbers of, verified, 179, 181, 194–95, 201; social, 192; US visas for, 200–204. *See also* adoption

Ōta Tenrei, 115–16

overpopulation, 21, 26, 108–11, 116–17

Ōyuki Yoshio, 77, 83–84

Palmer, Henry Spencer, 57

pan-Asianism, 8–9, 13–15, 29, 31, 45–48, 53, 56–57, 73, 78, 87–90; Ijichi and, 22–23; limits on, 15, 63, 69, 89; postwar leftists and, 159; rejected, 13, 60, 89–90, 144; Sakurai and, 65–66; Watsuji and, 26, 90

panpan, 120–21, 158, 159, 160, 171, 173–75, 182, 221; abortion and, 120, 171; *panpan* hunts, 120; *panpan seifu* ("government of whores"), 159; sterilization of, 120

patriarchy: Chinese, 47, 75–76; Japanese, 27, 44, 50–51, 64, 75, 76–77, 81, 140; pan-Asian, 22–23, 27, 44–50; threats to, 64, 75–77, 140–41; universal, 27; US, 187–90; white, 189

patriliny, 4, 75–76, 81, 97; and US law, 189–91

Patriotic Women's Association (*Aikoku fujinkai*), 98, 114

Patterson, Robert Sr., 100

Peking. *See* Beijing

Philippines, the: "blood mixing" and, 39, 43, 58, 83, 141, 161, 168; occupied by Japan, 58, 106; occupier of Japan, 141, 161, 168; as US ally, 62–63, 187–88; US immigration law and, 187–88; in World War II, 38, 58, 43, 62–63, 106

Photographic Weekly (*Shashin shūhō*, magazine), 47–50, 53–56

Pilcher, James, 194–96, 198, 201

polygyny, 19, 26–27, 70

Population Anguish (Okazaki), 132–33

population policy: All-Country Conference on Population Problems and, 68, 72–77; antinatal, 100–122; Diet and, 113–17, 121–22; Eugenic Protection Law and, 6, 16, 93, 117–20, 171; food supply and, 100–101, 105, 107–11, 115–16; Foundation-Institute for Research on Population Problems and, 72–73; Fukuda and, 115–18, 121, 180; Ichikawa and, 112; Ijichi on, 21–22; infanticide and, 106–8; Ishiwara Fusao on, 73–77; Katō and, 112, 114–16, 121; Konoe and, 73; Koya and, 77–82, 112–15, 119–20, 178; Miyake and Mizushima on, 37–38; MOW and, 51–52, 51, 52, 77, 98–105, 111–14, 117–18, 120, 132, 178; Nagai and, 112–15, 119–20; Nanba on, 24–26; National Eugenics Law and, 96, 115, 119; New Committee for Population Countermeasures and, 112–15, 120; Ōta and, 115–16; pronatal, 9–11, 51–52, 51, 52, 73, 77, 111; SCAP and, 98–102, 108, 117; Taniguchi Konen on, 42–43, 83; Taniguchi Yasaburō and, 115–18, 120–21; Ueno on, 75. *See also* abortion

Population Policy and Territorial Planning (book), 37

pregnancy, 23, 96–99, 105, 107, 114, 120–22, 208; "illegal," 101–6, 116, 118

private legislation, 188–189, 191, 197, 200. *See also* public law

pronatalism, 9–11, 51–52, 51, 52, 73, 77, 111

prostitution, 19, 75, 104, 180, 182, 184, 213–14, 215, 221. *See also* comfort stations; *panpan*

INDEX

Prostitution Prevention Law (*Baishun bōshihō*, 1956), 6, 174–75
protests, 12; *of Anpo*, 16, 151–55, *154*, 184–85, 221, 223–24; of "colonial culture," 150–55, 175; of "*panpan* politics," 158–59, 175, 221. *See also* Bloody May Day
public law, 188–89, 200–202. *See also* private legislation
Public Law 162 (1953), 200–201
"pure blood" (*junketsu*), xiii, 13–14, 16, 90; abortion and, 114, 122; children, 37, 42, 149, 195–96, 200, 202–4, 210; Hasebe on, 137–38; Korea and, 29–31, 33–35, 202–4; Koyama and, 100, 138–39; language and, 142–44; Mizushima on, 37, 39–40; Moriyoshi on, 84; Nagai on, 85–87, 89, 145–49; Nakasone on, 182, 185–86, 225; *Nihonjinron* and, 223; Okazaki on, 132–33; postwar politics and, 155–56, 159, 169–73, 180, 183, 185–86, 202–4, 210, 214, 216, 220, 227–28; Prostitution Prevention Law and, 175; repatriation and, 99; Robertson on, 18; Sakurai on, 64–65, 71–72; SCAP and, 100, 122, 132–34, 137–39; Takagi on, 66–67, 69, 71; Taniguchi Konen on, 41–43; Teng on, 59; Tsushima and, 136–37; Ueda on, 33–35. *See also* racial purity
purges: in imperial Japan, 34; within JCP, 157; MOW and, 100; under SCAP, 100, 113, 117, 120, 173, 182, 184, 186. *See also* Red Purge

Qing dynasty, 44–45, 68–69, 88

Race, Language, and Culture (Boas), 38
race hygiene (*minzoku eisei*). *See* eugenics
Race Hygiene (*Minzoku eisei*, journal), 82
Race Hygiene Association (*Nihon minzoku eisei gakkai/kyōkai*, RHA), 77, 82, 85, 112, 119–20, 146, 178, 240n43
race science, 4, 67–69, 73–74, 76, 85–87, 132–40; anti-mixing, during occupation, 136–49; anti-mixing, in imperial era, 63, 70–72, 77–82, 84–85, 87–90; 134–35, 149; anti-mixing, post-occupation, 149–50, 177–78, 213; Boas and, 25, 38–39; European, 38–49, 41, 143; pro-mixing, during occupation, 132–36; pro-mixing, in imperial era, 35–44, 82–84
race suicide, 63, 79–81, 88–89, 146
race war, 15–16, 62–63, 92–93, 95, 146–47, 183
racial nationalism. *See* nationalism
racial purity, 2, 5, 21, 25; ethnic cleansing and, 193; nonexistent, 39, 132, 177; in US, 16, 133, 189, 204. *See also* "pure blood"
racism, xiii–xiv, 1–9, 12–17; anti-Asian, 23, 187–92, 196–99, 225; anti-Black, 41, 86, 144, 148–49, 172–73, 176, 177–179, 197, 200, 208, 212–14; anti-Chinese, 15, 49, 60, 62–63, 66, 68–72, 79–85, 87–90, 93, 145, 178, 187, 228; anti-European, 23, 135; anti-Japanese, 187–92, 198, 225; anti-*konketsuji*, 6, 12, 14–17, 38–40, 79, 182, 187–92, 193–94, 198–200, 210–14, 216; anti-Korean, 31, 34, 221; anti-Mongolian, 23–24, 38, 88; anti-Semitic, 22, 41, 66, 72, 82, 178, 182, 185, 256n86; anti-white, 25, 41; British, 33–34; Han, 68–69; Japan supremacist, 22, 24, 44, 65–66, 85, 135; Nordic supremacist, 38, 43–44, 119; "polite," 7, 63; segregation and, 25, 34, 40, 63, 65, 78, 82–83, 128, 133, 204, 212, 231n23; US, 16–17, 25, 33–34, 187–92, 194, 196–99, 225; "vulgar," 7, 63, 224; white supremacist, 25, 38–41, 84, 86–87, 132–33, 216; xenophobic, 14, 22, 89, 137. *See also* discrimination; "pure blood"
rape. *See* sexual violence
Reagan, Ronald, 185, 224, 226
recessive genes. *See* neo-Mendelism
Red Flag (*Akahata*, newspaper), 160–65, 167, 175, 176, 211
Red Purge, 164–65, 254n42
Refugee Relief Act (RRA, 1953), 200–202

INDEX

refugees, 96, 194. *See also* repatriates
Repatriate Aid Bureaus, 97, 99, 102–4
repatriates, 95–99, 101–8, 111, 114
Republican Party, 225. *See also* Reagan, Ronald
reverse course, 156–57, 164–65
RHA. *See* Race Hygiene Association
Ridgway, Matthew, 229n5
Robertson, Jennifer, 18, 231n22
Rougier, Michael, *154*
RRA. *See* Refugee Relief Act
Rubin, Jay, 127–28, 132
Russell, John, 213
Russia. *See* Soviet Union
Russians, in Manchukuo, 125
Russo-Japanese War, 19
Ryūkyū Islands. *See* Okinawa.

Saipan, battle of, 93–95, 108, 127. *See also Nan'yō*
Saitō Makoto, 28
Sakai, Naoki, 8
Sakano Tōru, 85
Sakanoue no Tamuramaro, 74
Sakurai Hyōgorō, 63–66, 71–72, 77, 80
Sams, Crawford, 163–64, 210–11
San Francisco Peace Treaty, 16, 151–52
Satō Ei, 111
Satō Yoshiko, 143
Sawada Miki, 192–93, 199–201, 204–13, *207*, 216
Sawada Renzō, 199
SCAP (Supreme Commander for the Allied Powers), 5, 98–99, 113, 153; censorship by, 16, 116–17, 120–39, *124*, *130*, 141, 147, 149, 161–64, 168, 210–11, 248n13, 253n30; civil liberties and, 113, 125–26, 156; Hirohito and, 123–25, *124*; JCP and, 156–67, 254n42; on *konketsuji*, 129–32, *130*, 138, 163–64; MOW and, 99–101; population control and, 100–101; war crimes and, 65, 100, 182, 184
schizophrenia, 119
schools and schoolchildren, 21, 35, 36, 76, 90, 95, 106, 144, 164–66, 212
science, race. *See* race science

scientific nationalism, 77, 78, 140, 218, 249n34
Second Sino-Japanese War, 4, 8, *10*, 20, 24, 29, 47, 61–63, 65, 98; battlefield adoption and, 44, 47–56, *48*, *50*, *55*; biologizing defeat and, 15, 69–72, 79–82, 84–85, 87–91, 145, 152, 228; "blood mixing" and, 23–25, 63–66, 69–72, 79–90, 93, 96–97, 145, 152, 228; Chinese nationalism and, 61, 68–69, 72, 76; *konketsuji* and, 36–37, 56–59, 84, 73–77, 82, 149; Koreans in, 29–32; MOW and, 77; as race war, 15, 60, 63, 90–93; sexual violence and, 6, 14–15, 53, 75, 82, 93–97; Soviet entry into, 93–97; Takami and, 125; Wuhan in, 47–50, 54–56, 61
Sekigawa Hideo, 212
sexual sovereignty. *See* sovereignty, sexual
sexual violence, 14–15; under *Anpo*, 213, 219–21; Eugenic Protection Law and, 118–19; obstetrics and gynecology as, 102–8, *105*; under occupation, 97, 104–5, 107–8, 118, 127, 165, 167, 171, 213, 219–21, 246n64; repatriates and, 93–97, 101, 103–5, 107; war and, 26–27, 53, 75, 82, 93–97, 108, 118, 125, 243n12
sex work. *See* prostitution
shame, 17; rape and, 93–95; of family, 105–6, 208; of women, 14, 102, 104–8, 128, 158–160, 167–68, 171, 177, 205, 208. *See also* chastity suicide
Shanghai, China, 58, 73
Shimoji Rōrensu Yoshitaka, xiii–xiv, 4, 168–169, 196
Shimojima Tetsurō, 94–95, 108
Shinto: gods and myths, 26–27, 35; SCAP and, 138; shrines, 51, *169*, *174*
Shōji Tadashi, 139–45
Siddens, Dorothy, 57
Singapore, *10*, 38, 57
socialism, 1; and birth control, 110–11
Socialists, 114–17, 121, 167, 171–73, 175, 177, 180, 183–84, 186, 222

social orphans, 192, 195–96, 200, *207*
South Korea: international adoption and, 201–4; democratic activists in, 218–19. *See also* Korean War
South Seas. *See Nan'yō*
sovereignty, 1–4, 9, 97, 126, 151–59, 173, 182–85, 218, 225; of Japanese men, 168; of Japanese women, 119; racial, 32, 97–98; sexual, 1–7, 97–98, 103, 119, 151–52, 155–59, 168, 173–75, 182–89, 222–23, 226, 228; of US men, 187–89
Soviet Union, 13, 133, 161, 194, 202; *Anpo* and, 153; "blood mixing" and, 93, 96–97, 105, 168, 202; invasion of Manchukuo, 93–96; invasion of Korea, 93–97, 108, 156, 202; JCP and, 157–61; Korean War and, 157; Lysenkoism and, 161; San Francisco Peace Treaty and, 151; SCAP and, 126, 156–58, 248n13; sexual violence and, 93–97, 105, 243n12; war with Nazi Germany, 95. *See also* Cominform Criticism; Stalin, Josef
Stalin, Josef, 95, 153, 156–57
sterilization, 112, 115–16, 119–21
St. George, Katharine, 198
suffrage: of colonial men, 28; of Japanese women, 113, 128; minimum age, 113; suffragettes, 97, 114, 173
Sugawara En, 114
suicide, 206–7, 248n16; chastity, 93–6, 107–8, 127; group, 15, 93–96, 107–8; race, 63, 79–81, 88–89, 146
Supreme Commander for the Allied Powers. *See* SCAP
Suzuki Kantarō, 65, 113

Tai, Eika, 85
Taipei Imperial University, 68, 87
Taiwan, 33; "blood mixing" and, 18–19, 28, 69, 78, 85, 87; 140–41; Japanese colonization of, 2, 87, 140; Nagai and, 87, 146; Shōji in, 140–41; Taiwanese in postwar Japan, 146; in World War II, 7, *10*, 33, 59, 69

Takada Masami, 180
Takagi Tomosaburō, 66–71, 80, 90
Takami Jun, 125–28
Takamure Itsue, 27, 53
Takasaki Setsuko, 212–14
Taniguchi Konen, 40–44, 77, 83, 234n42, 236n74
Taniguchi Toratoshi. *See* Taniguchi, Konen
Taniguchi Yasaburō: Eugenic Protection Law and, 115–18, 120–21, 171–72; at Futsukaichi Sanatorium, 117; on *panpan*, 120–21, 171–72; on rape, 118
Tanka people, 68–69
Tatewaki Sadayo, 177
Teng, Emma, 59
Territory, Population, Blood (Koya), 78–79
Theory of Japanese Race Formation (Kiyono), 134–36
Thomas, Julia Adeney, 49
Tōjō Hideki, 62–63
Tokutomi Sohō, 89–90
Tokyo (Imperial) University, 77, 86–87, 137, 146
Tokyo, Japan: All-Country Conference on Population Problems in, 72–73; "blood mixing" in, 36, 73, 104, 160, 190, *190*, 200, 206, 210; Ministry of Welfare in, 99; occupied, 99, 104, 113, 156, 160, 168, 190, *190*, 200; press in, 35, 168, 210; protests in, 153–54, *154*; Ueda Tatsuo in, 33; US Congressional Subcommittee on International Operations in, 194–95, 198
Tokyo Family Court, 196
Tokyo Municipal Hygiene Examination Office, 36, 73
Tomita Fusa, 114
Toneman, Amelia Shidzee Nagamine, 187–89
Toneman, Paul, 188–89
treaty ports, 58, 214–15, *215*
Truman, Harry, 100, 197, 229n5
Tsuda Michio, 217, 221
Tsushima, 136–37

INDEX

Ueda Tatsuo, 31–35
Ueno Chizuko, 75
Umemori Naoyuki, 159
umeyo fuyaseyo (give birth and multiply), 111. *See also* pronatalism
United States of America (US):
　Americanization of Japan, 144–45, 218; Americanization of *konketsuji*, 156, 168–73, 186, 144–45, 218; anti-American nationalism, 122, 151–186, 154, 218–26, 228; China and, 156–57, 187; as colony of Japan, 225–26; Congress, 187–92, 194–201, 203–4, 210; Department of State, 65, 167, 197–98, 200; as empire, 6, 16–17, 72, 150–59, 167, 169, 175, 183–85, 216, 219, 220–21, 223–26; forces in occupied Japan, 6, 108, 127–28, 141, 156, 160–61, *171*, *174*, *190*, 200, 213, 250n54; immigration to, 16–17, 33, 174, 181, 186–204, *190*, 210–11, 223; internment in, 189; interracial sex and, 6, 13, 16, 22, 86, 92–95, 127–29, 150–52, 158–60, 162, 189, 220; *konketsuji* and, 6, 16–17, 86–87, 92–95, 108, 129–32, 141–46, 150–52, 155–56, 158–204, *190*, 206, 208–13, 216, 221–22; Korea and, 92–94, 156–57, 164–65, 196, 201–4; laws of, 16–17, 22, 76, 129, 177, 187–193, 196–204; newspapers, 193–97, 199, 201, 209–11; racism in, 16–17, 25, 33–34, 129, 133, 187–92, 194, 196–99, 216, 225; Sawada and, 199–200, 206, 208–11; Ueda in, 33; Vietnam War and, 92, 224; World War II and, 15, 41, 62–63, 71, 92–95, 131, 146–47, 156–58, 176, 187–89, 197, 216; yellow peril and, 225. *See also* Anpo; Cold War; SCAP; war brides
USSR. *See* Soviet Union
Utagawa (Gountei) Sadahide, *215*

venereal disease (VD), 97–99, 101–3, 120
victimhood nationalism, 14, 159, 161, 167, 171, 185–86, 206, 218–19, 225–28
Vietnam War, 92, 224
voting rights. *See* suffrage

Wakakuwa Midori, 51
Wakatsuki Reijirō, 65
war brides, *174*, 189–91, *190*; Hirohito as, 123–25, *124*
War Brides Act (1945), 187–90
war crimes, 100; Kishi and, 182, 184; Sakurai and, 65. *See also* sexual violence
Watari Shōzaburo, 53
Watsuji Tetsurō, 26–27, 90
"We the People," 2, 218–219
white *konketsuji*, 39, 43, 56–58, 143–44, 148–50, *190*, *207*, 213–16, 256n87; euthanasia of, 106–7; numbers of, 175, 179–80, 256n87
white patriarchy, 189
white race, 21, 25, 42, 187
white supremacy, 25, 38–41, 84, 86–87, 132–33, 216
women's suffrage. *See* suffrage
World War I, 66–67, Germany in, 6, 19; Japan in, 19
World War II: *10*, *12*, 193; Australia and, 9, *10*, 62–63, 169; China and, 4, 8, *10*, 29, 47–50, *48*, *50*, 55, 61–63, 65, 71, 87–90; Europe and, 6–7, 22, 41, 57–58, 62–63, 66–67, 93–97, 135, 146–47; Indonesia and, *10*, 38–39, 57–59, 182; Japan and, 2, 4–17, *10*, 20, 23, 29, 32, 38, 41–44, 54–55, 60–63, 65, 87, 93–97, 107, 123, 125, 131, 182, 214, 216–17, 225–26, 228; Korea and, *10*, 29–33, 157; Okinawa and, *10*, 93–95, 108, 127; the Philippines and, *10*, 38, 58, 43, 62–63, 106; as race war, 15, 92–93, 95, 146–47; Saipan and, 93–95, 108, 127; Singapore and, *10*, 38, 57; Soviet Union and, 93–97, 108, 156, 202; Taiwan and, 7, *10*, 33, 59, 69; US and, 15, 41, 62–63, 71, 92–95, 131, 146–47, 156–58, 176, 187–89, 197, 216. *See also* Second Sino-Japanese War
Wuhan, China, 47, 61
"Wuhan Lullaby" (article, Cabinet Information Bureau), 47–50, *48*, *50*, 52–56, *55*

INDEX

xenophobia. *See* racism, xenophobic
Xu Songshi, 69

Yamada Fūtarō, 127–28
Yamashita Gishin, 167–68, 171–72, 186
Yamato, 7, 9, 29, 37, 84; as "mixed blood," 44; as "pure," 64–65, 133, 136–37; as superior, 44, 65–66
yellow peril, 225
Yi Bangja, 27. *See also* Nashimoto Masako
Yi Jonson, 40

Yi Kwang-su, 29–30
Yi Un, 27, 124
Yi Yŏng-gŭn. *See* Ueda, Tatsuo
Yokohama, Japan, 57, *109*, 160, 214–15, *215*
Yoshida Shigeru, 151–53, 155–56, 158–59, 163–68, 173, 179–84; Nakasone on, 182
Yun Ch'i-ho, 29–30
Yūsei hogohō. See Eugenic Protection Law

Zengakuren, 151–53, 158
Ziomek, Kirsten, 19, 64
Zou Rong, 68

GPSR Authorized Representative: Easy Access System Europe, Mustamäe tee 50, 10621 Tallinn, Estonia, gpsr.requests@easproject.com

www.ingramcontent.com/pod-product-compliance
Lightning Source LLC
Chambersburg PA
CBHW022035290426
44109CB00014B/865